Orientalism

ORIENTALISM

A READER

Edited by
A. L. Macfie

EDINBURGH UNIVERSITY PRESS

Selection and editorial material
© A. L. Macfie, 2000. The texts
are reprinted by permission of
other publishers.

Transferred to digital print 2009

Edinburgh University Press Ltd
22 George Square, Edinburgh

Typeset in Sabon and Gill Sans
by Bibliocraft Ltd, Dundee, and
printed and bound in Great Britain by
CPI Antony Rowe, Chippenham and Eastbourne

A CIP record for this book is available
from the British Library

ISBN 0 7486 1442 7 (hardback)
ISBN 0 7486 1441 9 (paperback)

CONTENTS

PREFACE

In the early 1960s, as an amateur historian interested in the modern history of the Middle East, I was aware of the powerful critiques of orientalism mounted by Anouar Abdel-Malek and A. L. Tibawi. But it was only in the early 1980s, at a conference on a related subject I attended at the School of Oriental and African Studies, London, that I became aware of the furore provoked, in orientalist circles, by the publication of Edward Said's *Orientalism* (1978). The comments made on Said's book by the orientalists present at the conference, when the subject was raised during a question and answer session, appeared both sceptical and uneasy. It was evident that in his critique of orientalism Said had struck a raw nerve, and that the orientalists present did not know quite how to respond. Some suggested that Said's book did not warrant the attention it was receiving; others that the furore it had provoked would soon pass. Yet more than twenty years later Said's critique of orientalism continues to provoke great interest, not only in the world of orientalism but also in other related areas, including anthropology, sociology, history, media studies, feminism and the arts. It has been suggested that the continued interest that Said's book provokes is a consequence of its multi-disciplinary appeal. No doubt there is some truth in this suggestion. But I would suggest that the true explanation lies elsewhere, in the fact that the subject, as interpreted by Said, raises the age-old question, never convincingly answered by philosophers, of the nature of perception – that is to say, the relationship between subject and object, 'self' and 'other' and appearance and thing-in-itself.

May I take this opportunity of thanking Professor John MacKenzie, of Lancaster University, and Professor J. J. Clarke, of Kingston University, for their help and encouragement in the preparation of this anthology. I would also like to thank the librarians of the University of London and the School of Oriental and African Studies libraries for their help in assembling the various extracts.

A. L. Macfie

INTRODUCTION

In the eighteenth and nineteenth centuries, the word orientalism was, according to the *Oxford English Dictionary* (1971), generally used to refer to the work of the orientalist, a scholar versed in the languages and literatures of the orient (Turkey, Syria, Palestine, Mesopotamia and Arabia, later also India, China and Japan, and even the whole of Asia); and in the world of the arts to identify a character, style or quality, commonly associated with the Eastern nations. Moreover, according to John MacKenzie, the author of *Orientalism: History, Theory and the Arts* (Manchester University Press, 1995), in the final quarter of the eighteenth century the word came, in the context of British rule in India, to acquire a third meaning. There it was used to refer to or identify a 'conservative and romantic' approach to the problems of government, faced by the officials of the East India Company. According to this approach the languages and laws of Muslim and Hindu India should not be ignored or supplanted, but utilised and preserved, as foundations of the traditional social order. For a time this approach was adopted, but at the turn of the eighteenth century it was challenged by the combined forces of evangelicalism and utilitarianism; and in the 1830s it was supplanted by the new, so-called 'Anglicist' approach. Henceforth, as a minute on education presented by Thomas Macaulay, President of the Committee of Public Instruction, to the Supreme Council in Calcutta on 2 February 1835 made clear (see G. O. Trevelyan, *The Life and Letters of Lord Macaulay*, Oxford University Press, 1932, pp. 370–3), indigenous learning in India would be completely supplanted by British scholarship imparted through the English language.

The meaning of the word orientalism, as given in the *Oxford English Dictionary*, remained more or less unchanged until the period of decolonisation that followed the end of the Second World War (1939–45). Then, in a little more than twenty years, it came to mean not only the work of the orientalist and a character, style or quality associated with the Eastern nations, but also a corporate institution, designed for dealing with the orient, a partial view of Islam, an instrument of Western imperialism, a style of thought, based on an ontological and epistemological distinction between orient and occident, and even an ideology, justifying and accounting for the subjugation of blacks, Palestinian Arabs, women and many other supposedly deprived groups and peoples. This transformation, which as MacKenzie has remarked turned orientalism into one of the most highly charged words in modern scholarship, was accomplished by a series of scholars and intellectuals, many of whom lived in or came from the orient. Principal among these were Anouar Abdel-Malek, an Egyptian (Coptic) sociologist, attached to the CNRA (Centre National de la Recherche Scientifique) (Sociology), Paris; A. L. Tibawi, a Syrian student of Arabic history, employed at the Institute of Education, London University, and later at Harvard; Edward Said, a Palestinian (Christian-Protestant) student of English and Comparative Literature, employed at Columbia University, New York; and Bryan S. Turner, a leading sociologist and student of Marxism. The result was that orientalists – members of what had, in recent years, become an abstruse, dry-as-dust profession – were now accused of practising, not orientalism, but 'orientalism', that is to say a type of imperialism, racialism, and even, according to some accounts, anti-Semitism.

The conditions necessary for the launching of an effective assault on orientalism, as traditionally practised, were, as the eminent French orientalist Maxime Rodinson has pointed out – in an article entitled 'The Western Image and Western Studies of Islam', in S. Schacht and C. Bosworth, *The Legacy of Islam* (Oxford University Press, 1979) – already created well before the outbreak of the Second World War. The Iranian revolution of 1906, the Young Turk revolution of 1908, the defeat and destruction of the German, Austrian, Russian and Ottoman empires in the period of the First World War, the rise of the Kemalist movement in Turkey (1919–22), the rise of a national movement in Egypt (1919), the spread of Bolshevism – all these events and developments showed that the military and political hegemony imposed by the European powers, throughout large parts of Asia and Africa, could now be successfully challenged, and even on occasion undermined. There followed a period of rapid decolonisation, culminating in the independence of India (1947), the Algerian uprising (1952), the British withdrawal from Egypt (1954) and the collapse of the British-backed Hashemite regime in Iraq (1958). As a result of these and other developments, there arose in Asia and Africa, in the 1950s and 1960s, a climate of opinion that made possible an effective challenge to European hegemony, not only in the military and political but also in the intellectual sphere.

The assault on orientalism, when it finally came, was launched on four fronts: on orientalism as an instrument of imperialism, designed to secure the colonisation and enslavement of parts of the so-called Third World (Abdel-Malek; Chap. 9); on orientalism as a mode of understanding and interpreting Islam and Arab nationalism (Tibawi; Chaps 10 and 19); on orientalism as a 'cumulative and corporate identity' and a 'saturating hegemonic system' (Said; Chaps 12–16); and on orientalism as a justification for a syndrome of beliefs, attitudes and theories, affecting the geography, economics and sociology of the orient (Turner; Chap. 17).

The intellectual origins of the four principal assaults on orientalism, launched in the post-Second World War period, were somewhat narrower in scope than might have been expected. Abdel-Malek based his critique of orientalism on the work of Karl Marx, the nineteenth-century German philosopher and economist. Tibawi based his analysis on the traditional principles of mutual respect, scientific detachment and fairmindedness, much promoted in Europe in the nineteenth century. Said based his approach on the work of a number of European scholars and intellectuals, including Jacques Derrida (deconstruction), Antonio Gramsci (cultural hegemony) (Chap. 7) and Michel Foucault (discourse, power/knowledge, and epistemic field) (Chap. 8). Turner based his critique on a critical reading of Marx and the literature of anti-colonialism associated with his name (Chap. 17). All four critiques, that is to say, were either based on, or assumed the existence of, a European philosophy or thought system, derived for the most part from the work of two of the greatest German philosophers of the nineteenth century, G. W. F. Hegel, the transcendental idealist and precursor of Marx, and F. Nietzsche, the critic of idealism in all its manifestations (Chap. 6).

The motivation of the four principal assaults on orientalism, on the other hand, may be sought elsewhere, in a hatred of colonialism and imperialism (Abdel-Malek); a dislike of what was perceived by some to be the lack of respect, shown by many English orientalists, for Islam (Tibawi); a personal sense of loss and national disintegration (Said); and an aversion to the workings of the capitalist system (Turner). In the face of such resentment, exacerbated, it is said, in Tibawi's case by a sense of personal and professional marginalisation, it is not surprising that apologies for orientalism and defences of it – made by such eminent European orientalists as Claude Cahen, professor of Muslim history, Sorbonne University (Diogenes, 49, 2, 1965, not cited here) and Francesco Gabrieli, professor of Arabic languages and literature at the University of Rome (Chap. 11) – should have made so little impression.

What the four principal critics of orientalism hoped to achieve, according to their own account, was a critical re-evaluation of the methods employed by the orientalists (Abdel-Malek); a 'better understanding of an old problem' (Tibawi); an exposure of the 'subtle degradation of knowledge', accomplished by the orientalists (Said); and a reconsideration of the dispute between the orientalists, the sociologists and the Marxist, regarding the characterisation of the history and social structure of North Africa and the Middle East (Turner). What they actually succeeded, to a considerable extent, in achieving, in conjunction with other anti-European, anti-imperialist and anti-elitist groups (liberals, socialists, blacks, feminists and many others) active at the time, is what Nietzsche was wont to refer to as a 'transvaluation of all values'. What had previously been seen as being good (orientalism, text-based scholarship, knowledge of classical languages, concepts of absolute truth, ethnocentricity, racial pride, service to the state, and national pride) was now seen as being bad, or at least suspect. And what had previously been seen as being bad (anti-colonialism, racial equality, uncertainty regarding the nature of truth, resistance to imperialism, mixed race, and internationalism) was now seen as being good, worthy of promotion. Not that the victory achieved by the critics of orientalism was uncontested, as the debate which ensued, following the publication of Said's *Orientalism* in 1978, shows.

Of the four principal assaults launched on orientalism, as traditionally practised, that launched by Edward Said, in *Orientalism* (New York: Pantheon Books, 1978), proved to be by far the most effective. According to Said the orientalist, the heir to a 'narcissistic' tradition of European writing founded by, amongst others, Homer and Aeschylus, through his writing 'creates' the orient. In the process, he assists in the creation of a series of stereotypical images, according to which Europe (the West, the 'self') is seen as being essentially rational, developed, humane, superior, authentic, active, creative and masculine, while the orient (the East, the 'other') (a sort of surrogate, underground version of the West or the 'self') is seen as being irrational, aberrant, backward, crude, despotic, inferior, inauthentic, passive, feminine and sexually corrupt. Other 'orientalist' fantasies invented by the orientalist include the concept of an 'Arab mind', an 'oriental psyche' and an 'Islamic Society'. Together they contribute to the construction of a 'saturating hegemonic system', designed, consciously or unconsciously, to dominate, restructure and have authority over the orient – designed, that is to say, to promote European imperialism and colonialism.

In *Orientalism*, Said cites scores of examples of orientalism, as it appears in the works of European scholars, poets, philosophers, imperial administrators, political theorists, historians, politicians, travel writers and others. These include the Italian poet Dante, the French orientalists Barthélemy d'Herbelot and Abraham Hyacinthe Anquetil-Duperron, Sir William Jones, the East India Company official and founder of the Asiatic Society of Bengal, the English scholar and adventurer Sir Richard Burton, and the British Arabists Sir Hamilton Gibb and Bernard Lewis. Not that Said believes that the orientalism he discovers in Western thought and text is merely an imaginative phenomenon, a 'structure of lies and of myth', which might, if the truth were ever told, be quickly blown away. On the contrary, as we have seen, he believes that it is part of an integrated discourse, an accepted grid for filtering the orient into the Western consciousness and an 'integral part of European *material* civilisation and culture' – that is to say, an instrument of British, French and later American imperialism.

Other examples of orientalism, as defined by Said, may be found in James Mill, *The History of British India* (1817), which contains an early mention of an 'Asian model' (Chap.1); G. W. F. Hegel, *The Philosophy of History* (1837), an archetypal 'orientalist' text (Chap.2); and Karl Marx, 'The British Rule in India' (Chap.3), a significant text for Marxist sociologists.

Opinion regarding the validity of Said's thesis proved as diverse as it was contentious. A list of critics generally convinced by his thesis might include Stuart Schaar, 'Orientalism at the Service of Imperialism' (Chap. 21); Ernest J. Wilson III, 'Orientalism: A Black Perspective' (Chap. 25); and Ronald Inden, 'Orientalist Constructions of India' (Chap. 28). A list of critics opposed might include Bernard Lewis, 'The Question of Orientalism' (Chap. 26); C. F. Beckingham, 'Review of Orientalism' (*Bulletin of the School of Oriental and African Studies*, 42, 3, 1979, not cited here); David Kopf, 'Hermeneutics versus History' (Chap. 22); M. Richardson, 'Enough Said' (Chap. 23); John MacKenzie, 'Edward Said and the Historians' (*Nineteenth-Century Contexts*, 18, 1994, pp. 9–25, not cited here); and Keith Windshuttle, *The Killing of History* (New York: Free Press, 1996, not cited here). A list of critics generally sympathetic to the approach adopted by Said, but critical of some aspects of his work, might include Sadik Jalal al-'Azm, 'Orientalism and Orientalism in Reverse' (Chap. 24); AijazAhmad, 'Between Orientalism and Historicism' (Chap. 29) and 'Orientalism and After', in *In Theory* (London: Verso, 1992, not cited here); James Clifford, 'On Orientalism', in *The Predicament of Culture* (Harvard University Press, 1988, not cited here); and Fred Halliday, 'Orientalism and Its Critics' (*British Journal of Middle Eastern Studies*, 20, 2, 1993, pp. 145–63, not cited here). Donald P. Little, 'Three Arab Critiques of Orientalism' (Chap. 18), whilst in general critical of Said, effectively accepts his conclusions, as does Albert Hourani, 'The Road to Morocco' (*New York Review of Books*, 8 March 1979, not cited here).

What divides Said from many of his critics is the fact that while Said, in *Orientalism*, tends to view his subject through the prism of modern and postmodern philosophy (in particular the philosophies of Nietzsche, Foucault, Derrida and, surprisingly, the Marxist Gramsci), his critics remain, for the most part, firmly wedded to a traditional (realist) approach to the writing of history. Thus Bernard Lewis, in his article 'The Question of Orientalism' (Chap. 26), accuses Said of an 'arbitrary rearrangement of the historical background', a 'capricious choice of countries, persons and writings', and an 'unpolemical ignorance' of historical fact. Into the category of orientalist he, Said, introduces a number of writers and *littérateurs*, such as Chateaubriand and Nerval, whose work may have been relevant to the formation of Western cultural attitudes, but who had nothing to do with the academic tradition of orientalism. David Kopf, in his article 'Hermeneutics versus History' (Chap. 22), notes Said's failure to take account of the bitter Orientalist – Anglicist controversy, concerning cultural attitudes and policies, that took place in India in the 1830s. Said's notion of orientalism, Kopf remarks, is lacking in historical precision, comprehensiveness and subtlety. John MacKenzie, in his article 'Said and the Historians' (not cited here) points out that, in the eighteenth and early nineteenth centuries, Britain's principal 'other' was France; and in the century and a half that followed, France, Russia, Germany and the Soviet Union. Said's account of orientalism fails to take account of the instability, the heterogeneity and the 'sheer porousness' of imperial culture. His work is 'supremely a-historical'.

Critics of Said's *Orientalism* are, from their own point of view, no doubt, fully justified in drawing attention to Said's occasional lack of respect for historical fact. But in so emphasising the issue of historical fact, it can be argued that a number, including in particular Lewis, Kopf and MacKenzie, fail to make due allowance for the nature of the task undertaken by Said: the identification of orientalism as a Foucauldian discourse, a 'systemic discipline', without which it would be difficult, if not impossible, for European culture to 'manage – and even produce – the orient, politically, sociologically, militarily, ideologically, scientifically, and imaginatively'. Said, in other words, was not attempting to write a history of orientalism, similar to Pierre Martino, *L'Orient dans la littérature française* (see Chap. 4) and Raymond Schwab, *The Oriental Renaissance* (Chap. 5). Nor, as he makes clear in 'Orientalism Reconsidered' (Chap. 35), and the afterword of the 1995 edition of *Orientalism* (not cited here), was he attempting to write an anti-Western tract, a defence of Islam and the Arabs, a history of East–West relations, a history of British and French colonialism, or a history of European and Asian cultural relations and exchange. His concern was merely to identify the nature of the 'orientalist' discourse, as a 'created body of theory and practice', designed, consciously or unconsciously, to serve the interests of the European imperial powers. Not that, in exploiting the concepts of discourse and epistemic field, Said was necessarily following a model which Foucault would have recognised. According to Aijaz Ahmad, one of Said's most perceptive critics (Chap. 29), Foucault would not have accepted Said's view that a discourse – that is to say an epistemic construction – could span both the pre-capitalist and the capitalist periods of history. Moreover, Said's view, that an 'ideology of modern imperialist Eurocentrism' might be found, already inscribed, in the ritual theatre of ancient Greece, was radically anti-Foucauldian.

For Foucault, it may be noted, a discourse was a complexly dispersed historical phenomenon, a recalcitrant means of expression, burdened with historical sedimentation; while an epistemic field was a field of knowledge, created by a culture, which exercised control over what might, and might not, be said and written.

The debate about orientalism in the academic journals was not confined to merely intellectual issues. In Lewis's view (Chap. 26), Said's critique of orientalism was intended, not as a contribution to understanding, but as an attack on Zionism, Jewish scholarship and the West, particularly America. It was a polemic inspired by hostile motives. In Said's view, on the other hand (Chap. 35), Lewis, seen as a spokesman for the guild of orientalists, was a politically motivated zealot, masquerading as an impartial scholar. His defence of orientalism was an 'act of bad faith', covered with a 'veneer of urbanity'. In other words, it was pro-Zionist, anti-Islamic and anti-Arab.

Criticism of Said's *Orientalism* was not confined to reviews and review articles. In the twenty years or so following its publication, a number of scholars sought to test out Said's conclusions in what became in effect a series of case studies. The outcome proved once again remarkably inconsistent. Ali Behdad, *Belated Travelers* (Cork University Press, 1994, not cited here), Richard King, *Orientalism and Religion: Post-Colonial Theory and the 'Mystic East'* (London: Routlege, 1999) (Chap. 34), and most of the authors published in C. A. Breckenridge and P. van der Veer (eds), *Orientalism and the Post-Colonial Predicament* (Philadelphia: University of Pennsylvania Press, 1993), in particular Sheldon Pollock, 'Indology, Power, and the Case of Germany' (Chap. 31), generally found in Said's favour. Nevertheless, Ali Behdad concluded that in formalising orientalism's discursive regularities, Said failed to take full account of its micropractices, irregularities, historical discontinuities and discursive heterogeneity. European power over the orient should be seen as a productive and dynamic exchange between the two, an exchange that made colonial authority tolerable to those on whom it was being imposed. Richard King drew attention to inconsistencies in Said's argument, in particular his unwillingness to accept the full implications of the Foucauldian critique of representation. Breckenridge and van der Veer pointed out, in an introduction to their collection, that the essays contained therein suggest that significant discontinuities exist in the disciplinary project of the colonial and post-colonial periods; that colonised subjects were not passively produced by hegemonic projects; and that orientalism was constitutive not only of the orient but also of the occident. Others proved more critical. B. J. Moore-Gilbert, *Kipling and Orientalism* (London: Croom-Helm, 1986), (Chap. 27), showed that Said's conclusion could not reasonably be applied to the Anglo-Indians, whose knowledge of India was both personal and direct. Anglo-Indians, as their writings show, were as shocked at the ignorance, indifference and prejudice of their fellow countrymen regarding life in India as were many later oriental critics of Anglo-Saxon attitudes. Billie Melman, *Women's Orients* (London: Macmillan, 1992), showed that, while Said's conclusions may well have applied to most English travellers in the orient in the period with which he was concerned, they hardly ever applied to female travellers, such as Lady Blunt, the wife of Wilfred Scawen Blunt, who travelled widely in the Middle East in the second half of the nineteenth century (Chap. 30). Lisa Lowe, *Critical Terrains* (Cornell University Press, 1991), similarly showed that Lady Mary Wortley Montagu, in her 'Turkish Embassy Letters' (Chap. 32), challenged many of the preconceptions, concerning the lives of Turkish women, held by English male travellers in Turkey at the time. John MacKenzie, *Orientalism: History, Theory and the Arts* (Manchester University Press, 1995) (Chap. 33), found that, with regard to the arts, at least, Said's thesis was unsustainable. The artistic record of imperial culture had in fact been one of 'constant change, instability, heterogeneity and sheer porousness'. It was impossible to recognise either the 'essentialised, basically unchanging self' or the freezing of 'the Other in a kind of basic objecthood'. Finally Emily M. Weeks, 'About Face: Sir David Wilkie's Portrait of Mehmet Ali, Pasha of Egypt', in J. F. Codwell and D. S. Macleod, *Orientalism Transposed: The Impact of the Colonies on British Culture* (Aldershot: Ashgate, 1998, not cited here), found that an analysis of Wilkie's painting not only complicates a popular Saidian reading of a work of orientalist art, it demands a complete revision of it. That is to say, it demands a complete reversal of the expected coloniser – colonised, East – West relationship.

The writings of the three other principal critics of orientalism, Abdel-Malek, Tibawi and Turner, provoked no such storm of debate as that which followed the publication of Said's *Orientalism* in 1978; though, as we have seen, Abdel-Malek's critique of orientalism (Chap. 9) did provoke responses from Claude Cahen and Francesco Gabrieli (Chap. 11); and Tibawi's critique of English-speaking orientalists, together with the critiques of orientalism mounted by Abdel-Malek and Said, provoked a response from D.P. Little, an American historian (Chap. 18), which in turn elicited a somewhat ill-tempered riposte from Tibawi (Chap. 20). That is not to suggest that the attacks on orientalism, mounted by Abdel-Malek, Tibawi and Turner, are in any sense less interesting than those of Said; though it has to be conceded that they cannot compete with Said for sheer intellectual bravura. Abdel-Malek's 'Orientalism in Crisis' (Chap. 9), probably the most influential of the founding documents of the orientalist debate, deserves consideration for its careful identification of the principal features of orientalism and its long-standing relationship with the European, colonialist state. Tibawi's two critiques of 'English-Speaking Orientalists' (Chaps 10 and 19) deserve consideration again for their identification of the principal features of orientalism, and for their analysis of what Tibawi sees as the prejudices displayed by a number of English-speaking orientalists. Finally, Turner's 'Marx and the End of Orientalism' (Chap. 17) should be read for its careful analysis of the relationship which Turner believes exists between orientalism, capitalism and underdevelopment in parts of the Third World.

The debate about orientalism, sparked off in the 1980s and 1990s by the works of Abdel-Malek, Tibawi, Said and Turner, has proved both instructive and enlightening, inspiring new approaches to the study of many subjects, including the history of art, media studies, musicology, architectural history, the history of ideas, feminism (Chap. 34), translation studies and post-colonialism. Yet many questions remain unanswered. Is there a real orient or only an imaginary one? Is it possible to move briskly from Eurocentricism to anti-Eurocentricism? Is it sensible to equate traditional learning, however flawed, with colonial oppression? Do we want an alternative description of the orient, or only a better one? These are some of the questions Fred Dallmayr, 'Exit from Orientalism' (Chap. 36) and Bryan S. Turner, 'From Orientalism to Global Sociology' (Chap. 37) attempt to answer.

PART I
FOUNDATIONS OF A MYTH

Some scholars, in particular Edward Said, a Palestinian (Christian-Protestant) student of English and comparative literature, have traced the myth of the orient, Europe's exotic 'other', back as far as Homer and Aeschylus. In its more recent manifestation, it may be detected in the works of James Mill, G. W. F. Hegel and Karl Marx.

I

THE INDIAN FORM OF GOVERNMENT

James Mill

In his History of British India *(1817), James Mill, who never actually visited India, wrote an extremely critical account of Hindu civilisation, which in his view was much in need of redemption by 'European honour and European intelligence'. In the following extract, which includes an early reference to an 'Asiatic model', Mill betrays many of the preconceptions and prejudices later associated by its critics with orientalism. These include an exaggerated respect for classical text and an over-emphasis on the significance of oriental despotism.*

After the division of the people into ranks and occupations, the great circumstance by which their condition, character, and operations are determined, is the political establishment; the system of actions by which the social order is preserved. Among the Hindus, according to the Asiatic model, the government was monarchical, and, with the usual exception of religion and its ministers, absolute. No idea of any system of rule, different from the will of a single person, appears to have entered the minds of them, or their legislators. 'If the world had no king,' says the Hindu law, 'it would quake on all sides through fear; the ruler of this universe, therefore, created a king, for the maintenance of this system.' Of the high and uncontrollable authority of the monarch a judgment may be formed, from the lofty terms in which the sacred books describe his dignity and attributes. 'A king,' says the law of Manu, 'is formed of

James Mill, *The History of British India* (London: Baldwin, Cradock and Joy, 1820), p. 66.

particles from the chief guardian deities, and consequently surpasses all mortals in glory. Like the sun, he burns eyes and hearts; nor can any human creature on earth even gaze on him. He, fire and air; He, the god of criminal justice; He, the genius of wealth; He, the regent of waters; He, the lord of the firmament. A king, even though a child, must not be treated lightly, from an idea that he is a mere mortal: No; he is a powerful divinity, who appears in human shape. In his anger, death. He who shows hatred of the king, through delusion of mind, will certainly perish; for speedily will the king apply his heart to that man's destruction.' The pride of imperial greatness could not devise, hardly could it even desire, more extraordinary distinctions, or the sanction of a more un-limited authority.

2

GORGEOUS EDIFICES

G. W. F. Hegel

G. W. F. Hegel, in his Philosophy of History *(1837), concluded that reason (the world spirit, God) found its highest manifestation in the Germanic world, where 'All are free'. Previous empires (cultures, civilisations, nations), including the Chinese, Indian, Persian, Egyptian, Greek and Roman, were therefore by definition inferior, imperfect manifestations of the world spirit. In particular, the two great oriental empires, the Chinese and the Indian, were assumed to display all the characteristics later associated in the European mind with the orient: irrationality, immutability, despotism, childishness, sensuality, femininity, capriciousness, backwardness, cruelty and barbarism. In China, Hegel believed, the patriarchal principle ruled a people 'in a condition of nonage', while in India there prevailed a 'universal pantheism', inspired not by thought but by the imagination. The Indian world displayed the beauty of a 'flower-life', but should we approach it more closely, and examine it in the light of 'Human Dignity' and 'Freedom', we would ultimately find it unworthy in every respect.*

In the geographical survey, the course of the World's History has been marked out in its general features.

The *Sun* – the Light – rises in the East. Light is a simply self-involved existence; but though possessing thus in itself universality, it exists at the same time as an individuality in the Sun. Imagination has often pictured to itself the

G. W. F. Hegel, *The Philosophy of History* (New York: P. F. Collier & Son, 1902), pp. 163–6.

emotions of a blind man suddenly becoming possessed of sight, beholding the bright glimmering of the dawn, the growing light, and the flaming glory of the ascending Sun. The boundless forgetfulness of his individuality in this pure splendor is his first feeling – utter astonishment. But when the Sun is risen, this astonishment is diminished; objects around are perceived, and from them the individual proceeds to the contemplation of his own inner being, and thereby the advance is made to the perception of the relation between the two. Then inactive contemplation is quitted for activity; by the close of day man has erected a building constructed from his own inner Sun; and when in the evening he contemplates this, he esteems it more highly than the original external Sun. For now he stands in a *conscious relation* to his Spirit, and therefore a *free* relation. If we hold this image fast in mind, we shall find it symbolizing the course of History, the great Day's work of Spirit.

The History of the World travels from East to West, for Europe is absolutely the end of History, Asia the beginning. The History of the World has an East $x\alpha\tau'$ $'\varepsilon\xi o\chi\acute{\eta}^{\nu}$ (the term East in itself is entirely relative); for although the Earth forms a sphere, History performs no circle round it, but has on the contrary a determinate East, viz. Asia. Here rises the outward physical Sun, and in the West it sinks down: here consentaneously rises the Sun of self-consciousness, which diffuses a nobler brilliance. The History of the World is the discipline of the uncontrolled natural will, bringing it into obedience to a Universal principle and conferring subjective freedom. The East knew and to the present day knows only that *One* is Free; the Greek and Roman world, that *some* are free; the German World knows that *All* are free. The first political form therefore which we observe in History is *Despotism*, the second *Democracy* and *Aristocracy*, the third *Monarchy*.

To understand this division we must remark that as the State is the universal spiritual life, to which individuals by birth sustain a relation of confidence and habit, and in which they have their existence and reality – the first question is, whether their actual life is an unreflecting use and habit combining them in this unity, or whether its constituent individuals are reflective and personal beings having a properly subjective and independent existence. In view of this, *substantial* [objective] freedom must be distinguished from *subjective* freedom. Substantial freedom is the abstract undeveloped Reason implicit in volition, proceeding to develop itself in the State. But in this phase of Reason there is still wanting personal insight and will, that is, subjective freedom; which is realized only in the Individual, and which constitutes the reflection of the Individual in his own conscience.[1] Where there is merely substantial freedom, commands and laws are regarded as something fixed and abstract, to which the subject holds himself in absolute servitude. These laws need not concur with the desire of the individual, and the subjects are consequently like children, who obey their parents without will or insight of their own. But as subjective freedom arises, and man descends from the contemplation of external reality into his own soul, the contrast suggested by reflection arises, involving the Negation of Reality.

The drawing back from the actual world forms *ipso facto* an antithesis, of which one side is the absolute Being – the Divine – the other the human subject as an individual. In that immediate, unreflected consciousness which characterizes the East, these two are not yet distinguished. The substantial world is distinct from the individual, but the antithesis has not yet created a schism between [absolute and subjective] Spirit.

The first phase – that with which we have to begin – is the *East*. Unreflected consciousness – substantial, objective, spiritual existence – forms the basis; to which the subjective will first sustains a relation in the form of faith, confidence, obedience. In the political life of the East we find a realized rational freedom, developing itself without advancing to *subjective* freedom. It is the childhood of History. Substantial forms constitute the gorgeous edifices of Oriental *Empires*, in which we find all rational ordinances and arrangements, but in such a way that individuals remain as mere accidents. These revolve round a centre, round the sovereign, who, as patriarch – not as despot in the sense of the *Roman* Imperial Constitution – stands at the head. For he has to enforce the moral and substantial: he has to uphold those essential ordinances which are already established; so that what among us belongs entirely to subjective freedom here proceeds from the entire and general body of the State. The glory of Oriental conception is the One Individual as that substantial being to which all belongs, so that no other individual has a separate existence, or mirrors himself in his subjective freedom. All the riches of imagination and Nature are appropriated to that dominant existence in which subjective freedom is essentially merged; the latter looks for its dignity, *not* in itself, but in that absolute object. All the elements of a complete State – even subjectivity – may be found there, but not yet harmonized with the grand substantial being. For outside the One Power – before which nothing can maintain an independent existence – there is only revolting caprice, which, beyond the limits of the central power, roves at will without purpose or result. Accordingly we find the wild hordes breaking out from the Upland – falling upon the countries in question, and laying them waste, or settling down in them, and giving up their wild life; but in all cases resultlessly lost in the central substance.

NOTE

1. The essence of Spirit is self-determination or 'Freedom.' Where Spirit has attained mature growth, as in the man who acknowledges the absolute validity of the dictates of Conscience, the Individual is 'a law to himself,' and his Freedom is 'realized.' But in lower stages of morality and civilization, he *unconsciously projects* this legislative principle into some 'governing power' (one or several), and obeys it as if it were an alien, extraneous force, not the voice of that Spirit of which he himself (though at this stage imperfectly) is an embodiment. The Philosophy of History exhibits the successive stages by which he reaches the consciousness, that it is *his own inmost being* that thus governs him – *i.e.* a consciousness of self-determination or 'Freedom.' – *Tr.*

3

THE BRITISH RULE IN INDIA

Karl Marx

In an article entitled 'The British Rule in India', published in the New York
Daily Tribune, *on 25 June 1853, Karl Marx, a keen student of Hegel and
occasional observer of the Indian scene, continued to propagate the view, put
forward by his great predecessor, that India had no history, and that Hindu
society was 'undignified, stagnatory and vegetative'. Unlike Hegel, however, he
argued that the brutal interference of the British tax-gatherer and the British
soldier, combined with the working of 'English steam and English free-trade',
would in due course undermine the economic base of Indian society, and
produce 'the greatest, and to speak the truth, the only social revolution ever
heard in India'.*

Now, sickening as it must be to human feeling to witness those myriads of
industrious patriarchal and inoffensive social organizations disorganized and
dissolved into their units, thrown into a sea of woes, and their individual
members losing at the same time their ancient form of civilization and their
hereditary means of subsistence, we must not forget that these idyllic village
communities, inoffensive though they may appear, had always been the solid
foundation of Oriental despotism, that they restrained the human mind within
the smallest possible compass, making it the unresisting tool of superstition,
enslaving it beneath traditional rules, depriving it of all grandeur and historical

Karl Marx, 'The British Rule in India', *New York Daily Tribune*, 25 June 1853.

energies. We must not forget the barbarian egotism which, concentrating on some miserable patch of land, had quietly witnessed the ruin of empires, the perpetration of unspeakable cruelties, the massacre of the population of large towns, with no other consideration bestowed upon them than on natural events, itself the helpless prey of any aggressor who deigned to notice it at all. We must not forget that this undignified, stagnatory, and vegetative life, that this passive sort of existence evoked on the other part, in contradistinction, wild, aimless, unbounded forces of destruction, and rendered murder itself a religious rite in Hindustan. We must not forget that these little communities were contaminated by distinctions of caste and by slavery, that they subjugated man to external circumstances instead of elevating man to be the sovereign of circumstances, that they transformed a self-developing social state into never changing natural destiny, and thus brought about a brutalizing worship of nature, exhibiting its degradation in the fact that man, the sovereign of nature, fell down on his knees in adoration of Hanuman, the monkey, and Sabbala, the cow.

England, it is true, in causing a social revolution in Hindustan, was actuated only by the vilest interests, and was stupid in her manner of enforcing them. But that is not the question. The question is, can mankind fulfil its destiny without a fundamental revolution in the social state of Asia? If not, whatever may have been the crimes of England she was the unconscious tool of history in bringing about that revolution.

PART II
THE RISE OF ORIENTAL STUDIES

The history of oriental studies in Europe may be traced back to the year 1312, when the Church Council of Vienna decided to establish a series of chairs in Arabic, Greek, Hebrew and Syriac, in Paris, Oxford, Bologna, Avignon and Salamanca. Later, in the seventeenth and eighteenth centuries, following the great voyages of discovery undertaken by the European maritime powers, and the dispatch, by the Roman Catholic Society of Jesus, of Christian missions to the East, a series of institutes and academies were set up for the study of the languages and cultures of India, China and Japan. But it was only in the final quarter of the eighteenth century that orientalism, as a profession, became firmly established. Among the historians who have written substantial accounts of orientalism as a profession, Pierre Martino and Raymond Schwab must be considered two of the most significant.

4

LES COMMENCEMENTS
DE L'ORIENTALISME

Pierre Martino

In L'Orient dans la littérature française au XVIIe et au XVIIIe Siècle, *first published in Paris in 1906, Pierre Martino identifies many of the characteristics later associated by its critics with orientalism. These include the important part played in the development of the discipline by state subsidy, the emphasis placed by its practitioners on text-based scholarship ('le rapprochement, le commentaire, la glose, la compilation'), the lack of interest displayed in living languages, cultures and civilisations ('*ils ne se sentaient certes point de scrupules à parler de la Turquie sans même connaître Constantinople'*), and the close relationship established between French colonialism and '*l'exotisme littéraire' ('il y a là une relation immédiate de cause à effet'). In the following extract, taken from his chapter on the beginnings of orientalism, which he believes did not become fully constituted until the last quarter of the eighteenth century, Martino describes the way in which oriental studies developed in the seventeenth century.*

III

Le XVIIe siècle est «l'époque où se place la découverte, pour ainsi dire, du monde littéraire des contrées exotiques[1]». Les langues d'Orient, l'arabe du moins, n'étaient pas tout à fait inconnues aux hommes du moyen âge; on y était naturellement amené par l'étude de l'hébreu et du syriaque, indispensables à une

Pierre Martino, *L'Orient dans la littérature française* (Paris: Librairie Hachette, 1906), part I, ch. 5. section 3.

bonne connaissance de la Bible[2]; quelques grecs renégats, des musulmans convertis, avaient pu en instruire de rares savants; mais ceux-ci étaient déjà assez affairés devant cette dure besogne, et ils ne songeaient pas à publier leurs difficultueuses trouvailles : point de traductions véritables, point de grammaires, point de dictionnaires. La prise de Constantinople, l'exode vers l'Occident des Grecs instruits, l'élan donné par la Réforme aux recherches d'exégèse biblique, le prodigieux effort de travail auquel se livrèrent les érudits de la Renaissance, tels ont été les vrais prodromes de la future science orientaliste[3]. Dès le XVIe siècle il y eut des chaires d'arabe dans les principales universités d'Europe : le Collège de France ne manqua point à en créer une, lui aussi; et il se vérifia une fois de plus qu'il est, pour s'instruire, peu de moyens aussi profitables que d'enseigner la science qu'on veut acquérir! On pourra, si l'on veut, aller chercher dans *Gallia orientalis* du vieux bibliographe Colomiès[4], les noms, obscurs et rébarbatifs, sous leur forme latine, des savants français qui jetèrent sur les langues d'Orient toutes leurs ardeurs de travail; pour la plupart ils se bornèrent à l'étude de l'hébreu, mais quelques-uns déjà, comme Scaliger, Postel surtout, «lecteur des lettres grecques, hébraïques et arabiques» au Collège de France[5], parvinrent à une connaissance véritable de l'arabe. Il y avait des professeurs; il y eut des élèves, et avec les premières générations du XVIIe siècle, on put commencer le défrichement d'un domaine, jusque-là si broussailleux qu'on n'en devinait pas même l'étendue.

A vrai dire le travail orientaliste se fit à cette époque surtout hors de France, en Angleterre et en Hollande[6]; mais il existait déjà une sorte d'internationalisme de la science, et peu importait que les livres fussent édités à Leyde, à Cologne, à Rome ou à Paris, puisqu'ils étaient tous écrits en latin. Toutefois, même au XVIIe siècle, il y eut en France une série continue de savants qui furent d'assidus orientalistes : Du Ryer, le premier traducteur du Koran[7]; Thévenot, garde de la bibliothèque du roi[8], Vattier, professeur d'arabe au Collège de France; d'Herbelot, enfin, l'auteur de la *Bibliothèque orientale*, sont les moins inconnus parmi eux; mais il serait facile d'en citer d'autres qui collaborèrent obscurément à cette tâche, grammairiens, lexicographes et traducteurs.

Pendant cette première période, ce qu'on chercha surtout à produire, ce furent «des instruments de travail ... pour pouvoir plus tard sonder ces immenses mines littéraires de l'Orient[9]»: et l'on pourrait écrire à la suite, en une même liste, plus de vingt grammaires ou lexiques qui parurent entre les *Rudimenta grammatices linguæ turcicæ* de Du Ryer (1630) et la *Bibliothèque orientale* de d'Herbelot (1697)[10]. C'était là le plus pressé; aux troupes qui demandent la bataille il faut d'abord des armes et une théorie claire qui puisse en enseigner le maniement. Mais à quoi bon tous ces exercices d'assouplissement si l'on n'a pas occasion de les appliquer? Il n'était pas à la portée de tous d'acheter chèrement en Orient quelque manuscrit, pour le déchiffrer ensuite avec passion; on dut donc se préoccuper d'éditer les textes orientaux eux-mêmes, on grava les poinçons et les matrices nécessaires, on donna aux imprimeries les sinueux caractères arabes. Dès Louis XIII, on put publier quelques textes, et à la fin du

XVIIe siècle l'Imprimerie royale vint, avec ses belles éditions, soutenir cet effort de l'initiative privée[11].

Le travail des fouilles n'était pas achevé, que déjà s'élevèrent au-dessus des fondations, mal déblayées encore, quelques pièces de la bâtisse future; des traductions latines ou françaises vinrent apprendre au public à la fois l'existence des savants orientalistes et celle d'une littérature asiatique; on put, de bonne heure, connaître Sadi, Pilpay et Confucius, le Koran et quelques livres de philosophie chinoise[12]; alors les écrivains s'empressèrent de réfuter Mahomet ou d'exalter Confucius, après avoir lu cent verset de l'un ou dix sentences de l'autre. Si superficielle que fût celle érudition, trop prestement acquise, il n'y en avait pas moins là de quoi modifier beaucoup la notion de l'Orient.

A ces premiers orientalistes les encouragements royaux ne manquèrent pas. Sur ce point encore, Colbert s'intéressa beaucoup à la révélation de l'Orient. De même qu'il encourageait les voyageurs et surtout les commerçants, de même il fit donner des subventions aux savants; il créa des chaires au Collège de France, institua des "secrétaires interprètes du roi aux langues orientales"; des missions archéologiques furent envoyées en Égypte, en Asie Mineure, à Constantinople, plus loin même dans l'Orient[13]; des sommes importantes furent dépensées pour l'achat de médailles et d'objets exotiques; et le cabinet du roi s'enrichit peu à peu d'une masse considérable de manuscrits orientaux, que ne devaient pas épuiser, malgré leur féconde curiosité, les traducteurs du XVIIIe et du XIXe siècle.

Ce premier élan vers l'étude scientifique du monde oriental se termine à peu près à la fin du XVIIe siècle : la *Bibliothèque orientale* de D'Herbelot (1697) marque en effet non pas un arrêt, mais comme une étape dans le dévelopement de ces études : elle résume et codifie les efforts que pendant plus de cent cinquante ans avaient accumulés les savants de France et d'Europe. Cet énorme *in-folio* offre à sa première page un interminable sous-titre (honnête habitude qu'on avait alors d'inscrire en tête du livre tout son contenu!) : *Dictionnaire universel contenant généralement tout ce qui regarde la connaissance des peuples de l'Orient*[14], ... etc.; en effet, dans le livre, comme dans le titre, tout avait sa place : histoires, traditions, religions, politique, sciences, arts, biographies, ... etc., le tout disposé sous des rubriques commodes, accompagné de tables des matières qui en rendaient l'usage aisé même aux moins érudits. On s'attend bien qu'il y ait en ce livre beaucoup d'erreurs et que la critique y soit généralement insuffisante; néanmoins cette œuvre, aujourd'hui encore tenue en grande estime, était une richesse extraordinaire pour une science encore bien pauvre. Il va de soi qu'un tel instrument de travail facilitait la tâche des savants, et rendait possibles des découvertes nouvelles; on eût dit de multiples sondages, exécutés méthodiquement sur l'emplacement tout entier de la mine, jusque-là exploitée un peu au hasard. Mais le public en tira lui aussi avantage : le livre de D'Herbelot devint une *source* où directement chacun alla puiser, quand il voulut parler de l'Orient. Nombre d'auteurs dramatiques et de romanciers, d'historiens ou de philosophes, avouent ce qu'ils lui doivent; mais combien se taisent qui l'ont effrontément pillé!

Déjà au moment où paraît la *Bibliothèque orientale*, une nouvelle génération d'orientalistes est arrivée à maturité. Mais avant d'étudier cette seconde période, qui va de Galland et de Petis de la Croix jusqu'à Anquetil du Perron, il faut dire en peu de mots quelle contribution les orientalistes de la première heure apportèrent à la conception du public sur l'Orient. Comme ils furent les premiers à l'œuvre, ils purent la marquer au coin de leur esprit; et leur influence fut, sinon plus scientifique, du moins plus générale et plus profonde que celle de leurs disciples.

Or leur état d'esprit était bien singulier : à quelques exceptions près, ils n'avaient point voyagé en Orient : toute leur science était livresque. Tout ce qui était écrit leur paraissait vrai; si Confucius émettait de belles maximes, c'est donc que les Chinois les mettaient en pratique. Un livre de théologie, un traité de philosophie devenait l'image exacte de mœurs réelles[15]. Puis la lecture des manuscrits orientaux était assez difficile pour que le savant eût le droit de s'extasier sur son propre travail : à travers la fatigue de son esprit contracté, les pensées ordinaires revêtaient une beauté singulière, et les sentences remarquables devenaient des traits de sublime philosophie. Peu à peu l'érudit s'enthousiasmait[16] : et l'imprimeur n'était pas loin qui reproduirait son latin cicéronien ou ses phrases oratoires en l'honneur de Confucius. La Chine des savants fut plus merveilleuse encore que celle des missionnaires; elle ne devait être dépassée que par celle des philosophes!

Au frontispice d'une dissertation latine[17], l'érudit Spizelius fit représenter un mandarin assis, au travail, avec un serviteur tenant au-dessus de lui une grande ombrelle : c'était bien ainsi que les savants devaient imaginer la Chine, et avec elle un peu l'Orient tout entier. De la Chine des missionnaires ils avaient surtout retenu ce qui était dit des mandarins et des lettrés; ils admiraient ce pays étonnant où, l'empereur étant lui-même un érudit, toutes les gloires, tous les honneurs, toutes les charges publiques, et, avec elles, les richesses, allaient aux hommes d'étude. Leur enthousiasme débordait d'autant plus volontiers qu'en faisant l'éloge des mandarins, leurs collègues lointains, ils avaient vaguement conscience de rehausser leur propre dignité. Tout sujet leur était bon pour arriver à ce thème favori. Isaac Vossius[18], écrivant un traité sur l'antiquité du monde, est amené à parler des tables de chronologie chinoise, récemment révélées par les Jésuites. Immédiatement il s'exalte : le pays où l'on fait de si belle chronologie est un pays merveilleux; point de guerres, point de querelles, on s'adonne uniquement au plaisir et à la contemplation de la nature : les étrangers qui y vont n'en veulent plus revenir[19]. Tous les savants répétaient le même cantique de doctes louanges[20].

Mais une autre raison les inclinait à tant de bonne volonté vers l'Orient. En général, malgré une déférence tout extérieure, ils n'avaient pas beaucoup de sympathie pour l'Église qui, un siècle auparavant, persécutait leurs devanciers, et surveillait encore leurs propres travaux avec hostilité. Or ils s'aperçurent que cet Orient, si vanté par les Jésuites, on pouvait le retourner aimablement contre la religion, sans que d'abord personne prît garde à ce détour : on dirait de

Mahomet ce qu'on n'osait dire de Jésus-Christ, et l'on constaterait que Confucius avait fort bien agi en pratiquant des maximes tout opposées à celles de Rome. De cette tactique les érudits du XVIIe siècle usèrent en général prudemment, mais parfois des scandales éclatèrent, assez bruyants pour que les libertins et les philosophes fussent avertis de l'excellence de cette méthode. Ainsi le mathématicien Wolff fut accusé, condamné et exilé, pour avoir à Hall, dans une cérémonie académique, prononcé l'éloge de Confucius[21]; ne le mettait-il pas en effet au rang des grands prophètes de toutes les religions, et parmi eux de Jésus-Christ[22]! L'affaire eut assez de retentissement pour que Voltaire en ait dit quelque chose dans son *Dictionnaire philosophique*[23]; s'il avait fallu lui faire un procès, à lui, toutes les fois qu'il eut recours à cet ingénieux procédé, il aurait lassé les juges par ses récidives.

Cette vision d'un Orient idéal et d'une Chine philosophe ne pouvait que plaire aux hommes du XVIIIe siècle. Aussi les nouveaux orientalistes, s'ils ont perfectionné admirablement la science qu'ils avaient héritée de leurs ancêtres, n'ont pas manqué de l'entreprendre dans le même esprit. Pendant tout le siècle des Encyclopédistes, la révélation scientifique de l'Orient fut plus d'une fois détournée au profit de la libre pensée; les orientalistes eux-mêmes n'y faisaient point difficulté ; et si cela risquait de devenir une faiblesse plus tard, cela fut d'abord une force, puisqu'il fut ainsi possible au public de s'intéresser à des sciences un peu rébarbatives.

Notes

1. [G.] Dugat, *Histoire des orientalistes de l'Europe* (ouvrage inachevé), t. 1, Préface, p. iii. Voir, dans Langlois, *Manuel de Bibliographie historique*, [1896,] p. 334, quelques indications sur les études orientalistes au XVIIe et au XVIIIe siècle.
2. Pendant longtemps on ne sépara guère l'étude de l'arabe de celle de l'hébreu, du syriaque et du chaldéen. Nombre de dictionnaires et de grammaires, au XVIe et au XVIIe siècle, unissent ces quatre langues. Par exemple, et comme type, voir l'ouvrage de Hottinger, *Grammatica quatuor linguarum hebraïca, syriaca, chaldaïca et arabica*, Heidelberg, 1658.
3. Le terme lui-même parait bien tard. L'Académie l'admet en 1835, et il n'a guère paru qu'à la fin du XVIIIe siècle, au moment où précisément se constituait le véritable orientalisme.
4. Colomesius, *Gallia orientalis*, 1665.
5. Auteur, en particulier, d'une grammaire arabe. Il avait voyagé en Orient. Voir A. Lefranc, *Histoire du Collège de France*, [1893,] p. 159 et 184.
6. Erpenius, Bocharl, Castell, Golius, Hottinger.
7. Avait été consul en Égypte.
8. Oncle du voyageur.
9. Dugat, *ouvrage cité*, Préface, p. xxviii.
10. Parmi les principaux : Grammaire arabe d'Erpenius, 1631; – Une grammaire et un dictionnaire japonais publiés en 1632 par la Congrégation *De propaganda fide*; – Une grammaire persane, 1649; – Golius, *Dictionnaire arabe*, 1653; – Hottinger, *Grammatica quatuor linguarum*, 1659; – *Bibliotheca orientalis* et *Etymologium orientale*, 1661; – Thévenot, *Grammaire tartare*, 1682. – Un dictionnaire persan, 1684.
11. Dugat, *ouvrage cité*, Préface. Les poinçons furent donnés en 1691 à l'Imprimerie royale.

12. Voir plus loin dans le cours du chapitre.
13. Osmont, *Missions archéologiques*, Paris, 1902 : il y eut au XVIIe siècle au moins huit missions en Asie.
14. Voir en 1658, du même genre, mais moins considérable : Hottinger, *Promptuarium seu Bibliotheca orientalis*. Le dictionnaire de D'Herbelot a été publié après sa mort et achevé par Galland. Il y eut plusieurs rééditions, 1776 et 1777. En 1780 paraît un *Supplément*, par Visdelou et Galland. Il y eut un abrégé en 1782 – et une nouvelle réédition en 1797.
15. Voir, par exemple, Lettre du P. Parennin au directeur de l'Académie des Sciences, 11 avril 1730.
16. Voir, dans Marmontel, *Mémoires*, liv. VI, un amusant portrait de Mairan. "Il était quelquefois soucieux de ce qui se passait à la Chine; mais lorsqu'il en avait reçu des nouvelles, ... il était rayonnant de joie. ... Quelles âmes que celles qui ne sont inquiètes que des mœurs et des arts des Chinois!"
17. Spizelii *de Re litteraria Sinensium Commentarius*, Leyde, 1660.
18. Voltaire, *Essai sur les Mœurs*, chap. II : 'Dans le siècle passé nous ne connaissions pas assez la Chine. Vossius l'admirait en tout avec exagération. ...'
19. *De vera aetate mundi*, 1665, p. 44. Voir Spizelius, *Ouvrage cité*, p. 1.
20. Sur les contradicteurs, voir Voltaire, *Essais sur les Mœurs*, chap. II, et l'article de l'*Encyclopédie* de D'Alembert sur les Chinois. – Au XVIIIe siècle encore Le Beau citera, comme comble de gloire pour l'*Abrégé chronologique* du président Hénault, ce fait qu'il a été traduit en Chine. (*Histoire de l'Académie royale des Inscriptions et Belles-Lettres*, XXVIII, 135.)
21. *Oratio de Sinarum philosophia practica* (12 juillet 1721). Francfort-sur-le-Mein, 1726.
22. P. 24.
23. Au mot CHINE section II.

[The seventeenth century is 'the period in which the literary world discovered, as it were, exotic lands'.[1] The oriental languages – Arabic at least – were not altogether unknown in the Middle Ages as scholars were drawn to them through their studies of Hebrew and Syriac, which a good knowledge of the Bible demanded.[2] A few rare scholars who had been taught by Greeks or converted Muslims were fully occupied with this difficult task and did not dream of publishing their findings: there were no real translations, grammars or dictionaries. The real precursors of the future oriental science were the taking of Constantinople, the exodus of educated Greeks to the West, the impetus the Reformation gave to critical interpretation of the Bible and prodigious efforts undertaken by Renaissance scholars.[3] From the sixteenth century the main European universities had chairs in Arabic: one of them was created by the Collège de France; and it proved once again that there is no more beneficial way to learn than by teaching the scientific knowledge one wishes to acquire. The obscure, daunting Latin names of the French scholars who devoted their most fervent endeavours to the study of oriental languages can be found in the *Gallia orientalis* by the bibliographer Colomesius;[4] the majority studied only Hebrew but some, like Scaliger and particularly Postel, 'lector in Greek, Hebrew and Arabic' at the Collège de France,[5] had already acquired a genuine knowledge of Arabic. The first generation of seventeenth-century teachers and pupils could begin exploring a field which was previously so obscure that the very extent of it was unknown.

During this period, work on orientalism in fact took place outside France, in England and Holland;[6] but it was already a kind of international science, and it mattered little whether the books were edited in Leiden, Cologne, Paris or Rome as they were all written in Latin. However, in seventeenth-century France, there was a stream of diligent orientalist scholars. The best-known among them were: Du Ryer, who first translated the Koran;[7] Thévenot, custodian of the king's library;[8] Vattier, professor of Arabic at the College de France; and finally D'Herbelot, author of the *Bibliothèque orientale*. In addition there were grammarians, lexicographers and translators whose contribution to the work is less known.

The aim of this early period was to produce 'the tools with which to be able to plum the literary depths of the Orient at a later stage'.[9] Consequently more than twenty grammars and glossaries appeared between Du Ryer's *Rudimenta grammatices linguae turcicae* in 1630 and D'Herbelot's *Bibliothèque orientale* in 1697.[10] There was a pressing need for these; soldiers ready for battle need an army first and a clear strategy on which to base their drills. But what purpose do all their training exercises serve without the opportunity to put them into practice? Not everyone had the means to buy an expensive manuscript in the Orient before passionately deciphering the text. They would have to set about printing the oriental texts themselves, to carve the punches and matrixes required, to give the printing presses Arabic's sinuous characters. From the reign of Louis XIII a few texts could be published and the royal stationery office, with its beautiful editions, lent its support to this private initiative at the end of the seventeenth century.[11]

Before excavations were complete, parts of the future building rose from the foundations which had barely been cleared; through Latin or French translations the public learnt of the existence of orientalist scholars and Asian literature. They were soon able to read Sadi, Pilpay and Confucius, the Koran and some Chinese philosophy books:[12] writers then jostled to contradict Mohammed or praise Confucius after reading a hundred lines of one or ten sayings of the other. Superficial though their swiftly acquired erudition was, it was sufficient to change the notion of the Orient radically.

The Crown encouraged the work of the early orientalists and the discovery of the Orient was of great interest to Colbert. He encouraged travel and particularly commerce but also granted subsidies to scholars. He created professorships at the Collège de France and 'interpreters in oriental languages as secretaries to the king'. Archaeological expeditions were sent to Egypt, Asia Minor, Constantinople and even further afield;[13] huge sums of money were lavished on jewellery and exotic objects; and the king's court gradually amassed a valuable collection of oriental manuscripts which would sustain the thirst for knowledge of translators in the eighteenth and nineteenth centuries.

This first impetus of scientific oriental study ended around the end of the seventeenth century: D'Herbelot's *Bibliothèque orientalis* (1697) represents a stage in its development rather than an end to it, the codification of French and European scholars' endeavours over more than a hundred and fifty years. The enormous tome has a lengthy subtitle on the first page (in accordance with the common practice of outlining an entire book's contents at the beginning!): *A universal dictionary of general knowledge pertaining to oriental countries*[14] ... etc. Indeed the clarity of the title was reflected in the book itself with sections on history, traditions, religion, politics, science, art, biography ... etc., along with a table of contents which even the less erudite found easy to use. Despite the work's many errors and lack of depth of analysis, it is still considered an important work and was an extremely valuable resource in what was then a humble science. Naturally it served as a reference facilitating research and new discoveries. It was as if exploitation of the mine had been haphazard until then and now became systematic and wide-ranging. D'Herbelot's book became an authoritative text to which any member of the public could refer when commenting on the Orient. While numerous playwrights and novelists, historians and philosophers acknowledge their debt to him, how many plagiarists remain silent?

Just as the *Bibliothèque orientale* appeared, a new generation of orientalists came into its own. But before studying this second wave from Galland and Petis de la Croix to Anquetil du Perron, let us sum up how the public's perception of the Orient was influenced by the early orientalists. Pioneers in the field, they left their mark; and in comparison with their disciples, they exerted a less scientific but deeper and more widespread influence.

The way in which their entire science was derived from books reflected a strange way of thinking: with few exceptions they had never travelled. They believed everything they read: surely the Chinese practised Confucius' beautiful sayings? Theology books and philosophical treatises were considered a precise reflection of real life.[15] They allowed themselves to be carried away by the oriental manuscripts they strained to decipher.[16] In their tense, fatigued minds everyday thoughts took on an extraordinary beauty and remarkable sayings turned into magnificent philosophical tracts. Learned men grew more and more enthusiastic and their Ciceronian Latin and oratory in Confucius' honour was soon in print. They had a more idealised view of China than the earlier missionaries which was surpassed only by the later philosophers!

The frontispiece of a Latin dissertation by Spizelius shows a mandarin seated at work with a large shade held above his head by a servant:[17] this was exactly how scholars imagined not only China to be but perhaps the entire Orient. From missionary times in China they remembered above all what was said about the mandarins and men of letters. They admired this amazing country where, the emperor himself being erudite, glory, honour and the wealth of public office were bestowed on the men of letters. They were all the more willing to be carried away with their enthusiasm given that, by praising their faraway mandarin colleagues, they were vaguely aware of boosting their own self-esteem. Any pretext served to discourse on their favourite theme. In his treatise on antiquity Isaac Vossius comments on the Chinese calendars recently discovered by the Jesuits.[18] He launches into praise for the marvellous country in which there are no wars or conflicts, life is devoted to pleasure and contemplating nature and from which foreigners are reluctant to return.[19] This same song of praise was repeated by other scholars.[20]

There was another reason for their leaning so favourably towards the Orient. Despite showing outward signs of respect, they generally had little sympathy for the Church which, only a century before, had persecuted their predecessors and which remained hostile to their own work. They then realised that the Orient, held in such high regard by the Jesuits, could be used to subtly challenge religion without at first causing alarm. What they did not dare say about Jesus Christ, they said about Mohammed; and they claimed that Confucius had acted wisely in practising a doctrine opposed to the Church of Rome. The tactic was generally used with caution by seventeenth-century erudites, but scandals did at times occur which were enough to alert libertines and philosophers to its effectiveness. Thus the mathematician Wolff was accused, condemned and exiled for having praised Confucius in an academic ceremony at Halle.[21] He had claimed that he was among the great religious prophets including Jesus Christ.[22] The repercussions of the affair were such that Voltaire commented in his *Dictionnaire philosophique* that if he himself had been subjected to trial every time he had had recourse to the same technique, the judges would have grown weary of his offences.[23]

In the eighteenth century the vision of an idealised Orient and the association of philosophy with China could not fail to please. So the new orientalists, in much the same spirit as their ancestors, succeeded admirably in perfecting the science they had inherited. During the period of Diderot's Encyclopedists, scientific discovery of the Orient was on more than one occasion manipulated in the cause of freethinking. The orientalists themselves were not opposed to it and though it later became a weakness, it was initially a strength, allowing the public to develop an interest in this somewhat daunting science.

NOTES

1. G. Dugat, *Histoire des orientalistes de l'Europe* (unfinished work), Preface, p. iii. For references to orientalist studies in the seventeenth and eighteenth century, see Langlois, *Manuel de Bibliographie historique*, 1896, p. 334.
2. For a long time Arabic was not separate from the study of Hebrew, Syriac and Chaldean. The four languages are grouped together in many dictionaries and grammars. For a typical example see Hottinger, *Grammatica quatuor linguarum hebraïca, syriaca, chaldaïca et arabica*, Heidelberg, 1658.
3. The term hardly appeared until the end of the eighteenth century and was admitted by the Academy in 1835 when orientalism became fully constituted.
4. Colomesius, *Gallia orientalis*, 1665.
5. The author of an Arabic grammar, he had travelled to the Orient. See A. Lefranc, *Histoire du Collège de France*, 1893, pp. 159 and 184.

6. Erpenius, Bochart, Castell, Golius and Hottinger.

7. He had been consul in Egypt.

8. The traveller's uncle.

9. Dugat, *op. cit.*, Preface, p. xxviii.

10. Among the main ones: an Arabic grammar, Erpenius, 1631; a Japanese grammar and dictionary published in 1632 by Congrégation *De propaganda fide*; a Persian grammar, 1649; Golius, *Dictionnaire arabe*, 1653; Hottinger, *Grammatica quatuor linguarum*, 1659; *Bibliotheca orientalis* and *Etymologium orientale*, 1661; Thévenot, *Grammaire tartare*, 1682. A Persian dictionary, 1684.

11. Dugat, *op. cit.*, Preface. The punches were given to the royal stationery office in 1691.

12. See later in the chapter.

13. Osmont, *Missions archéologiques*, Paris, 1902. There were at least eight missions to Asia in the seventeenth century.

14. See the less important work by Hottinger, *Promptuarium seu Bibliotheca orientalis*, 1658. D'Herbelot's dictionary was published after his death and finished by Galland. There were several re-editions in 1776 and 1777. In 1780, a *Supplément* appeared by Visdelou and Galland. There was an abridged version in 1782 and a new re-edition in 1797.

15. See, for example, Letter from Père Parennin to the director of the Académie des Sciences, 11 April 1730.

16. See Marmontel, *Mémoires*, book VI, for an amusing portrait of Mairan. 'He sometimes worried about what was happening in China, but after receiving news ... he appeared delighted ... Those lucky souls who only concern themselves with Chinese art and culture!'

17. Spizelius, *de Re litteraria Sinensium Commentarius*, Leiden, 1660.

18. Voltaire, *Essai sur les Mœurs*, chap. ii: 'In the last century not enough was known about China. Vossius' admiration for everything about it was excessive ...'

19. *De vera aetate mundi*, 1665, p. 44. See Spizelius, *op. cit.*, p. 1.

20. For critics, see Voltaire, *Essai sur les Mœurs*, chap. ii, and D'Alembert's article on the Chinese in the *Encyclopédie*. In the eighteenth century, Le Beau cited – as the epitome of its success – the fact that Hénault's *Abrégé chronologique* had been translated into Chinese. (*Histoire de l'Académie royale des Inscriptions et Belles-Lettres*, XXVIII, 135.)

21. *Oratio de Sinarum philosophia practica* (12 July 1721). Francfort-sur-le-Mein, 1726.

22. P. 24.

23. Under the entry for CHINA, section ii.]

5

THE ASIATIC SOCIETY OF CALCUTTA

Raymond Schwab

Raymond Schwab's La Renaissance Orientale *(1950) remains essential reading for the student of oriental studies. In his account of the origins of oriental studies in Europe, Schwab describes the contributions made by the 'old Catholic' schools in Holland and Switzerland, individual French scholars such as Barthélemy d'Herbelot and Abraham Anquetil-Duperron, Portuguese and Spanish explorers, and Jesuit missionaries dispatched to India and China in the seventeenth and eighteenth centuries. But it was not until the British, following the conquest of Bengal, instituted a thoroughgoing research programme designed to produce an understanding of the laws and customs of the Hindus that a real breakthrough was made, led by three great scholars, William ('Oriental') Jones, Charles Wilkins and Henry Thomas Colebrooke.*

The decisive period in Indic studies began with the arrival of English civil servants in Calcutta around 1780, who supported by the governor, Warren Hastings, began an extraordinary undertaking. Learning does not determine its own course alone, and the initial intention, conversion, yielded to or was intermingled with another intention, conquest. The aim in this period was no longer to clear a path for knowledge but for administration. For this reason, fact-finding teams were encouraged, which could produce conclusive results more quickly than individual efforts, however talented.

Raymond Schwab, *The Oriental Renaissance: Europe's Discovery of India and the East, 1680–1880* (New York: Columbia University Press, 1984), pp. 33–6.

William Jones, following in Anquetil's footsteps, made many linguistic discoveries. While still a young man, Jones had attacked Anquetil's *Avesta*, although he later recognized his injustice. In the interim Jones had come to reconsider matters he had once thought settled. Only twelve years separated his quarrel with Anquetil from his own departure for India. During those years, Jones yearned to travel to India, but did not make the journey until he was thirty-eight. Curiosity about the Orient and its languages was seething everywhere, and Jones was already a polyglot linguist and had mastered Persian grammar, an achievement rare for his time. The English conquest gave him his opportunity. Jones wanted to administer justice in Calcutta and, from Pondicherry to Bombay, he was able to accomplish what Anquetil had first set out to achieve. The stir created by the apocryphal *Ezour-Vedam* and the false shastras of Holwell and Alexander Dow during the interval of waiting had reanimated Jones's desire to carry out research on the spot. In his preface to *Sakuntala; or, The Fatal Ring: an Indian Drama*, Jones acknowledged what his vocation owed to the *Lettres édifiantes*, although he did not hold them in high esteem.

When British authority was installed in Bengal, its first priority was to thread the labyrinth of local custom and legislation, and its representatives realized that languages would be the key to dominion. These representatives fortunately included such men as Robert Clive, Henry Vansittart, and, above all, Warren Hastings. Hastings – despotic, discredited, disputed, and legendary – was a *cause célèbre* who provoked some of the finest judicial and political oratory in English parliamentary history. Colebrooke, who began his career as a minor employee of the Exchequer in Bengal, embarked upon his own study of languages at the same time that Edmund Burke, in London, was vehemently denouncing Hastings' mistakes – with such disturbing evidence that Colebrooke considered leaving the colony because of its ill repute. Two years later Hastings was recalled to London for trial and, although exempted from corporal punishment, languished for years in public scorn.

One's judgment of Hastings becomes more complex if one considers the assessment of Thomas Babington Macaulay, who was himself a member of the Supreme Council for India from 1834 until 1838 and who served as president of the commission that created the criminal code for India. Writing in the *Edinburgh Review* (October 1841) Macaulay, who clearly did not scruple to take the side of India against its governors, writes 'Our feeling towards him [Hastings] is not exactly that of the House of Commons which impeached him in 1787; neither is it that of the House of Commons which uncovered and stood up to receive him in 1813.' Macaulay goes on to state simply that Hastings 'had great qualities, and he rendered great services to the state.' In the history of Indic studies Hastings ranks as a great benefactor. Drawn to poetry, which was his daily joy during his forced retirement, impassioned on the subject of oriental languages, and 'deeply skilled in Persian and Arabic literature,' Hastings had, since 1764, 'conceived that the cultivation of Persian literature might with advantage be made a part of the liberal education of an English gentleman; and he drew up a plan with that view. It is said that the University of Oxford, in which oriental learning had never, since the revival of letters, been wholly neglected, was to be the seat of the institution which he contemplated. ... Hastings called on Samuel Johnson,' a man whose attainments in similar capacities were certainly no less than those of Jones, 'with the hope, it would seem, of interesting in this project a man who enjoyed the highest literary reputations, and who was particularly connected with Oxford. The interview appears to have left on Johnson's mind a most favorable impression of the talents and attainments of his visitor.' Moreover, as Hastings was, in spite of his excesses, the most popular of the authorities among the Hindus because of his interest in them, it was only natural that he would eventually conceive of establishing the study of their languages on the subcontinent. As Macaulay said, 'The Pundits of Bengal had always looked with great jealousy on the attempts of foreigners to pry into those mysteries which were locked up in the sacred dialect. ... That apprehension, the wisdom and moderation of Hastings removed. He was the first foreign ruler who succeeded in gaining the confidence of the hereditary priests of India, and who induced them to lay open to English scholars the secrets of the old Brahminical theology and jurisprudence.'

Hence, one must acknowledge that even if Hastings proved a bit lavish with the local wealth in regard to this or that mistress, his mind also encompassed intellectual concerns. In his *Recherches*, Anquetil, who was not sparing in his criticism of British imperialism, treated Hastings with justice during his trial – in defiance of his enemies in London – and, speaking of the ingratitude that was destined for colonial conquerors, compared Hastings to the French governor Dupleix. Anquetil attested that the pandits who taught Sanskrit to the English refused any remuneration beyond the rupee a day necessary for their sustenance. If they had previously forbidden access to their books it was because, prior to Anquetil and to Hastings' employees, Europeans had approached them with a negative bias. Langlès noted: 'It was in response to a direct summons from Hastings that the Brahmans versed in the Shastras ... came to Calcutta from all parts of India. Gathering at Fort William and supplied with the most authentic texts, they drafted a comprehensive treatise on Indic law in the Hindu language. This was subsequently translated into Persian, and into English by Halhed under the title *Code of Gentoo Laws*. It was also under Hastings' auspices that Charles Wilkins studied Sanskrit and had the distinction of publishing the first translation in a European language based directly on a Sanskrit text.'

In fact it was Wilkins who, after Halhed had furnished the rudiments of Bengali, changed the course of linguistic history by going directly to Sanskrit, which was to reveal the structure of secondary languages although the reverse had been hoped for. Jones later asserted that he would not have learned Sanskrit without Wilkins. Within ten years – the ten years he had left to live – Jones attained a knowledge of Sanskrit that astounded his instructors. It was Hastings who had sparked the research upon which his own political success depended.

Destiny's natural consent to human exigency placed in the offices of the East India Company two men who seemed only to be waiting for their cue: Charles Wilkins, who was employed there from 1770, and Henry Thomas Colebrooke, who arrived in 1783. In this same year everything came together with the arrival in Calcutta of William Jones, who had at last obtained a judgeship on the Supreme Court, where Colebrooke later sat.

These three, men of the most widely divergent character, pursued an identical vocation. One of them, a well-read jurist, affable and brilliant, enthusiastic and spontaneous, the 'harmonious Jones' already well known as a gifted poet and scholar, was called by Samuel Johnson one of the most enlightened of the sons of man. Jones, the son of a professor of mathematics, had authored and published poems in Greek at the age of fifteen. At the age of sixteen, having learned Persian from a Syrian in London, Jones translated Hafiz into English verse. In 1771, at the age of twenty-five, Jones produced a remarkable Persian grammar which he translated into French. It was also in the language – and, as much as possible, in the style – of Voltaire that Jones penned his famous *Lettre* to Anquetil concerning the latter's *Avesta*. It was a witty, impudent, and ultimately unjust attack. No other orientalist, Pauthier later affirmed, had so broad a range of knowledge at his disposal as Jones did. Jones himself acknowledged that he had a thorough knowledge of thirteen of the twenty-eight languages he had studied. His open-hearted nature and his curiosity, his penetrating intuition, his ardor, and his grace can all be read in his features, preserved, fortunately, in the portrait by Joshua Reynolds and reproduced in engravings as early as 1779 and 1782. It seems fitting that his name should be given to a formerly mythical tree: *Jonesia asoka*.

Jones was interested in everything, uncovering and compiling information in many fields: Indian chronology, literature, music, fauna and flora. He discovered and guided others to the summits of poetry and philosophy, although the study of local law alone seemed entirely serious to him. But since his interests were so widely scattered, Jones, like others whose disposition it is to be easily fascinated, was not a creator of methods. His impact on the new science, which owed so much to him, was less that of the founder of a school of thought than a sower of vast fields that his successors would harvest. In 1794 he died in Calcutta at the age of forty-eight, and he was buried there. A monument was raised in his memory at Saint Paul's Cathedral by the East India Company, and a second was placed at Oxford by his widow. The bicentennial of Jones's birth in 1946 was celebrated in London, Calcutta, and New York, and by Indic scholars everywhere. The nineteenth-century English poets read and frequently quoted Jones as an orientalist and admired him as a poet.

PART III
FOUNDATIONS OF A CRITIQUE

Many of the concepts employed by Edward Said in his study of orientalism, such as canonical discourse, epistemic power, logocentric thought and truth-as-illusion, are ultimately derived from the work of Friedrich Nietzsche, the nineteenth-century German philosopher. Nietzsche's ideas were transmitted to Said by way of the work of Michel Foucault, the French historian and philosopher, who in his article 'Nietzsche, Genealogy, History', in *Hommage à Jean Hyppolite* (Paris: Presses Universitaires de France, 1971), attempted to work out the implications for the writing of history of Nietzsche's philosophy. Other continental writers who influenced Said in his work include Antonio Gramsci and Jacques Derrida.

6

APPEARANCE AND THE THING-IN-ITSELF

Friedrich Nietzsche

In the following extract from Human, All Too Human, *Nietzsche explains that the world of appearance, far from being a product of the 'thing-in-itself', is actually the product of man's imagination, of his 'erroneous' conceptions. Such an analysis, as Nietzsche makes clear, points eventually to the abolition of essence, the metaphysical world and the 'thing-in-itself'.*

Appearance and the thing-in-itself. Philosophers tend to confront life and experience (what they call the world of appearance) as they would a painting that has been revealed once and for all, depicting with unchanging constancy the same event. They think they must interpret this event correctly in order to conclude something about the essence which produced the painting, that is, about the thing-in-itself, which always tends to be regarded as the sufficient reason for the world of appearance. Conversely, stricter logicians, after they had rigorously established the concept of the metaphysical as the concept of that which is unconditioned and consequently unconditioning, denied any connection between the unconditioned (the metaphysical world) and the world we are familiar with. So that the thing-in-itself does *not* appear in the world of appearances, and any conclusion about the former on the basis of the latter must be rejected. But both sides overlook the possibility that that painting – that which to us men means life and experience – has gradually *evolved*, indeed is

Friedrich Nietzsche, *Human, All Too Human* (London: University of Nebraska Press, 1984), Section 1.16, pp. 23–4.

still *evolving*, and therefore should not be considered a fixed quantity, on which basis a conclusion about the creator (the sufficient reason) may be made, or even rejected. Because for thousands of years we have been looking at the world with moral, aesthetic, and religious claims, with blind inclination, passion, or fear, and have indulged ourselves fully in the bad habits of illogical thought, this world has gradually *become* so strangely colorful, frightful, profound, soulful; it has acquired color, but we have been the painters: the human intellect allowed appearance to appear, and projected its mistaken conceptions onto the things. Only late, very late, does the intellect stop to think: and now the world of experience and the thing-in-itself seem so extraordinarily different and separate that it rejects any conclusion about the latter from the former, or else, in an awful, mysterious way, it demands the *abandonment* of our intellect, of our personal will in order to come to the essential by *becoming essential*. On the other hand, other people have gathered together all characteristic traits of our world of appearances (that is, our inherited idea of the world, spun out of intellectual errors) and, *instead of accusing the intellect*, have attacked the essence of things for causing this real, very uncanny character of the world, and have preached salvation from being.

The steady and arduous progress of science, which will ultimately celebrate its greatest triumph in an *ontogeny of thought*, will deal decisively with all these views. Its conclusion might perhaps end up with this tenet: That which we now call the world is the result of a number of errors and fantasies, which came about gradually in the overall development of organic beings, fusing with one another, and now handed down to us as a collected treasure of our entire past – a treasure: for the *value* of our humanity rests upon it. From this world of idea strict science can, in fact, release us only to a small extent (something we by no means desire), in that it is unable to break significantly the power of ancient habits of feeling. But it can illuminate, quite gradually, step by step, the history of the origin of that world as idea – and lift us, for moments at least, above the whole process. Perhaps we will recognize then that the thing-in-itself deserves a Homeric laugh, in that it *seemed* to be so much, indeed everything, and is actually empty, that is, empty of meaning.

7

ON HEGEMONY AND DIRECT RULE

Antonio Gramsci

According to Richard Bellamy, who edited Antonio Gramsci: Pre-Prison Writings *(Cambridge University Press, 1994), the concept of hegemony had a long history in the Russian labour movements, going back to the writings of Plekhanov. In the following extract, from his prison writings, Gramsci employs the concept – later used by Edward Said, in* Orientalism *– in the context of social class. According to Gramsci, hegemony is exercised in society by the ruling class, supported by the intellectuals, the 'officers' of the ruling class, and the apparatus of state coercion.*

The relationship between intellectuals and the world of production is not immediate, as is the case for fundamental social groups; it is 'mediated', in different levels, by the whole social fabric, and by the complex of the superstructure of which the intellectuals are in fact the 'officials'. One could measure the 'organic position' of the different intellectual strata, their more or less close connection with a fundamental social class, fixing a gradation of functions and of the superstructure from bottom to top (from the structural base upwards). For the moment we can fix two great 'floors' of the superstructure: that which can be called 'civil society', i.e. all the organisations which are commonly called 'private', and that of 'political society or the State', which corresponds to the function of 'hegemony' which the ruling class exercises over the whole of

A. Gramsci, *The Modern Prince* (New York: International Publishers, 1957), p. 124.

society and to that of 'direct rule' or of command which is expressed in the State and in 'juridical' government. Intellectuals are the 'officers' of the ruling class for the exercise of the subordinate functions of social hegemony and political government, i.e. (1) of the 'spontaneous' consent given by the great masses of the population to the direction imprinted on social life by the fundamental ruling class, a consent which comes into existence 'historically' from the 'prestige' (and hence from the trust) accruing to the ruling class from its position and its function in the world of production; (2) of the apparatus of State coercion, which 'legally' ensures the discipline of those groups which do not 'consent' either actively or passively, but is constituted for the whole of society in anticipation of moments of crisis in command and direction when spontaneous consent diminishes.

8

TRUTH AND POWER

Michel Foucault

In the period of the Cold War, when millions were spent on propaganda, English and American intellectuals can hardly have remained ignorant of the fact that a close relationship existed between power and knowledge. But it was left to Michel Foucault, the French historian and philosopher – in a series of works, commencing with Madness and Civilisation *(1965) and* The Archaeology of Knowledge *(1970) – to persuade them of just how insidious the relationship was. According to Foucault, until the period of the Renaissance people had assumed that language reflected reality (objects, things). But in the late eighteenth and nineteenth centuries language came to be seen, not as a reflection of reality, but as a transparent 'film', dissociated from it. As a result it became possible to identify words and statements not as signs, representing objects and things, but as events, floating in a space, field or* episteme. *In this strange world, knowledge became not so much a matter of fact as the outcome of a struggle for power, in which events and discourses, vehicles of 'economies of power', created new 'networks' and 'regimes' of knowledge – regimes which would themselves survive only until such time as new ones arose, capable of taking their place. Truth, therefore, as Foucault remarked in a conversation regarding power and knowledge (later published in* Power/Knowledge*), was not outside power or lacking in it.*

Michel Foucault, *Power/Knowledge* (New York: Pantheon Books, 1980), pp. 131–3.

The important thing here, I believe, is that truth isn't outside power, or lacking in power: contrary to a myth whose history and functions would repay further study, truth isn't the reward of free spirits, the child of protracted solitude, nor the privilege of those who have succeeded in liberating themselves. Truth is a thing of this world: it is produced only by virtue of multiple forms of constraint. And it induces regular effects of power. Each society has its régime of truth, its 'general politics' of truth: that is, the types of discourse which it accepts and makes function as true; the mechanisms and instances which enable one to distinguish true and false statements, the means by which each is sanctioned; the techniques and procedures accorded value in the acquisition of truth; the status of those who are charged with saying what counts as true.

In societies like ours, the 'political economy' of truth is characterised by five important traits. 'Truth' is centred on the form of scientific discourse and the institutions which produce it; it is subject to constant economic and political incitement (the demand for truth, as much for economic production as for political power); it is the object, under diverse forms, of immense diffusion and consumption (circulating through apparatuses of education and information whose extent is relatively broad in the social body, not withstanding certain strict limitations); it is produced and transmitted under the control, dominant if not exclusive, of a few great political and economic apparatuses (university, army, writing, media); lastly, it is the issue of a whole political debate and social confrontation ('ideological' struggles).

It seems to me that what must now be taken into account in the intellectual is not the 'bearer of universal values'. Rather, it's the person occupying a specific position – but whose specificity is linked, in a society like ours, to the general functioning of an apparatus of truth. In other words, the intellectual has a three-fold specificity: that of his class position (whether as petty-bourgeois in the service of capitalism or 'organic' intellectual of the proletariat); that of his conditions of life and work, linked to his condition as an intellectual (his field of research, his place in a laboratory, the political and economic demands to which he submits or against which he rebels, in the university, the hospital, etc.); lastly, the specificity of the politics of truth in our societies. And it's with this last factor that his position can take on a general significance and that his local, specific struggle can have effects and implications which are not simply professional or sectoral. The intellectual can operate and struggle at the general level of that régime of truth which is so essential to the structure and functioning of our society. There is a battle 'for truth', or at least 'around truth' – it being under-stood once again that by truth I do not mean 'the ensemble of truths which are to be discovered and accepted', but rather 'the ensemble of rules according to which the true and the false are separated and specific effects of power attached to the true', it being understood also that it's not a matter of a battle 'on behalf' of the truth, but of a battle about the status of truth and the economic and political role it plays. It is necessary to think of the political problems of intellectuals not in terms of 'science' and 'ideology', but in terms of 'truth' and 'power'. And thus the question of the professionalisation of intellectuals and the division between intellectual and manual labour can be envisaged in a new way.

All this must seem very confused and uncertain. Uncertain indeed, and what I am saying here is above all to be taken as a hypothesis. In order for it to be a little less confused, however, I would like to put forward a few 'propositions' – not firm assertions, but simply suggestions to be further tested and evaluated.

'Truth' is to be understood as a system of ordered procedures for the production, regulation, distribution, circulation and operation of statements.

'Truth' is linked in a circular relation with systems of power which produce and sustain it, and to effects of power which it induces and which extend it. A 'régime' of truth.

This régime is not merely ideological or superstructural; it was a condition of the formation and development of capitalism. And it's this same régime which, subject to certain modifications, operates in the socialist countries (I leave open here the question of China, about which I know little).

The essential political problem for the intellectual is not to criticise the ideological contents supposedly linked to science, or to ensure that his own scientific practice is accompanied by a correct ideology, but that of ascertaining the possibility of constituting a new politics of truth. The problem is not changing people's consciousnesses – or what's in their heads – but the political, economic, institutional régime of the production of truth.

It's not a matter of emancipating truth from every system of power (which would be a chimera, for truth is already power) but of detaching the power of truth from the forms of hegemony, social, economic and cultural, within which it operates at the present time.

The political question, to sum up, is not error, illusion, alienated consciousness or ideology; it is truth itself. Hence the importance of Nietzsche.

PART IV
ORIENTALISM IN CRISIS

As the noted Indian scholar Aijaz Ahmad points out – in his article 'Orientalism and After', published in *In Theory* (New York: Verso, 1992) – attacks on colonial cultural domination are almost as old as colonialism itself. But it was only in the period of decolonisation following the end of the Second World War that they began to make much impact.

9

ORIENTALISM IN CRISIS

Anouar Abdel-Malek

Anouar Abdel-Malek, whose article 'Orientalism in Crisis' (published in Diogenes *in 1963) must be considered one of the most influential, if not the most influential, of the many critiques of orientalism written in the period immediately following the end of the Second World War, was born in Cairo in 1923. After studying at the University of Aim-Chams, Cairo, and the Sorbonne, and teaching philosophy at the Lycée al-Hourriyya, Cairo, in 1960 he was appointed to a post at the Centre Nationale de la Recherche Scientifique (CNRS) (Sociology), Paris. In 'Orientalism in Crisis', Abdel-Malek explains that, in the period immediately following the end of the Second World War, the 'resurgence' of the peoples of Asia, Africa and Latin America, and the victories achieved by a series of national liberation movements, made a new approach to the problem of understanding the orient necessary. The victories of many of the national liberation movements had plunged the orientalist profession into crisis. Henceforth orientalists would have to treat the 'objects' of their studies as 'sovereign subjects'. No longer would they enjoy direct control of their 'terrain'.*

Let us examine the subject closer. Our study deals naturally with the Arab world, and more particularly with Egypt; it will also touch upon the sector of China and Southeast Asia, in a related fashion.

A. Abdel-Malek, 'Orientalism in Crisis', *Diogenes*, no. 44, winter 1963, pp. 104–12.

Numerous works[1] are at the disposal of scholars, disparate material, full of suggestions, rarely precise, on the history of traditional orientalism – from its foundation, decided on by the Council of Vienna in 1245, and from the first chairs of Oriental languages at the *Universitas magistrorum et scolarium Parisiensium*, until World War II.

One will note with interest, however, that the real impetus of Oriental studies in the two key sectors, that of the Arab world and the Far East, dates essentially from the period of colonial establishment, but, above all, from the domination of the 'forgotten continents' by the European imperialisms (middle and second half of the nineteenth century): the first wave was marked by the creation of orientalist societies (Batavia 1781; Société Asiatique, Paris 1822; Royal Asiatic Society, London 1834; American Oriental Society, 1842; etc.); the second phase witnessed the appearance of orientalist congresses, the first of which took place in Paris in 1873; sixteen congresses were then held up to World War I (the last congress was the one in Vienna in 1912); since then only four have taken place ...

Precisely what kind of studies were these?

The orientalist – 'a scholar versed in the knowledge of the Orient, its languages, its literatures, etc.'[2] – what kind of man, what kind of scholar is he? What are his motivations? What occupies him? What objectives does he set himself to attain?

Michelangelo Guidi (1886–1946) placed himself in the perspective of a philosophy of history as opposed to that of the hellenocentric peoples, upheld, notably, by Werner Jaeger:[3] 'By orientalists, I understand those who study the Near East; for the thought of India and China is certainly of the greatest interest in understanding the spiritual paths (...), but they have no vital contact with us;"We orientalists, in fact, look towards the cultures in which the Oriental element appears in its most complete expression, that is, towards the pure national cultures, towards Islam, for instance, not only with the aim of recreating a foreign world, very high nevertheless, very worthy of scientific consideration, but also as the only means that would enable us to understand fully the nature of the elements of the admirable and very fecund fusion that occurred *in the zone of hellenism*;'[4] 'The orientalist, if he wants to be complete, must start with the classic world. But it would be anti-historical to disregard completely a period which is situated between us and pure antiquity. A *homo classicus* and a *homo orientalis* become, at a certain moment, a recollection or an abstraction. Only a *homo novus* of hellenism is a 'living' product of 'living' movements and not of movements artificially created by the scholars; all have been created by an original historical force.' Therefore 'we do not study these worlds to arrange a new series of phenomena in the show window of the human museum, to describe exotic and marvelous forms, in order to understand the βαρβαρῶν σοφια; we study these worlds rather to relive in their fullness the phases of intimate union of two different traditions, endeavoring to distinguish the modes and functions of one of them, with eyes made more keen by the contemplation of the manifestations of Oriental culture in its total expression, with the possibility of a more precise estimation, with a livelier sensibility,'[5] etc. Is it exaggerated to speak here of romantic 'europeocentrism,'[6] which animates scientific investigation, while one finds in a Raymond Schwab identical themes,[7] and while the seven portraits of English orientalists – S. Ockley, W. Jones, E. H. Palmer, E. G. Browne, R. A. Nicholson, A. J. Arberry – drawn by this latter very recently,[8] are moving essentially in the same sense? But we must see that we are – historically – at the epoch of European hegemony; the retrospective criticism must take this into account.

The most notable works of the principal Western orientalist schools spring from this current of thought, from this vision of orientalism (France, Great Britain, Germany, Spain, Italy, Russia and the United States). Their contribution has been multiple and fruitful. The Lebanese bibliographer Youssef Assaad Dagher distinguishes eight positive elements in the field of Arabic and Islamic studies: the study of ancient civilization; the collection of Arabic manuscripts in European libraries; the establishment of catalogues of manuscripts; the publication of numerous important works; the lesson of method thus given to Oriental scholars; the organization of orientalist congresses; the editing of studies, frequently deficient and erroneous from a linguistic point of view, but precise in the method; and finally, 'this movement has contributed to arousing the national consciousness in the different countries of the Orient and to activating the movement of scientific renaissance and the awakening of the ideal.'[9] We will see further on what is in it.

This vision of traditional orientalism, however, was not the dominant vision; or, rather, it represented, in part, the essential segment of the work, accomplished in the universities and by scholarly societies, without however ignoring the whole range of the work that has been carried out and published within this framework and elsewhere. On the other hand, this study itself was profoundly permeated by postulates, methodological habits and historico-philosophical concepts that were to compromise, often, the results and the scientific value of arduous work, and to lead, *objectively*, a great number of genuine orientalist scholars to the politico-philosophical positions of the other group of researchers.

This latter group was formed by an amalgam of university dons, business-men, military men, colonial officials, missionaries, publicists and adventurers, whose only objective was to gather intelligence information in the area to be occupied, to penetrate the consciousness of the people in order to better assure its enslavement to the European powers. 'The optic of the Arab bureau,' as Jacques Berque rightly observed, has led to the result that, 'sustained, nourished at the same time and limited by action, the study of the North African societies has been oriented from the start.'[10] One may guess in which sense ... The phenomenon is general, since it is built into the structure of the social science of the European countries in the period of imperialist penetration and implantation: Italian orientalism under Mussolini, the psycho-political penetration as practiced by T. E. Lawrence and his school, and previous to them the reports of missionaries, business circles and orientalists (a notable instance being the third provincial congress of orientalists at Lyons, in 1878), etc. – the examples abound, multiply, for we are still in the epoch of humiliation, of occupation, before the great liberating revolutions.[11]

Can one speak, however, despite these very real differences, of a certain similarity in the general conception, the methods and the instruments intro-duced by these two schools of traditional orientalism?

We will answer in the affirmative: the community of interest, and not only of interests, is fundamental, in the face of the other, the world which later was to be called 'third' with regard to the present as history.

1. *General conception*, that is, the vision of the Orient and of Orientals by traditional orientalism:

a) On the level of the *position of the problem*, and the *problematic*, the two groups consider the Orient and Orientals as an 'object' of study, stamped with an otherness – as all that is different, whether it be 'subject' or 'object' – but of a constitutive otherness, of an essentialist character, as we shall see in a moment. This 'object' of study will be, as is customary, passive, non-participating, endowed with a 'historical' subjectivity, above all, non-active, non-autonomous, non-sovereign with regard to itself: the only Orient or Oriental or 'subject' which could be admitted, at the extreme limit, is the alienated being, philosophically, that is, other than itself in relationship to itself, posed, understood, defined – and acted – by others.

b) On the level of the *thematic*, both groups adopt an essentialist conception of the countries, nations and peoples of the Orient under study, a conception which expresses itself through a characterized ethnist typology; the second group will soon proceed with it towards racism.

According to the traditional orientalists, an essence should exist – sometimes even clearly described in metaphysical terms – which constitutes the inalienable and common basis of all the beings considered; this essence is both 'historical,' since it goes back to the dawn of history, and fundamentally a-historical, since it transfixes the being, 'the object' of study, within its inalienable and non-evolutive specificity, instead of defining it as all other beings, states, nations, peoples and cultures – as a product, a resultant of the vection of the forces operating in the field of historical evolution.

Thus one ends with a typology – based on a real specificity, but detached from history, and, consequently, conceived as being intangible, essential – which makes of the studied 'object' another being, with regard to whom the studying subject is transcendent: we will have a *homo Sinicus*, a *homo Arabicus* (and, why not, a *homo Aegypticus*, etc.), a *homo Africanus*,[12] the man – the 'normal man' it is understood – being the European man of the historical period, that is, since Greek antiquity. One sees how much, from the eighteenth to the twentieth century, the hegemonism of possessing minorities, unveiled by Marx and Engels, and the anthropocentrism dismantled by Freud are accompanied by europeocentrism in the area of human and social sciences, and more particularly in those in direct relationship with non-European peoples.

Among the masters of traditional orientalism, none have expressed this theme better, in speaking of the Arabs, dear to his mystic heart, than the great scholar Louis Massignon (1883–1962). In one of his last texts, a short time before his death, he wrote: 'I think that for the problem of the future of the Arabs, it must be found in semitism. I think, that at the base of the Arab difficulties there is this dramatic conflict, this fratricidal hatred between Israel and Ismaël. I think that it must be surmounted. Can we succeed in surmounting it? I believe it must be placed less in the drama of the mechanical incidence of actual technocracy in which Israel, in the final analysis, pulls the strings of the entire world, for due to its superiority of thought and technique in the construction of the problems – because Israel has never ceased posing these problems to itself, it is its strength of hope, an intellectual speculation in a pure state – the Arabs find themselves in collision with it in the claim of exclusivity among the semites, the privileged semites of the right. They, on the contrary, are the outlaws, the excluded; for many reasons, they proved themselves inferior to the task Israel had known how to overcome, but it seems to me that between brothers there should be a reconciliation, for Israel as the Arabs can bring internal testimony to bear; it is the testimony of their language, which is a sacred language, and which is also an instrument of abstract scientific research. The Jewish elite thought and wrote in Arabic during the entire Middle Ages. That is the essential problem.'[13]

The generosity of the sentiment could not hide the nature, profoundly erroneous and capable of pernicious extensions, of this thematic. It would be, almost, comparable to seeing the history of contemporary Europe through the deforming prism of Aryanism.

2. *Methods of study and research.*

These are inevitably determined by the general conception:
a) The past of Oriental nations and cultures quite naturally constitutes the preferred field of study:[14] in 'admitting implicitly that the most brilliant periods of the Orient belong to the past,' one admits, by the same token, 'that their decadence is ineluctable.' And Jean Chesneaux rightly notes that 'the road followed since the second half of the nineteenth century, by the Greco-Latin studies and their rebirth as studies of "dead" civilizations, completely cut off from their contemporary heirs, furnished an eminent model to the orientalists.'[15]
b) This past itself was studied in its cultural aspects – notably the language and religion – detached from social evolution. If the general offensive of anti- and post-Hegelian irrationalism in Europe explains the accent placed on the study of the religious phenomenon, as well as its para-psychical, esoteric aura,

this is tantamount to the rebirth of the studies of Antiquity, at the end of the last century, in the light of the historical method, and more precisely of historical philology, which explains the primacy accorded simultaneously to linguistic and philological studies by traditional orientalists. But the study of Oriental languages – such as Arabic, very much a living language – as dead languages was bound to cause a great number of mistakes, contradictions, errors, just as if one intended to furnish a commentary on the French language (of R. Martin du Gard, of Sartre, or of Aragon) on the basis only of the knowledge of the 'Chansons de geste,' of the English of Shaw or Russell on the basis of Saxon, or of the Italian of Croce, Gramsci or Moravia on the basis of Church Latin.[16]

c)   History, studied as 'structure' was projected, at its best, on the recent past. That which re-emerged, appeared as a prolongation of the past, grandiose but extinct. From historicizing, history became exotic.

d)   The scientific work of the scholars of different Oriental countries was passed over in silence, and for the most part completely ignored, except for a few rare works which are conceived in the sense of orientalism of the cities. The rest was declared to be without value, denigrated, and the retardation, imputable to historical conditions, notably to colonialism, became a specific constitutive characteristic of Oriental mentalities.

3. *The instruments of study and research:*

a)   These are constituted essentially by the accumulation and concentration of the treasures belonging to the countries of Asia, Africa and Latin America in the great European cities: the history of the Cernuschi and Guimet museums in Paris, of the great collections of the British Museum, for example, follows the same trajectory, which is that of the immigration of the scholarly treasures of Europe in the direction of the United States, since 1919. In the field of Arabic studies, especially, the situation is particularly serious: several tens of thousands of manuscripts (the number 140,000 has been mentioned) are outside the Arab world, that is, practically out of reach of Arab researchers themselves; hence, they must work most of the time on the basis of indirect sources dealing with the matters at the core itself of their own national and cultural history. The League of Arab States, as well as several countries, principally Egypt, has established various organisms, publications and projects, whose aim is to restitute to the Arab world its irreplaceable sources.[17]

b)   In the field of modern and contemporary history, the greatest and even the essential part of the materials concerning the colonial and dependent countries (notably India, Egypt and the Arab Near East, the Maghreb, dark Africa, etc.), which are collected in the state archives of the great ex-colonial powers, are for the most part inaccessible, subject to various kinds of interdictions (the least serious being the famous rule of 'fifty years'). The approximative knowledge of the past is thus prolonged into a quest of one's self, full of perilous gaps.

c) The secondary sources used by traditional Western orientalists – reports by colonial administrators,[18] by Catholic or Protestant religious missions,[19] balance sheets and reports of boards of directors of companies, travel descriptions, etc. – are profoundly tainted by all the variants of ethnism and racism; the most moderate are exotic and paternalistic. One may see that, though furnishing numerous data, these secondary sources hide many other facts and could not, in any case, validly sustain scientific research work.

These are the main characteristics of traditional orientalism, that which represented the whole of orientalism up to the end of World War II, and which continues to occupy a disproportionate place to the present day.

But the rebirth of the nations and peoples of Asia, Africa and Latin America, since the end of the nineteenth century, and the very rapid acceleration of this process due to the victory of the national liberation movements in the ex-colonial world but also to the appearance of the group of socialist states and the subsequent differentiation between the 'two Europes,'[20] has shaken the edifice of traditional orientalism to its foundations. Suddenly, specialists and the public at large became aware of the time-lag, not only between orientalist science and the material under study, but also – and this was to be determining – between the conceptions, the methods and the instruments of work in the human and social sciences and those of orientalism.

Rejected by history and the national rebirth of the Orient, traditional orientalism found itself out of step with regard to the progress of scientific research.

Therefore, the whole problem had to be thought anew.

NOTES

1. On the general history of traditional orientalism, more particularly in the Arab and Islamic field, is an abundant bibliography, notably: V. V. Barthold, *La découverte de l'Asie, histoire de l'orientalisme en Europe et en Russie*, Fr. tr., Paris, 1947; nothing in the *Encyclopédie de l'Islam*, nor in the *Encyclopedia Britannica*; 'Orientalistika,' *Soviet Encyclopedia*, Moscow, 1951, Vol. IX, 193–202; Giovanni Vacca, 'Orientalismo,' *Enciclopedia italiana di scienze, lettere ed arti*, Rome, 1935, vol. XXV, 537; G. Levi della Vida, 'Per gli studi arabi in Italia,' *Nuova Antologia*, Dec. 1912, 1–10; A. Bausani, 'Islamic Studies in Italy in the XIXth and XXth Centuries,' *East and West*, VIII, 1957, 145–155 and *Journal of Pakistani Historical Society*, V, 1957, 185–199; P. M. Holt, 'The Origin of Arabic Studies in England,' *al-Kulliyya*, Khartum, 1952, No. 1, 20–7; A. J. Arberry, *Oriental Essays*, London, 1960; M. Horten, 'Die Probleme der Orientalistik,' *Beiträge zur Kenntnis des Orient*, XIII, 1916, 143–61; G. Germanus, 'Hungarian Orientalism – Past and Present,' *Indo-Asian Culture*, VI, 1957, 291–8; L. Bouvat, 'Les Hongrois et les études musulmanes,' *Revue du monde musulman*, I, 1907, No. 3, 305–24; Naguîb Al-'Aqîqi, *Al-moustachriqoûn*, Cairo, 1947; Youssef A. Dagher, *Dalîl al-A'âreb ilâ 'ilm'al-koutoub wa fann al-makâteb*, Beyrouth, 1947, bibl. trav. étrangers, 150–60, Arabes, 161–7; Y. A. Dagher, *Fabâress al-maktaba al-'Arabiyya fîl-khâfiqayn*, Beyrouth, 1947, 105–12; Y. A. Dagher, *Massâder al-dirâssa al-adabiyya*, vol. II, 1800–1955, Beyrouth, 1955, 771–84; J. Fueck, *Die arabischen Studien in Europa*, Leipzig, 1955; etc.
2. 'Orientaliste,' *Grand Larousse encyclopédique*, Paris, 1963, VII, 1003–4.

3. This is the famous book of the master from Berlin: *Paideia, Die Formung des griechischen Menschen* (I, Berlin-Leipzig, 1934), thus synopsized by M. Guidi, 'No broadening of the historical horizon can change anything of the fact that our history starts with the Greeks(...). Evidently, this history cannot have the whole planet for its theatre, but only the 'hellenocentric' peoples(...), since it is they who have taken from the Greeks the conscious principle of the true *Kultur*(...). It is not at all difficult to draw the practical consequences from this theoretical formula: the absolute and central value of antiquity, as the eternal and unique source of the constitutive principle of our culture, and, consequently, as the force of formation and education. Total humanism.' (M. Guidi, 'Trois conférences sur quelques problèmes généraux de l'orientalisme,' *Annuaire de l'Institut de philologie et d'histoire orientales – volume offert à Jean Capart*, Brussels, 1935, 171–2.)

4. Our italics. They point out well the reference to one's own self, i.e., to Europe.

5. M. Guidi, *op. cit.*, 171–80. He defined thus orientalism in 1954: 'The scholar from the Orient, or orientalist worthy of this name, does not limit himself to the knowledge of certain ignored languages, or who can describe the foreign customs of some peoples, but he is the one who unites rather the study of certain sides of the Orient to the knowledge of the great spiritual and moral forces which have influenced the formation of human culture, the one who has been nourished on the lesson of ancient civilizations and who has been able to evaluate the role of the different factors which have participated in the constitution of the civilization of the Middle Ages, for example, or in the course of the modern Renaissance.' ('Ilm al-Charq wa târikh al-'oumrân,' *Al-Zabrâ*', rabie awwal 1347 H., August-September 1928, quoted by Y. A. Dagher, *Massâder* ... , 771.)

6. On the definition of 'europeocentrism,' cf., among others, J. Needham, 'Le dialogue entre l'Europe et l'Asie,' *Comprendre*, No. 12, 1954, 1–8; equally, the preface of our *Egypte, société militaire*, Paris, 1962, 9–13.

7. R. Schwab, 'L'orientalisme dans la culture et les littératures de l'Occident moderne,' *Oriente Moderno*, XXXII, 1952, Nos. 1–2, 136.

8. A. J. Arberry, *op. cit.*

9. Y. A. Dagher, *Massâder* ... , 779–80.

10. J. Berque, 'Cent vingt-cinq ans de sociologie maghrébine,' *Annales*, XI, 1956, No. 3, 299–321.

11. 'The advanced studies, and in particular Oriental, philological and historical studies, are they not, on the contrary, the most valuable auxiliary of the colonial expansionist policies of Italy?' (A. Cabaton, 'L'orientalisme musulman et l'Italie moderne,' *Rev Md. Mus.* VII, 1914, No. 27, p. 24); the moving postscript of Lawrence in *The Seven Pillars of Wisdom* (London, 1926), showing how he was caught himself at his own game, is known: 'Damascus had not seemed a sheath for my sword, when I landed in Arabia; but its capture disclosed the exhaustion of my main springs of action. The strongest motive throughout had been a personal one, not mentioned here, but present to me, I think, every hour of these two years. Active pains and joys might fling up, like towers, among my days: but, refluent as air, this hidden urge re-formed, to be the persistent element of life, till near the end. It was dead before we reached Damascus;' 'The French nation works, accumulates. From its adventurous consuls to its utopian designers of railroad lines, to its moved travelers, a Lamartine, a Barrès, it edifies in the Orient a work, of which the Champollions, Sacys and Renans erect the scientific counterpart. In this period the Arabs neglect their own past, and stammer their noble language. Contemporary orientalism was born from this vacancy. The exploration, the resurrection of such moral treasures was the chance of the erudite Christian, who as well as the Christian of the Bank concurrently revived the wasted space and filled the warehouses(...). For instance, look at the Arab tribe, at beduinism in general, Orientalism approaches them through three great political thrusts: the phase of our "Arab Bureau," in Algeria, until about 1870; the phase of the "revolt in the desert,"

the triumph of British agents in the Near East; the contemporary petroleum expansion.' (J. Berque, 'Perspectives de l'Orientalisme contemporain,' *Ibla*, XX, 1957, 220–1); in 1822, the founders of the 'Société Asiatique' pledge themselves to 'permit to the historians the explanation of the Antiquities of the peoples of the Orient,' and to collect a 'valuable documentation on the diplomatic operations in the Levant and the commercial operations in all of Asia;' among the questions posed to the orientalists, at Lyon, let us point out the following: 'Is it in the interest of the Europeans to demand that treaties give them the right of residence in the interior of China, in order to buy themselves cocoons and silk directly from the producers; in order to establish spinning factories, and to engage in business in general? What are the advantages and disadvantages of the coming of Chinese coolies into foreign countries?' (Texts quoted by J. Chesneaux: 'La recherche marxiste et le réveil contemporain de l'Asie et de l'Afrique,' *La Pensée*, No. 95, Jan.–Feb. 1961, 4–5.)

12. On ethnist typology, cf. M. Rodinson, 'L'Egypte nassérienne au miroir marxiste,' *Les Temps Modernes*, No. 203, April 1963, 1859–65.

13. J. Berque and L. Massignon, 'Dialogue sur *Les Arabes*,' *Esprit*, XXVIII, 1960, No. 288, 1506. On the relationship between orientalism and colonialism, these words from L. Massignon, 'I myself, strongly colonial at the time, wrote to him about my hopes for a coming conquest of Morocco by arms, and he answered me approvingly (letter No. 1 from In-Salah, Oct. 2, 1906). Let us admit that Morocco then was in a terrible state. But fifty years of occupation, without Lyautey and his high Franco-Moslem ideal, would have left nothing that was essential.' ('Foucauld in the desert before the God of Abraham, Agar and Ismaël,' *Les mardis de Dar el-Salam*, 1959, p. 59.)

14. Precise criticisms in *University Grants Committee: Report of the Subcommittee on Oriental, Slavonic, East European and African Studies* (London, HMSO, 1961), under the presidency of Sir William Hayter; 'Modern Far Eastern studies are a closed book in almost every other history or social science faculty.' (p. 38) 'The more inward looking characteristics of the language departments and their lack of interest in modern studies and languages have contributed to a number of unfortunate results.' (p. 46), etc. A very recent selection, *Etudes d'orientalisme dédiées à la mémoire de Lévi-Provençal* (2 vol., Paris, 1962), groups sixty-one articles, only eight of which deal with the modern period, and three are of a bio-bibliographical nature related to it.

15. J. Chesneaux, *La recherche* . . . , 5.

16. Omar Al-Dassoûqui, *Fî-'l-adab al-hadîth*, 3rd edit., Cairo, 1954, 325–6; Y. A. Dagher, *Massâder* . . . , 779; N. al-Aqîqî, *op. cit.*, 207–9; Mohamed Hussein Heykal, '*Hayât Mo'hammad*, preface to the 2nd edit. (6th edit., Cairo, 1956), 60–1; Anouar al-Guindî, *Al-adab al-'Arabi al-'hadith fî ma'rakat al-mouqâwama wa'l-tagammo' min'al-mou'hît ila'l-khalîg*, Cairo, 1959, 621–4; then: *Al-fikr al-'Arabi al-mou'âsser fî maarakat al-taghrîb wa'l taba'iyya al-thaqâfiyya*, Cairo, s.d.c., 1962, 271–85, etc.

17. Particularly the 'Institute of Arab Manuscripts,' directed by Prof. Salah Eddine al-Mounajjed, attached to the Arab League; the review *Magallat al-makhtoûtât al-'Arabiyya*, which has been published in Cairo since 1955; the creation of the new 'Institute of Islamic Research,' at the University Al-Azhar, under the direction of Prof. Abdallah al-'Arabî (*Al-Ahram*, Nov. 23, 1961); the effort of restoration undertaken by the Ministry of Culture and National Guidance of Egypt, mainly under the impetus of Fat'hi Radouân, Hussein Fawzi and Tharwat 'Okâcha, must be mentioned; similar efforts in Syria and Iraq, in particular. In Egypt, the existentialist philosopher 'Abd al-Ra'hman Badawî has undertaken, since 1940, a gigantic work of publication and has given the impetus to many works on Moslem thought, while the great philologist, Mourad Kâmel, authoritatively cleared the ground in the Coptic, Ethiopian and Semitic field.

18. J. Berque mentions it at length, critically, both in *Le Maghreb entre les deux guerres* (Paris 1962), and in his lectures at the Collège de France. Equally, J. P. Naish, 'The Connection of Oriental Studies with Commerce, Art and Literature during the XVIIIth and XIXth Centuries,' *Journ. Manch. Eg. and Or. Soc.*, XV, 1930, 33–9; J. Chesneaux, 'French Historiography and the Evolution of Colonial Vietnam,' in D. G. E. Hall, *Historical Writing on the Peoples of Asia – Historians of South-East Asia*, Oxford – London, 1961, 235–44.

19. Cf. M. Khalidi and O. Farroûkh, *Al-tabchîr wa'l-isti'mâr fî'l-bilâd al-'Arabiyya*, Sayda-Beyrouth, 1953.

20. On this idea, cf. R. Makarius, *La jeunesse intellectuelle d'Egypte au lendemain de la Deuxième Guerre Mondiale* (Paris – The Hague, 1960), and our article 'La vision du problème colonial par le monde afro-asiatique,' publ. in *Cahiers inter. de sociologie*, vol. 35, 1963, 145–56.

10

ENGLISH-SPEAKING ORIENTALISTS

A. L. Tibawi

Whereas Abdel-Malek approaches the question of orientalism from a left-wing point of view, A. L. Tibawi – a Palestinian Arab historian, educated at the University of London – approaches it from the point of view of a student of Islam and a believer. In his 'Critique of English-Speaking Orientalists', first published in 1963, Tibawi draws particular attention to the deep-seated hostility towards Islam displayed in the Christian world; and to the fact that in the nineteenth century Christian missionaries formed a close alliance with academic orientalists. For these and other reasons, he concludes, many orientalists have failed to display a proper sense of 'scientific detachment' in their work. Not only have they adopted 'fixed' ideas about Islam, they have also shown a complete misunderstanding of the nature of the Koran, interpreting it, not as the 'speech of God, eternal and uncreated', but as a mere, human composition, incorporating elements drawn from Christianity and Judaism.

PART I

(1)

There is scarcely any academic pursuit, in the realm of the humanities, which has more unfortunate antecedents than Islamic and Arabic studies in the West.

A. L. Tibawi, 'English-Speaking Orientalists', *Islamic Quarterly*, 8, 1–4, 1964, pp. 25–45.

It is no purpose of this paper to go into details of its sad history. Suffice it, therefore, to give below a mere synoptic view of that history in very rough outline to serve as a general introduction to our limited subject.[1]

From the beginning, the roots of Judaeo-Christian hostility to Islam were seen in the Qur'ān. The 'People of the Book' were quick not only to deny but to challenge Muḥammad's role as the bearer of a divine message, and thus began a chain of polemics that continued, parading under different banners, almost to our own times. With the political and military actions of the Islamic state under Muḥammad and his successors the hostility was extended from the confines of Arabia to embrace the Byzantine Empire and later still Western Christendom.

The Byzantine polemicists were not ignored by triumphant Islam, nor did it neglect to reciprocate their venomous effusions. But the Byzantines were in due course even surpassed by their medieval European successors in cultivating hatred and prejudice through the dissemination of abusive and false accounts. Thus to them Islam was 'the work of the devil', the Qur'ān 'a tissue of absurdities', and Muḥammad 'a false prophet', 'an impostor', or 'antichrist'. The Muslims were some sort of brutes with hardly any human qualities.

To what extent such propaganda conditioned Western Europe to respond to the call for the Crusades is hard to determine. But one of the most spectacular, and paradoxically less obvious, failures of this long contest between Christendom and Islam is that it did not induce Christendom, despite close and prolonged contact with Islam in the Holy Land and the neighbouring countries, to soften its prejudices or at least to correct its factual image of the enemy. Two centuries of strife ended with both sides even more hostile to one another, and not less prejudiced or ignorant.

But the Crusades had a chastening influence on Christendom. Instead of attempting to regain former Christian territory by force of arms, instead of fighting the 'Saracen', a new approach had gradually been gaining recognition. Thus Francis of Assisi sought, through missionary persuasion, to evangelize the 'infidel', and Raymond Lull, with similar motives in mind, was instrumental in the introduction of the teaching of Arabic in Christian institutions of higher learning.[2] But the aim was still largely destructive, hostile: to know more about Islam so as to be better equipped to expose its 'defects'. Indeed, Peter the Venerable, who encouraged the first Latin translation of the Qur'ān, was himself the author of a vehement polemic against Islam.[3]

No appreciable advance towards a better understanding is discernible until comparatively very recent times. The first serious attempts, such as they were, were overshadowed by renewed fighting. Both the Christian reconquest of Spain and the Ottoman penetration deep into Europe seem to have rekindled the flames of hatred and prejudice and retarded the possibility of fair representation. The old world was as divided as ever between the 'abode of Islam' and 'the abode of war', and the twain could never meet except on the battlefield or in the pages of squalid polemics.

And yet meet they did. For meanwhile two great historical developments took place. First, there had developed in Western Europe certain forces which culminated in the fifteenth-century Renaissance, and had called for the translation of Greek science from Arabic physicians, mathematicians, philosophers, &c. Although this 'scientific' contact was prolonged and profound, it does not seem to have greatly influenced the doctrinal, theological, or even historical image of Islam in Christian eyes. Secondly, the unity of Christendom under the Church was disrupted by new political, economic, and religious forces. There emerged from the upheaval of the Reformation national, often rival, states, some of which entertained ambitious schemes of overseas expansion. Once more there was a violent conflict with Islam. But these new smaller nation-states tended to seek to advance their own interests irrespective of the interests of other Christian states or of Christendom as a whole. And this was the practical beginning of closer diplomatic and commercial relations with the lands of Islam than were ever possible before.

Although the religious polemicists were still as bitter and active as ever, although the missionary aim was increasing its hold on the imagination of ecclesiastical authorities, new secular motives had now been recognized as equally, if not more, valid. For the purpose of this paper, the change is perhaps exemplified by the statement formulated by the academic authorities in the University of Cambridge in connexion with the founding of the chair of Arabic. In a letter dated 9 May 1636 addressed to the founder of the chair they state:

> The work itself we conceive to tend not only to the advancement of good literature by bringing to light much knowledge which as yet is locked up in that learned tongue, but also to the good service of the King and State in our commerce with the Eastern nations, and in God's good time to the enlargement of the borders of the Church, and propagation of Christian religion to them who now sit in darkness.[4]

But it must be acknowledged that any Arabic or Islamic studies that were cultivated for any of these reasons – polemic, missionary, commercial, diplomatic, scientific, or academic – continued for a long time to be coloured by some measure of the same deep-rooted animosity. Indeed, the very first holder of the chair of Arabic at Cambridge planned, even though he never completed, a refutation of the Qur'ān. One of his early successors in the eighteenth century wrote a pioneering *History of the Saracens*, but also recommended that the Qur'ān should be read in order to contradict or refute it. Thus increased knowledge seems to have made little headway in dispelling a tradition which had developed during the course of centuries.

Nor was the situation improved by new historical developments. The expansion of Europe overseas embraced, in the course of time, large areas of the lands of Islam, and a climax was reached in the nineteenth century when Europe became master of extensive Muslim territory inhabited by many millions of Muslims. Political domination was accompanied, or followed, by more subtle cultural subordination. The fortunes of the Muslim world had reached a very low ebb and the future of its civilization was to a great extent in the hands of Christian powers.[5]

Under the new dispensation secular education struck root and missionary work among the Muslims became possible. Secular education and Christian missions between them tended to foster at least a sceptical attitude to the Muslim way of life.[6] Both the 'empire-builder', the Christian gentleman, and the 'ambassador of Christ', the Christian missionary, came to exert direct or indirect influence on the course of education in Muslim lands. These two classes of workers, to be sure, supplied a number of the new Arabic (or Persian or Turkish) and Islamic specialists, the forerunners of the academic orientalists.

The way was also more safely open to the curious traveller, the leisurely romantic, and the rich connoisseur who wrote rather shallow books about the Orient, acquired antiques, or collected manuscripts. But through this tangle the figure of the disinterested scholar is discernible, for example in the indefatigable E. W. Lane.[7] Of all these types, at least the missionary was convinced that if the political power of Islam could be shaken, spiritual collapse and eventual conversion to Christianity was near at hand.

Such were the forecasts when British (and other) missionary societies commenced operating in the East, in Africa and the Mediterranean lands. From the beginning there was, if not an affinity of aims, at least some mutual sympathy and active co-operation between the academic orientalist and the evangelizing missionary. In England this was particularly true of the Arabists at the two ancient universities where Arabic was cultivated as an aid to theological and biblical studies by scholars who were themselves usually in holy orders. Thus both McBride of Oxford and Lee[8] of Cambridge worked for the Church Missionary Society on a 'Protestant' translation of the Gospels and Psalms into Arabic.

The loose alliance between the two sides was continued throughout the nineteenth century and, in a sense, down to the days of Margoliouth at Oxford well into this century. It has never been dissolved. To be sure, both sides learnt to revise their objectives and methods. But somehow there persisted an undercurrent of common thought – perhaps now largely unconscious – that Islam might be transformed through 'westernization' or 'modernization', or 'reformation'. The missionary prayed, and the orientalist speculated, and both wrote and continue to write, with varying degrees of subtlety and insight, on the subject.

The discussion has now been narrowed down to Great Britain and that is on purpose to suit the subject of the paper. But oriental studies in Great Britain, as in other countries, were in some way related to the development of the humanities in European universities as it affected the 'scientific' study of history in general and the 'academic' approach to Islam in particular. English, French, and German scholars, as well as scholars from other nations, contributed greatly to Arabic and Islamic studies through teaching, writing, and publication of texts. Their combined efforts created conditions favourable to the adoption of a detached, disinterested, and truly academic approach to Islam.[9]

There is no doubt that considerable advance towards this goal has been made. But there is also little doubt that the goal has not yet been reached by a considerable number of contemporary students of Islam, those who have died recently and those who are still alive. Their work divides itself into two distinct departments: editing of texts and analytical studies. Details will be given below. But here it may be stated, in a summary fashion, that English-speaking students of Islam – and from now on the discussion will be restricted to them – have been less scholarly objective in their studies than in their publication of texts. Instances of insufficient scientific detachment are not lacking even in the editing or translating of certain texts, where the subject lends itself to the ventilation of those 'fixed ideas' about Islam which still exist in the minds of certain Western scholars.[10]

It may be considered unusual for a paper like this one to concern itself with living rather than dead orientalists. But if it is an accepted custom to review a book by a living author soon after its publication, and to quote it later on with approval or disapproval, surely it is a legitimate pursuit to inquire into any author's contributions in part or as a whole, particularly if they are on subjects of vital interest. The living, not the dead, are capable of reflecting on the consequences of their published ideas. That is one of the objects of this study: to remind some scholars of the impact of their ideas on the Muslim mind in this scientific age.

A word of warning must now be given. The following analysis, the fruit of long and careful study and reflection, is not conceived in any spirit of controversy. It must not be mistaken for an apology for any creed, religious or national. It is offered simply as a sincere contribution to a better understanding of an old problem. The writer believes that on the whole old prejudices, greatly diminished since the dawn of this century, are still strong and widely disseminated by some Arabic and Islamic scholars in the West. Moreover, he fears that 'religious' prejudices have more recently been reinforced by new 'national' prejudices. There is evidence that the feeling of hatred long reserved for Islam has now been extended to the Arabs or more particularly Arab nationalism. It is idle to speculate, but this feeling may develop, on medieval patterns, to such a degree that it may prove disastrous to oriental scholarship and human relations alike. Genuine concern for both prompts the following discussion.

(2)

Some contemporary English-speaking orientalists – and this generic term is from now on used to cover not only those in Great Britain but also those in North America – came to the study of Islam via biblical or theological studies, and indeed a number of them are at present in holy orders. Others found themselves in this department of study in consequence of accident of residence, missionary or military service in an Islamic country. Others still – and this is perhaps more true of the younger generation – chose to study Islam deliberately as a career. If we were to describe in a word the kind of training they had received, it would be generally correct to say that, apart from theological background in certain cases, most of them had linguistic or literary training, and that very few among them are trained historians. One or two have recently made rather experimental ventures in the vague realms of sociology and psychology.

This is perhaps one of the most serious handicaps. Many of the studies on Islam written by English-speaking orientalists are distinguished by erudition, but if one penetrates beneath the apparatus of the learned footnotes and the array of sources one is bound to detect an alarming degree of speculation, guesswork, and passing of judgement, for which little or no concrete evidence is produced. It is, of course, one thing to be skilful in deciphering documents in Arabic (or Persian or Turkish) and quite another to be able to integrate the material culled therefrom into an historical contribution in the accepted professional sense. History in general is one of the most vulnerable of disciplines to the invasion of people from outside; it is often assumed that anyone who wields a pen can write history. In Islamic sources, the linguistic, literary, and historical materials are so intertwined that scholars are prone to attempt too much and find themselves writing history, almost unconsciously, with scant qualification for the task. Hence it is easy to understand why the subject of Islam has been far better treated by the few 'historians' among the orientalists than by the majority who are in actual fact linguists.

In the following discussion we shall take a few of the 'fads' in the works of orientalists which seem to fall short of scientific historical standards. But to keep the discussion within manageable limits we shall restrict our attention to the Arabists. There is no question of ascribing polemic or open missionary motives to any one of them. All of them are taken as engaged in an academic activity which should be its own justification and reward. Of course orientalists train, in the normal course of their duties, diplomatists, missionaries, and business men, in addition to perpetuating their kind by training their successors in teaching and research. Hence the added significance and relevance of whatever ideology they may hold. It is precisely the ideology as revealed in published works that we propose to examine with a view to pointing out where, in our opinion, the accepted canons of scientific investigation have not been strictly observed.

Perhaps the most significant matter in which the rules of the games are often disregarded is the conception which most orientalists entertain of the role of Muḥammad as a messenger of God and the nature of the message, enshrined in the Qur'ān, which he was commanded to convey. To the community of Islam, Muḥammad is the last of God's messengers to mankind sent to confirm and complete earlier messages conveyed through former prophets. To the community the Qur'ān is the Speech of God, eternal and uncreated, transmitted to Muḥammad, at intervals, through the agency of the angel Jibrīl. Not only the message itself but also the call to preach it is of divine origin.

Any writer, even though he is not a believing Muslim, who ignores the vital necessity to take note of these beliefs in what he writes about Islam runs the risk of exposing himself to the charge of lack of objectivity. In writing on the subject, a fair way would be to state the Muslim view in its entirety so fully and clearly as to leave no room for complaint of misrepresentation. If the writer holds another view, or if he wishes to refer to still other views, he would be fully justified in introducing such matters, separately and distinctly, after he had stated the traditional Muslim view.

But unfortunately this logical and natural order of representation is seldom followed and is often inverted, with the result that unless he is well-instructed the reader will, in effect, be subjected to some 'indoctrination' or at least to such confusion that he will be unable to distinguish between native tradition and the opinion of the writer. For many orientalists, assuming in others the great learning they themselves possess, often neglect to observe such simple elements of objective treatment of historical questions. They assert, for example, that the Qur'ān is Muḥammad's own composition.[11] Then they proceed to base on this assertion far-reaching judgements, historical, theological, literary, &c., which by sheer repetition are elevated to the dignity of facts.

This is perhaps one of the major factors, if not *the* major factor, in creating an attitude of suspicion, if not hostility, towards the work of orientalists adopted by the 'ulamā' as well as by educated Muslims, including some who were trained in Western institutions or even under well-known orientalists. Gone are the days when orientalists used to write largely for the benefit of other orientalists. Apart perhaps from specialized monographs, much of the present output is read and weighed by large numbers of scholars and intelligent readers in the West and perhaps even more of these in the Muslim world. In their present mood, after repeated polemic and missionary onslaughts against their faith, and after prolonged Western political and cultural domination of their lands, the Muslims are more prone to take offence than ever before.

Offensive ideas never cease to be published, however. Surely the authors must be aware that it offends Muslim sentiment to brush aside the cardinal Muslim belief that Islam is of divine origin, and to suggest, whether obliquely or bluntly, that Muḥammad laid false claims to be the bearer of a divine message, and that the Qur'ān itself is thus the composition of an impostor. Is it not more conducive to human understanding, and more scholarly, to leave matters of faith alone, and to turn to more tangible pursuits in such fields as literature, art, and the sciences which despite the orientalists' own efforts still bristle with question-marks? Surely it is possible for a Christian (or Jewish) orientalist, having a different faith from a Muslim, to state the Muslim's conception of his religion in Muslim terms.[12] If he does so he will not only be more accurate, but he will place himself in a better position to comprehend Islam's manifestation in history.

The believing Muslim and the sceptical orientalist are also poles apart as regards the 'origins' of Islam. Here again the views of the majority of orientalists,

English-speaking and otherwise, tend to create ill-feeling among Muslims, and in consequence place serious obstacles in the way of intellectual traffic between the two sides. For, having on the whole rejected the Muslim doctrine of the divine origin of Islam, and having moreover decided that Muḥammad the man, and not any divine agency, was responsible for the composition of the Qur'ān, the orientalist has been busy, since the dawn of the scientific historical method, in trying to discover Judaeo-Christian 'origins' without reaching conclusive results beyond pointing out obvious 'parallels' and in the process producing learned, if speculative, discourses on the obvious.

'Speculative' has been used with due consideration for the following reason. Let us forget for a moment what the Muslims believe, and let us consider the problem as a purely historical one.[13] Granted, for the sake of argument, that the Qur'ān is Muḥammad's own composition. How is a student of history to prove Muḥammad's borrowing from previous sources? If by guesswork, then it is not profitable to waste any time examining details; if by the rigour of strict historical discipline, then any evidence produced is worthy of serious attention. However, any contemporary evidence that may have existed and might have been used to support the Judaeo-Christian thesis is lost beyond recall.

Surely parallels cannot be accepted in lieu of what might have been conclusive evidence. Scraps, clues, inferences, intelligent guesswork, are never satisfactory in this case and possibly in any case. It would therefore be highly imaginative to assume that Muḥammad – who according to tradition was unable to read and write though in the scheme of things constructed by the orientalists he was so – sat down 'in his study' to consult and 'quote'[14] previous authors for the composition of the work known as the Qur'ān. No doubt this is an exaggerated way of putting it, but this is in brief what the thesis proclaims in detail.[15]

Parallels are very deceptive; they are not necessarily scientific proof of identity of two similar compositions, still less of conscious adoption by the successor from the predecessor. Both may be derived from a third common source. Indeed, a scholar who holds that the Bible and the Qur'ān are human documents may be tempted, with good reason, to trace some of their contents in earlier Semitic traditions of the Near East. However, in order to prove actual adoption more convincing evidence than has hitherto been produced is necessary.

It was Vico who said that ideas are propagated by the independent discovery by each nation (or culture) of what it needs at any given stage in its development.[16] A leading orientalist had said much the same thing, with illuminating elaboration, when he insisted that a borrowing culture – or in the present case simply religious system – must itself feel the need, through its own internal development, for external nourishment. Whatever it borrows in this way can only be useful if it is sustained by those elements in the native culture (or religion) which called for the borrowing. A living culture (or religion) rejects automatically all foreign elements which conflict with its own fundamental values.[17]

In the voluminous effusion about the 'origins' of Islam there is, in the writer's opinion, no convincing evidence, in the historical sense, which proves that such a borrowing did in fact take place. On the contrary, the only surviving contemporary evidence is that of the Qur'ān itself, and it rules out any such possibility in most categorical terms. It is surprising that this evidence is too often brushed aside. Thus an acute scholar, who has made valuable contributions to Islamic studies, has remarked that 'Islam has always combined a capacity for absorption of foreign elements with a certain reluctance to admit their origin.'[18]

This remark deserves to be examined even out of context, since it has already been quoted out of context. If by Islam is meant civilization or culture, then neither the fact of absorption of foreign elements nor their source has ever been denied.[19] On the other hand, if by Islam is meant its dogma and creed, then the writer of that statement hardly needs any reminder that if Islam were to remove the cause of his complaint it would cease to be itself and would have to renounce the explicit teaching of its holy book. As a *faith* Islam is of course indivisible; one has to take it or leave it as a whole.

This is one illustration among many where insufficient precision is only slightly concealed beneath catchy and therefore quotable phrases which lose their lustre on close examination. Even orientalists who resigned themselves to admitting the sincerity of Muḥammad and to recognizing that he preached a fundamentally new religion assert at the same time that his message was not wholly of divine origin. Here is a quotation from another scholar who has made valuable researches into the life of Muḥammad. 'Islam', he writes, 'would have to admit the fact of its origin – the historical influence of the Judaeo-Christian religious tradition.'[20] Here the question of the 'origins' is taken as settled and referred to as 'fact' without any qualification or discussion.[21] To borrow the phraseology of the quotation one might say that its author would have to admit that he cannot have it both ways: to consider Muḥammad as a sincere prophet and to impute dishonesty to him since he, the supposed author of the Qur'ān, does not admit that he appropriated somebody else's ideas.

Such a duality of approach is bound to be self-contradictory; it is moreover unsatisfactory from either point of view of the problem, for it neither fully supports the one nor completely refutes the other. The faithful Muslim will still be consistent within his system; so also will the polemicist. But not the professed writer of history who attempts to ride two horses at the same time. Respectable as his attempt at a compromise may be, the result of his effort is frustrating to protagonist and antagonist alike, and not strictly acceptable to the neutral historian who has no axe to grind. Indeed, despite the advance made in the writing of scientific history, the new 'dualists' in Islamic studies have produced contributions – distinguished in themselves – which have proved less comprehensible than those of the extremists, whether believers or polemicists, whom they try, consciously or unconsciously, to supplant.

(3)

It is evident that the divergence between the meaning of Islam to its adherents and its image as drawn by orientalists touches the very fundamentals of the Islamic faith. Despite the undoubted advance made towards an academic approach it is clear that, in this matter, the late medieval image of Islam remains substantially unaltered; it has only discarded old-fashioned clothes in favour of more modern attire. Illustrations of the persistence of the old ideas abound, not only concerning the Qur'ān and Muḥammad but also quite logically concerning Islamic theology, law, and history. It is neither desirable nor profitable to dwell more on the subject here. Instead we propose to consider it from another angle.

One of the results of Western penetration into the lands of Islam has been the exposure of the mind of the young, largely through secular education and missionary effort, to seductive arguments – patterned partly on those that had undermined faith in Christianity in Western Europe. But, unlike the method of the medieval polemicist, the new method had, to the missionary at any rate, the positive aim of conversion to Christianity. In its simplest form this is the method of the student of 'comparative religion' who endeavours to compare Christianity with Islam, almost always to the disadvantage of the latter. This method of approach is still with us, even though it does not any longer profess open evangelical aims.

Here again it is more instructive to take concrete examples. But some general principles may be stated first. The origin of comparative religious studies in the West is rooted in controversy. Judaism had already been compared with Christianity, but instead of promoting understanding the comparison engendered further hostility. Similar were the results of comparing Judaism and Christianity with Islam by those Jews and Christians who claim it as an offspring of the one or the other religion, or of both. While, however, there is between Judaism and Christianity an admitted organic relationship, there is no such admitted, or scientifically proved, relationship between either and Islam. Jewish and Christian hostility to it springs rather from political and doctrinal conflicts in history. It is a sad commentary on the collective wisdom of the learned among the adherents of these faiths that they never succeeded in removing the causes of their mutual discord and orientalists must accept a share in perpetuating this regrettable state of affairs.

Unless therefore the aims of comparative religion in the Islamic field are clearly defined, and unless some rules of the method of comparison are accepted by those who wish to engage in it, there is a risk that comparison might degenerate into fruitless controversy. It may be assumed that those who wish to undertake such pursuits harbour no polemic or missionary aims and that their chief interest is purely academic. If this is really the case, they will surely recognize that comparison requires tolerance, sympathy, and respect in the one who undertakes it. For the principal aim is to deepen both one's understanding of one's native culture (or tradition) and of the other culture (or tradition) with which it is to be compared. Such understanding is bound to foster a critical approach not only to this other culture (or tradition) but also to one's own.

Therefore any matter that is to be studied comparatively must be stated in terms acceptable to those from whose tradition (or in this case religion) it is taken. It must also be related to its circumstances and judged according to the values of its own native system. If these elementary principles should be accepted, then any writer who feels any hostility to, repulsion from, even contempt for a foreign tradition should be considered – nay, he should honestly consider himself – as mentally and emotionally unfit to attempt a comparison which could contribute no tangible benefit to scholarship.

While mercifully none of the contemporary English-speaking orientallists betrays such rancour and vindictiveness as disfigures, for example, the late Lammens's distinguished work, nevertheless some of those among them who attempt comparison betray here and there theological or doctrinal prejudices which tend to diminish the value of their contributions and to shake confidence in their scholarship.

At first sight Islam has some similarities with Christianity, but closer examination reveals fundamental differences. This fact has often irritated missionaries in the past, and still tempts a few in the academic world to chase such elusive hares as the 'origins of Islam'. Both the missionary and the academic scholar tended to forget, when directly or indirectly they abused Muḥammad, how deeply pious Muslims venerate Jesus.

In a recent volume in the 'Penguin Books' an orientalist, who is an Anglican Clergman, sought by numerous comparisons to show that Islam was virtually an imperfect or distorted form of Christianity.[22] He has, however, given us reason to justify our questioning his competence as an impartial judge, not so much by the inconclusiveness or otherwise of his suggestions as by what he confesses of his feelings concerning the message enshrined in the Qur'ān. He admitted in one place that to him and to like-minded people (he uses the pronoun 'us') the Qur'ān has a 'repellent content'.[23] In another place he speaks of 'our repugnance' being excited by unspecified aspects of Islam.[24] That should be enough reason for him to keep away from the subject. But he was not 'repelled' from attempting to translate the *Sīrah* into English and to use it, by annotation and other means, to air his prejudices. Since a detailed critique of this translation has already been published[25] there is no need to say more about it here.

A student of Islam, who is also a clergyman, deserves mention here principally because of his introduction of further speculation concerning the similarity between Christianity and Islam. 'Muslims and Christians', he writes, 'have been alienated partly by the fact that both have misunderstood each other's faith by trying to fit it into their own pattern.'[26] Like many generalizations, this quotation is not as fair as it sounds. For it is only Christians who have for centuries been attempting to understand, or misunderstand, Islam in Christian terms. The basic Muslim view of Christianity has always been the same because it is part of the divine revelation in the Qur'ān[27] No believing Muslim ever tried to fit Christianity into any other pattern. The Christian has no such explicit restrictions in his holy books to preclude his acceptance of the Muslim view of Islam, and yet he rejects not only the Muslim view of Christianity but also the Muslim view of Islam, and attempts, moreover, to change both views.

The author of the quotation in the paragraph above is a trained theologian who began his career as a teacher in a missionary institution in Lahore. He used his words as an apology for attempting to achieve at least one of the Christian objectives. For this purpose he argues that it is a common error on the part of Christians and Muslims to suppose 'that the roles of Jesus Christ in Christianity and Muḥammad in Islam are comparable'. This statement too is misleading, since such comparison is only valid for Muslims who believe in Jesus as one of God's messengers to mankind. On the other hand Christians in general, and orientalists in particular, either do not recognize Muḥammad as a prophet or resort to equivocation as was shown above. Under these circumstances for whom is the comparison valid? The previous account will have shown to what extent the study of Islam and the life of Muḥammad is already too complicated by what the orientalists introduced of controversial, unresolved problems. Far from extricating us from this mess the new comparative hypotheses, if taken seriously, will only get us even more entangled.

The hypotheses are briefly that the role of Muḥammad in Islam and that of St. Paul in Christianity 'are much more comparable', that the Qur'ān is comparable to the person of Christ, and that the Hadīth is comparable to the Bible. More parallels were also suggested.[28] We are not concerned here with what reception these 'heresies' might have in Christian theological circles; we are rather interested in the declared objective of their author, which is, in his own terms, 'communication' or 'intercommunication' between enlightened Muslims and Christians. Are these analogies conducive to this object? Very often honest people are singularly oblivious of the implication of their ideas when confronted with the beliefs, sentiments, or prejudices of other people. It is difficult in this case to imagine that the devisor of the analogies expects them to be welcomed by learned Muslims. Let there be no misunderstanding of the intent of these words. It is not so much the analogies themselves that are here in question, as it is the pretentious banner, 'meaningful and enlightening to Muslims', under which they are paraded.

The realities of verifiable Muslim reaction do not seem to deter or to interest the author. He himself confesses that he offered only one of his analogies to a 'liberal' Muslim, a doctor of philosophy from the University of London, who was very much shocked and had no hesitation in repudiating it. But that did not convince the author. We need not go to Al-Azhar to discover stronger rejection. Three so-called 'Westernized' Muslims, noted for their scholarship and liberalism, were consulted separately by the present writer. Each returned much the same answer even though using stronger or milder adjectives: 'superficial', 'impertinent', and 'blasphemous'. With whom to 'communicate' then, and whom to 'enlighten'?

Bold speculation, drawing of parallels, and formulation of analogies may be attractive to a professor of comparative religion who understandably must somehow find subjects for comparison. Such purely imaginary exercises may likewise be interesting to the missionary who may employ the analogies to 'soften' the resistance and to open the way. They may also be useful to the non-Muslim teacher in a Western university as a diversion to enliven his task. But as the product of a Christian theological mind couched in Christian terms they are, to say the least, pointless to educated Muslims.[29] The matter is almost like a social conversation; in order to be fruitful it must cover subjects agreeable and interesting to both sides.

With less insight and subtlety, and apparently very little respect for the intelligence of the reader, a former missionary who lectures on Islamic law in the University of London managed to include in a single article almost all the medieval objections to Muḥammad and Islam. What is surprising is that he professes in the foreword to provide 'factual information', to treat the subject 'objectively', to be 'scrupulously fair', and to avoid 'adverse comparison with Christianity'.[30] But soon after these professions of objectivity he writes, 'there can be no manner of doubt, that Muḥammad absorbed his ideas from Talmudic and apocryphal sources, and that 'it seems overwhelmingly probable' that he derived inspiration from Christianity.

The use of such language alone may raise doubt concerning the author's competence to judge, but his actual treatment of the subject as a whole is even more revealing. Muḥammad's character is defamed on many counts, but chiefly on the vital matter of his 'representing' the Qur'ān as the speech of God while it was not. Islam itself is similarly treated. Thus pilgrimage to Mecca, one of the five pillars, has 'no moral uplift', and the whole religion 'is at best cold and formal'. Like another writer quoted above, he says he is 'repelled' by Islam's moral standards.

Whether this measures up to the promised objectivity or not is quite clear. The author is a former Christian missionary writing from that point of view. The 'defects' of Islam are judged by Christian, modern European, standards. The aim is frankly evangelical. Among the possible developments in Islam in the modern world the author speculates on the chances of Communism, but evidently hopes for 'a turning, on a wholly unprecedented scale, to Christianity, which has never yet been adequately presented to the Muslim world'. Using some standard missionary arguments he finds that among the obstacles 'to the evangelization of Islam' are the law of apostasy and, in recent times, lack of provision in modern codes for a Muslim to change his faith.[31] 'The world has yet to see', he concludes lyrically, 'what would happen if the Gospel of the living Christ was adequately presented to the millions of Islam.'

There is no need to examine this author's professional works. They are on the whole descriptive of contemporary legal practice in a number of Muslim countries. Apart from repeated moral judgement, according to Christian standards, there is a main idea which is soon explained. Far from being an immutable divine law, the *Sharī ʿah* has in practice been amended – drastically in recent times. This interpretation obviously takes little account of the history of Islamic law. Because the main origins of the law are the Qur'ān and the Traditions, it has a divine character; because it was partly derived from these and other sources through the exercise of human judgement it has also a human character. This being so the law has always been subject to revision from the days of early Islam to the present time.[32]

Consider, for contrast, the approach of the scholar who has made distinct contributions to the study of Islamic law. He does not prejudice his conclusions with an emotional hostility to the background of his subject.[33] Although some Muslim authorities may find his analysis too sceptical and may question his work on points of detail, his main thesis, despite appearance, is not entirely irreconcilable with tradition. For whether according to the traditional view Islamic law was derived, in the first instance, from the Qur'ān and the Traditions or, as demonstrated in the thesis in question, was the outcome of sifting and codification by the jurists of existing customary law and administrative practice, the outcome was bound to be the same. To the early Muslim community the eventual result was bound to be a legal system in accord with its holy book, traditions, and approved practice.

Similar scholarly neutrality is adopted in the approach to contemporary legal practice, with neither moral judgement nor preaching. Modern legislation, concludes a neat survey,[34] must be tested by Islamic standards. To be successful according to these standards modern legislation must, as in the classical period, achieve a synthesis. Neither mechanical re-shaping of tradition nor secular structure behind an Islamic façade will do. What is required is an 'evaluation of modern social life and of modern legal thought from an Islamic angle'.

(4)

When the early polemicists indulged in abuse and misrepresentation of Islam their aim was simply destructive. With the introduction of missionary aims, however, a measure of objectivity was necessary. The method of approach became a mixture of abuse and demonstration of the 'defects' of Islam, but on the basis of more solid facts for the purpose of comparison with Christianity. The first method has now been practically abandoned; the second has either been weakened or dressed in new garments. One of its mild manifestations is the suggestion that Islam must be 'reformed'. It is not clear who first made the suggestion or used the term 'reform' in its Western sense. But it is abundantly clear that so much nonsense has been written on this subject that it is necessary to discover briefly what it means.

Orientalists, and more particularly those who are Protestants, cannot free themselves from what might be called the inevitability of the Reformation. It is perhaps no accident that at present Jewish (and Roman Catholic) orientalists seldom take an active part in this subject, which is almost entirely monopolized by Protestant scholars. Although various contributions touching on the subject of 'reformation' in modern Islam have poured from the press, and although there still seems no cessation or abatement of the effusion, stating or re-stating one or two ideas in different words, genuinely clear and coherent formulation of these ideas has yet to be published. Stripped of its unconscious disguise, the suggestion of 'reforming' Islam, if it is an external suggestion, looks like another attempt to change the Muslim view of Islam, and to bring it as near as possible to Christianity, or, better still, to the Protestant form of Christianity.

Apart from being a civilization and a culture, Islam has essentially two aspects, the creed and the law. The first is precise and universally comprehensible and is subject to no mutation. The second is partly derived from revelation, partly from the prophetic tradition through the exercise of human judgement. It has therefore been, from the days of the early caliphate down to the present time, subject to interpretation and adjustment through administrative rules, concession to customary law and practice, and, in recent times, through parallel civil legislation. Where do the advocates of 'reform' wish to introduce it, and what exactly do they propose to introduce, and for what purpose?

There is no wish to quibble over small details, but it must be clear to anyone with genuine knowledge of Islam that perceptible 'reform' cannot be effected in the doctrines of the faith without diminishing or cancelling their validity. It is therefore most unlikely that any Muslim thinker should harbour such designs, still less is it likely that any religious authority would tolerate him if he did. No such authority will countenance, for example, such a 're-statement' as would accommodate the Christian doctrines of original sin or incarnation in the body of Muslim theology.

As evidence of the muddle concerning 'reforms' one has only to consider the equivocal attitude of those non-Muslims who advocate it. On the one hand they allege that Islam is too 'rigid' and admits of little change in its system. On the other, when far-reaching changes are made in the application of Islamic law, those same advocates miss no opportunity to point out that such changes undermine the *Sharī'ah*. Surely this is a matter which the Muslim community can judge better. Its two guiding principles have always been that change should be in accordance with the interests of the community (*maṣlaḥah'*) and the principles of justice (*'adl*). There have indeed been protests against even such a change, and our own time is no exception. The essential test of validity in our own time is still the old one, the consensus of the community and the approval of the *'ulamā'* in the region concerned. There is good evidence that these authoritative elements have now, as in the past, shown their resilience and tolerance in accommodating the new measures.

The first English-speaking orientalist to produce a thoughtful contribution on Islam in the modern age, whose ideas continue to provide many followers with texts for expansion, is careful to avoid meddling or patronizing. What the Muslims are doing, or will do, with their systems of beliefs and laws he assigns to where it belongs, the *'ulamā*'.[35] Other scholars are not as careful; they boldly proceed from the descriptive survey to the prescriptive 'remedy' and even to the prophetic forecast of the future. A stranger to a religious system cannot so easily dispense with elementary courtesy and yet expect to be listened to with respect.

Religious perception is a spiritual, intuitive experience. It cannot be comprehended by analytical or critical methods. Those outside a religious system can never capture the significance of the experience of those inside it.[36] It is a thing which cannot be learnt from books. Hence the confusion about the nature and aims of 'reform' among its non-Muslim advocates. Hence also the difficulty of those inside the religious community in explaining their religion to those outside it vainly trying to appreciate its emotional and intuitive undertones. And yet these simple matters are often overlooked by orientalists whose knowledge of Islam is chiefly derived from books.

On those rare occasions when they discuss aspects of Islam with learned Muslims, the result is seldom satisfactory. The Muslim takes so much for granted that the orientalist ends by assuming ignorance in him without justification. Furthermore there is the language difficulty. Very few indeed are the orientalists who can conduct and sustain a discussion in an Arabic (or Persian or Turkish) intelligible to an educated Muslim. Those Muslims who have acquired facility of expression in a European tongue are still at a disadvantage; they seldom can match the orientalist in borrowing the cultural allusions of that tongue, let alone appropriating and utilizing its classical heritage.

These are some of the obstacles which render suggestions from orientalists either unwelcome or offensive. While the writer was collecting material for this paper the issues involved were discussed with a number of orientalists and Muslim and Arab scholars in Europe, America, and the Arab world. One example is pertinent to the subject of this section; it is the opinion of a scholar who combines a traditional Muslim education with a training in a Western university. 'I have known some orientalists', he said, 'who approach Muslim scholars with an air of superiority and arrogance. When sometimes they ask a question on an Islamic problem they seem to imply that they know more about it already, whereas they simply have a different point of view with little real insight.'

It was in connexion with the subject of 'reform' that this remark, somewhat toned down in translation, was made. It must not be supposed however that this sort of resentment is caused by superficial social or academic encounters such as are described above. One may even venture to suggest that it does not spring primarily from immediate religious motives. Both the unfortunate history of Islamic studies, which were, in effect, born from polemic and missionary parents, and the legacy of the long military conflict between Christendom and Islam, still play their part, consciously or unconsciously, in determining Muslim attitudes. Of more recent date, and certainly with more bitter taste, is the feeling that the ideas of 'reform' came with, or in consequence of, Christian political domination of many parts of the lands of Islam.[37] The early encounter between Islam and Greek thought was a different matter; Islam then ruled supreme, and adopted or rejected foreign elements as a discriminating master. In modern times its discrimination has been, in part at least, suggested, urged, or limited by foreign non-Muslim individuals or agencies, acting, as Muslims sometimes suspect, according to the dictates of foreign interests.

This may explain why those 'reformists' who had Western inspiration or encouragement never gained a firm hold on the imagination of authoritative Muslim opinion. They have been admired chiefly by orientalists and their followers. On the other hand, genuinely native reformers, with substantial followings, are frequently branded as mere 'reactionaries'. Nor were those who chose a middle way, more or less like their predecessors in the golden age, accorded unqualified approval, because, we are told, they did not go far enough. But they could not go further than they did. The 'ulamā' in all ages possess that collective instinct which indicates to them how far to go, what compromises to accept and where to stand firm in upholding the system. Muḥammad 'Abduh and his disciples were the authors of such a compromise. Neither the extreme 'puritanism' of the Wahhabi movement nor the extreme 'liberalism' of some Indian Muslims was acceptable to them or to the Muslim community as a whole.

The first essential prerequisite for any successful change (or reform) is therefore native initiative, independent of foreign control or suggestion. The second essential prerequisite is that all change must be acceptable to learned orthodox authority. Ever since Salim III initiated preliminary innovations in the Ottoman Empire before the end of the eighteenth century, ever since British legal practice in India compelled some Indian Muslim thinkers to adapt the religious law to the realities of non-Muslim sovereignty, the change in the application of Islamic law has continued down to our own time. The rate of change has even been accelerated, not retarded, with the restoration of sovereignty to, or the attainment of independence by, Muslim nations. If protest at the initial change was loud, it was due in no small measure to the fear that the sacred law was not safe under foreign non-Muslim manipulation. If despite the greater change the protest has become fainter, this is due partly to the feeling of security under Muslim government and partly to a realistic and accommodating religious authority.

It is therefore incorrect to continue to assert that Islam is too rigid and sanctions no change. Outside the central doctrine of the faith and the postulates of a simple theology, Islam has undergone revolutionary change in that very department of its system which controls the life of the individual and the community. However, a Christian theologian qualified to be counted as an enlightened missionary or as a missionary Islamist has very recently written:[38] 'Islam must either baptize change in its spirit or renounce its own relevance to life.' It is difficult to discover what exactly this means. In the light of the discussion in this section, the first part of this statement is clearly untenable, and the second sounds like preaching by an outsider to Muslims on what to do with their religion. Such is the extent of the confusion among the advocates of 'reform'. Unaware of its implications in detail, they confine themselves to vague generalizations that do not bear examination.[39]

NOTES

1. Oriental studies in the Islamic and Arabic fields are, of course, an international discipline built up by Western orientalists: English, French, German, Italian, and others. This critique may generally apply to most of them; its limitation to English-speaking orientalists is merely for convenience of treatment. Even within this limited scope only those scholars with published views bearing directly on the specific themes of the critique are mentioned.
2. The Council of Vienne held in 1312 directed that Arabic, among certain other languages, should be introduced at the Universities of Paris, Bologna, Oxford, Salamanca, and the Roman Curia. See H. Rashdall, *The Universities of Europe in the Middle Ages* (Oxford, 1895), ii, pt. I, pp. 30, 81–82, 96, who states (p. 30) that 'the objects of the measure were purely missionary and ecclesiastical, not scientific'.
3. Cf. Émile Dermenghem, *La Vie de Mahomet* (Paris, 1929), p. 136; R. W. Southern, *Western Views of Islam in the Middle Ages* (Harvard University Press, 1962), p. 37.
4. Quoted by A. J. Arberry, *The Cambridge School of Arabic* (Cambridge, 1948), p. 8 – spelling has been modernized.
5. Cf. *Proceedings of the Church Missionary Society, 1882–3*, p. 57: '. . . The Egyptian campaign and the dominant influence it has given to England over the destinies of the country much enhance the responsibility of English Christians to give Egypt the Gospel of Christ.'
6. Cf. Dr. Muḥammad Al-Bahiy's introduction to Shaikh Maḥmud Shaltut's *Al-Islam 'Aqidatun wa-Shari'a* (Al-Azhar Press, 1379/1959), pp. iii and v.
7. Lane was greatly assisted in his lexicography by an Azhar Shaikh, Ibrāhīm Dasūqī, who was a *muṣaḥḥiḥ* at the Bulaq Press. See A. A. Paton, *History of the Egyptian Revolution* (London, 1870), ii. 270, quoted by J. Heyworth-Dunne, 'Printing and Translation under Muhammad Ali of Egypt', in the *Journal of the Royal Asiatic Society* (July, 1940), p. 345.
8. Samuel Lee was educated at Queens' College while holding a scholarship from the Church Missionary Society as is recorded in the C.M.S. *Committee Minutes*, ii. 91, 349.
9. For an historical survey see J. Fück, *Die arabischen Studien in Europa bis in den Anfang des 20. Jahrhunderts* (Leipzig, 1955).
10. Cf. section (3) below.
11. See, however, H. A. R. Gibb, *Mohammedanism* (Oxford, 1950), pp. 35–37, who quite clearly states the traditional Muslim point of view first before he proceeds to elaborate the view that the Qur'ān is Muhammad's 'utterances'. A. J. Arberry, to take the other most perceptive of living English orientalists, considers the Qur'ān as 'a supernatural production', but he does not subscribe to the Muslim view that it is of divine origin. See *The Holy Koran* (London, 1953), p. 32.
12. Cf. a similar suggestion made by N. Daniel, *Islam and the West – The Making of an Image* (Edinburgh, 1960), p. 305.
13. An English bishop who was also a distinguished mathematician, E. W. Barnes, *The Rise of Christianity* (London, 1948), has shown how deep-rooted is the origin of Christianity, and Judaism before it, in the ancient Near Eastern tradition of myth, legend, and fact. The historian who holds that the Bible and the Qur'ān are human documents may ask the orientalist, speculating on the 'Judaeo-Christian origins' of Islam, to note and reflect.

14. Cf. A. Guillaume, *The Life of Muhammad* (Oxford, 1955), p. 86: 'a quotation from the Gospel'; p. 655: 'an allusion to Matt. xxi. 33 f.'. See also W. Montgomery Watt, *Islam and the Integration of Society* (London, 1961), p. 262: 'quotations from the Bible begin to appear in Muslim works ...'. All this when there was no Arabic Bible to 'quote' from!

15. Cf. F. Rosenthal, 'The Influence of Biblical Tradition on Muslim Historiography', in B. Lewis and P. M. Holt (eds.), *Historians of the Middle East* (Oxford, 1962). While subscribing to the theory that the Qur'ān is Muhammad's composition and that he derived at least its historical parts from 'ultimate Judaeo-Christian origin', he is more careful than many other scholars holding similar views. He indicates an historical sense by the use of the word 'ultimate', and mental neutrality by the warning against 'speculation' and 'preconceived ideas', even though by his acceptance of unproved hypotheses he somewhat succumbs to the same temptation (see pp. 35–36 *et passim*). The editors of this valuable collection of articles might have exercised more care in this matter. In their Introduction (pp. 2, II) they state that the Middle East 'saw the birth of three of the great religions of humanity, Judaism and its two offspring, Christianity and Islam'. See discussion of this point in the opening remarks of section (3).

16. Quoted in R. G. Collingwood, *The Idea of History* (Oxford, 1951), pp. 69, 71.

17. H. A. R. Gibb, 'The Influence of Islamic Culture on Medieval Europe', in the *Bulletin of the John Rylands Library* (Manchester), xxxviii (1955–6), pp. 85–87.

18. G. E. von Grunebaum, *Islam: Essays in the Nature and Growth of a Cultural Tradition* (London, 1961), p. 228.

19. Hence the validity of another remark made by Grunebaum must be questioned. See 'Problems of Muslim Nationalism', in R. N. Frye (ed.), *Islam and the West* (The Hague, 1957), p. 29: '... conservative pressure will force the concealment of the borrowing wherever possible behind the veil of orthogenetic legend'. ...

20. W. Montgomery Watt, *Islam and the Integration of Society* (London, 1961), p. 263.

21. Cf. B. Lewis, *The Arabs in History* (London, 1960), who in this short and undocumented volume might have used more guarded language when he wrote (p. 39): '... probably from Jewish and Christian traders and travellers whose information was affected by midrashic and apocryphal influences'.

22. A. Guillaume, *Islam* (1954), pp. 192–6 *et passim*.

23. Ibid., p. 74.

24. *The Listener* (London, 16 October 1952), p. 635a.

25. A. L. Tibawi, 'The Life of Muhammad: A Critique of Guillaume's English Translation' (*Islamic Quarterly*, iii, No. 3, pp. 196–214).

26. W. C. Smith, *Islam in Modern History* (Princeton, 1957), p. 17.

27. This is a suitable place to evaluate W. C. Smith's lyrical review of G. Cragg's *City of Wrong (A Friday in Jerusalem)* published in *The Muslim World*, li (April, 1961), pp. 134–7. The book is, of course, a translation of the Arabic philosophical novel by Muhammad Kāmil Husain, *Qaryatun Zālimah*. The reviewer, even more than the translator, exaggerates the intentions of the novel as a 'major move' by a notable Muslim towards the Christian view of Good Friday. H. A. R. Gibb, more soberly, perceived that theology was 'irrelevant to the purpose' of the novel, that it upholds all the essential Islamic positions, and that moreover it omits all reference to the Christian symbolism associated with the story. See *Religion in Life*, xxix (1959–60), pp. 158–9. Equally judicious is Albert Hourani's review, which finds that the novel gave 'the orthodox Muslim answer' to the two fundamental questions: whether Jesus was the Son of God, and whether he was actually crucified. See *Frontier*, ii (Summer 1960), p. 129. My own review of the translation and the translator's introduction makes a similar assessment. See *Die Welt des Islams*, vi, Nos. 3–4 (1961), pp. 280–1.

28. *The World of Islam, Studies in Honour of Philip K. Hitti* (London, 1960), pp. 47–59.

29. Cf. Dr. Muḥammad Al-Bahiy, *Al-Fikr al-Islāmī: al-Ḥadīth wa-Ṣilatuhu bi al-Isti'mār al-Gharbi* (Cairo, 1376/1957), p. 181.
30. J. N. D. Anderson (ed.), *The World's Religions* (London, 1950). Only the article on Islam (pp. 52–98) is by the editor, who also contributes a foreword and an epilogue. The quotations in the text above appear on pp. 7–8, 54, 56, 58, 59, 60 (n. 5), 82 (n. I), 85 (n. I), 92, 93, 97–98.
31. Cf. J. N. D. Anderson, *Islamic Law in the Modern World* (New York, 1959), p. 98.
32. Cf. the opening remarks of section (4).
33. J. Schacht, *The Origins of Muhammadan Jurisprudence* (Oxford, 1950).
34. Id. 'Problems of Modern Islamic Legislation', in *Studia Islamica*, xii. 129.
35. H. A. R. Gibb, *Modern Trends in Islam* (Chicago, 1947), p. 122, cf. 129.
36. Cf. P. Ferris, *The Church of England* (London, 1962), p. 10: 'The Outsider who asks about the Church is told that he cannot understand it unless he is inside it, even, sometimes, that it is impertinent of him to try.'
37. Cf. Aḥmad Amïn, *Yaum al-Islām* (Cairo, 1952), p. 215.
38. K. Cragg, *The Call of the Minaret* (New York, 1956), p. 17.
39. Cf. the equally misleading expression 'reform of the religion of Islam' used by C. C. Adams, *Islam and Modernism in Egypt* (Oxford, 1933), pp. 2, 187.

PART V
AN APOLOGY FOR ORIENTALISM

11

APOLOGY FOR ORIENTALISM

Francesco Gabrieli

In his 'Apology for Orientalism', written in response to Abdel-Malek's 'Orientalism in Crisis', Francesco Gabrieli, a professor of Arabic languages and literatures at the University of Rome, suggests that not only have orientalists added greatly to our knowledge of the civilisations and cultures of the east (as shown in Raymond Schwab, La Renaissance orientale, *1950), they have also contributed substantially to the inner development of Europe, particularly in the period of the Enlightenment. Some orientalists, he admits, may have colluded with 'Western exploiters'; remained too dependent on classical text; and been disinclined to engage directly with the lives and cultures of the people they were studying. But the great majority remained committed to the highest values, engaged in a 'disinterested and impassioned search for the truth'.*

Until a few decades ago the study of the peoples and civilizations of the Orient did not appear to require any apology, since it was considered one of the most uncontroversial and innocuous branches of the science. The orientalist was, and still is in some of the less up-to-date sectors of European *communis opinio*, a scholar who chooses as the object of his research one of the most remote fields of knowledge, far removed in space or time, or both, barred from access by incomprehensible languages and writings, whose religions, philosophies and literatures are quite apart from the main stream of classical and Western

F. Gabrieli, 'Apology for Orientalism', *Diogenes*, No. 50, Summer, 1965, pp. 128–36.

tradition. This was the conception of orientalism among the Bouvards or Pecuchets of the nineteenth and early twentieth centuries. In reality, the interest in oriental civilizations itself constitutes a brilliant chapter in contemporary European culture and civilization, developing from this modest level of estimation to a more important historical concern. This is illustrated in certain respects, if not yet in its entirety, by works that are at the same time a history of ideas and a balance sheet of the results achieved.[1] Orientalism has been respectively an aspect of Enlightenment and of Romanticism, of Positivism and of European historicism, and to sketch its complete history would be tantamount to going through the entire evolution of Western culture. It was precisely in this latter field that it had projected itself outside of itself, toward something other than itself, and by this very act (this should appear obvious and should not be the object of polemics or raised eyebrows) establishing its own view of civilization and history, politics and religion, society and poetry.

Alongside this internal evolution, tied to the development of the entire historiographical, philosophical and religious thought of the nineteenth century, orientalism had another external evolution, a consequence of its own growth, differentiation and deepening. From a discipline originally considered as unitary, it was articulated in many other branches which became increasingly autonomous, and which corresponded to the various civilizations of the Afro-Asian East. Sinology and Indology, Iranistics and Turcology, Semitistics and Islamistics, Aegyptology and Africanistics, and other groupings that are convenient or that correspond to well-delimited linguistic, historical and ethnological divisions of civilization, have been substituted for the generic term orientalism, which has remained a fairly vague common denominator and common matrix. Specialization has headed gradually toward isolating and subdividing further these fields, perhaps even more than would lead to a correct historical view. Hence, to the ancient scientific associations and organs, generically called 'orientalistic' (the *Deutsche Morgenländische Gesellschaft*, the British *Royal Asiatic Society*, the French *Société Asiatique*, all with their respective well-known reviews), have been added more modern and more specific denominations of study and publications in the various specialized fields. The traditional 'orientalist congresses,' which up to now have gathered every three years an indiscriminate crowd of scholars in oriental studies, tend to be joined by specialized meetings and congresses on Arabistics and Islamistics, Indology and Sinology, and so on for the different sectors. From this standpoint, it seemed that the old generic term of orientalism was destined to disappear.

But what the *gnosis* inclined to distinguish, articulate and finally almost dissolve, the *eris* of our time, paradoxically, turns about to reunite. The orientalism that was purely scientific was on the point of vanishing, or rather subdividing into too narrow, single disciplines. Today it is reunified and reconceived in a precise, even if in our opinion not entirely authentic and legitimate, ideological, sociological and political personality; and as such it is in the dock of the accused, on trial for its origins, intentions, methods and results.[2] The accuser in this trial, needless to say, is now the East itself, which from a passive object of history and study has revived as a subject, which seeks with profound travail its own soul and does not recognize it in its past or present in the mirror of European orientalistic investigation. Nor does it recognize the accuracy of the vision nor the honesty of the statements of this European and Western science, which for three centuries has been concerned with it. It tends precipitately to make of European orientalism a scapegoat for its own problems, anxieties and pains.

The most ancient and general accusation in this indictment of orientalism is that of having been the instrument, or at least the collaborator and ally, of European colonial penetration and exploitation. The orientalist, according to this view, is now the foretunner, now the associate and the technical advisor, of the merchant, the politician, the Western exploiter, and the co-responsible if not directly the primary cause of the evil that European domination brought to the Eastern peoples. Without intending in the least to raise again the general historical problem of the nature and function of colonialism, we would like merely to observe that *this* specific claim – that orientalism was its accomplice in its proclaimed misdeeds –, if it is not entirely unfounded, is unjustly exaggerated, generalized and embittered. That the discovery and the scientific exploration of oriental civilizations in the past (where, incidentally, the highest values appear that the East has contributed to the history of humanity), was *at times* accompanied with the economic and political penetration of the modern East by Europe, for its subjection and exploitation, is a fact that may honestly not be denied; but it would be as just and honest not to generalize specific cases and episodes in an indiscriminate act of accusation which, insofar as it aims at laying the blame on orientalistic studies in their entirety, is born of a misunderstanding and an untruth. It is mistaken and untrue that the exclusive or main motive for the historical and linguistic, the literary and religious interest of Europe in the East was in function of its plans for political and economic penetration of the area. If there were, and there definitely were, orientalists who were at the same time agents and instruments of this penetration (consuls and ambassadors, businessmen and missionaries, military or technical personnel, whose trial will take place eventually in 'another sphere', innumerable other important and outstanding investigators of the East held their scientific interests entirely distinct from the practices, if such there were, of their countries, and at times even opposed these practices. The oriental critics of orientalism are free, if they are so persuaded, to reserve their appreciation and gratitude for Soviet orientalism, which officially hoists the anti-colonialist banner. But it is not correct to regard every orientalist of the non-Soviet world as an agent of colonialism, and to forget for example the names of Edward Browne, who gave his life fighting for the independence and freedom of Persia, of Louis Massignon who was beaten by fascists and police for keeping faith in the word given to the Arab world, of Leone Caetani who was scoffed at in Italy as the 'Turk' for having opposed the conquest of Libya. And how surprised the finest among them, from Theodor Neoldeke to Ignaz Goldziher and Julius Wellgausen, from Sylvestre de Sacy to Sylvain Levy, Oldenberg and Pischel, from Amary to Dozy, from Pelliot and Le Coq to Bartold, would be in the Elysian fields to see the pure scientific passion that animated their lives and works debased to the level of low services to a nascent or triumphant colonialism. Colonialism has risen, it has celebrated its misdeeds and its splendors (and not only misdeeds, friends from the East, with or without your permission). It is dead and buried as, everything considered, it deserved to die. But this fact has no bearing whatever on the work of the greatest and most important European scholars who did not see their work as a contribution to political or commercial interest, but as a disinterested and impassioned search for the truth. This is an affirmation worthy of a 'verité de M. de La Palice,' if it is recalled (as it is moreover well recalled in the anti-orientalistic indictment, to the point of making of it, as we will see, one of the summary points of the accusation) that most, in fact the major part, of European orientalistic work on the civilizations and peoples of the Orient was directed toward illuminating the events of the past. It was concerned with the history of civilizations now buried, and of others that still continue, some as stubborn survivals but whose original and vital motives are all or almost all to be sought in a distant past, beyond any modern polemics. The suspicion and hostility of some Eastern milieu toward certain scholars of the ancient East have no more justification than if analogous feelings were to be entertained by modern Greeks or Italians toward the great investigators and reconstructors of the classical civilizations of Greece and Rome.

But, continues the accusation of the modern East, let us admit that there are merits to your study of our past. It is our present that poses your crisis, you and your science and its antiquated or reactionary methods. It is this Orient, very much alive, which today rises to confront you with its problems, its needs, its as yet unsatisfied yearning for a just share of the goods of the earth. What interest do you have in it, what measure will you use to judge it, and to aid it, once your hateful world of subjection and exploitation has fallen to pieces? How will you pretend still to write our history, to analyze our feelings and aspirations with your old west-centered vision, which made Europe, the present-day, degraded Europe, the axis and the center of world history?

These are passionate words, whose sincere feeling cannot and should not be ignored, but which, we believe, should be answered not emotionally but with calm reason. First of all, the right of the modern peoples of the Orient to feel themselves again a subject of history and to demand that their present be given dignity as an object of study is incontestable. This the 'classical' conception of orientalism was inclined to ignore. Today, that disproportion between the past and the present as material for investigation has been largely counterbalanced by the work of the truest and best prepared scholars and writers of the East itself, and of European scholars, among whom the new generations of Soviet orientalists are emerging in greater number if not always higher quality. Also the invitation to consider the history of oriental peoples and civilizations not from a west-centered point of view is fully justified, if one intends to take care not to judge this history merely as complementary to that of the West, almost as a prelude, a counterpoint and epilogue of the 'great history,' the history par excellence, which evolved precisely in Europe. If from this viewpoint the condemnation of historiography and of orientalism as west-centered reaches the point of contending the right of the West to apply, in considering the East, the concepts which the West has elaborated in its modern history, of what precisely is history, civilization, philosophy and poetry – the demand, in other words, that it renounce the results of its secular study on the evolution of humanity and the correlative interpretation in order to look at the Orient *with oriental eyes and mentality* – , this the West could never accept without repudiating itself and its self knowledge, its own *raison d'être*. For at least four centuries modern concepts of history, science, evolution, and of all that makes up the spiritual heritage of man, have been elaborated in the West. *During this same period* the East contributed nothing in any way to this labor. Hence the 'unjustified' pride of the West in its own cultural superiority, which has been recently candidly thrown in its face.[3] It would be strange to say the least to expect that the West renounce the use of such concepts in considering the history of the East, through a sense of *fair play* toward the object of its study, adapting to it relevant concepts that doubtless have had a high and sometimes the highest historical value, but which are by now implied in and surpassed by the further development of human thought. Because, so far as *modern* conceptions, master-ideas, interpretations of history or of life that have been developed in the East are concerned, we confess that we are still waiting to know of them. We know of only one of major importance, which however is an isolated instance, that does not seem to be followed any more in its own country of origin: we refer to the doctrine and work of Gandhi, a lofty personal formulation, grafted onto the traditional influences of the East, from which the West itself would still have a great deal to learn. Other than this, the East is theoretically a desert, if the obvious historical fact is borne in mind that Marxism to which it seems to cling in search of a new philosophy of life, in opposition to the repudiated myths of the West, is also itself a fruit of the West, since Hegel, Marx and Lenin do not belong to the history of oriental thought but properly to Western thought, which has thus demonstrated itself to be fertile with implications and applications in the troubled contemporary history of the Afro-Asiatic peoples. When they now preach hatred and contempt of the West in dogmatic Marxist formulas, they are adopting a weapon that the West itself forged and applied to itself, for its own revival or decline and impoverishment, according to the point of view. Certainly, there is no question here indeed of a genuine product of the East, even if the East has accepted it with such ingenuous and avid enthusiasm.

Our friends from the East should therefore not come to ask us to start studying their past and present in the light of a modern Eastern historiography, philosophy, aesthetics and economics, inasmuch as these are today nonexistent. They should indicate, if they are themselves sure of them, the relevant Marxist doctrines as correct canons of interpretation, but they should not delude themselves that with this they have counterposed something to Western thought that the latter does not already have, indeed that it did not itself generate. And as far as the 'systematic denigration' of the contribution of the orientals themselves to orientalism – another subject of complaint and recrimination –, we take the liberty of considering this question too in the same terms that we have just specified. The original contributions of some oriental civilizations to the study of their own languages and literature, their philosophy and history, were great in the past, while the West was arrogantly and candidly ignored by them. Today, while maintaining contact with this past and pertinent technique, the way to scientific progress and intellectual maturation in the study of these same civilizations still passes through Western orientalism, that is, European histor-ical, philological and sociological thought. And this is the way that intelligent and courageous orientals have taken, and in some cases they have achieved full parity with their Western colleagues. The names, to remain in the field more familiar to those who write, of Abd al-Wahhab Qazvini, Abbas Iqbal and Taqizade in Persia, Faud Koprulu in Turkey, Taha Husein and Ibrahim Madkur in Egypt, Munaggid in Syria, Tangi in Morocco, and many others, are considered by every European orientalist to be on a footing of perfect equality, united by the assimilation of a common mentality, technique and method of work, in which really 'there is no more oriental nor occidental' with opposite programs, but one scientific ideal only, and one sole modern method of work. If many others in the East have not risen to this level, the affirmation does not imply any absurd kind of exclusivism of culture or race, but a simple, verified statement of fact which the future could well modify.

More and more scholars have arrived at an *historical* and not a polemical conception of their great heritage, they have gained a capacity to interpret it and relive it, which includes in itself and surpasses if possible the interpretation of Western orientalism; and a further deepening and progress of this sort would be happily conceded to the most vital forces of the modern East. But so long as the East does not succeed in overcoming this complex of suspicion and ill-feeling that also prejudices friendly cooperation with the West, it should not speak with so much presumption of an 'orientalism in crisis,' blaming it for what is its own agonizing crisis.

This writer has spent what one could call by now a lifetime in dedicated, impassioned study of at least one among the oriental civilizations, the Arabic-Islamic, precisely from which come the most inflammatory and for the most part unjust accusations and recriminations against the *istishràq*. As a son of the West, and tied to its civilization with the most intimate fiber, I have always recognized the dignity and the greatness of the oriental component in history and in humanity. Rectifying and rejecting, where it has been possible and necessary, an inequitable appraisal of the disinterested work of generations in the knowledge of the East, I can but voice one wish: that the East express new, original values that may serve to enrich the common viaticum on earth, or that, welcoming with the necessary adaptations those that have matured in the West, it be able to choose among them only the most generous, the richest in critical ferments, and (to use the words of a great Italian poet) 'the most compassionate of themselves and of others,' rather than the most corrosive and destructive. But if necessity of free choice lead it to prefer the latter, it should at least be able to recognize and not falsify the origin.

NOTES

1. The book by R. Schwab, *La Renaissance orientale* Paris 1950, should be mentioned here. Many other studies on this subject are mentioned in the recent article in *Diogenes*, No. 44, 'Orientalism in Crisis,' by Anouar Abdel-Malek, an article with whose thesis we for the most part differ, as the reader may gather, but which we do not deny contains broad information, sincere feeling and singularly acute observations. For an overall historical perspective we refer to our article 'Oriente e Occidente, e la loro conoscenza reciproca,' in *La comunità internazionale*, XVII [1962], No. 2.

2. The process is extended to the concept of orientalism itself, which the East no longer accepts, sensing a note of condescension in it. And in fact the words Orient and orientalism tend to disappear from the Soviet scientific and propagandistic terminology, which is most sensitive to these moods. For example, the former *Institut Vostokovedenja* in the Academy of Sciences the USSR has become the *Institut Narodov Asii*, and the official line is precisely 'to disorientalize the study of Asia.'

3. In the above-mentioned article by Anouar Abdel-Malek, which is presumed to be familiar to the reader. Of a considerably more measured tone, but not any less instructive in this regard are the observations of M. Arkoun, 'L'Islam moderne vu par le professeur G. E. Grunebaum' in *Arabica*, XI [1964], 113–124, which contest the legitimacy of the Western islamist's diagnosis of Islam, by taking as its point of departure an explicit or implicit consciousness of the superiority of the West.

PART VI
AN ELABORATE ACCOUNT

Edward Said's *Orientalism* (1978) and his numerous other writings on the subject, which now span more than two and a half decades, have provoked considerable interest, not only in the field of oriental studies, but also in many other areas, including anthropology, sociology, Indology and imperial history, where his approach has been much copied. Cited here are parts of an article entitled 'Shattered Myths', published in Naseer H. Aruri (ed.), *Middle East Crucible* (1975); 'Arabs, Islam and the Dogmas of the West', a review article published in the *New York Times Book Review* (1976); and three short pieces from *Orientalism* (1978).

In an afterword to the 1995 Penguin edition of *Orientalism*, Said – a Palestinian Arab, born and brought up in Palestine and Egypt (both then under British occupation), and educated in Palestine, Egypt and America (Princeton and Harvard) – admits that his account of the subject was written out of an 'extremely concrete history of personal loss and national disintegration'. It was no doubt for this reason that, in *Orientalism* and his many other works on the subject, he generally concentrates his attention on British, French and American orientalism, largely ignoring the impressive contributions made to the subject by German, Russian and other orientalists.

12

SHATTERED MYTHS

Edward Said

In 'Shattered Myths' (1975), Said explains how myths work and how from time to time they break up. In particular, he wonders whether, in the aftermath of the Arab – Israeli war of 1973, a change may have occurred in the 'myths of Arab society' preserved in the discourse of orientalism.

The myths of Arab society under discussion here are those preserved in the discourse of Orientalism, a school of thought and a discipline of study whose focus includes 'the Arabs,' Arabism, Islam, the Semites, and 'the Arab mind.' It should be immediately evident that Arab society *in fact* cannot be discussed, because the Arabs all told number over a hundred million people and at least a dozen different societies, and there is no truly effective intellectual method for discussing all of them together as a single monolith. Any reduction of this whole immense mass of history, societies, individuals, and realities to 'Arab society' is therefore a mythification. But what it is possible to do is to analyze the structure of thought for which such a phrase as 'Arab society' is a kind of reality – and this structure as we shall soon see, is a myth, with its codes, discourse, and tropes. This structure has a history (albeit a far simpler one than the subject it purportedly treats) and is upheld by a set of institutions that give it whatever power and validity it seems to have. For this myth the October war was a surprise, but not because 'the Arabs' fought well, rather because the Arabs,

Edward Said, 'Shattered Myths', in Naseer H. Aruri (ed.), *Middle East Crucible* (Wilmette, IL: Medina University Press, 1975), pp. 410–27.

according to the myth, were not supposed to fight at all, and because the war seemed therefore to be a deviation out of context, a violation of a well-established logic. This is a chorus found in many places; it is worth examining in some detail because today the myths of Orientalism surface there most readily.[1]

MYTHS UNLEASHED BY THE OCTOBER WAR

One of the commonest motifs to appear in discussions of the October war was not that the war took place, but rather that it took place in the form of a Western and Israeli intelligence failure. This is as inventive as saying that the American use of napalm in Vietnam was really the natives' failure to use suntan oil. On October 31, 1973 the *New York Times* quoted Henry Kissinger as follows: 'the gravest danger of intelligence assessments' is in trying 'to fit the facts into existing preconceptions and to make them consistent with what is anticipated.' The *Times* went on by itself: 'This is a judgement widely shared in the intelligence community.' True, and what is interesting is that such a community can exist because it speaks a common language of myths for which 'intelligence' is possible with regard to the Middle East because of a hoard of practical knowledge, historical lore, and unshakable conviction ultimately derived from Orientalism. According to Orientalism, Orientals can be observed as possessing certain habits of mind, traits of character, and idiosyncrasies of history and temperament; the sum total of these characteristics inclines Orientals towards certain types of action. Kissinger objected to the rigidity of these inclinations, not as unreal objects, but as mistakenly formulated. In other words what mattered here was the sophistication and flexibility of a formula for predicting human behavior (and congruently, the bases in social scientific attitudes of the formula) not the notion that any formula for prediction will necessarily be inadequate, so long as it relies on such schools of thought as Orientalism.

A startling piece of Orientalism clarifies the problem with which Kissinger was trying (hopelessly, I think) to deal. In its February, 1974 issue *Commentary*, the leading Jewish intellectual journal in the United States, gave its readers an article by Professor Gil Carl Alroy entitled 'Do the Arabs Want Peace?' Alroy teaches political science at Hunter, and is the author of two works, *Attitudes Towards Jewish Statehood in the Arab World*, and *Images of Middle East Conflict*, so he is a man who professes to know the Arabs, and he is obviously some sort of expert on image-making. His argument is quite predictable: that Arabs want to destroy Israel, that Arabs really say what they mean (and Alroy makes ostentatious use of his ability to cite evidence from Egyptian newspapers, evidence which he everywhere identifies with 'Arabs' as if the two, Arabs and Egyptian newspapers, are but one), and so on and on, with unflagging, one-eyed zeal. Quite the center of his article, as it is the center of previous work by other 'Arabists' (synonymous with 'Orientalists') like General Y. Harkabi whose province is something called the 'Arab mind,' is a working hypothesis on what Arabs, if one peels off all the outer nonsense, are really like. In other words

Alroy must prove that because Arabs are first of all as one in their bent for bloody vengence, second, psychologically incapable of peace, and third, congenitally tied to a concept of justice that means the opposite of that, because of these then they are not to be trusted and must be fought interminably as one fights any other fatal disease. For evidence Alroy's principal exhibit is a quotation taken from an essay modestly entitled 'The Arab World' and written by Harold W. Glidden for the February, 1972 issue of the *American Journal of Psychiatry*. Alroy finds that Glidden 'captured the cultural differences between the Western and the Arab view' of things 'very well.' Alroy's argument is clinched therefore, the Arabs are unregenerate savages, and thus an authority on the Arab mind has told a wide audience of presumably concerned Jews that they must continue to watch out. And he has done it academically, dispassionately, fairly, using evidence taken from the Arabs themselves – who, he says with Olympian assurance, have 'emphatically ruled out ... real peace' – and from psychoanalysis.

Harold Glidden turns out to be a retired member of the Bureau of Intelligence and Research, US Department of State, a Ph.D. graduate of Princeton, Department of Oriental Languages, and no doubt he is an instance of those legendary Arabists of whom one has always heard so much. What his work is doing in a reputable psychiatric journal is beyond me, and Alroy – or any other social scientist for that matter – would never dare to quote such trash about any other nationality. It is not only naked racism; it is also the poorest sort of scholarship, even though it is essentially a repetition of canonical Orientalist myths. Glidden's article is nothing less than a four page, double-columned psychological portrait of over one hundred million people, considered for a period of 1300 years, and he cites exactly four sources for his views: a recent book on Tripoli, one issue of *Al-Ahram*, *Oriente Moderno*, and a book by Majid Khadduri. The article itself, purports to uncover 'the inner workings of Arab behavior' which from Glidden's or the Western point of view is 'aberrant' but for Arabs is 'normal.' This is an auspicious start, for thereafter we are told that Arabs stress conformity and that the Arabs inhabit a shame culture whose 'prestige system' involves the ability to attract followers and clients. (As an aside we are told that 'Arab society is and always has been based on a system of client-patron relationships.') The analysis further states that Arabs can function only in conflict situations, that prestige is based solely on the ability to dominate others, and that a shame culture – and Islam itself – makes of revenge a virtue. (Here Glidden triumphantly cites the June 29, 1970 *Ahram* to show that 'in 1969 (in Egypt) in 1070 cases of murder where the perpetrators were apprehended, it was found that 20 per cent of the murders were based on a "desire to wipe out shame," 30 per cent on a desire to satisfy real or imaginary wrongs, and 31 per cent on a desire for blood revenge.') We are told that if from a Western point of view 'the only rational thing for the Arabs to do is to make peace ... for the Arabs the situation is not governed by this kind of logic, for objectivity is not a value in the Arab system.'

Glidden continues now, heady with the power of his analysis: 'it is a notable fact that while the Arab value system demands absolute solidarity within the group, it at the same time encourages among its members a kind of rivalry that is destructive of that very solidarity'; in Arab society only 'success counts' and 'the end justifies the means'; Arabs live 'naturally' in a world 'characterized by anxiety expressed in generalized suspicion and distrust, which has been labelled free-floating hostility'; 'the art of subterfuge is highly developed in Arab life, as well as in Islam itself'; the Arab need for vengence overrides everything, otherwise the Arab would feel 'ego-destroying' shame. Therefore if 'Westerners consider peace to be high on the scale of values' and if 'we have a highly developed consciousness of the value of time,' this is not true of Arabs. 'In fact,' we are told, 'in Arab tribal society (where Arab values originated), strife, not peace, was the normal state of affairs because raiding was one of the two main supports of the economy.' The purpose of this learned disquisition is merely to show how on the Western and Arab scale of values 'the relative position of the elements is quite different.'

When Alroy was challenged for his use of this shabby stuff he replied with the supreme innocence of a man confident in the tradition of his learning that 'what is said [in his article and in Glidden's] is about as controversial amongst Orientalists as the multiplication table.'[2]

Alroy is altogether too trivial an intelligence to bother with for long. He is, however, useful as a symptom. Anyone who refers blithely to a humanistic tradition whose uncontroversial tenets are as irrefutable as multiplication tables can only be expected mindlessly to repeat their underlying code. Neither Glidden nor Alroy disappoints. As with all mythologies theirs is a structure built around a set of simple oppositions, which initiate the distinction between Orientalism and every other form of human knowledge. This then is the key reduction. On the one hand there are Westerners and on the other there are Orientals; the former are (in no particular order) rational, peaceful, liberal, logical, capable of holding real values, without natural suspicion and distrust, and so forth. Orientals are none of these things. These are explicit distinctions. Less explicit is the difference between *us* (Europeans, whites, Aryans) and *them* (non-Europeans, blacks or browns, Semites). The great irony of course is that in many cases non-Europeans – Arabs or Jews – may be Orientalists who consider themselves part of the European, non-Oriental camp; the political meaning of such a confusion will be alluded to from time to time in this essay. The point here is how the myths of Orientalism rely upon a set of differences that may even scant the really real, or empirical, distinction between a European and a non-European Orientalist.

The Oriental as Seen by the Orientalist

A still more implicit and powerful difference posed by the Orientalist as against the Oriental is that the former writes about, whereas the Oriental is written about. For the latter passivity is the presumed role, for the former, the power to observe, study, and so forth. As Barthes said, a myth (and its perpetuators) can invent itself (themselves) ceaselessly. The Oriental is given as fixed, stable, in need of investigation, and in need even of knowledge about himself. There is no dialectic either desired or allowed. There is a source of information (the Oriental) and a source of knowledge (the Orientalist): in short, a writer and a subject matter otherwise inert. The relationship between the two is radically a matter of power, for which there are of course numerous images. Here is an instance taken from Raphael Patai's *Golden River to Golden Road: Society, Culture, and Change in the Middle East*:

> In order properly to evaluate what Middle Eastern culture will *willingly accept* from the embarrassingly rich storehouses of Western civilization, a better and sounder understanding of Middle Eastern culture *must first be acquired*. The same prerequisite is necessary in order to gauge the probable effects of *newly introduced traits on* the cultural context of tradition directed peoples. Also, the ways and means *in which new cultural offerings can be made palatable* must be studied much more thoroughly than was hitherto the case. In brief the only way in which *the Gordian knot of resistance* to Westernization in the Middle East *can be unraveled* is that of studying the Middle East, *of obtaining a fuller picture* of its traditional culture, a better understanding of *the processes of change taking place* in it at present, and *a deeper insight* into the psychology of human groups brought up in Middle Eastern culture. *The task is taxing, but the prize, harmony between the West* and a neighboring world area of crucial importance, is well worth it. (italics added)[3]

The metaphorical figures running through this passage (indicated by italics) come from a variety of human activities, some commercial, some horticultural, some religious, some veterinary, some historical. Yet in each case the relation between the Middle East and the West is really defined as sexual. The Middle East is resistant, as any virgin would be, but the male-scholar wins the prize by bursting open, penetrating through the Gordian knot (the hymen, clearly), despite the taxing task (energetic foreplay?). 'Harmony' is the result of the conquest of maidenly coyness; it is not by any means the coexistence of equals. The underlying power relation between scholar and subject-matter is never once altered: it is uniformly favorable to the Orientalist. Study, understanding, knowledge, and evaluation, masked as blandishments to harmony, are instruments of conquest.

The verbal operations in such writing as Patai's (who has outstripped even his previous work in his more recent *The Arab Mind*)[4] aim at a very particular sort of compression and reduction. Much of his paraphernalia is anthropological – he describes the Middle East as a culture area – but the result is to eradicate the plurality of differences among the Arabs (whoever they may be in fact) in the interest of one difference, that one setting Arabs off from everyone else. As a subject matter for study and analysis they can be controlled more readily.

Moreover, thus reduced they can be made to permit, legitimate, and valorize such general nonsense as that found in Sania Hamady's *Temperament and Character of the Arabs*:

> The Arabs so far have demonstrated an incapacity for disciplined and abiding unity. They experience collective outbursts of enthusiasm but do not pursue patiently collective endeavors, which are usually embraced half-heartedly. They show lack of coordination and harmony in organization and function, nor have they revealed an ability for cooperation. Any collective action for common benefit or mutual profit is alien to them.[5]

The style of this prose tells more perhaps than Hamady intends. Verbs like *demonstrate*, *reveal*, and *show* are used without an object: to whom are the Arabs revealing, demonstrating, showing? To no one in particular, obviously, but to everyone in general. This is another way of saying that these truths are self-evident only to a priviledged or initiated observer, since nowhere does Hamady cite generally available evidence for her observations. Besides, given the inanity of the observations what sort of evidence could there be? As her prose moves along her tone increases in confidence, e.g., 'any collective action ... is alien to them.' The categories harden, the assertions are more unyielding, and the Arabs have been totally transformed from people into no more than the putative subject of Hamady's style. The Arabs exist only as an occasion for the tyrannical observer.

And so it is throughout the work of the contemporary Orientalist – assertions of the most bizarre sort dot his pages, whether it is a Halpern arguing that even though all human thought processes can be reduced to eight, the Islamic mind is capable of only four,[6] or a Berger assuming that since the Arabic language is much given to rhetoric Arabs are consequently incapable of true thought.[7] These assertions are myth in their function and structure, and yet one must try to understand what other imperatives govern their use. Here one speculates of course. Orientalist generalizations about the Arabs are very detailed when it comes to critically itemizing Arab characteristics, far less so when it comes to analyzing Arab strengths. The Arab family, Arab rhetoric, the Arab character, etc., despite copious descriptions by the Orientalist, appear denatured, that is, without human potency, even as these same descriptions possess a fullness and depth in their sweeping power over the subject matter. Hamady again:

> Thus, the Arab lives in a hard and frustrating environment. He has little chance to develop his potentialities and define his position in society, holds little belief in progress and change, and finds salvation only in the hereafter.[8]

What the Arab cannot achieve himself is to be found in the writing about him. The Orientalist is supremely certain of his potential, is not a pessimist, and is able to define not only his own position, but the Arab's as well. The picture of the Arab-Oriental that emerges is determinedly negative; yet why this endless series of works on him? What grips the Orientalist, if it is not – as it certainly is not – love of Arab science, mind, society, and achievement?

Orientalist Fascination with the Arab

Two factors attract the Orientalist: number and generative power. Both qualities are reducible to each other ultimately, but are separated for the purposes of analysis. Almost without exception, every contemporary work of Orientalist scholarship (especially in the social sciences) has a great deal to say about the family, its male-dominated structure, its all-pervasive influence in the society. Patai's work is a typical example. A silent paradox immediately presents itself, for if the family is an institution for whose general failures the only remedy is the placebo of modernization, it must be acknowledged that the family continues to produce itself, it is fertile, and it is the source of Arab existence, such as it is, in the world. What Berger refers to as 'the great value men place upon their own sexual prowess'[9] suggests the lurking power behind Arab presence in the world. If on the one hand Arab society is represented in almost completely negative and generally passive terms – to be ravished and won by the Orientalist hero – we can assume on the other that such a representation is a way of dealing with the great variety and potency of Arab diversity, whose source is if not intellectual and social then sexual and biological. Yet the absolutely inviolable taboo in Orientalist discourse is that that very sexuality must never be taken seriously. It can never be explicitly blamed for the absence of achievement and 'real' rational sophistication the Orientalist everywhere discovers among the Arabs. And yet this is the missing link in arguments whose main project is criticism of 'traditional' Arab society, such as Hamady's, Berger's, Lerner's, and others. They recognize the power of the family, note the weaknesses of the Arab mind, remark on the importance of the Oriental world to the West, but never say what their discourse implies, that what is really left to the Arab after all is said and done is an undifferentiated sexual drive. On rare occasions – as in the work of Leon Mugniery – the explicit is made clear: that there is a 'powerful sexual appetite . . . characteristic of those hot-blooded southerners.'[10] Most of the time, however, the belittlement of Arab society and its reduction to platitudes inconceiveable for any except the racially inferior is carried on over an undercurrent of sexual exaggeration: the Arab produces himself, endlessly, sexually, and little else. The Orientalist says nothing about this, although his argument depends on it. 'But cooperation in the Near East is still largely a family affair and little of it is found outside the blood group or village.'[11] Which is to say that the only way in which Arabs count is sexually; institutionally, politically, and culturally they are nil, or next to nil. Numerically and sexually Arabs are actual.

The difficulty with this view is that it complicates the passivity among Arabs assumed by Orientalists like Patai, and even Hamady, and the others. But it is in the logic of myths, like dreams, exactly to welcome radical antitheses. For a myth does not analyze or solve problems. It represents them as already analyzed and solved; that is, it presents them as already assembled images, in the way a scarecrow is assembled from bric-a-brac and then made to stand for a man. Since the image uses all material to its own end, and since by definition the myth displaces life, the antithesis between an over-sexed Arab and a passive doll is not functional. The discourse papers the antithesis over. An Arab is that impossible creature whose sexual energy drives him to paroxysms of overstimulation, and yet, he is as a puppet in the eyes of the world, staring vacantly out at a modern landscape he can neither understand nor cope with.

Just preceding the October war such an image of the Arab seemed to be notably relevant, and it was often occasioned by scholarly discussion of those two recent favorites of Orientalist expertise: revolution and modernization. Under the auspices of the School of Oriental and African Studies there appeared in 1972 a volume entitled *Revolution in the Middle East and Other Case Studies* edited by Professor P. J. Vatikiotis. The title is overtly medical, for we are expected to think of Orientals as finally being given the benefit of what traditional Orientalism had usually avoided: psychosexual attention. In this imposing compilation of studies by noted scholars the argument is obviously vulnerable as knowledge and as reading of the modern Arab world. At this point it is not of interest to examine the book's failures: the distortions, the willful slanting of scholarly evidence, the unbending desire to discredit and debunk the Arabs as a people and as a society. What is interesting is how close to the surface defensive fear of Arab sexuality has come. Having exhausted his timeworn arsenal of racial criticism made with scholarly detachment, the Orientalist now sheds his disguise, and attacks the very thing he fears most.

Professor Vatikiotis sets the tone of the collection with a quasi-medical definition of revolution, but since Arab revolution is in his mind and in his readers', the naked hostility of the definition seems acceptable. There is a very clever irony here about which I shall speak later. Vatikiotis's theoretical support is Camus, whose colonial mentality was no friend of revolution or of the Arabs, as Conor Cruise O'Brien has recently shown, but the phrase 'revolution destroys both men and principles' is accepted from Camus as having 'funda-mental sense.' Vatikiotis continues:

> ... all revolutionary ideology is in direct conflict with (actually, is a head-on attack upon) man's rational, biological and psychological makeup.
>
> Committed as it is to a methodical metastasis, revolutionary ideology demands fanaticism from its adherents. Politics for the revolutionary is not only a question of belief, or a substitute for religious belief. It must stop being what it has always been namely, an adaptive activity in time for survival. Metastatic, soteriological politics abhors adaptiveness, for how else can it eschew the difficulties, ignore and bypass the obstacles of the complex biological-psychological dimension of man, or mesmerize his subtle though limited and vulnerable rationality. It fears and shuns the concrete and discrete nature of human problems and the preoccupations

of political life: it thrives on the abstract and the Promethean. It subordinates all tangible values to the one supreme value: the harnessing of man and history in a grand design of human liberation. It is not satisfied with human politics which has so many irritating limitations. It wishes instead to create a new world not adaptively, precariously, delicately, that is, humanly, but by a terrifying act of Olympian pseudodivine creation. Politics in the service of man is a formula that is unacceptable to the revolutionary ideologue. Rather man exists to serve a politically contrived and brutally decreed order.[12]

Whatever else this passage is – purple writing of the most extreme sort, counterrevolutionary zealotry – it is nothing less than fascism proclaimed in the name of the human, and a brutal identification of sexuality (pseudo-divine act of creation) with cancerous disease. Whatever is done by the 'human' according to Vatikiotis is rational, right, subtle, discrete, concrete; whatever the revolutionary proclaims is brutal, irrational, mesmeric, cancerous. Procreation, change, and continuity are identified with sexuality and madness; not only with that but, wonder of wonders, with abstraction.

Vatikiotis's terms then are weighted and colored emotionally (from the right) by appeals to humanity and decency, and (against the left) by appeals to safeguard humanity from sexuality, cancer, madness, irrational violence, and revolution. Since it is Arab revolution that is in question the passage is to be read as follows: this is what revolution is, and if the Arabs or the Middle East want it, then that's a fairly telling comment on them, on what kind of inferior race they are. They are capable only of sexual incitement not Olympian (and Western or modern) reason. The irony of which I spoke earlier now comes into play. For a few pages later we find that the Arabs are so inept that they cannot even aspire to, let alone consummate, the ambitions of revolution. By implication, too, Arab sexuality need not be feared for itself, but for its failure. In short we are asked to believe with Vatikiotis, who has an almost Wildean skill with delicate paradoxes, that revolution in the Middle East is a threat precisely because revolution cannot be attained.

> The major source of political conflict and potential revolution in many countries of the Middle East, as well as Africa and Asia today, is the inability of so-called radical nationalist regimes and movements to manage, let alone resolve, the social, economic, and political problems of independence.[13]
>
> Until the states in the Middle East can control their economic activity and create or produce their own technology, their access to revolutionary experience will remain limited. The very political categories essential to a revolution will be lacking.[14]

Damned if you do, and damned if you don't. In this masterful, sneering series of dissolving definitions revolutions emerge as figments of sexually crazed minds which on closer analysis turn out not to be capable even of the craziness Vatikiotis truly respects – which is human not Arab, concrete not abstract, asexual not sexual.

Myth and the Arabic Language

The scholarly centerpiece of Vatikiotis's collection is Bernard Lewis's essay, 'Islamic Concepts of Revolution.' The strategy here is extremely refined. Most readers will know that for Arabic-speakers today the work *thawra* and its immediate cognates means revolution; they will know this also from Vatikiotis's introduction. Yet Lewis does not describe the meaning of *thawra* until the very end of his article, after he has discussed concepts such as *dawla*, *fitna* and *bughat* in their historical and mostly religious context. The point there is mainly that 'the Western doctrine of the right to resist bad government is alien to Islamic thought'[15] which led to 'defeatism' and 'quietism' as political attitudes. At no point in the essay is one sure where all these terms are supposed to be taking place except somewhere in the history of words. Then near the end of the essay:

> In the Arabic-speaking countries a different word was used for [revolution] *thawra*. The root th-w-r in classical Arabic meant to rise up (e.g., of a camel), to be stirred or excited, and hence, especially in Maghribi usage, to rebel. It is often used in the context of establishing a petty, independent sovereignty; thus, for example, the so-called party kings who ruled in eleventh century Spain after the breakup of the Caliphate of Cordova, are called *thuwwar* (sing. *tha'ir*). The noun *thawra* at first means excitement, as in the phrase, cited in the Sihah, a standard medieval Arabic dictionary, *intazir hatta taskun hadhihi 'lthawra* – wait till this excitement dies down – a very apt recommendation. The verb is used by al-Iji, in the form of *thawaran* or *itharat fitna*, stirring up sedition, as one of the dangers which should discourage a man from practising the duty of resistance to bad government. *Thawra* is the term used by Arabic writers in the nineteenth century for the French Revolution, and by their successors for the approved revolutions, domestic and foreign, of our own time.[16]

The entire passage reeks of condescension and bad faith. Why introduce the idea of a camel rising as an etymological root for modern Arab revolution except as a clever way of discrediting the modern? One can tolerate this sort of ploy when it is used by Vico in the *New Science* (1744) as he tries to show the etymological relations between the word for father and a shriek of fear; Vico's interest is in polemically attacking Cartesian rationalism. Yet Lewis's reason is patently to bring down revolution from its contemporary valorization to nothing more noble (or ugly) than a camel about to raise himself from the ground. Revolution is excitement, sedition, setting up a petty sovereignty and nothing more. One's best counsel (presumably only a Western scholar and gentleman can give it) is 'wait till the excitement dies down.' One wouldn't know from this slighting account of *thawra* that innumerable people have an active commitment to it, in ways too complex even for Lewis's pseudo-Gibbonian sarcasm and scholarship. But it is this kind of essentialized description that is canonical for students and policymakers concerned with the Middle East: that the upheavals and the energies among 'the Arabs' are as consequential as a camel rising, as worth attention as the babblings of yokels. When Lewis's wisdom about *thawra* suddenly appears in a *New York Times* article on modern Libya (by Eric Pace, January 30, 1974) in the throes of revolutionary agitation, we are comforted to know that *thawra* originally – how contemptible is the adverb here – means a camel getting up, and so all the fuss about Libya and Qaddafi is pretty funny.

Lewis's association of *thawra* with a camel rising, and generally with excitement, hints much more broadly than is usual for him that the Arab is scarcely more than a neurotic sexual being. Each of the words he uses to describe revolution is tinged with sexuality: stirred, excited, rising up. But for the most part it is a bad sexuality he ascribes to the Arab. In the end, since Arabs are really not equipped for serious action, their sexual excitement (an erection) is no more noble than a camel's rising up. Instead of revolution there is sedition, setting up a petty sovereignty, excitement, which is as much as saying that instead of copulation the Arab can only achieve foreplay, masturbation, coitus interruptus. These are Lewis's implications, no matter how innocent his air of learning or parlor-like his language. Since he is so sensitive to the nuances of words he must be aware that his words have nuances as well.

Lewis's quasi-philology links him to a fairly widespread method among contemporary Orientalists, especially those specialists in Arab affairs whose work is connected to government intelligence agencies (Harkabi with Israeli intelligence)[17] or government propaganda machines (Alroy with the Zionist movement). For such specialists Arabic indicates the nature of the Arab mentality. Words are unmediated indices of irreducible character traits, regardless of culture, history, or social and economic circumstances. Arabic words reveal the Arab's obsession with oral functions (note the sexual motif creeping in again, ascribing sexuality to the Arab, then showing it to be an impaired, or immature sexuality) and the words' meanings are instances of either a malicious hidden significance (proving that Arabs are innately dishonest) or a fundamental inability to be like the 'normal' Westerner.

The contemporary *locus classicus* for these views of Arabic is E. Shouby's 'The Influence of the Arabic Language on the Psychology of the Arabs.'[18] The author is described as 'a psychologist with training in both clinical and social psychology.' His views have wide currency, probably because he is an Arab (a self-incriminating one at that) himself. The argument Shouby proposes is lamentably simpleminded, perhaps because he has no notion of what language is and how it operates. Nevertheless the subheadings of his essay tell a good deal of his story; accordingly Arabic is 'General Vagueness of Thought,'

'Overemphasis on Linguistic Signs,' 'Overassertion and Exaggeration.' Shouby is frequently quoted as an authority because he speaks like one and because what he hypostatizes is a sort of mute Arab who, at the same time, is a great word-master playing games without much seriousness or purpose. Muteness is an important part of what Shouby is talking about, since during his entire paper he never once quotes from the literature of which the Arab is so inordinately proud. Where then does Arabic influence the Arab mind? Exclusively within the mythological world created for the Arab by Orientalism. The Arab is a sign for dumbness combined with hopeless over-articulateness, impotence with hyper-sexuality, poverty with excess. That such a result can be attained by philological means testifies to the sad end of a once noble learned tradition, exemplified today only in individuals like M. M. Bravmann.[19] Today's Orientalist by and large is the last infirmity of a once-great scholarly discipline.

Language plays the dominant role in all the myths under discussion. It brings opposites together as 'natural'; it presents human types in scholarly idioms and methodologies; it ascribes reality and reference to objects (other words) of its own making. Mythic language is discourse, that is, it cannot be anything but systematic; one does not really make discourse at will, nor statements in it, without first belonging – in some cases unconsciously, but at any rate involuntarily – to the ideology and the institutions that guarantee its existence. These latter are always the institutions of an advanced society dealing with a less-advanced society. The principal feature of mythical discourse is that it conceals its own origins as well as those of what it describes. Arabs are presented in the imagery of static, almost ideal types, neither as creatures with a potential in the process of being realized nor as a history being made. The exaggerated value heaped upon Arabic as a language permits the Orientalist to make the language equal to mind, society, history, and nature. Undoubtedly the absence in Arabic of a full-fledged tradition of reported informal personal experience (auto-biography, novel, etc.) makes it easier for the Orientalist to let the language as a whole have such uncontrolled significance; thus for the Orientalist the language speaks the Arab, not vice versa. There are historical and cultural reasons for this distortion.

MYTH-SUSTAINING INSTITUTIONS OF THE WEST

Most universities and institutes in the West have confined Orientalism since World War II to the culturally decadent thesis of the regional studies program. The reasons for this confinement are obvious, as all combinations of political expediency with unimaginative intellectual bureaucracy are obvious. The particularity of literary tradition, which is the way cultures survive, are transmitted, and exist (for the purposes of a scholar), was completely violated. Instead quite stupid bulks of knowledge began to appear masquerading as information about The Middle East, The Communist World, The Latin American countries, and Southeast Asia. New identities, quite without ontological validity, were created, each laced with fraudulent descriptions. One striking result is that nowhere in the West today is there a flourishing school of traditional Oriental philology or a serious attention paid to literary-humanistic Arab literature since the classical period. Near East institutes, Middle East area programs, Oriental studies or Oriental languages and civilization programs hash and rehash the same sociopolitical cliches about the Arab – Israeli conflict, Arab nationalism, the Arab mind, and Islamic institutions. Very few programs include a study of the traditions of Orientalism, let alone critiques of Orientalist methodology, or rational examination of what in fact is the material of Orientalism; it is only the occasional scholar who seriously asks himself why things are this way. Whole generations of Arab and Jewish students, whose stake in Orientalist theory and practise is very large, are educated into this corrupt racism, believing themselves to be gaining the 'objective' methods of analysis their teachers have urged upon them. The result is Jews talking about 'the Arab mind' and Arabs talking about 'the Jewish mind': in the long run, both are equally bad.

We are very far from knowing today what true expense the people of the Middle East have paid for this kind of knowledge and for the kind of political action it has prompted. Nevertheless certain assessments can be made. To say that Orientalism is simply an academic school of thought and that it has no political, social, and even economic significance is unacceptable. For one thing is sure: the study of the Middle East in the West has not been disinterested. The oil and strategic wealth of the region as well as its historic importance have made scholarship an act of acquisition in the grossest way. Conversely to say that Orientalism is near the root of the Middle East problem is as great an exaggeration. As a thesis the cultural imperialism of the West (a form of which is Orientalism) is attractive, yet analytically and methodologically it is still a very gross, even crude notion. Since the modern history of the Middle East is very tightly linked to the history of Orientalism, two systems of knowledge supporting each other, it is difficult to detach them from each other and proclaim one the unilateral bloodsucker and the other the blood. What must not be forgotten, but rather investigated, is that the Orient was available as a subject matter; if Orientals were not informants to Orientalism in the traitorous way such a noun implies, they were nevertheless participants in a process they helped create. Moreover because Orientalists themselves have not often bothered with the matter of their work, its origins, its purposes, they cannot be excused for adhering to the traditions of their caste. Recent attempts to streamline Orientalism with contemporary techniques (like psychoanalysis) merely increase complicity in the mythology of the Oriental, his mind, race, and character. An accurate assessment would have to recognize the dialectic between Orientalist and Oriental. And also the restorative dialectic by which the Oriental asserts his actuality. As Fanon put it in describing a parallel situation: 'It is the white man who creates the Negro. But it is the Negro who creates negritude. To the colonialist offensive against the veil, the colonized opposes the cult of the veil.'[20]

The value of such events as the October war is that they highlight the prevailing system of ideas with which these events form a radical discontinuity. The mythology, in its detail as much as in its global structure, denied the Arabs a possibility for any sort of action. Vatikiotis visited Egypt in early 1973 and saw what he wanted to see: a sort of emblem of Oriental despondency. The army, he said, was 'in a state of high combat readiness, I would suggest for military *in* action'; the regime was dependent 'on the condition of no war no peace.'[21]

No matter how much or how little one thinks of Anwar Sadat's political tactics since the war there can be no gain-saying the fact that his people moved from inaction to action, and it is precisely this rupture of continuity which Vatikiotis, Orientalism, and their joint myths, cannot account for. Not only does the rupture present insuperable epistemological problems for a discourse made up of legends of a supine and impotent Oriental, but it also casts many doubts upon the whole notion of political stagnation between 1967 and 1973. What in the history of Orientalism produced the myths so disturbed by the October war? Why were those myths so acceptable culturally and politically to the schools of thought for whom the October war was a shock?

NOTES

1. My strategy in this essay will be in three parts. First I shall analyze the myths and their structures of Orientalism summoned by the war. What I can discuss will be a few cases that clearly are reasons why Orientalism found the war, specially the fact that the Arabs went to war, a surprise. I shall generalize of course, leaving it to be understood that I will discuss the discourse as a systematic whole, and not every instance of it. Space dictates such a procedure, as well as a conviction that exceptions to the rules of Orientalism as a discourse prove the rules. Secondly, the present institutions that sustain Orientalism are analyzed as the result of the modern history of Western scholarship of the Orient. And finally my concern is with ways of dealing methodologically and practically with Orientalism as a myth system and as a type of thought.
2. This statement was made by Alroy in a response following a letter of mine to *Commentary*, LVII, No. 5 (May, 1974).
3. Raphael Patai, *Golden River to Golden Road: Society, Culture and Change in the Middle East* (3rd ed.; Philadelphia: University of Pennsylvania Press, 1969), p. 406.
4. Raphael Patai, *The Arab Mind* (New York: Scribner's, 1973).
5. Sania Hamady, *Temperament and Character of the Arabs* (New York: Twayne Publishers, 1960), p. 100. Hamady's book is a favorite among Israelis and Israeli apologists; Alroy cites her approvingly, and so too does Amos Elon in *The Israelis: Founders and Sons* (New York: Rinehart and Winston, 1971). Monroe Berger (see note 7) also cites her frequently. Her model is a book like Edward William Lane's *Account of the Manners and the Customs of the Modern Egyptians* (1833–35), but she has none of Lane's literacy, wit, or general learning.
6. Halpern's thesis is presented in 'Four Contrasting Repertories of Human Relations in Islam: Two Pre-Modern and Two Modern Ways of Dealing with Continuity and Change. Collaboration and Conflict and the Achieving of Justice,' a paper presented to the 22nd Near East Conference at Princeton University on Psychology and Near Eastern Studies, May 8, 1973. This treatise was prepared for by Halpern's 'A Redefinition of the Revolutionary Situation,' *Journal of International Affairs*, XXIII, No. 1 (1969), 54–75.

7. Monroe Berger, *The Arab World Today* (New York: Anchor Books, 1964), p. 140. Much the same sort of implication underlines the clumsy work of quasi-Arabists like Joel Carmichael and Daniel Lerner; it is there more subtly in political and historical scholars who include Theodore Draper, Walter Laquer, Elie Kedourie. It is strongly in evidence in such highly-regarded works as Gabriel Baer, *Population and Society in the Arab East*, trans. Hanna Szoke (New York: Frederick A. Praeger, 1964) and Alfred Bonne, *State and Economics in the Middle East: A Society in Transition* (London: Routledge and Kegan Paul Ltd. 1955). The rule seems by consensus to be that if they think at all Arabs think differently, i.e. not necessarily with reason, and often without it. See also Adel Daher's RAND study, *Current Trends in Arab Intellectual Thought* (RM–5979–FF, December, 1969) and its typical conclusion that 'the concrete problem-solving approach is conspicuously absent from Arab thought,' p. 29. In a review–essay for the *Journal of Interdisciplinary History*, IV, No. 2 (Autumn, 1973), 287–298, Roger Owen attacks the very notion of 'Islam' as a concept for the study of history. His focus is *The Cambridge History of Islam* which, he finds, in certain ways perpetuates an idea of Islam (to be found in such writers as C. H. Becker and Max Weber) 'defined essentially as a religious, feudal, and antirational system, [that] lacked the necessary characteristics which had made European progress possible.' For a sustained proof of Weber's total inaccuracy see Maxim Rodinson's *Islam and Capitalism*, trans. Brian Pearce (New York: Pantheon Books, 1974), pp. 76–117. There is a useful short account of Orientalist myths militarily in operation before and during the October war by Yassin el-Ayouti, 'Al-jabha al-ma 'anawiya fi harb October,' *Siyassa Dowaliya*, No. 35, January, 1974, pp. 66–72.
8. Hamady, *op. cit.*, p. 197.
9. Berger, *op. cit.*, p. 102.
10. Quoted by Irene Gendzier, *Frantz Fanon: A Critical Study* (New York: Pantheon Books, 1973), p. 94.
11. Berger, *op. cit.*, p. 151.
12. P. J. Vatikiotis (ed.), *Revolution in the Middle East, and Other Case Studies; proceedings of a seminar* (London: Allen and Urwin, 1972) pp. 8–9.
13. *Ibid.*, p. 12.
14. *Ibid.*, p. 13.
15. *Ibid.*, p. 33.
16. *Ibid.*, pp. 38–9. Lewis's study *Race and Color in Islam* (New York: Harper and Row, 1971) expresses similar disaffection with an air of great learning; more explicitly political – but no less acid – is his *Islam in History: Ideas, Men and Events in the Middle East* (London: Alcove Press, 1973).
17. General Yehoshafat Harkabi, *Arab Attitudes Toward Israel*, trans. Misha Louvish (New York, 1972). Harkabi is the former chief of Israeli intelligence.
18. Originally published in the *Middle East Journal*, V (1951). Collected in *Readings in Arab Middle Eastern Societies and Cultures*, eds. Abdulla Lutfiyya and Charles W. Churchill (The Hague: Mouton and Company, 1970), pp. 688–703.
19. See in particular his *The Spiritual Background of Early Islam: Studies Ancient Arab Concepts* (Leiden: E. J. Brill, 1972).
20. Fanon, *A Dying Colonialism*, trans. Haakon Chevalier (New York: Grove Press, 1967), p. 47. For a more recent analysis of the relationship between Arab and Westerner in common myths see Sadek G. al-Azm, *Nagd al-thaty ba'd al-hazima* (Beirut, 1969).
21. P. J. Vatikiotis, 'Egypt Adrift: A Study in Disillusion,' *New Middle East*, No. 54, March, 1973, p. 10. See also his hostility to Jacques Berque – stated on the basis of Berque's 'ideological' approach, Vatikiotis being of course beyond ideology – in 'The Modern History of Egypt Alla Franca,' *Middle Eastern Studies*, X, No. 1 (January, 1974), 80–92.

13

ARABS, ISLAM AND THE DOGMAS OF THE WEST

Edward Said

In his review article 'Arabs, Islam and the Dogmas of the West' (1976) Said sets out, with great clarity, the essential features of his case against orientalism: its dogmas, its origins, its prejudices, its collusion with imperialism and its failure to reform – a case later elaborated in Orientalism *(1978).*

Orientalism is the learned study of what Disraeli called the great Asiatic mystery, which included Arab, Indian, Chinese and Japanese civilizations. The roots of modern Orientalism as a discipline are philological and can be found in the late 18th century.

The principal dogmas of Orientalism persist in their purest form today in Western studies of the Arabs and Islam. One is the absolute and systematic difference between the West (which is rational, developed, humane, superior) and the Orient (which is aberrant, undeveloped, inferior). Another dogma is that abstractions about the Orient, particularly those based on texts representing a 'classical' Oriental civilization, are always preferable to direct evidence drawn from modern Oriental realities. A third dogma is that the Orient is eternal, uniform, incapable of defining itself; therefore it is assumed that a highly generalized and systematic vocabulary for describing the Orient from a Western standpoint is inevitable and even scientifically 'objective.' A fourth dogma is that the Orient is at bottom something either to be feared (the

Edward Said, 'Arabs, Islam and the Dogmas of the West', *The New York Times Book Review*, 31 October 1976.

yellow peril, the Mongol hordes, the brown dominions, etc.) or to be controlled (by pacification, research and development, outright occupation whenever possible).

The interesting thing is that popular stereotypes about niggers, wogs, Semites, Ay-rabs, babus, gooks and the Oriental mentality have derived not from uninformed lower middle-class Occidental red-necks but from the Orientalists' dogmas. The racial distinction between Oriental Semites (Moslems and Jews) and Indo-Germanic Aryans, for example, was first made respectable by Friedrich Schlegel, not by some crude Bavarian beerdrinker. In most Orientalist work since there has always lurked a value judgment decreeing the Oriental to be a discrete specimen of something resembling (but never attaining the status of) a normal – that is, Western and white – human being.

Historically, Islam and the Arabs were always an additional problem for the West as it thought about the Orient. Between the seventh and 16th centuries either the Arabs or Islam (or both) dominated the Mediterranean; thereafter the Ottoman Empire figured prominently as part of the so-called Eastern Question. Moreover, because Islam as a faith is somehow part and yet not really part of the Judeo-Christian tradition, Western Christianity has never seriously been able either to accommodate Islam or to subdue it completely. There is an unbroken tradition in European thought of profound hostility, even hatred, toward Islam as an outlandish competitor; one finds it in Dante (who placed Mohammed in the eighth circle of the Inferno), in Voltaire, in Renan. Yet during the early 19th century Islam and the Arabs became fully fledged members of the Semitic branch of Orientalism, and I for one am fully certain that Western anti-Semitism has always included both the Jews and the Muslims. The latter have yet to be released from that ideological prison, which has had an objective equivalent in Western colonial and imperialist dominion over all of the Islamic world.

Middle East and Islamic specialists in England and the United States have never ideologically re-educated themselves; neither have they been re-educated. The Concerned Asian Scholars, as they are called, led a revolution during the 1960's in the ranks of East Asian specialists; the African studies specialists were challenged by revisionists; so too were other Third-World area specialists. Only the Arabists and Islamologists still function unrevised. For them there are still such things as *an* Islamic society, *an* Arab mind, *an* Oriental psyche. Even those whose specialty is the modern Islamic world anachronistically use texts like the Koran to read into every facet of contemporary Egyptian or Algerian society. Islam – or a seventh-century ideal of it – is assumed to possess the unity that eludes the more recent and important influences of colonialism, imperialism, and even ordinary politics. Clichés about how Muslims (or Mohammedans as they are still insultingly called by some Orientalists) behave are bandied about with an abandon no one would risk in talking about blacks or Jews. At best, the Muslim is a 'native informant' for the Orientalist. Secretly, however, he remains a despised heretic who for his sins must additionally endure the entirely thankless position of being known negatively, that is, as an anti-Zionist.

14

MY THESIS

Edward Said

In his conclusion to the first part of chapter 2 of Orientalism, *Said summarises the way in which orientalism became a systematic discipline capable of exercising authority over the orient.*

My thesis is that the essential aspects of modern Orientalist theory and praxis (from which present-day Orientalism derives) can be understood, not as a sudden access of objective knowledge about the Orient, but as a set of structures inherited from the past, secularized, redisposed, and re-formed by such disciplines as philology, which in turn were naturalized, modernized, and laicized substitutes for (or versions of) Christian supernaturalism. In the form of new texts and ideas, the East was accommodated to these structures. Linguists and explorers like Jones and Anquetil were contributors to modern Orientalism, certainly, but what distinguishes modern Orientalism as a field, a group of ideas, a discourse, is the work of a later generation than theirs. If we use the Napoleonic expedition (1798–1801) as a sort of first enabling experience for modern Orientalism, we can consider its inaugural heroes – in Islamic studies, Sacy and Renan and Lane – to be builders of the field, creators of a tradition, progenitors of the Orientalist brotherhood. What Sacy, Renan, and Lane did was to place Orientalism on a scientific and rational basis. This entailed not only their own exemplary work but also the creation of a vocabulary and ideas

Edward Said, *Orientalism* (London: Pantheon Books, 1978), pp. 122–3.

that could be used impersonally by anyone who wished to become an Orientalist. Their inauguration of Orientalism was a considerable feat. It made possible a scientific terminology; it banished obscurity and instated a special form of illumination for the Orient; it established the figure of the Orientalist as central authority *for* the Orient; it legitimized a special kind of specifically coherent Orientalist work; it put into cultural circulation a form of discursive currency by whose presence the Orient henceforth would be *spoken for*; above all, the work of the inaugurators carved out a field of study and a family of ideas which in turn could form a community of scholars whose lineage, traditions, and ambitions were at once internal to the field and external enough for general prestige. The more Europe encroached upon the Orient during the nineteenth century, the more Orientalism gained in public confidence. Yet if this gain coincided with a loss in originality, we should not be entirely surprised, since its mode, from the beginning, was reconstruction and repetition.

One final observation: The late-eighteenth-century and nineteenth-century ideas, institutions, and figures I shall deal with in this chapter are an important part, a crucial elaboration, of the first phase of the greatest age of territorial acquisition ever known. By the end of World War I Europe had colonized 85 percent of the earth. To say simply that modern Orientalism has been an aspect of both imperialism and colonialism is not to say anything very disputable. Yet it is not enough to say it; it needs to be worked through analytically and historically. I am interested in showing how modern Orientalism, unlike the precolonial awareness of Dante and d'Herbelot, embodies a systematic discipline of *accumulation*. And far from this being exclusively an intellectual or theoretical feature, it made Orientalism fatally tend towards the systematic accumulation of human beings and territories. To reconstruct a dead or lost Oriental language meant ultimately to reconstruct a dead or neglected Orient; it also meant that reconstructive precision, science, even imagination could prepare the way for what armies, administrations, and bureaucracies would later do on the ground, in the Orient. In a sense, the vindication of Orientalism was not only its intellectual or artistic successes but its later effectiveness, its usefulness, its authority. Surely it deserves serious attention on all those counts.

15

ON FLAUBERT

Edward Said

Said admits that the work of the French novelist Gustave Flaubert – who visited Egypt in 1849–50 and later published a collection of travel notes and letters, recording his impressions – is, in some respects, too vast and complex to be easily characterised. Nevertheless, he identifies Flaubert as an archetypal orientalist, determined to identify the orient with sexual promise, untiring sensuality and unlimited desire. In the following extract, from the chapter in Orientalism *entitled 'Orientalist Structures and Restructures', he describes Flaubert's complex reaction to the orient as he experienced it.*

Despite the energy of his intelligence and his enormous power of intellectual absorption, Flaubert felt in the Orient, first, that 'the more you concentrate on it [in detail] the less you grasp the whole.' and then, second, that 'the pieces fall into place of themselves.'[1] At best, this produces a *spectacular* form, but it remains barred to the Westerner's full participation in it. On one level this was a personal predicament for Flaubert, and he devised means, some of which we have discussed, for dealing with it. On a more general level, this was an *epistemological* difficulty for which, of course, the discipline of Orientalism existed. At one moment during his Oriental tour he considered what the epistemological challenge could give rise to. Without what he called spirit and style, the mind could 'get lost in archaeology': he was referring to a sort of

Edward Said, *Orientalism* (London: Pantheon Books, 1978), pp. 189–91.

regimented antiquarianism by which the exotic and the strange would get formulated into lexicons, codes, and finally clichés of the kind he was to ridicule in the *Dictionnaire des idées reçues*. Under the influence of such an attitude the world would be 'regulated like a college. Teachers will be the law. Everyone will be in uniform.'[2] As against such an imposed discipline, he no doubt felt that his own treatments of exotic material, notably the Oriental material he had both experienced and read about for years, were infinitely preferable. In those at least there was room for a sense of immediacy, imagination, and flair, whereas in the ranks of archaeological tomes everything but 'learning' had been squeezed out. And more than most novelists Flaubert was acquainted with organized learning, its products, and its results: these products are clearly evident in the misfortunes of Bouvard and Pécuchet, but they would have been as comically apparent in fields like Orientalism, whose textual attitudes belonged to the world of *idées reçues*. Therefore one could either construct the world with verve and style, or one could copy it tirelessly according to impersonal academic rules of procedure. In both cases, with regard to the Orient, there was a frank acknowledgment that it was a world elsewhere, apart from the ordinary attachments, sentiments, and values of *our* world in the West.

In all of his novels Flaubert associates the Orient with the escapism of sexual fantasy. Emma Bovary and Frédéric Moreau pine for what in their drab (or harried) bourgeois lives they do not have, and what they realize they want comes easily to their daydreams packed inside Oriental clichés: harems, princesses, princes, slaves, veils, dancing girls and boys, sherbets, ointments, and so on. The repertoire is familiar, not so much because it reminds us of Flaubert's own voyages in and obsession with the Orient, but because, once again, the association is clearly made between the Orient and the freedom of licentious sex. We may as well recognize that for nineteenth-century Europe, with its increasing *embourgeoisement*, sex had been institutionalized to a very considerable degree. On the one hand, there was no such thing as 'free' sex, and on the other, sex in society entailed a web of legal, moral, even political and economic obligations of a detailed and certainly encumbering sort. Just as the various colonial possessions – quite apart from their economic benefit to metropolitan Europe – were useful as places to send wayward sons, superfluous populations of delinquents, poor people, and other undesirables, so the Orient was a place where one could look for sexual experience unobtainable in Europe. Virtually no European writer who wrote on or traveled to the Orient in the period after 1800 exempted himself or herself from this quest: Flaubert, Nerval, 'Dirty Dick' Burton, and Lane are only the most notable. In the twentieth century one thinks of Gide, Conrad, Maugham, and dozens of others. What they looked for often – correctly, I think – was a different type of sexuality, perhaps more libertine and less guilt-ridden; but even that quest, if repeated by enough people, could (and did) become as regulated and uniform as learning itself. In time 'Oriental sex' was as standard a commodity as any other available in the mass culture, with the result that readers and writers could have it if they wished without necessarily going to the Orient.

It was certainly true that by the middle of the nineteenth century France, no less than England and the rest of Europe, had a flourishing knowledge industry of the sort that Flaubert feared. Great numbers of texts were being produced, and more important, the agencies and institutions for their dissemination and propagation were everywhere to be found. As historians of science and knowledge have observed, the organization of scientific and learned fields that took place during the nineteenth century was both rigorous and all-encompassing. Research became a regular activity; there was a regulated exchange of information, and agreement on what the problems were as well as consensus on the appropriate paradigms for research and its results.[3] The apparatus serving Oriental studies was part of the scene, and this was one thing that Flaubert surely had in mind when he proclaimed that 'everyone will be in uniform.' An Orientalist was no longer a gifted amateur enthusiast, or if he was, he would have trouble being taken seriously as a scholar. To be an Orientalist meant university training in Oriental studies (by 1850 every major European university had a fully developed curriculum in one or another of the Orientalist disciplines), it meant subvention for one's travel (perhaps by one of the Asiatic societies or a geographical exploration fund or a government grant), it meant publication in accredited form (perhaps under the imprint of a learned society or an Oriental translation fund). And both within the guild of Orientalist scholars and to the public at large, such uniform accreditation as clothed the work of Orientalist scholarship, not personal testimony nor subjective impressionism, meant Science.

NOTES

1. *Flaubert in Egypt: A Sensibility on Tour*, trans. and ed. Francis Steegmuller (Boston: Little, Brown & Co., 1973), p. 79.
2. Ibid., pp. 211–12.
3. For a discussion of this process see Michel Foucault, *Archaeology of Knowledge* (New York: Pantheon Books, 1972); also Joseph Ben-David, *The Scientist's Role in Society* (Englewood Cliffs, NJ: Prentice-Hall, 1971). See also Edward W. Said, 'An Ethics of Language,' *Diacritics* 4, no. 2 (Summer 1974): 28–37.

16

LATENT AND MANIFEST ORIENTALISM

Edward Said

In a chapter in Orientalism, *entitled 'Latent and Manifest Orientalism', Said describes the relationship of orientalism with racialism, Darwinianism, sexism and imperialism. Orientalist notions of the orient, he concludes, whether latent or manifest, depend on what he sees as a total absence, in Western culture, of the orient as a 'genuinely felt and experienced force'.*

On several occasions I have alluded to the connections between Orientalism as a body of ideas, beliefs, clichés, or learning about the East, and other schools of thought at large in the culture. Now one of the important developments in nineteenth-century Orientalism was the distillation of essential ideas about the Orient – its sensuality, its tendency to despotism, its aberrant mentality, its habits of inaccuracy, its backwardness – into a separate and unchallenged coherence; thus for a writer to use the word *Oriental* was a reference for the reader sufficient to identify a specific body of information about the Orient. This information seemed to be morally neutral and objectively valid; it seemed to have an epistemological status equal to that of historical chronology or geographical location. In its most basic form, then, Oriental material could not really be violated by anyone's discoveries, nor did it seem ever to be revaluated completely. Instead, the work of various nineteenth-century scholars and of imaginative writers made this essential body of knowledge more clear, more

Edward Said, *Orientalism* (London: Pantheon Books, 1978), pp. 205–9.

detailed, more substantial – and more distinct from 'Occidentalism.' Yet Orientalist ideas could enter into alliance with general philosophical theories (such as those about the history of mankind and civilization) and diffuse world-hypotheses, as philosophers sometimes call them; and in many ways the professional contributors to Oriental knowledge were anxious to couch their formulations and ideas, their scholarly work, their considered contemporary observations, in language and terminology whose cultural validity derived from other sciences and systems of thought.

The distinction I am making is really between an almost unconscious (and certainly an untouchable) positivity, which I shall call *latent* Orientalism, and the various stated views about Oriental society, languages, literatures, history, sociology, and so forth, which I shall call *manifest* Orientalism. Whatever change occurs in knowledge of the Orient is found almost exclusively in manifest Orientalism; the unanimity, stability, and durability of latent Orientalism are more or less constant. In the nineteenth-century writers I analyzed in Chapter Two, the differences in their ideas about the Orient can be characterized as exclusively manifest differences, differences in form and personal style, rarely in basic content. Every one of them kept intact the separateness of the Orient, its eccentricity, its backwardness, its silent indifference, its feminine penetrability, its supine malleability; this is why every writer on the Orient, from Renan to Marx (ideologically speaking), or from the most rigorous scholars (Lane and Sacy) to the most powerful imaginations (Flaubert and Nerval), saw the Orient as a locale requiring Western attention, reconstruction, even redemption. The Orient existed as a place isolated from the mainstream of European progress in the sciences, arts, and commerce. Thus whatever good or bad values were imputed to the Orient appeared to be functions of some highly specialized Western interest in the Orient. This was the situation from about the 1870s on through the early part of the twentieth century – but let me give some examples that illustrate what I mean.

Theses of Oriental backwardness, degeneracy, and inequality with the West most easily associated themselves early in the nineteenth century with ideas about the biological bases of racial inequality. Thus the racial classifications found in Cuvier's *Le Règne animal*, Gobineau's *Essai sur l'inégalité des races humaines*, and Robert Knox's *The Dark Races of Man* found a willing partner in latent Orientalism. To these ideas was added second-order Darwinism, which seemed to accentuate the 'scientific' validity of the division of races into advanced and backward, or European-Aryan and Oriental-African. Thus the whole question of imperialism, as it was debated in the late nineteenth century by pro-imperialists and anti-imperialists alike, carried forward the binary typology of advanced and backward (or subject) races, cultures, and societies. John Westlake's *Chapters on the Principles of International Law* (1894) argues, for example, that regions of the earth designated as 'uncivilized' (a word carrying the freight of Orientalist assumptions, among others) ought to be annexed or occupied by advanced powers. Similarly, the ideas of such writers as Carl Peters, Leopold de Saussure, and Charles Temple draw on the advanced/backward binarism so centrally advocated in late-nineteenth-century Orientalism.

Along with all other peoples variously designated as backward, degenerate, uncivilized, and retarded, the Orientals were viewed in a framework constructed out of biological determinism and moral-political admonishment. The Oriental was linked thus to elements in Western society (delinquents, the insane, women, the poor) having in common an identity best described as lamentably alien. Orientals were rarely seen or looked at; they were seen through, analyzed not as citizens, or even people, but as problems to be solved or confined or – as the colonial powers openly coveted their territory – taken over. The point is that the very designation of something as Oriental involved an already pronounced evaluative judgment, and in the case of the peoples inhabiting the decayed Ottoman Empire, an implicit program of action. Since the Oriental was a member of a subject race, he had to be subjected: it was that simple. The *locus classicus* for such judgment and action is to be found in Gustave Le Bon's *Les Lois psychologiques de l'évolution des peuples* (1894).

But there were other uses for latent Orientalism. If that group of ideas allowed one to separate Orientals from advanced, civilizing powers, and if the 'classical' Orient served to justify both the Orientalist and his disregard of modern Orientals, latent Orientalism also encouraged a peculiarly (not to say invidiously) male conception of the world. I have already referred to this in passing during my discussion of Renan. The Oriental male was considered in isolation from the total community in which he lived and which many Orientalists, following Lane, have viewed with something resembling contempt and fear. Orientalism itself, furthermore, was an exclusively male province; like so many professional guilds during the modern period, it viewed itself and its subject matter with sexist blinders. This is especially evident in the writing of travelers and novelists: women are usually the creatures of a male power-fantasy. They express unlimited sensuality, they are more or less stupid, and above all they are willing. Flaubert's Kuchuk Hanem is the prototype of such caricatures, which were common enough in pornographic novels (e.g., Pierre Louÿs's *Aphrodite*) whose novelty draws on the Orient for their interest. Moreover the male conception of the world, in its effect upon the practicing Orientalist, tends to be static, frozen, fixed eternally. The very possibility of development, transformation, human movement – in the deepest sense of the word – is denied the Orient and the Oriental. As a known and ultimately an immobilized or unproductive quality, they come to be identified with a bad sort of eternality: hence, when the Orient is being approved, such phrases as 'the wisdom of the East.'

Transferred from an implicit social evaluation to a grandly cultural one, this static male Orientalism took on a variety of forms in the late nineteenth century, especially when Islam was being discussed. General cultural historians as respected as Leopold von Ranke and Jacob Burckhardt assailed Islam as if they were dealing not so much with an anthropomorphic abstraction as with a religio-political culture about which deep generalizations were possible and warranted: in his *Weltgeschichte* (1881–1888) Ranke spoke of Islam as defeated by the Germanic-Romanic peoples, and in his 'Historische Fragmente' (unpublished notes, 1893) Burckhardt spoke of Islam as wretched, bare, and trivial. Such intellectual operations were carried out with considerably more flair and enthusiasm by Oswald Spengler, whose ideas about a Magian personality (typified by the Muslim Oriental) infuse *Der Untergang des Abendlandes* (1918–1922) and the 'morphology' of cultures it advocates.

What these widely diffused notions of the Orient depended on was the almost total absence in contemporary Western culture of the Orient as a genuinely felt and experienced force. For a number of evident reasons the Orient was always in the position both of outsider and of incorporated weak partner for the West. To the extent that Western scholars were aware of contemporary Orientals or Oriental movements of thought and culture, these were perceived either as silent shadows to be animated by the Orientalist, brought into reality by him, or as a kind of cultural and intellectual proletariat useful for the Orientalist's grander interpretative activity, necessary for his performance as superior judge, learned man, powerful cultural will. I mean to say that in discussions of the Orient, the Orient is all absence, whereas one feels the Orientalist and what he says as presence; yet we must not forget that the Orientalist's presence is enabled by the Orient's effective absence. This fact of substitution and displacement, as we must call it, clearly places on the Orientalist himself a certain pressure to reduce the Orient in his work, even after he has devoted a good deal of time to elucidating and exposing it. How else can one explain major scholarly production of the type we associate with Julius Wellhausen and Theodor Nöldeke and, overriding it, those bare, sweeping statements that almost totally denigrate their chosen subject matter? Thus Nöldeke could declare in 1887 that the sum total of his work as an Orientalist was to confirm his 'low opinion' of the Eastern peoples. And like Carl Becker, Nöldeke was a philhellenist, who showed his love of Greece curiously by displaying a positive dislike of the Orient, which after all was what he studied as a scholar.

PART VII
A MARXIST INTERPRETATION

17

MARX AND THE END OF ORIENTALISM

Bryan S. Turner

Critics of orientalism have generally confined their attention to the political and cultural aspects of Europe's relationship with the orient. It was left to the Marxists, fascinated by Karl Marx's concept of an Asiatic Mode of Production (AMP), to attempt an analysis of East–West relations based on economic principles. In the following passage, cited from the conclusion of Bryan S. Turner, Marx and the End of Orientalism *(1978), Turner argues that Marxism is well equipped to perform this task, but first Marxism itself must be cleansed of its own internal theoretical problems, in particular those which tie it to Hegelianism, nineteenth-century political economy and Weberian sociology.*

The controversy which constitutes this study [*Marx and the End of Orientalism*] concerns the dispute between Orientalists (historians, Arabists and Islamicists), sociologists, and Marxist political economists as to the characterisation of the history and social structure of North Africa and the Middle East. By 'Orientalism', I mean a syndrome of beliefs, attitudes and theories which infects, not only the classical works of Islamic studies, but also extensive areas of geography, economics and sociology. This syndrome consists of a number of basic arguments: (i) social development is caused by characteristics which are internal to society; (ii) the historical development of a society is either an evolutionary progress or a gradual decline; (iii) society is an 'expressive

Bryan S. Turner, *Marx and the End of Orientalism* (London: George Allen and Unwin, 1978), pp. 81–2 and 85.

totality' in the sense that all the institutions of a society are the expression of a primary essence. These arguments allow Orientalists to establish their dichotomous ideal type of Western society whose inner essence unfolds in a dynamic progress towards democratic industrialism, and Islamic society which is either timelessly stagnant or declines from its inception. The societies of the Middle East are consequently defined by reference to a cluster of absences – the missing middle class, the missing city, the absence of political rights, the absence of revolutions. These missing features of Middle East society serve to explain why Islamic civilisation failed to produce capitalism, to generate modern personalities or to convert itself into a secular, radical culture.

My approach to the Orientalist picture of the Middle East has not been primarily to argue that their assertions turn out to be empirically false but to show the absurdity of the problems which are produced by their premises. My counterattack is based on the argument that once the global centres of capitalism had been established, the conditions for development on the periphery were fundamentally changed. The internalist theory of development fails to grasp the significance of this global relationship and consequently persists in posing futile questions about spontaneous capitalist development. The dominant character of development on the periphery is combined inequality and unevenness. Capitalism intensifies and conserves pre-capitalist modes of production so that there is no unilinear, evolutionary path from 'traditional society' to 'modern society'. On the basis of these arguments about capitalism on the periphery, all the assumptions about the universal relevance and significance of European models of development ('the bourgeois revolution', secularisation, modernisation) fall to the ground.

The critique of Orientalism, however, persistently runs into the difficulty that Marxism itself contains a heavy dosage of Orientalism, or that Marxism can be interpreted in such a manner as to make it compatible with certain aspects of Orientalism. This situation arises partly because of the overlap between Hegelian versions of Marxism and Orientalism which is illustrated by the view of history as an unfolding essence and by the specification of the static nature of 'Asiatic society'. . . .

[. . .]

The criticism of Orientalism in its various forms requires something more than the valid but indecisive notion that at its worst Orientalist scholarship was a rather thin disguise for attitudes of moral or racial superiority (Asad, [Talal, *Anthropology and the Colonial Encounter* (Ithaca Press,] 1973) and thereby a justification for colonialism. What is needed is something other than the objection that some Orientalists were less than neutral and objective, or that they retired from the real world of Middle East politics to the ivory tower of philology, poetry and aesthetics. The end of Orientalism requires a fundamental attack on the theoretical and epistemological roots of Orientalist scholarship which creates the long tradition of Oriental Despotism, mosaic societies and the

'Muslim City'. Modern Marxism is fully equipped to do this work of destruction, but in this very activity Marxism displays its own internal theoretical problems and uncovers those analytical cords which tie it to Hegelianism, to nineteenth-century political economy and to Weberian sociology. The end of Orientalism, therefore, also requires the end of certain forms of Marxist thought and the creation of a new type of analysis.

PART VIII
AN AMERICAN RESPONSE

18

THREE ARAB CRITIQUES
OF ORIENTALISM

Donald P. Little

Donald P. Little, of the Institute of Islamic Studies, Montreal, Canada, was one of the first of the North American scholars to respond to the critique of orientalism mounted by Anouar Abdel-Malek in 'Orientalism in Crisis', A. L. Tibawi in 'English-Speaking Orientalists', and Edward Said in 'Shattered Myths'. In 'Three Arab Critiques of Orientalism', Little questions Tibawi's willingness to display the 'courtesy, tolerance and moderation' he demands of others; calls attention to Abdel-Malek's left-wing bias; and wonders at Said's failure to draw 'subtle distinctions'. Yet, in his concluding paragraphs, paradoxically, he implicitly accepts the validity of many of the criticisms of orientalism made by its critics.

Given the absence among Arab intellectuals of a strong impulse to analyze themselves, their culture and what it means to them,[1] it may be instructive for those of us in the West who want to understand Arabs to study what they have written about *us*. Instructive in at least two ways. First, more often than not, Arab critics of Western scholarship on Arab-Islamic culture have been devastatingly critical, in the patent conviction that Western scholars do not understand Arabs. Surely if we want to understand them and their culture we should know why our past attempts have been rejected by the subjects of our study. This is especially true now when mutual understanding between Arab and

D. P. Little, 'Three Arab Critiques of Orientalism', *Muslim World*, 69, 2, 1979, pp. 110–31.

non-Arabs is increasingly important for economic and political reasons. Second, this attempt to acquaint ourselves with Arab attitudes will inevitably lead us to question the validity of their judgments of the strengths and weaknesses of the methodology which we use and prompt us to ask if, or how, these methods can be improved. Thus, even if this exercise does not teach us much about Arabs, hopefully it will deepen our understanding of ourselves.

There is a considerable body of literature on the subject of *istishrāq* (Orientalism) and *al-mustashriqūn* (Orientalists), which, being written in Arabic and other Islamic languages, is intended primarily for domestic consumption.[2] All of this literature I have chosen to ignore for the present in order to focus instead upon three articles on this subject which have been composed in English or in French and which are intended therefore for a different – foreign – audience. Since all three articles appeared in scholarly format and were published in the West, I assume that they were designed for the edification of Western scholars. It is also worth noting that all three authors are themselves Western scholars in the sense that they were trained in Western educational institutions and have, accordingly, intimate acquaintanceship with the subject of their concern. One indication of this familiarity with the West is the ease and force with which they express themselves in a Western language.

Without quibbling over the meaning of terms, I should state what I mean by *Arab* and *Orientalist*. Since all three authors are, or have been, expatriates, I am clearly not referring to present nationality. Unless I am mistaken, however, all three would identify themselves as Arabs in most contexts, linguistic and cultural contexts in particular. By *Arab*, then, I mean anyone who feels this linguistic and cultural identity. This does not mean that the authors I have chosen are stereotypes or that they are representative of Arabs or even of Arab intellectuals; nevertheless, I would suggest that the views which they express about Orientalism are by no means peculiar to themselves and are, in fact, widespread in certain quarters.[3] *Orientalist* is also an elusive term; for present purposes I shall adopt a definition formulated by Abdallah Laroui because it is plainly the one which our three authors have in mind: 'An Orientalist is defined as a foreigner – in this case a Westerner – who takes Islam as the subject of his research.'[4] It is perhaps worth noting that all three of our critics qualify as Orientalists under a broad interpretation of this definition; also, that I realize that the definition is simplistic in that it ignores the distinction between philologists and social scientists, the latter of whom reserve the term *Orientalism* for the former and do not themselves like to be associated with it at all, but this is a complex subject which deserves separate treatment.

Professor A. L. Tibawi, a distinguished educator and scholar on subjects Islamic and Arab who has recently reached the end of his teaching career, is the first critic whom we shall consider,[5] through his article, 'English-Speaking Orientalists: A Critique of their Approaches to Islam and Arab Nationalism.'[6] It is Tibawi's complaint that almost all Orientalists, both past and present, if not actually hostile to Islam and the Arabs, lack an elementary sympathy for the Islamic religion and the nationalistic aspirations of the Arab people. In the religious sphere this negative attitude impedes, Tibawi claims, a true understanding of what Islam really means, that is, what Islam means to Muslims, and results, inevitably, in errors and distortions, or even downright blasphemy, that is bound to offend Muslim sensibilities. In a secular context, if indeed it is possible from Tibawi's point of view to make a distinction between Islam and the Arabs, this negativism is manifest in thinly disguised contempt for the Arabs and their struggle to free themselves from imperialist, including Zionist, interference and control.

These two dimensions of Orientalism are discussed separately. Western interest in Islam as a religion has been tainted from the beginning, Tibawi believes, by hostility to Islam as a rival religion to Judaism and Christianity. This hostility was first displayed openly, in the form of polemics, holy war and missionary activities aimed at converting or destroying Muslims. Later, however, commercial and political considerations led Westerners to study Islam and Muslim peoples in order to subject them to imperialist control. Those few figures in the West who studied the Islamic East for its own sake were far outnumbered by those who were inspired by missionary or colonialist motives, which, in the last analysis, were one and the same. Eventually, however, thanks to the development of a 'scientific' approach to the humanities, a detached and truly academic approach to Islam appeared in the West, but this approach has not been mastered, much less adopted, by many scholars. Indeed, much to Tibawi's dismay, religious prejudice against Islam has by no means disappeared and is still being propagated in the works of Orientalists of the most seemingly impeccable credentials, marring to a greater or lesser degree the pronouncements of such eminent Orientalists as A. Guillaume, Montgomery Watt, G. E. von Grunebaum, Bernard Lewis, Wilfred Cantwell Smith, J. N. D. Anderson, and Kenneth Cragg, to name only a few.

Prejudice emerges most clearly in scholarship on the Prophet Muḥammad and the origins of Islam. Tibawi objects vehemently to Orientalists' implicit assumption or explicit assertion that the Qur'ān was composed by Muḥammad rather than revealed to him by Allāh. This he regards as denial of the 'cardinal Muslim belief that Islam is of divine origin' and therefore suggests that it is 'more conducive to human understanding, and more scholarly, to leave matters of faith alone. ...'[7] Or, failing that, and it is doubtful that he seriously expects non-Muslim scholars 'to leave matters of faith alone,' Tibawi insists that they should at least state 'the traditional Muslim view' on such matters before stating contrary views of their own. In the same vein he decries the perennial attempts of Orientalists to seek the origins of Islam in Christianity and Judaism. Not only do such attempts presuppose ideas that are unacceptable to Muslims and thus 'tend to create ill-feeling among Muslims, and in consequence place serious obstacles in the way of intellectual traffic between the two sides';[8] these attempts are also futile since they are speculative and are incapable of historical proof. Also doomed to failure are attempts even to compare Islam with Christianity since most who have applied the methods of comparative religion to Islam have tried to fit it into a Christian mold, to make Islam compatible with Christianity, with the ultimate object of persuading Muslims to abandon or soften their beliefs in order to embrace Christianity. Of the same stripe are those Orientalists who advocate the reform or reformation of Islam as the prerequisite for its survival in modern times. For Tibawi Islamic *beliefs* are immutable; Islamic *law*, on the other hand, has its own instrumentalities by which change can be, and has been, effected and has no need of alien guidance.

In the end, one cannot escape the impression that Tibawi would prefer it if non-Muslims did not study Islam at all; in fact, at one point he does declare that 'those outside a religious system can never capture the significance of the experience of those inside it.'[9] Since religious experience is intuitive in nature, it cannot be understood by scholars' 'analytical and critical' methods.[10] Thus it does no good to study Islam from books. Furthermore, since few Orientalists can speak an Islamic language properly and few Muslims have mastered a Western tongue, it is of no avail for Orientalists to study by talking to Muslims. What is left? This is difficult to determine. Although Tibawi expresses approval on several occasions of the scholarship of H. A. R. Gibb and, surprisingly, of Joseph Schacht's work on Islamic law, he has in effect closed most of the doors by which Orientalists have tried to gain access to Islam. What is more discouraging is the fact that while pleading for a more sympathetic, tolerant approach to Islam on the part of Orientalists, he has gone out of his way to denounce the work of those very Orientalists who have leaned over backwards to avoid offending Muslim sensibilities, a group which has recently been labelled 'irenic.'[11] Thus, Wilfred Cantwell Smith, who founded the McGill Institute of Islamic Studies for cooperative study of Islam by Muslims and non-Muslims, is denounced for his attempt to find common ground between Islam and Christianity, and Montgomery Watt, whose two-volume study of Muḥammad is generally so favorable to the Prophet that it often seems apologetic, is dismissed as a 'new dualist' in Islamic Studies, whose works 'have proved less comprehensible than those of the extremists'![12] If consciously conciliatory scholarship is not acceptable to Tibawi, there would seem to be little hope for work of a more neutral character. Indeed, on Tibawi's ground there is only scant hope for neutrality at all. Although he claims to be seeking only 'courtesy, tolerance, and moderation' from non-Muslim students of Islam, he puts the Orientalist in a most compromising position when he advises him that to teach Muslim students involves 'a moral responsibility, for his teaching might shake the faith of his students in his religion.'[13] The perils implicit in this admonition for an education of any but the most blatantly limited sort are surely too obvious to require comment.

The religious hostility which Tibawi sees in Western scholarship on Islam he finds transmuted into 'national or ideological antipathy' in scholarship on Arab nationalism. In fact, this new hostility is merely an extension of the old, as the conflict between Christendom and Islamdom has narrowed into a political struggle between the West and the Arab nations fighting for their independence. In this case the most conspicuous villain is the Zionist or the Zionist sympathizer, whose studies of Arabs are immediately suspect for political reasons. An equally dangerous foe is the Western scholar who judges the Arabs by Western liberal standards and condemns the Arabs for abandoning parliamentary democracy, failing to realize that the Arabs, like other Muslims, are guided by Islamic norms even in politics. Surely few Orientalists would quarrel with Tibawi's plea that Arab politics should not be judged, or even analyzed, within the context of rigid Western norms and standards. But, by the same token, few of us would follow him to the next step, where he reduces his political argument again to a religious, moral, one by insisting that since Arab nationalism 'is inseparable from Islam,' 'what is hostile to Arab nationalism is then automatically hostile to Islam, and vice versa,'[14] and, furthermore, that the Western scholar is therefore once again faced with a moral problem when he attempts to appraise Arab nationalism. If, as would seem to be the case, Tibawi is suggesting that Islam requires Muslims to support Arab nationalism and that Orientalists should therefore pause before criticizing it lest they disturb an Arab Muslim's faith, he is making a proposal which would not commend itself to many.

Professor Tibawi's objections to Orientalism are religious; those of Professor Anouar Abdel-Malek are markedly different. Of Coptic background, Abdel-Malek identifies himself as a Marxist who left Egypt, his homeland, because of government repression of the Left.[15] Not surprisingly, his analysis of 'Orientalism in Crisis'[16] is expressed in terms of conflict between Right and Left, Imperialism and Socialism, reactionary dogma and progressive ideology.

Orientalism for Abdel-Malek has been from the beginning the intellectual handmaiden of colonialism and has been dominated by its assumptions and tools whether it consciously espoused its goals or not. It divided early into two branches, one cultivated by academicians who were interested in the Arab world primarily as the heir of Hellenism, the other dominated by amateur gatherers of intelligence which they hoped to use 'to penetrate consciousness of the people in order to better assure its enslavement to the European powers.'[17] The two groups did not remain distinct, and the goals of the latter permeated and subverted those of the former. So far Abdel-Malek has said nothing that Tibawi did not say; at this point, however, he proceeds in a different vein to define more precisely the distinguishing characteristics of Orientalism. These are two: conceptional and methodological. He observes that Orientalists conceive of Orientals as essential objects which can be reduced to an ethnic, racist type. This is a theme which we shall see reiterated by our third critic. Methodologically, Orientalists confine their attention to the past, mainly to the languages and the religions of the past, which they study either through manuscripts (plundered from the East!) and archives (stored in the West!) or through the racist observations of visiting imperialists. Tibawi presumably would find little in this characterization to quarrel with and would probably accept it as valid for the whole range of Orientalists, both past and present. I am not so sure that he would accept Abdel-Malek's more characteristically Marxist contention that the nature of Orientalism has changed in the recent past as a direct result of 'the victory of the national liberation movements in the ex-colonial world ... [and] the appearance of the group of socialist states and the subsequent differentiation between the "two Europes". ...' [18]These profound political changes led to the development of two new types of Orientalism, one of which arose among the former colonial master-states of western Europe and the other in the new socialist states of eastern Europe. Given Abdel-Malek's intellectual and political orientation, it is not difficult to predict which of the two types he prefers. Western neo-Orientalism has flowed since the end of World War II in two streams: the French and the Anglo-Saxon. As representative of the new French approach Abdel-Malek chooses Jacques Berque, the French sociologist who is known for his impressionistic, highly individualistic studies of Egypt and the Maghreb. Berque's approach, according to Abdel-Malek, differs very little from that of traditional Orientalism except in attitude: rather than viewing Arabs as objects to be studied from a distance, Berque tries to understand them by participating with them in their human condition and submitting his systematization of their history to them for their judgment and criticism. Anglo-Saxon neo-Orientalism, on the other hand, still regards the Arabs as objects – things – of study from whom the researcher must remain aloof. The only new element in this brand of Orientalism can be seen in the formation of institutes and commissions in Great Britain and America for the study of the Oriental present in order to define and guarantee these countries' political and economic interests in the newly emerging world order. Although the importance of the present has at long last been recognized as well as the necessity of collaboration with indigenous scholars, the main thrust remains ethnocentric, with the Western governments building up depots of source materials and training Western scholars to use them efficiently. The indigenous scholars are to be left the menial task of organizing 'local documentary materials.'[19]

Thus, in Abdel-Malek's view, Western neo-Orientalism, especially but not exclusively the Anglo-Saxon variety, remains as exploitative, as imperialistic as before, only more concerned with the present and better financed and organized to serve the ends of Western powers. In contrast, the main feature of Socialist Orientalism as proclaimed by Anastas I. Mikoyan at the Twenty-Fifth Congress of Orientalists held in Moscow in 1960 is to serve the exploited peoples of the Orient by helping them to help themselves. More specifically, it is the duty of Orientalists 'to contribute in a creative manner to the elaboration of the fundamental problems of the struggle of the peoples of the Orient for their national and social liberation and to recover from their economic backwardness.'[20] This contribution necessarily takes the form of collaboration with the Oriental peoples, now that, by gaining their freedom, they have elevated themselves from objects of study to creators of their own science, history, culture, and economy. Only in this way can the new Orientalism free itself from the blinders of Europocentrism which have limited the vision of the old Orientalism since its inception. In this joint endeavor it will be necessary for foreign researchers to yield primacy to Orientals, especially in the field of contemporary studies, which, of course, will displace the study of the past in the socialist order of priorities. In order to break the 'monopoly of the colonial powers' over source materials, the socialist states, led by the Soviet Union, have mounted 'a truly colossal effort' in establishing bodies for the study of the peoples of the Orient and Africa within the traditional disciplines of socialist scholarship so as to keep these studies in the mainstream and to avoid their 'orientalization' as has occurred in the West.[21] Skeptics might suspect that Oriental studies have been incorporated within the already existing academic bodies for even more practical reasons, but this I am not in a position to judge.

Nor do I have any way of knowing whether the results of socialist neo-Orientalism have met Abdel-Malek's obviously high expectations, whether, that is, this new scholarship has actually ameliorated the political and economic conditions of Oriental peoples. Certainly the Soviet experiment in assisting Abdel-Malek's own compatriots does not seem to have been an unqualified success, though it may well be that the new scholarship was not really involved in what was essentially technical and military assistance. In this respect, perhaps it would be more meaningful to investigate the role of socialist neo-Orientalism in improving the lot of the people of the Soviet Muslim republics, where it is undeniably true that remarkable progress has been made in assimilating Muslims into Soviet society at the expense of pre-existing cultures, though this process began considerably before 1945.

Many of Abdel-Malek's assumptions and judgments are shared by the third Arab critic whom we shall consider, Edward Said, professor of English and comparative literature at Columbia University.[22] But whereas Abdel-Malek is careful to distinguish types of Orientalists according to time and place and the evolution of a discipline, Said unceremoniously dumps every Westerner who has ever studied the Arabs into one big basket. Thus we find mixed with such traditional scholars as Gibb, von Grunebaum, and Lewis, others with decidedly different interests and approaches – General Yehoshafat Harkabi, Gil Carl Alroy, and Harold Glidden, for example. Though it is perfectly legitimate from Said's point of view to lump such diverse scholars into one indistinguishable group and certainly makes it easier for him to tar all of them with the same brush, this procedure is as meaningful as it would be to attack T. S. Eliot for the foibles of Rudyard Kipling, even though a good case can certainly be made that both are bona fide poets. But Said is clearly not interested in drawing subtle distinctions, since to him all Orientalists have been, and are, the same, because they share the same beliefs and assumptions which invariably distort their vision. This conviction Said has declared most blatantly as follows:

> The principal dogmas of Orientalism persist in their purest form today in Western studies of the Arabs and Islam. One is the absolute and systematic difference between the West (which is rational, developed, humane, superior) and the Orient (which is aberrant, undeveloped, inferior). Another dogma is that abstractions about the Orient, particularly those based on texts representing a 'classical' Oriental civilization, are always preferable to direct evidence drawn from modern Oriental realities. A third dogma is that the Orient is eternal, uniform, incapable of defining itself; therefore it is assumed that a highly generalized and systematic vocabulary for describing the Orient from a Western standpoint is inevitable and even scientifically 'objective.' A fourth dogma is that the Orient is at bottom something either to be feared (the yellow peril, the Mongol hordes, the brown dominions, etc.) or to be controlled (by pacification, research and development, outright occupation whenever possible).
>
> The interesting thing is that popular stereotypes about niggers, wogs, Semites, Ay-rabs, babus, gooks and the Oriental mentality have derived not from uninformed lower middle-class Occidental red-necks but from the Orientalists' dogmas.[23]

This manifesto, published in the *New York Times Book Review* presumably for popular consumption, Said earlier expounded in an article entitled 'Shattered Myths,' by which he means Orientalists' myths about the Arabs, which were shattered by the October War of 1973.[24] Chief of these myths is the Orientalist racist delusion that the Arabs are passive and powerless. On one level this myth reflects the Orientalists' habit (already identified by Abdel-Malek) of viewing Orientals as inert objects to be studied and manipulated. But on a deeper level this Western concern with Arab passivity and impotence Said thinks is related to Western fear of Arab sexual prowess. Since both these contradictory beliefs are myths and are therefore irrational it is not necessary for Said to explain how Orientalists manage to reconcile them except to say that they do manage. Rather, having raised the issue of sexuality, he is far more interested in subjecting Orientalist scholarship to Freudian literary analysis, a mode of criticism which enables him to reduce to absurdity the writings of such establishment scholars as P. J. Vatikiotis and Bernard Lewis. Using this technique, whereby the sexual connotations of words undercut the denotative sense in which their author thinks he is using them, Said is able to claim that Vatikiotis's denunciation of revolutionary ideology is 'purple writing of the most extreme sort, counter-revolutionary zealotry – it is nothing less than fascism proclaimed in the name of the human, and a brutal identification of sexuality ... with cancerous disease'.[25] This outburst was occasioned by Vatikiotis's declaration that revolutionary ideology is irrational. Bernard

Lewis, on the other hand, is castigated for revealing that the Arabic word for revolution, *thawra*, is derived, like many other Arabic words, from a root associated with the activities of a camel, in this case rising up or 'to be stirred or excited.' From this Said insists that Lewis is discrediting the Arabs by ascribing 'bad sexuality' to them:

> In the end, since Arabs are really not equipped for serious action, their sexual excitement (an erection) is no more noble than a camel's rising up. Instead of revolution, there is sedition, setting up a petty sovereignty, excitement, which is as much as saying that instead of copulation the Arab can only achieve foreplay, masturbation, coitus interruptus. These are Lewis's implications, no matter how innocent his air of learning or parlor-like language.[26]

Worse yet, Lewis's manipulation of philology as an insidious psychological attack is by no means atypical but, according to Said, is 'a fairly widespread method among contemporary Orientalists, especially those specialists in Arab affairs whose work is connected to government intelligence agencies ... or government propaganda machines. ...'[27]

From this observation Said launches a discussion of Orientalists' use of philology to propagate another racist myth about the Arabs, namely, that Semites, in comparison with other people, are simple folk who have been incapable of producing a civilization beyond that of tent and tribe. The evidence for this myth Said traces to the racial theories of Renan and Gobineau, which rested ultimately on the argument that since Semitic languages are simple, agglutinative systems based on the triliteral root, Semites must have simple minds and are capable of producing only a simple civilization. Furthermore, since they are simple, they do not change, so that general, eternal truths can be formulated about Semitic people which are universally valid. Thus Orientalists are able to write palpably absurd books about such subjects as Arab mentality and the Arab mind as if such imaginary objects actually existed. By the same logic Said would undoubtedly conclude that Orientalism is also simple because it has made no advance over these simplistic nineteenth-century views. 'It scarcely needs mention,' he says, 'that what Renan and Gobineau say about the Semites is practically identical with what one finds in works by the contemporary Orientalists.'[28] As proof of this assertion Said recapitulates Laroui's contention that the scholarship of von Grunebaum is 'reductive' because it reduces many Islams to one Islam, a whole complex of cultural phenomena to one central determining core. In other words, because von Grunebaum can be demonstrated to be reductive he must share the nineteenth-century racist belief that Arabs and Islam are simple. The Jews, Said avers, have recently exempted themselves from this blanket characterization of the Semites by adopting Zionism, whereby they identified themselves with Europe, produced an 'advanced quasi-Occidental society' and adopted the myth of Indo-European superiority to all other peoples. This explains why, in Said's words, 'Orientalism governs Israeli policy towards the Arabs throughout.'[29]

At this point I hope that enough has been said to set forth Said's chief complaints against Orientalism and to suggest how they differ from those of Abdel-Malek and Tibawi. As I indicated earlier, Said shares a great deal with Abdel-Malek in the conceptualization of Orientalism as a tool of imperialism; he differs from Abdel-Malek, however, in his preoccupation with the intimate relationship that he detects between Orientalism and Zionism, a subject on which Abdel-Malek is for the most part silent; in this respect Said is closer to Tibawi. Said differs conspicuously from both, of course, in his approach to Orientalism as a literary phenomenon which can be analyzed with the apparatus of the literary critic. His style is also distinctive, especially when he is discussing the works of Orientalists whom he particularly detests. It is also significant that Abdel-Malek and Tibawi are themselves Orientalists by profession and, as such, have spent their careers reading and digesting Orientalism. Accordingly, their familiarity with the subject lends their criticism an authority which Said's lacks, so that it is unclear, when he accuses Orientalism of dogmatism, for example, whether he has merely failed to read as widely in Orientalist scholarship as he should or whether he has simply chosen to ignore the vast body of literature which he cannot conveniently cut to his pattern.

For my purposes it is not so instructive to dwell on differences among the three as it is, as an Orientalist, to come to grips with the similarities which unite them. The first of these is the deep bitterness and resentfulness with which all three regard Western studies of the Arab-Islamic world. Tibawi is bitter at the religious and political hostility which he detects in Western scholarship; Abdel-Malek is bitter at the capitalist exploitation of Orientals with the advice and consent of the scholarly establishment. Said is most bitter of all at the racism that he finds in Orientalism toward the character, achievements, and aspirations of a people with whom he has chosen to identify himself. In each case the bitterness is visibly present, on the surface, and has undoubtedly contributed to the sense of alienation which each writer feels. Connected with this feeling of bitterness is the belief shared by all three that Orientalism is virtually useless, the conviction that Orientalism as it is being practiced at present is prevented by its very nature from yielding results which are valid for Orientals or anyone else. While each critic does concede that Orientalists have made contributions to knowledge of Arabs and Islam, these contributions are seen to be few in number and limited in scope. Tibawi singles out only a handful of scholars who over the past two centuries have succeeded in writing about Islam and the Arabs objectively. Among these he numbers E. W. Lane, von Grunebaum, Watt, and Schacht, but his approval even of these is qualified, except for the latter. Said's list is also short, though less discriminating than Tibawi's, including as it does such disparate writers as Gibb, Berque, and Bravmann on the one hand, and Fred Halliday on the other. Abdel-Malek also finds a few individual scholars to commend; otherwise he is content to list the general fields to which Orientalists have made a positive contribution: the study of ancient civilization; the cataloguing, editing, and publishing of texts; the convening of Orientalist congresses; the teaching of methodology; and the awakening of national consciousness.[30] In other words. Orientalism has achieved very little of a substantive nature except for the study of ancient civilization and is to be otherwise commended only for its preservation of the texts of the Arab-Islamic heritage, a labor which, it is true, was instrumental in sparking nationalist movements in the Islamic world and is therefore praiseworthy even though this result was accidental. The implication is that the creative task of interpreting the present, as opposed to the mechanical work of preserving the past, has been beyond the reach of those who are observers of, rather than participants in, the realities of the present, an echo of Tibawi's insistence that non-Muslims cannot really understand Islam.

In the face of this bitter rejection of the labors and achievements of Orientalism, it is tempting to search for an explanation beyond the arguments that its critics have employed, all the more so since such explanations lie close at hand. The closest is, of course, political. All three critics are advocates of a cause, and, rightly or wrongly, they have cast Orientalists in the role of adversaries. For Said and Tibawi this cause is Palestine, and the passion of their commitment underlies their attack against scholars in the West, who, they believe, have contributed to, or acquiesced in, the betrayal of the Palestinian homeland. In this regard the main distinction between the two is Tibawi's Islam, which, as we have seen, he confuses with his Arabness, so that his critique has a dimension that is absent in Said. Abdel-Malek, on the other hand, who is also a supporter of the liberation of Palestine, has wider loyalties, and since the political cause to which he is committed comes equipped with a carefully structured system of thought, his critique is more reasoned and dispassionate. Nevertheless, to recognize the political inspiration of these attacks against Orientalism does not justify dismissing the criticisms they contain, and these will have to be judged on their own merits. Beyond the immediate political contexts which inform and to a certain extent explain the thrust of these critiques there is also the historical fact of a strong tradition in modern Arab and Islamic thought of rejecting European civilization. This attitude toward cultural borrowing is by no means peculiar to Arabs and Muslims, of course, and is a characteristic response of people who feel threatened by a stronger civilization. In the Muslim world this tradition is associated with conservative intellectuals of the late nineteenth century who were intent on counteracting the threat of European political domination by repudiating Western materialism and the Western science which makes materialism possible; even in reformists like al-Afghānī and 'Abduh who were willing to borrow very selectively from the West there is a strain of ambivalence to be found. In order to achieve Islamic autonomy and self-sufficiency, they advocated a turning inward and back, a return to the first principles of Islam and the reconstruction of a militant faith which would protect Muslims from European attempts to exploit them by undermining their unity and subverting their religion.[31] This attitude toward the West, though it has undergone many permutations during the past century, has by no means vanished and, indeed, is evident in the stance of aggressive defensiveness adopted by Tibawi toward Western scholarship. More typical at this time is the feeling of disillusionment expressed by the Arab poet Adonis, who speaks for a generation of Arabs who turned to the West for inspiration and guidance and found it wanting:

> We no longer believe in Europe. We no longer have faith in the political system or in its philosophies. Worms have eaten into its social structure as they have ... its very soul. Europe for us – we backward, ignorant, impoverished people – is a corpse.[32]

Seen from this perspective, the critics of Orientalism might simply be grouped with all those other Arabs who, resenting either the political and cultural arrogance of the West and its interference in their affairs or the failure of the West to provide solutions to their problems, have turned elsewhere, seeking fulfillment or revival in other traditions.

As another way to counter the arguments of these critics, it might be pointed out that the number of Arab intellectuals who have raised their voices against Orientalism are outnumbered by those who have not only joined its ranks but actually lead it. I am thinking of such prominent Arab scholars as Philip Hitti, Albert Hourani, Muhsin Mehdi, Hisham Sharabi, Aziz Atiyeh, George Makdisi, and G. C. Anawati, to mention only some of the most famous Arab scholars who have embraced Western methodology and a Western approach to the Arabs and Islam which is virtually indistinguishable from that of non-Arabs. In this respect it is worth mentioning that Albert Hourani has published his own critique of Orientalism, 'Islam and the Philosophers of History.'[33] Hourani, though certainly aware of the shortcomings of the study of Islam as it has evolved in Europe, is far more ready to acknowledge the positive aspects of that tradition at any given stage of its development, including the present one. But the mere fact that some Arabs have embraced Orientalism, have joined rather than succumbed to the forces of cultural imperialism as our critics would put it, is not very instructive unless we compare the reasons why these individuals accepted Orientalism with the reasons which lay behind its rejection by others. All this is beyond the scope of this paper.

Instead we shall return to the question raised at the beginning, namely, what can be learned about Orientalism from these three critiques? Let us look at the validity of the charges laid against Orientalism, which, I think, can be narrowed to three: one, that Orientalism as practiced in the West is a tool of imperialism; two, that Orientalists are hostile to Islam and Arab nationalism; three, that Orientalists, being ethnocentric, treat Orientals as passive, unchanging objects. From these three interrelated premises the conclusion follows that Orientalism is worthless.

In refutation of the first charge, the Italian Orientalist Francesco Gabrieli argues that while it can be conceded that the study of eastern civilizations by Western scholars was at times connected with Western political and economic campaigns against the East, *Description de l'Égypte* being the most conspicuous example, 'it is mistaken and untrue that the exclusive or main motive for the historical and linguistic, the literary and religious interest of Europe in the East was in function of its plans for political and economic penetration of the area.'[34] No, Gabrieli insists, although there are examples of Orientalists who were also ambassadors, missionaries, soldiers, or merchants, they are outnumbered by European scholars whose interest in the East was sparked by 'pure scientific passion' and 'a disinterested and impassioned search for the truth.'[35] Furthermore, since the interest of most Orientalists was limited to the distant past, a point conceded by the critics, their scholarship could hardly have contributed to imperialistic policies. These protestations, justified as they may well be from the point of view of Orientalists who regard themselves as scientists, are not likely to convince Abdel-Malek that Louis Massignon, for example, was any less racist simply because, as Gabrieli points out, he 'was beaten by fascists and police for keeping faith in the word given to the Arab world'.[36] For Abdel-Malek the point to remember about Massignon is not his generosity of spirit but his pernicious belief that the Arabs are Semites who are intellectually and technologically inferior to Israeli Jews. Besides, to claim, as Gabrieli does, that imperialism is 'dead and buried' and thereby to imply that Orientalism in the service of the state is also dead is a naïve claim at best. If this were indeed the case it would be difficult to explain why European Orientalists continue to publish such works as *Gli studi sul Vicino Oriente in Italia dal 1921 al 1970.*[37] But much clearer testimony to the continuing interest of governments in Middle Eastern scholarship comes from the United States, where massive support has been given by the federal government through the National Defense Education Act, which, since the late fifties, has helped to set up and support a dozen or more Near/Middle Eastern centers and to subsidize the training of scores of Middle Eastern scholars. The financial support of private foundations, Ford and Rockefeller in particular, has also been impressive. Having funded the centers and subsidized the students, the U.S. government has been equally generous in supporting research in which it has an interest.[38] Nevertheless, it cannot be reasonably argued, much less proved, that every, or even any, scholar who has accepted government funds has sold himself to U.S. government policy in the Middle East; in fact, it might well be argued that some have used that support to try to change that policy. Speaking for myself, I fail to see how my own research on Mamlūk historiography, financed by the U.S. government in some form or another for a period of six years, can possibly lend aid and comfort to the forces of imperialism, and I would hazard the guess that few of the dissertations produced by a generation of National Defense Scholars have any but the most peripheral connection to U.S. political and economic policies, which, it should be added, have shown little change, much less improvement, since the NDEA program began. Furthermore, while it is true that the United States has made vast sums available to encourage the study of the Middle East for the national interest and that students and scholars have been quick to accept these funds, the program has been administered in a spirit of benign neglect, and very little control has been exerted over the way that scholars have used public money to further their own academic interests. Orientalist scholarship in the United States is remarkably heterogeneous, and it is inconceivable that the highly individualistic scholars engaged in Oriental studies could be mobilized to serve national goals, even assuming that well defined goals exist.

Are Orientalists hostile to Islam and Arabs? Unquestionably, many students of Islam have been less than sympathetic toward their subject, in part, no doubt, because of the difficulty that Westerners encounter in understanding Islam, whether it be as a theological system, mystical experience, or a comprehensive set of laws. No wonder, then, that they often resort to rethinking it, reformulating it in terms that they *do* understand in a misguided attempt to initiate communication on a common basis. Charles J. Adams speaks of 'the negative tone,' 'the tone of personal disenchantment that runs through the majority of writing about Muslim faith,' the lack of 'attraction of Islamic civilization for the Western mind that Indian and Chinese civilizations are able to exercise,' and, worst of all, 'the frequent note of condescension that creeps into western expositions of Muslim religiousness.'[39] All of these observations are equally true, I am afraid, of much Western writing on the Arabs, and Tibawi is probably correct in his judgment that much of the hostility toward the Arabs is of political inspiration and derives from Western sympathy for Zionism; more recently this hostility has been fed by Western resentment of the militant new role that Arabs have begun to play in our economic and political destiny. Still, admitting that some, even a great deal, of Orientalist scholarship is negative in tone, we need not conclude that all of it is; indeed, judging from the perspective of a medievalist, I would judge that most of it is decidedly neutral.[40] And though it is true that the energy crisis has incurred Western resentment of the Arabs, it has also increased the interest of the West in Islamic and Arab civilization. That scholars have not failed to respond to this interest is indicated by the recent glut of scholars' coffee table books recently on the market, most of which were intended, and are accepted, as celebrations of the glories of Islamic and Arab civilization for the edification of the general reading public.[41] The fact that several of these books have been categorically denounced by Said indicates that he is not to be satisfied by eulogies which stop short of political commitment. Moreover, whether it is possible or even desirable in the plural world of scholarship to reindoctrinate scholars who are unsympathetic to certain aspects of Arab and Islamic civilization and persuade them to adopt a more positive line is a dubious question at best. It is at any rate a healthy sign that voices like Tibawi's, Abdel-Malek's and, Said's are heard, raising questions which may eventually result in the development of a more measured tone in Orientalism where such is needed.

A third major criticism is leveled against the distinction which Orientalism allegedly draws between Western observers and Eastern objects of study, reducing Muslims and Arabs to the level of unchanging, uniform things to be described, analyzed, and judged according to European standards and modes of thought. At this level Said in particular objects to scholars who ascribe a national character to the Arabs and lump the great diversity of people who constitute the Arabs into one undifferentiated mass, all thinking and acting in the same way because they are Arabs. To works on Arab character Said objects not only in principle but also in terms of the specific traits which are attributed to the Arabs: irrationality, disunity, excitability, love of rhetoric, etc. Much of what he says about specific works of this genre is undoubtedly true. Scholars such as Patai, Hamady, Berger, Carmichael,[42] and others do tend to generalize and to make observations about the Arabs which are unflattering to the image which Arabs have of themselves. Nevertheless, national-character historiography cannot be totally dismissed merely because some historians have abused it or produced conclusions which are unacceptable to the people described.[43] In this respect it might be enlightening if Said would address himself to recent studies which are concerned with aspects of Arab society limited in time and place and which are based, to some extent at least, on the interaction between the observer and the observed, works such as those by Robert and Elizabeth Fernea, Kenneth Brown, Dale Eickelman, Michael Gilsenan, and John Waterbury,[44] to mention only a few recent works among the many of this genre which Orientalists have produced.

Finally, what of the judgment that most, if not all, Orientalist scholarship is worthless? I shall not attempt to list any of what I regard as the monuments of Orientalism erected by scholars in the past nor the services that these scholars have performed for Arabs and Muslims and the world of scholarship at large because I realize that their critics reject the assumptions and methodology of these works and decry the motives of the men who wrote them. Instead I would point to a basic characteristic of Orientalism and of all Western scholarship, which, however obvious it may be, seems to have been overlooked by the three critics in question. I am referring to the implicit assumption that all knowledge, all learning, is tentative and that what scholars believe to be true is constantly evolving and growing and is subject to change in the light of new knowledge and new theories of knowledge, and as the result of new political, economic, and social conditions. I would suggest that this assumption underlies the work of most, if not all, scholarship on the Muslim world, whether it is stated or not. Recently it has been made explicit by Orientalists themselves in two publications. The first is a book entitled *The Study of the Middle East: Research and Scholarship in the Humanities and Social Sciences*, produced by the Middle East Studies Association, one of the professional societies for Orientalists based in the United States, but having an international membership.[45] Starting from the position that 'Middle Eastern Studies are beset by subjective projections, displacements of affect, ideological distortion, romantic mystification, and religious bias, as well as by a great deal of incompetent scholarship,'[46] this volume aims to survey the present state of the various disciplines which comprise Middle Eastern Studies – history, literature, religion, art, philosophy, and the social sciences – an aim which assumes that Orientalism has had a history, that its present state has been influenced by attitudes of the past, and that its future can be guided and directed by its present practitioners. Thus, each contributor surveys the various approaches and methodologies used by scholars of each discipline in the past and at present, then surveys and appraises the scholarship so far published, and, finally, maps out priorities for future research. Although I cannot attempt to evaluate the book here nor judge the accuracy of the image of past, present, and future Orientalism that it projects, I do want to stress that all of the contributors show an awareness that the study of the Middle East is an imperfect art, one which suffers from many liabilities but primarily from its isolation from the mainstream of scholarship and the legacy of the allegedly moribund tradition of Orientalism dominated by philological studies.[47] The cures recommended by the experts are various, but one dominates the plan of the book as conceived by its editor, the political scientist Leonard Binder: the notion of Orientalism as a discipline in its own right should be abandoned; henceforth the student of the Middle East must be trained in any one of the disciplines into which scholarship is compartmentalized in the West, be it history, religion, political science, sociology, economics, linguistics, or art and archeology. Whether or not we agree with this diagnosis we cannot but welcome this evidence of self-awareness on the part of Orientalists and of their realization that changes need to be made. While it is true that their perception of the changes that are needed may not coincide with those of Tibawi, Abdel-Malek, or Said, these signs of discontent should give the critics heart. Even more encouraging, I should think, is the launching in England of the *Review of Middle East Studies*, which aims to compensate for Orientalism's 'politically-motivated bias . . . and its profound methodological limitations' by encouraging 'the production of theoretically relevant work informed by a critical appreciation of the Middle East and its history.'[48] The first two issues of this journal are devoted to articles that criticize the assumptions and methodology of Orientalism and suggest what its authors consider to be more fruitful, less conservative, lines of analysis. It should not be a cause of surprise or alarm that one of the editors of the *Review*, an Arab anthropologist, despairs at Binder's 'retreat to the authority of persons and institutions where sustained intellectual argument is called for'[49] or that a *MESA Bulletin* reviewer decries the 'scarcely concealed (albeit different) political biases' which underlie the contributions to the *Review of Middle East Studies*.[50] This disagreement and the ferment it engenders only underscore the fact that Orientalism is not as static as its critics claim and that it is, indeed, currently undergoing a stage of self-analysis and reorientation. Whether the changes will be of the kind or extent to satisfy Arab critics of Orientalism cannot be answered at this point, but change Orientalism most certainly will.

NOTES

1. H. A. R. Gibb, 'Social Change in the Near East,' *The Near East: Problems and Prospects*, ed. Philip W. Ireland (Chicago: University of Chicago Press, 1942), p. 60, wrote some thirty-five years ago as follows: 'But I have not yet seen a single book written by an Arab of any branch in any Western language that has made it possible for the Western student to understand the roots of Arab culture. More than that, I have not seen any book written in Arabic for Arabs themselves which has clearly analyzed what Arabic culture means for Arabs.' Quoting this judgment sixteen years later, G. E. von Grunebaum, in 'Attempts at Self-Interpretation in Contemporary Islam,' *Islam: Essays in the Nature and Growth of a Cultural Tradition*, 2nd ed. (London: Routledge & Kegan Paul, 1961), p. 185, observed: 'This statement could be extended to include the non-Arab Muslim and his failure to interpret his culture to both himself and the West. It holds good today as it did when it was written, and it is likely to hold good for some time to come.' Today that rule could be proved with some exceptions.

2. See Anouar Abdel-Malek, 'Orientalism in Crisis.' *Diogenes*, XLIV (1959), 130, and, for later references, William G. Millward, 'The Social Psychology of anti-Iranology,' *Iranian Studies*, VIII (1975), 48–69. It is interesting, as Millward observes, p. 52, that recent critiques of Orientalism written in Arabic have been 'for the most part restrained and temperate,' especially when compared with counterparts in Persian.

3. Consider, for example, the following statement from a preface to a collection of papers delivered at the 1974 convention of the Association of Arab-American University Graduates: 'The problem of bias against Arabs is not limited to the news media. The "discourse of Orientalism" is probably a standard source of information about the Arabs and Islam for American students at all levels. Edward Said exposes some of Orientalism's "facts" about Arabs and Islam for what they really are: myths garbed in the protective cover of what appears to be "scientific" analysis. Other scholars at the convention underlined structural factors associated with the perpetuation of serious deficiencies in the Orientalist perspective and in regional studies programs whose focus includes the Middle East, the Arabs, and Islam. With disappointment, these scholars pointed to the entrenchment of Orientalism in American educational and political institutions'; Baha Abu-Laban and Faith T. Zeadey, *Arabs in America: Myths and Realities* (Wilmette, Illinois: The Medina University Press International, 1975), p. xi.

4. *The Crisis of the Arab Intellectual: Traditionalism or Historicism?* Tr. by D. Cammell (Berkeley: University of California Press, 1976), p. 44.

5. Born in Palestine in 1910, Tibawi holds academic degrees from the University of London; he has held administrative and academic posts in Palestine, England, and America and, most recently, lectured on Islamic education at the University of London Institute of Education. His publications include three works on foreign (British, American, and Russian) influence in Syria and Palestine as well as a general history of modern Syria; also several studies of Arab and Islamic education, besides books and articles on aspects of Arab and Islamic history.

6. *The Muslim World*, LIII (1963), 185–204, 298–313; reprinted, with only a few stylistic changes, in *Islamic Quarterly*, VIII (1964), 25–45, 73–88.

7. *MW*, LIII (1963), 192; *IQ*, VIII (1964), 32.

8. *Ibid.*

9. *MW*, LIII (1963), 202; *IQ*, VIII (1964), 42.

10. *Ibid.*

11. Charles J. Adams, 'Islamic Religious Tradition,' *The Study of the Middle East*, ed. Leonard Binder (New York: John Wiley and Sons, 1976), pp. 38–41.

12. *MW*, LIII (1963), 195; *IQ*, VIII (1964), 35.

13. *MW*, LIII (1963), 301; *IQ*, VIII (1964), 76.

14. *MW*, LIII (1963), 307; *IQ*, VIII (1964), 82.

15. Abdel-Malek was born in Cairo in 1924, educated in Egypt at the French Jesuit College and 'Ain Shams University; in France he earned a doctorate at the Sorbonne and, since 1960, has held teaching and research positions in Paris. His chief publications focus on the history of modern Egypt, contemporary Arabic literature, and contemporary Arab political thought.

16. *Diogenes*, XLIV (1959), 103–40; this is an English translation of the French original. It should be noted that Abdel-Malek's discussion of Orientalism includes Far Eastern as well as Near Eastern studies, though I have focussed on the latter for the purposes of this article.

17. *Ibid.*, 107.

18. *Ibid.*, 111–12.

19. *Ibid.*, 119.

20. *Ibid.*, 122.

21. *Ibid.*, 127.

22. Born in Jerusalem in 1935, Said was educated in Egypt, then in the U.S. at Princeton and Harvard. He has published books on Conrad and Swift as well as more general works on literary criticism, and also writes on the Palestine problem. [His *Orientalism* (New York: Pantheon Books, 1978) appeared after this manuscript was accepted for publication and is, therefore, not taken into account in the present article. Ed. Note]

23. 'Arabs, Islam and the Dogmas of the West,' *The New York Times Book Review*, October 31, 1976, p. 4.

24. *Middle East Crucible: Studies on the Arab-Israeli War of October 1973*, ed. Naseer H. Aruri (Wilmette, Illinois: The Medina University Press International, 1975), pp. 408–47; an abridged version appeared in *Arabs in America*, pp. 83–112, with the title, 'Orientalism and the October War: The Shattered Myths.'

25. *Middle East Crucible*, p. 420.

26. *Ibid.*, p. 422.

27. *Ibid.*, p. 423.

28. *Ibid.*, p. 433.

29. *Ibid.*, p. 436.

30. This list Abdel-Malek credits to Youssef Assaad Dagher, a Lebanse bibliographer, *Diogenes*, XLIV (1959), 106.

31. For a discussion of the different varieties of Arab intelligentsia, see Hisham Sharabi, *Arab Intellectuals and the West: The Formative Years, 1875–1914* (Baltimore and London: The Johns Hopkins Press, 1970); pp. 24–40, for the conservatives and reformers.

32. Quoted *Ibid.*, p. 136.

33. *Middle Eastern Studies*, III (1967), 206–68.

34. 'Apology for Orientalism,' *Diogenes*, L (1965), 131.

35. *Ibid.*, 132.

36. *Ibid.*, 132.

37. (Rome: Istituto per l'Oriente, 1971).

38. For an exposé of the role of government and foundations in American Orientalism, see Peter Johnson and Judith Tucker, 'Middle East Studies Network in the United States,' *Middle East Research and Information Project Reports*, XXXVIII (1975), 3–20.

39. 'Islamic Religious Tradition,' *Study of the Middle East*, pp. 3–4.

40. Jacques Waardenburg, 'Changes of Perspective in Islamic Studies over the Last Decades,' *Humaniora Islamica*, I (1973), 249–52, sees five ways that Islam has been viewed and studied by scholars, only one of which is decidedly negative. For a fuller exposition of Waardenburg's ideas on Orientalism see his *L'islam dans le miroir de l'occident* (Paris and The Hague: Mouton and Co., 1962).

41. E.g., Philip Bamborough, *Treasures of Islam* (Poole, Dorset: Blandford Press, 1976); Wilfrid Blunt, *Splendours of Islam* (London: Angus and Robertson,

1976); John R. Hayes, *The Genius of Arab Civilization* (New York: New York University Press, 1976); Bernard Lewis, *Islam and the Arab World: Faith, People, Culture* (New York: Knopf/American Heritage, 1976); Husayn Nasr, *Islamic Science: An Illustrated Study* (London: World of Islam Festival, 1976); Michael Rogers, *The Spread of Islam* (Oxford: Elsevier–Phaidon, 1976).

42. Raphael Patai, *The Arab Mind* (New York: Scribners, 1973); Sania Hamady, *Temperament and Character of the Arabs* (New York: Twayne, 1960); Morroe Berger, *The Arab World Today* (Garden City, N.Y.: Doubleday, 1962); Joel Carmichael, *The Shaping of the Arabs: A study in Ethnic Identity* (London: Allen and Unwin, 1969).

43. This problem is discussed in *Psychological Dimensions of Near Eastern Studies*, ed. Norman Itzkowitz and L. Carl Brown (Princeton: The Darwin Press, 1977), in which Hisham Sharabi and Mukhtar Ani, in 'Impact of Class and Culture on Social Behavior: The Feudal Bourgeois Family in Arab Society,' p. 240, point specifically to the resistance which Arab authors can expect from an Arab readership when they publish works critical of Arab society.

44. Robert A. Fernea, *Shaykh and Effendi: Changing Patterns of Authority among the El Shabana of Southern Iraq* (Cambridge: Harvard University Press, 1970); Elizabeth W. Fernea, *A Street in Marrakech* (Garden City, N.Y.: Doubleday, 1976); Kenneth L. Brown, *People of Salé: Tradition and Change in a Moroccan City, 1830–1930* (Cambridge: Harvard University Press, 1976); Dale F. Eickelman, *Moroccan Islam: Tradition and Society in a Pilgrimage Center* (Austin and London: University of Texas Press, 1976); Michael Gilsenan, *Saint and Sufi in Modern Egypt: An Essay in the Sociology of Religion* (Oxford: Clarendon Press, 1973); John Waterbury, *The Commander of the Faithful: A Study in Segmented Politics* (New York: Columbia University Press, 1970), and *North for the Trade: The Life and Times of a Berber Merchant* (Berkeley and Los Angeles: University of California Press, 1972).

45. Ed. Leonard Binder (see note 11). Besides sponsoring this book, the Middle East Studies Association, or certain elements of it, have been active in regenerating, or abandoning, traditional Orientalism in other ways. For example, the plenary session of the 1974 MESA annual meeting was devoted to a discussion of 'Whither Orientalism? The Future of Middle East Studies.' For a wry report on this discussion see Issa J. Boullata's 'Notes of the Quarter,' *MW*, LXV (1975), 69, in which it is observed that 'the commentators seemed all to agree on the death of Orientalism, apparent or real, but each emphasized in his or her own way the necessity for greater attention in the future to humanism in the approach and in the depth of interest when studying Middle East society and culture.' Also, Leonard Binder's address to the 1974 MESA annual meeting was directed to what he termed 'an area of embarrassment,' viz., 'the continued domination of our field by Orientalism and by area studies and to the misguided attacks still frequently made upon systematic disciplinary studies in the humanities and the social sciences'; '1974 Presidential Address.' *MESA Bulletin*, IX, 1, (Feb., 1975), 1.

46. Binder, 'Area Studies: A Critical Reassessment,' *The Study of the Middle East*, p. 16.

47. This view of philological Orientalism is not restricted to North America. See, for example, Maxime Rodinson, 'The Western Image and Western Studies of Islam,' *The Legacy of Islam*, 2nd ed., edited by Joseph Schacht and C. E. Bosworth (Oxford: The Clarendon Press, 1974), p. 62: 'Taking an extreme view, some have spoken of the end of Orientalism. The question must, however, be examined very delicately. What is at stake is the dominance of philology. There are signs of the abandonment of the view held implicitly for over a century that a philological training is adequate to the solving of all the problems arising within a linguistically defined field. This idea, which cannot be maintained on rational grounds, sprang from the pressing necessity of a philological training for the serious study of the problems raised within that field. That vast increase in available material, together

with the tools of research and the progress of methods of study, now enables one, if not to by-pass the philological stage, at least to devote less time to it.' Cf. C. A. O. van Nieuwenhuijze, 'The Trend in Middle East Studies as illustrated by the Dutch Case' (unpublished paper, December, 1976), p. 13: 'There is reason to wonder, from a methodological point of view, whether a typically historical-philological islamology remains an acceptable proposition.' It is also worthy of note that after considerable controversy it was decided in 1974 to transform the 30th International Congress of Orientalists (held in 1976) into the 30th International Congress of Human Sciences in Asia and North Africa. Subsequent meetings of that body will presumably share the same fate.

48. Talal Asad and Roger Owen, 'Introduction,' *Review of Middle East Studies*, I (1975).

49. Talal Asad, Review of *The Study of the Middle East*, in *MESA Bulletin*, XI, 3 (Oct., 1977), 37.

50. Michael A. Marcus, Review of Volume 1, *Review of Middle East Studies*, in *MESA Bulletin*, XI, 1 (Feb., 1977), 53.

PART IX
FURTHER CRITIQUES

In the decade or so following the publication of 'English-Speaking Orientalists', A. L. Tibawi looked further into the work of a number of English-speaking orientalists. As 'A Second Critique of English-Speaking Orientalists' shows, he was not impressed with what he found. Nor was he impressed by the arguments put forward by Donald P. Little in 'Three Arab Critiques of Orientalism'.

19

A SECOND CRITIQUE OF ENGLISH-SPEAKING ORIENTALISTS

A. L. Tibawi

In his 'Second Critique of English-Speaking Orientalists', Tibawi concentrates his attention on the works of a number of English orientalists and 'pseudo-orientalists' who, in his view, continue to fight against Islam and Arabic nationalism. As a result of their 'colossal failures' those who graduate at their hands – heavily indoctrinated – often find it necessary to adopt a fresh point of view when they come into actual contact with Arabs and Muslims in the course of their business.

II

It will be the task in this second monograph to re-examine the problems raised in the first one, to review progress or regress during the past sixteen years and to go into more detailed review of the publications by Orientalists and pseudo-Orientalists. As in the previous contribution here again most of the attention will be directed to the works of living authors, for the practical reason that the living and not the dead are capable of reflecting on the impact of their published opinions on the Arab or Muslim mind. But it is not intended to be inclusive: only writers with pronounced opinions indicative of bias will be covered. They all have merits, but these are not the subject of this critique. The coverage is naturally in direct proportion to the volume of offending matter in the works of individual writers.

A. L. Tibawi, 'Second Critique of English-Speaking Orientalists and Their Approach to Islam and the Arabs', *Islamic Quarterly*, 23, 1, 1979, sections II–V.

Any careful scrutiny of recent works by English Orientalists and pseudo-Orientalists is bound to reveal that they still fight, with varying degrees of subtlety or crudeness, against Islam and Arab nationalism on two fronts. On the first the fight is now kept alive with greatly reduced forces in comparison with the legions marshalled by previous generations. This is a remarkable retreat, but I do not accept the suggestion that the relaxation of the 'academic' and missionary onslaughts was the direct result of the recession of colonialism, even though it accompanied and followed, and was not entirely unrelated to, the eclipse of the power of the West in Arab and Muslim countries.

On the second front, the war is waged with increased fury reminiscent of that with which the early attacks on Islam and Muḥammad were maintained for centuries. To a great extent the motives and methods are still the same: animosity and prejudice using distortion and misrepresentation. One difference is the employment of the deceptive apparatus of footnotes. This will be discussed in detail later, but first let us deal with some of those who are still fighting on the first front.

The few chosen for the consideration of their views on the subject to the exclusion of any other include two clergymen, one Jew who is an ardent Zionist and two lay Christians. Like many of their predecessors, they are responsible for pronouncements concerning the Judaeo-Christian 'origins' of Islam and the related question of Muḥammad's sincerity. But unlike their predecessors who presented their opinions with some array of scholarship, they offer their judgment of these weighty questions summarily in the form of assertions as if they were established facts. None of them is judicious enough to introduce his bold statements with at least a reference to the Islamic point of view. Because these men are also teachers in Arabic and Islamic studies the danger of propagating their prejudices is great, misleading non-Muslim, and challenging the beliefs of Muslim students.

The first clergyman is professor of Arabic at Edinburgh University. Some of his pronouncements and assertions are objectionable to Muslims. For example when he says that Muḥammad 'was aware of the Jewish teaching', that he 'was trying to make his religion more Jewish' and that the Qur'ān shows dependence on 'Biblical tradition'.[1] It is difficult to believe that the writer is not aware that all these assertions are contrary to the letter of the Qur'ān, and that they ill accord with his own recognition of Muḥammad's sincerity as a prophet of God. Surely an author so steeped in the study of Islam must know that his judgment is offensive to orthodox Islam and does not satisfy the canons of weighing historical evidence.

The second clergyman, a reader in religious (not necessarily Islamic) studies in Sussex University, is frankly a missionary whose object is to convert Muslims to Christianity or at least to make them accept Jesus not simply as one of God's prophets but as Christ, the son of God. This attempt is the more remarkable because there is no Christian reciprocal recognition of Muḥammad. The aim of this modern missionary is plainly 'to arouse and inform a Muslim discovery of

Christ'. He hopes to succeed where generations of missionaries before him failed in taking Islam to the end of the road, since in his estimation 'it halted at a half-way house'.[2] He does not explain, however, how this Herculean task is to be accomplished. Nor does he estimate the chances of success among people he obviously antagonizes.

It is not so easy to sum up the Jewish writer if only because he is more audacious and extreme. He taught Arab and Islamic history at London and now teaches these subjects at Princeton to, among others, Arab and Muslim students. And yet he chose to join the ranks of those who denigrate Islam and Arab nationalism. On his attitude to Arab nationalism and his defence of Israel details will be given later. In this place only his view of Islam is considered. In a work that seems to be teaching notes, and hence an instrument of indoctrination, the writer asserts categorically that 'it is clear (to whom and on what evidence?) that he (Muḥammad) was subject to Jewish and Christian influences. The very ideas of monotheism and revelation and many biblical elements in the Qur'ān attest this ... His version of Bible stories suggest that his biblical knowledge was indirectly acquired, probably (sic) from Jewish and Christian traders and travellers whose information was affected by midrashic and apocryphal influences'[3]. In short the Qur'ān is not a divine revelation and Muḥammad is a false prophet! Exactly as the medieval polemicists proclaimed.

Less endowed with arrogant assurance but not less ready with summary judgment is the fourth participant in the old game of denigrating Islam. He worked under the former and participated with him in editing a collection of ill-assorted articles on Arab and Islamic history. In the introduction they asserted in one place that Islam, like Christianity, was an 'offspring' of Judaism, and in another they took 'the Judaeo-Christian inheritance of Islam' as an established fact.[4] (Need it be repeated that there is an admitted organic relationship between Christianity and Judaism, but that such relationship with either and Islam is categorically denied? Need it be added that such an assertion is in the circumstances nothing but a provocative and unnecessary challenge?) The two joined also in editing a history of Islam, again a collection of more ill-assorted articles. This time the introduction was written by the junior partner, but approved by the senior. In it the writer insists on Islam's 'kinship' with Judaism and Christianity, and described, rather irrelevantly, the two as 'more developed' than Islam.[5] As professor of Arab history at the time, the writer neglected to 'develop' and support this sweeping statement with other than subjective prejudice. It is with such unconscious asides that writers discredit themselves as impartial historians.

The case of the fifth writer singled out for consideration is more outrageous because his offensive opinion was published in the journal of the Islamic Cultural Centre in London! Since its inception this journal was edited by successive learned directors of the Centre who each combined training at al-Azhar with at least one doctorate from a Western university. But it was unfortunate that in the early 1970s a Pakistani businessman with no academic qualifications became director. The circumstances of his reliance for unofficial editing of the journal on a Christian lecturer in Manchester University are mysteriously obscure. This same lecturer had to my knowledge at least one of his articles rejected by a former editor. And yet once he became 'unofficial editor' himself, he filled the journal with his own articles and reviews and with contributions by friends and teachers. A book review by one of these stated that Muslims (and Christians) 'shared a common background of ethical monotheism derived from the Judaic religious tradition'.[6] The reckless writer and his presumptuous pupil[7] might have refrained from abusing, after exploiting, Islamic hospitality and trust to this extent.

The views of the five writers cited above were introduced with the remark that unlike their learned predecessors they dispensed with discussion in making far-reaching assertions. In two recent works by hitherto unknown authors the process is varied in that daring assumptions are put forward and 'evidence' is sought to support them. The two books, published simultaneously, may be regarded as proceeding from one source: an American recruited as lecturer in the history department of the School of Oriental and African Studies but for obscure reasons was moved to that of Arabic. He wrote one of the two books, and two of his pupils (a female art specialist and a lecturer in economic history) wrote the other.[8]

They profess to have done so 'with inordinate regard for infidel sources', and influenced by 'exposure to the sceptical approach' of their tutor. The essence of the rambling and ill-digested topics is the hoary controversy regarding the Judaeo-Christian 'origins' of Islam, with much greater emphasis on the former. Even allowing for inexperience it is difficult not to notice the rash and jumpy assurance of the pupils, and the inept and pedantic linguistic display of the tutor. There is no originality in either work except extremism. The teacher and pupils managed to resurrect the old prejudices and to parade them under modern academic auspices. (Who were 'the Arabist and Islamist' advisers to the two university presses that produced the two books?) While deploring an undercurrent of fanaticism in these two works the present writer finds them far less impressive as partisan theses than the earlier attempts by much more scholarly hands. They are indeed a comic reminder of the remark supposed to have been made by an oriental visitor to an occidental institution: he found Jews teaching the Qur'ān to Christians.

Since writing the above paragraph widespread resentment among the Muslims in Britain has been caused by the appointment of the female co-author of the second book as lecturer in Islamic history at Oxford, combined with a fellowship at Jesus College. Because any censorship or control of teaching is out of the question, surely the lecturer is entitled by virtue of her appointment to propagate her thesis among undergraduates and others. Reliable reports name a Christian Arab born in England as 'the moving spirit' behind this appointment. If so, there is a serious question for 'the Arab' and for the other dons concerned: Do you intend to revive the offensive controversy at Oxford?

But what Arabic is studied or taught by specialists in Arabic? It has long been an academic scandal that the professor of Arabic teaches no Arabic and neglects to write on Arabic subjects, is moreover never seen to write or heard to speak Arabic, and yet engages in theological and political controversy touching on the Arabs and Islam. There are few who stick to their speciality and fewer who accept the Islamic traditions generally as the Muslims see it. None of these exceptions is less, indeed some are more, distinguished than their bigoted predecessors and contemporaries in satisfying academic independence and personal integrity.

At the two old English universities and at the oldest of the new universities the chairs of Arabic had chequered histories under men of varied calibres. The present holder of the chair at Oxford, whose retirement was announced while this paper was in draft, is a rare type of the Orientalist who remains within his own limits. Long before he occupied the chair he published an admirable study of Sabaean inscriptions and short pieces on South Arabic. Since occupying the chair he continued on similar lines and as aids to his teaching produced two textbooks on modern Arabic.[9] But he was never tempted to stray into the dangerous realm of religion and politics.

The same cannot be said of the relative newcomer to the chair at Cambridge. After rising to occupy the chair of Arabic in the University of London he relinquished it to become lecturer in Islamic history at Cambridge where soon he succeeded to the chair of Arabic after the premature death of the holder. Before attaining professorial rank he published his only work on a strictly Arabic subject, an anthology of colloquial pieces.[10] Before and since he became professor he published opinions on contemporary Arab politics and on Islam. The former will be noted in the right place below. Here his opinion of the Qur'ān and the 'origins' of Islam is more directly relevant. Assuming that the Qur'ān was Muḥammad's composition, he asserted that its early chapters consisted of 'self-justification', and that for this purpose 'he (Muḥammad) resorted to episodes culled from Jewish and Christian literature and legend...'[11] With these categorical statements one of the younger generation of English Orientalists sinks to the level of the medieval depreciation of Islam. A disclaimer in another context that no 'attack' on Islam and Muḥammad was intended is revealing, but without a retraction rather unconvincing.[12]

Less well known than either the Oxford or Cambridge professors of Arabic is the present occupier of the chair of Arabic in the University of London. He was a student of the latter at London and under him wrote a thesis on the dialects of Eastern Arabia for the degree of doctor of philosophy. This was published in a revised form.[13] Except for articles on the same subject in the journal of his school he published nothing else. But according to reports, and unlike his teacher, he studiously avoids in his teaching the thorny questions that bedevilled Arab and Islamic studies for centuries.

Another teacher in the University of London deserves credit not only for avoiding controversial subjects but also for steering a course quite close to

Islamic tradition. The reference is to the professor of Islamic law who succeeded a professed missionary who made no secret of his hatred of Islam.[14] No two men could be so different in their approach and perception. The successor is obviously more detached and betrays no commitment to causes that might prejudice his treatment of the subject of his speciality. His first book is a testimony to his independence.[15] Neither in discussing the origins of Islamic law nor in tracing its historic development is there any sign of the rancour that disfigured the work of his predecessor.

It is noteworthy that, whatever the range of their pursuits, none of the present generation of Orientalists shows the keen interest of their predecessors in the call for the 'reform' of Islam. This call is now sustained by the lone and rather feeble voice of a missionary on the fringe of academic Orientalism. His zeal to convert Muslims to the Christian view of Jesus has been noted above. He is the author of the ridiculous dictum that 'Islam must baptize change in its spirit or renounce its own relevance to life'.[16] Neither alternative is of course his business, but he is obviously ignorant of the extent of the continuous change in Islam through Islamic agencies. That apparently is not the change he advocates.

It is rather strange to observe that all those non-Muslims who advocated in the past or are still now advocating the 'reform' of Islam had in mind its virtual secularization. They seem unconsciously to reduce the present impact of modern European thought on Islam to a one-way process. Islam must come into line with that thought, but there is no question of modern thought adapting itself to Islam. That is an arrogant assumption which has a built-in reason for its failure to materialize. Hence the fainter voices of its advocates.

Yet another important activity in the field of Orientalism is greatly diminished or entirely abandoned. The critical edition and publication of manuscript texts was one of the most useful services earlier generations of Orientalists rendered to Arabic and Islamic scholarship. Their successors apparently do not wish to make the greater effort of continuing it. Nor is their neglect compensated by utilizing the texts already edited. Such efforts as have been made in this direction are on the whole disappointing. The results of the last decade or so lack originality in ideas or depth in methods of treatment. Few if any of the new works advance knowledge or increase understanding of their subjects. Their authors are famous for nothing in particular, except in adapting or adopting well known ideas. Hence their works would not be greatly missed were they to disappear in a general disaster. The Arabic poet must have had them in mind when he said: 'We say only that which is borrowed or words we have uttered before.'

A great many of this new race of academic writers are prolific in an area where little effort is required. Either as individuals or in small groups, they show some enthusiasm in assembling articles by different hands, purported to be studies of one general subject, and then publishing the whole in one or more volumes. The editor or editors write introductions that introduce very little, sum up even less of the heterogeneous contents, synthesize next to nothing and even neglect to correct factual mistakes. I have discussed such an introduction in my review of *The Cambridge History of Islam.*[17]

A worse editor is the one who neglects to edit, and irresponsibly sponsors the publication, with his introduction, of works with blatant factual mistakes. Worst of all is the editor who had failed as a tutor to detect factual mistakes in the thesis of a pupil and compounds his failure by sponsoring the publication of the thesis with the undetected and uncorrected mistakes. A word may be added here about an irresponsible practice at some universities of allowing tutors, without the requisite specialist knowledge, to supervise the work of students preparing for higher degrees. Such students are known to seek assistance from specialists elsewhere, but there is little evidence of their tutors taking the trouble to instruct themselves with a view to giving useful advice and checking the sources cited by students.[18]

In concluding this section I would note that nothing comparably provocative on the Qur'ān, Islam and Muḥammad has been published by European scholars, nor in America and Canada since the writing of the first Critique. Of those that were covered in it two have since died and the other two published nothing new on these subjects. But the views of one of them bear repetition, if only because of the reservation in presenting them which contrasts very sharply with the categorical expression by all the others. In an article on 'The Influence of the Biblical Tradition on Muslim Historiography' the writer repeats the familiar view prevailing among Orientalists that the Qur'ān was Muḥammad's composition and that he derived its historical parts from 'ultimate Judaeo-Christian origin'. By the use of the word 'ultimate' he is more cautious than most. By the warning against 'speculation' and 'preconceived ideas' he shows some mental neutrality. But neither saved him from subscribing to an unproven hypothesis.[19]

III

Perhaps the greatest damage that is still being done is not so much in the summary repetition of medieval theological prejudices but in the continuous adulteration of Islamic history. It has already been remarked that most of those who meddle in this history are not trained historians and possess little auxiliary skills other than some linguistic proficiency. Indeed many are still learning the skills by trial and error. To go into great details would require more space than the scope of a short monograph. A few illustrations must suffice.

Take first one who taught Islamic history all his academic life. In dealing with the past he seldom manages to free himself from his Jewish prejudices, and when he ventures into contemporary political controversy, and he does so quite often, he is nakedly an ardent Zionist. Instead of asking how can such an historian, with such tendencies, establish a valid claim to authority and impartiality it is more to the point to let his treatment of a few sensitive episodes be the test. These are chosen at random and can eaily be multiplied.

In an article, in a collective volume of little coherence and less comprehensiveness or depth, on Egypt and Syria from the end of the Umayyads to the advent of the Turks, replete with bold exaggerations and generalizations that bear little examination, he stresses al-Ma'mūn's visit to Egypt in order to install a governor! But surely the caliph did not fly from Baghdad to Cairo, and his prior visit to Palestine was more important and should not have been omitted altogether. The major repairs he ordered in the Dome of the Rock in Jerusalem should figure more prominently than the confirmation of a provincial governor in Cairo. That this was so to al-Ma'mūm himself is clear from the fact that he had special coins minted with Jerusalem inscribed on them to commemorate the occasion.

Another sensitive subject befogged by the same writer is Saladin. While on the whole the Muslim hero is treated with relative brevity, the writer goes out of his way, even in a brief reference, to belittle him. He asserts that 'the Muslim historians' represented Saladin either as 'a ruthless, ambitious adventurer, bent on personal aggrandizement' or as 'a champion of Islam'. The precedence given to strong adjectives contrasts very sharply with the rather general and vague 'champion of Islam'. Not a word is said about Saladin's fame in the West no less than in the East for humanity, clemency and chivalry. It is very strange that none of 'the Muslim historians' is named, still less quoted by a writer who cites detailed references in the same article for very trivial matters such as the name 'Shajar ad-Durr'. He is probably the only Western writer who, by silence and otherwise, stripped Saladin of his proverbial qualities.[20]

One more example from the same writer. Writing on the Ottoman Empire in the nineteenth century he asserts that poll-tax (*jizyah*) 'was solemnly abolished' by an imperial rescript (*firman*). No source was cited. This is rather odd from one who examined the Ottoman archives in Istanbul while preparing the book in which this bold statement occurs. But this book is notorious for the absence of Turkish archival material and dependence on secondary sources, Turkish and European. Its author was content with the easier task of writing a descriptive article on the contents of a section of the Ottoman archives. Having used a great deal of the same archives in one of my works, I was curious to discover where the said imperial decree could be found. A written application to the author produced no more than reference to secondary printed works. I recorded these facts in more than one place before, but until now the location of the decree, if it exists, is still unknown.[21]

Less qualified to write Islamic history is the professor of Arabic at Cambridge. Unlike his counterpart at Oxford he published nothing on the Arabic language or its literature, classical or modern. His anthology of colloquial south Arabic succeeded only in scandalizing the purists. I recall a conversation in Damascus with Khalīl Mardam Bey, President of the Arabic Academy when he questioned the wisdom and utility of publishing such an anthology and the propriety of sending it for review in the journal of the Academy, devoted to the promotion of the classical and suppression of the colloquial. 'It is funny', he added 'that the author asked us to return the book if we do not review it'.

Reference has been made above to this author's unsubstantiated opinion of the Qur'ān and Muḥammad, simple reproduction of earlier opinions born of prejudice and hatred. He wrote a few articles but not on Arabic. The most substantial of these, in some forty pages, deals with the document drawn up by Muḥammad regulating tribal relations in Medina after the Hijrah and usually called by Orientalists 'the Constitution of Medinah'.[22] Now the professor of Arabic turned historian maintains that this brief document of about two printed pages was really eight 'distinct documents', drafted and redrafted before being issued on different occasions over a period of seven years! This fantastic theory starts with a more fantastic claim that 'words and expressions', in the document were 'not easily understood, even sometimes by the ancient Arab commentators and philologists'.[23]

Obviously he claims to know better, but is too presumptious to say why. He was briefly in south Arabia first as a research student and later in connection with the British colonial administration. His product is a painstaking and heavily documented account, disjoint, digressive and rambling. Despite an array of footnotes, often more pedantic than relevant, the article remains largely speculative and its thesis unconvincing. No useful purpose would be served in pursuing here its many untenable claims and far-fetched interpretations. An indication of these may be seen in the phraseology of a typical paragraph on the sixth page. It is scarcely more than five lines in which the writer, consciously or unconsciously, used 'may' four times. That is some of the outcome when non-historians attempt to write history. The writer of the article states that his theory has been the object of research and teaching since 1955. No disrespect is intended, but on completing a careful study of a virtually unreadable article I could not help recalling the Arabic proverb: 'After prolonged labour the camel gave birth to a mouse!'

There is no need to continue on these lines. It may be more in consonance with the purpose of this monograph to consider some major collective works on Islam by Orientalists. The oldest is of course *The Encyclopaedia of Islam* which carried articles or items by Orientalists of various countries and nationalities, and one single Arab contributor from Algeria admitted with a French ticket. It began publication in instalments in 1913 from the well-known Leiden publishing house, E. J. Brill, under an impressive editorial board. Needless to say that its articles reflected the prevailing views on Islam, Muḥammad, the Qur'ān, Islamic law, Islamic history, the Arabic language and literature, held by contributors and their approving colleagues. Nor is it necessary to say that the articles varied in depth and perception as mostly they do in works of this nature.

But it is important to record that the key articles aroused a great deal of protest and even anger in the world of Islam. A practical reaction was the issue of corrective publications in Egypt and also in secular Turkey. In Egypt *Dā'irat al-Ma'ārif al-Islāmiyyah*, consisting of translations with comments and corrections, was undertaken by enthusiastic young men with the active collaboration of scholars and financial assistance from the Ministry of Education. This movement was surprisingly more successful in Turkey as the pages of the authoritative *Islâm Ansîklopedîsi* clearly demonstrate.

The issue of the second edition of this European encyclopaedia began in 1954 and is still in progress. The project is under the patronage of the International Union of Academies with the same publisher. If the completion of the first edition in four volumes and a supplement took twenty-five years, the present edition looks like requiring double if not triple that number of years to complete. Meanwhile the progress of knowledge continues and several of the already published articles require revision or addition. The inevitable change in the personnel of the editorial board is sometimes reflected in the standard of the articles. Through death and other factors the English element in the editorial board is now stronger than the European. But there is no doubt that the present board is less authoritative than any previous one since 1913. The decline began after the reconstitution of the board that launched the second edition in 1954.

Both editions are of course 'on' Islam but not 'of' it, largely derived from books with little or no account of the Muslims as a human society or human beings. The first was practically without Muslim contributors, while in the second the editors managed to sprinkle a few Muslim or Arab writers among an overwhelming majority of Christians and Jews, writing *on* Islam and quite often disfiguring, misrepresenting and undermining its tradition as the Muslims know it. The editors learned nothing of Muslim criticism of the first edition. Having failed to give any of the significant articles to the handful of Muslim contributors the editors might have taken the precaution of submitting sensitive articles to selected Muslim scholars for comment. To continue to publish offensive opinion about Islam without balancing it with the opposite view is both arrogant and irresponsible.

Next to be considered is *The Legacy of Islam*. It purports to give a picture of Islamic contribution to the total of human civilization excluding the modern era after 1800. The present second issue published in 1974 succeeded far less in achieving this object than the first issue that appeared in 1931. Some of the articles bear little or no relation to the subject of the legacy and their inclusion in the volume is questionable. Not only the standard of scholarship in the main articles is lower than that of those in the first issue, but also there is a disturbing evidence of an insidious campaign to adulterate Islamic history at least in one of the key articles.

The most obvious shortcoming of a collective volume on Islam is the absence of articles by Muslim scholars, except for a section of an article on India in about thirteen pages out of 530. If in 1931 it could be claimed that there was a dearth of Muslim scholars acceptable to the European editors no such excuse can be valid now forty years later – unless the Orientalists admit their failure in adequately educating the hundreds, if not thousands, of Muslims and Arabs that qualified under their supervision. The volume has sixteen out of its eighteen articles by Christian or Jewish writers, and much of its contents calls for criticism and some for correction. But it is not proposed to offer detailed review of the whole book. Only two contributions are chosen for the contrast they offer in the art of detached or partisan treatment.

The first on 'Philosophy, Theology and Mysticism' is by an Eastern Christian theologian. In the first edition mysticism was treated separately by the then leading English authority on the subject. The article on philosophy and theology was written by an Anglican clergyman who became afterwards professor of Arabic in the University of London, no friend of Islam. There is no question that the present article is superior in perception and sympathetic understanding to the previous one on these two subjects, if not also on mysticism.

The new article on the three subjects was probably written in French and then translated into English. This circumstance and the writer's training in Christian theology may account for the use of some expressions that offend the ear of the Muslim, but there is no reason to suspect intentional bias or indifference to the susceptibilities of Muslim readers. To very different subjects the writer brought much learning, insight and tolerance.

His powerful analysis demonstrates convincingly the unity (he calls it one-ness) of Islamic knowledge and wisdom. The concluding section on 'the legacy to the West' might have been adopted by the editors and other contributors as a relevant and necessary part of every article in the book. The eight pages on this question repay careful study and deserve expansion by the same writer or another with equal learning.[24]

The second article on 'Politics and War' calls for more detailed notice. Its learned and seductive, almost dramatic, exposition conceals many serious defects. Apart from a few howling anachronisms it contains tendentious statements, stands guilty of suppression of facts and of untenable assertions. It is in short as the Arabic proverb has it: a mixture of poison with fat. Whenever the facts compel the writer to give an approximation of the truth on the Arabs and Islam, he manages at the same time to tarnish his words with far-fetched glosses and vitiates them by damaging asides. Here are a few random examples.

The native Arabic word 'ummah' is declared as 'probably' derived from the Hebrew. Muḥammad, as a head of state, is stated to have derived his authority 'not from the governed' (who else did in the seventh century AD?). His letters to the rulers of Byzantium and Persia are judged as 'apocryphal'. The Arab armies in Syria and Iraq faced mostly 'mercenary' armies. The Arab failure to capture Constantinople 'saved' the Byzantine and Western Christendom. (How reveal-ing, coming from a Jew!) The forces that defeated the Crusades did not 'originate' in the regions occupied by them. Saladin was a 'Kurd' and his army was of 'Turkish-type'. The Abbasid caliphate of Baghdad was abolished (by whom?). The Mongol destruction was 'sometimes exaggerated'. (Never heard of the destruction of Baghdad?) Most of this material and much else bears little or no relation to the 'legacy'. The writer concludes with a political sermon. He deplores that Western Europe, through what he calls failure of will and faith, relinquished its hold on Islamic territory, while Eastern Europe (circumlocution for Russia) still maintains its sway. The future of Islam, he speculates, depends on the choice its leaders make between the East and West.[25] What has this cheap journalese to do with the legacy of Islam? ...

Mention has been made above of *The Cambridge History of Islam* and of my critical review of it. Here it must suffice to recapitulate other important points covered in that review. The contents of the two volumes of the so-called history reveal a serious imbalance in the coverage and the distribution of articles among contributors. Western writers preponderate, not only in number but also in monopolizing most of the key articles. As if by design Arab Muslim writers are made conspicuous by their exclusion. There is not a single article from the heartlands of Islam where Islamic history was made. Such seats of Islamic learning as Baghdad, Damascus, Jerusalem and Cairo are apparently assumed to be devoid of scholars. The editors surely missed an opportunity of cooperation between occidental and oriental scholarship in this project.

Here is a summary of the shortcomings of one of the articles covered by the review just mentioned. It is by one of the three editors, who was at the time professor of Arab history in the University of London. His article on 'Ottoman Rule in Egypt and the Fertile Crescent' is stifled with dates and names and attempts little or no analysis and advances no ideas at all. The first three pages, for example, are literally covered with double dates in AH and AD even for insignificant events. In addition to eleven double dates expressed in centuries these three pages have also twenty-one double dates expressed in years. The remaining space is dotted, between dates, with many and largely obscure names and a few facts. There is nothing on social, economic and cultural aspects of history. As one of the editors who wrote in the preface that the book was 'not a repository of facts, names and dates' the writer must have little respect for the intelligence of his readers or be unaware how useless his writing was.

Nor are his meagre facts always accurate or accurately expressed. Thus it is incorrect to assert that the books translated under Muḥammad 'Ali Pasha in Egypt in the 1830s were one of the principal channels by which 'European culture was communicated to the Near East'. Equally inaccurate is the assertion that the Pasha's schools provided 'Western education'. The Ottoman Sultan surely did not 'cede' Syria to his vassal; he merely appointed him governor over it. The writer is also mistaken when, without seeing the British archival material now open for inspection, he follows slavishly popular views of the McMahon Pledge, the Sykes-Picot Agreement and the Balfour Declaration. The British archives reveal abundant evidence that Palestine was not 'clearly' excluded from the area of Arab independence, that there were no 'negotiations' with the Sharif of Mecca and that he was not 'informed' of the Agreement.[26] The facts are as follows: Britain declared the exclusion of Palestine only in 1921. The Foreign Office resisted all suggestions for negotiations. With the approval of Balfour, the Foreign Secretary, the Sharif was formally 'informed' that the Agreement did not even exist!

IV

Enough examples have been given above to show that there are two versions of Islam as a religion and as a civilization. The one version is derived from love, faith and tradition, and the other from hatred, scepticism and speculation. There is complete divorce between the one and the other on almost all essentials. Islam is perhaps the only religion to be thus maltreated by outsiders. The scheme of things created by the Orientalists placed formidable barriers between themselves and the enlightened Muslims including those educated by the Orientalists, and fostered prejudice against Islam and misunderstanding of the Muslims in the Western mind. Consider the consequences when the false pictures drawn by the Orientalists filter through as they often do to the textbooks used in schools and influence those responsible for the media of public information.

Redress is virtually impossible, for if misrepresentation is to be effectively eliminated its source must first be corrected. To correct all the objectionable matter in the sources of the textbooks would require the unlikely cooperation of the Orientalists, for revision and sometimes even rewriting. As this is a remote possibility, the misrepresentation and misunderstanding will persist with their harmful results. The mutual non-recognition between the Orientalists and the Muslims will also persist. Its outward signs are on the one side ignoring protest and criticism and on the other questioning the integrity and competence of the arrogant.

Some of the evidence of ignoring criticism, even by the younger generations of Orientalists, was given above. It remains to give one or two concrete examples of the reaction by thoughtful Muslims. The founder and first president of the Arabic Academy in Damascus, who acknowledges the useful work of Orientalists in editing and publishing Arabic texts, castigated them on almost all other aspects of their work. He wrote in the introduction of one of his well known books that his colleagues in the Arabic Academy were incensed by the partisan and unscientific treatment of Islam and the Arabs by the Orientalists.

He himself thought it was manifestly unjust for contemporary Orientalists to continue writing under the influence of the bigoted medieval polemicists. 'Even those of them', he added, 'who employ the modern technique of investigation and analysis cannot free themselves from powerful racial, religious and political motives, and accordingly stand condemned for their unjust opinions of Islam and the Muslims. No admiration of their methods of study can spare them condemnation for their faulty and biased opinions.' Elsewhere he also questions their academic capacity and accused them of being the political tools of their governments. 'I know', he wrote, 'that most of them have political aims inimical to our interests, that some of them are priests, missionaries or spies using Orientalism as means to other ends.'[27]

Equally uncomplimentary is the assessment by a well known Egyptian littérateur and a member of the Arabic Academy in Cairo. He referred to Christian missionaries as the 'professional' and the Orientalists as the 'unprofessional' enemies of Islam. Some of the latter 'concoct' useless Islamic studies which they teach to their students, imparting to them what they had learned from their own teachers. Some of these student-teachers are well-intentioned and ready to acknowledge the truth when confronted with it. Others are ill-intentioned because they are employed in the service of colonialism (isti'mār) and state propaganda. Seldom did he read a criticism of the Arabic language or of Islam by such foreigners except to find it mistaken. The cause of the error in every case is 'ignorance' of the Arabic language or of Islam. Some Orientalists are ignorant of the Arabic language because they memorize some of its vocabulary but cannot feel it or capture its spirit through the rules of grammar.[28]

A degree of ignorance of the Arabic language on these lines is not altogether an extravagant criticism of some of those who teach it in Western universities. I could support it by two examples among many from personal experience. In 1948 the Professor of Arabic in the University of London was going to Damascus and desired to give a speech in Arabic there, and requested my assistance for translating it from English. He gave me the English text and a few lines of his own translation of a paragraph or two. Its very poor quality removed my puzzlement why he sought my help and not that of a competent Iraqi Arab on his staff.

The professor's translation had to be discarded and I started from scratch, both translating and editing. For example I advised the omission of a rash reference to the events of 1860 as inappropriate in Damascus. The professor and I went over the English original and my translation and editing and he enthusiastically approved all that I did. As I heard him reading I found it necessary to add vowel signs to many words that I assumed he ought to know. A few years later he began preparing a translation of the Sīrah of the Prophet. He persuaded two of his Arab students to take for their theses each an aspect of the subject. Despite the active and acknowledged help of one of these students the professor's product contained many defects including misunderstanding of the original Arabic, faulty translation and even slips in English.[29]

Less serious but rather ludicrous is the second example. In 1960 I met at Harvard a visiting scholar from the University of California. He told me he was working on an edition and translation of a unique Bodleian Arabic manuscript by a Damascene author concerned with the reign of the Mamluk Sultan Barqūq. One day he asked me whether I could help him to understand a sentence in which the key word was written alif–lām–'ain–yā'–nūn (= the eye) preceded by the name of Tamerlane. After a glance I told the enquirer that there was an orthographical mistake by the omission of another lām: the key word should read al-la'īn (the accursed). I saw immediate signs of subdued humiliation in his face. I forgot the episode till the edited text and its translation were published, when I had a quick look, not to find an acknowledgment for I did not expect one, and at any rate it would have been very embarrassing to an editor who became professor of Arabic. The correction and its accurate translation are there.[30]

But to return to the two general assessments of Orientalists given above. To appreciate them, and to allow for the strong expression, it is important to place them in the emotional context of their time: the conflict between the Arabs and the colonial powers, principally France and Britain. The first assessment was probably written with a famous French Orientalist, now dead, in mind. Despite his profound learning he meddled in politics and acted as unofficial adviser to his government. The second assessment may be related to at least one British Orientalist who was also an Anglican clergyman. He wrote a rash letter, signed with his official title as professor of Arabic in the University of London, in which he attacked al-Azhar in connection with disorders in Egypt arising from the political dispute with Britain.[31] What connection this professor had with his government's policy cannot be established. But it was an open secret that a number of British Orientalists at the time of Suez were directly involved as advisers and must have supported the aggression at least by their silence which was very conspicuous in relation to the vociferous protest of half the English nation.

And yet neither of the two Arab Muslim critics quoted above took any practical steps to ostracize the Orientalists. On the contrary the first critic welcomed except the most bigoted of them as corresponding members of the Arabic Academy, and in due course Cairo followed suit. Furthermore both Cairo and Damascus invited a number of Orientalists to lecture in their universities and bestowed honours on them. These courtesies, let it be remembered, were extended during the colonial period, and as a sign of the times were never reciprocated. No visiting scholars from Arab or Muslim countries to Western institutions were accorded comparable honour. No one was elected even to an honorary fellowship in any Western institutions. No Arab or Muslim student trained at such institutions and retained for assistance in teaching was given security of tenure. One in particular was a witness of his European students promoted over his head. There was a slight improvement after the Second World War, but even now it is still symbolic in British universities. In this matter the United States is much more liberal.

In general the present generation of Arabic and Islamic specialists in British and American universities exhibit far less scholarship and humility than the previous generation. With all their faults the giants of the previous generation usually searched for and expounded new ideas, while the pigmies of the present are on the whole content to ruminate what has already been said by their predecessors and indeed by themselves. But they are more jealous of their privileges and take incredible measures to protect what they and their colleagues publish – a clear sign of lack of confidence. While they are on the whole lyrical in their approval of one another, they are often extremely partial in reducing the eternal truth they study to simple dismissals of the alternative point of view. Naturally such attitudes fall short of true academic integrity and lack the essential tolerance in true scholarship.

It is well known that the School of Oriental and African Studies in the University of London issues a journal under a board of its staff. There is another journal controlled by a board of British Orientalists but now has less prestige. In the United States there is at least one similar journal of comparable standard. But in Britain much more than in America the control of these publications is very tight. There is an unavowed fraternity of mutual congratulation whose members restrict publications to their own product and that of their colleagues and protégés. The members of this fraternity confidently confer honours on one another and on whom they favour. What they publish is generally an echo of their collective mind. Members seldom, if ever, criticize the works of one another, even when criticism is necessary. But they set themselves as judges of outsiders and deny them any comment or factual correction.

When the editorial board of the Bulletin of the school mentioned above was under the chairmanship of a Zionist Jew it was noticeable that the number of articles by still unknown Israeli writers was proportionately great, so much so that one of the students of the chairman of the editorial board nicknamed it the 'Bulletin of the Hebrew University'. Ideally learning ought to have no national or racial boundaries, but such was not the policy while a Zionist Jew was in charge. He had an article published with the title 'The Influence of the Hebrew Language on the Contemporary Israeli Art Music' with tendentious howlers confusing facts and dates, such as 'Israeli soil' in 1930, 'Israeli composers' between 1930 and 1940, and 'music composed in Israel since 1930'. I pointed out these and other defects in a short letter to the editor which he refused to publish. A singularly silly note merely said that the defects 'had escaped notice at the time of publication'. Did they indeed?[32] (Sixteen years later the chairman was another Jew, a protégé of the former, and the policy was still the same).

Political not academic motives could be suspected for this editorial prevarication. The political speculation of the editor behind it will be discussed in the next section. Here the special circumstances of a book on Islam he edited will be noted. After three years of preparation 'The World of Islam Festival' was held in London for three months in 1976. With a fund of two million pounds contributed by Arab and Muslim governments the Festival sought, in the words of the official announcement, 'to contribute towards a new understanding of Islam' and to remove 'the ignorance and prejudice that have characterized the Western approach to it and are still widely held'.

By a number of exhibitions in London and the provinces to which many priceless exhibits were loaned by Arab and Muslim countries, by series of lectures delivered by Muslim scholars from different parts of the world, by special radio and television programmes, and by several works issued by the Festival from its own publishing company, the wealth and variety of Islamic civilization was presented to the public. Her Majesty Queen Elizabeth II, wearing a turban-style hat, inaugurated the Festival on 8 April when she opened the section of the Arts of Islam at the Hayward Gallery.

The Festival was not, however, spared political propaganda. A campaign by the Board of Deputies of British Jews and the Zionist Organisation, aided by some individuals who were neither Jews nor Zionists, asserted that the Festival had political aims connected with the cause of the Palestine Arabs. These allegations were authoritatively and publicly denied and the course of events proved them false. Yet the campaign continued even after the inauguration of the Festival by the Queen. 'The Festival is very anti-Israel' said one, and 'there is no question that it is political' said another.[33]

Despite these accusations a Jewish firm of publishers offered their services to the Festival, but were refused for the simple reason that it had its own publishing company managed by the British director of a well known Oriental publishing house in London. This circumstance may explain the issue, under the imprimatur of the spurned firm, of a volume entitled *The World of Islam*, suggesting to the inattentive that it was connected with the Festival. Half text and half pictures, many in colour, the book has thirteen contributions, the majority by Jewish writers. To a great extent its contents duplicate those of *The Legacy of Islam*, of a number of works issued by other British publishers, and of much of the material and illustrations that appeared in special issues in the British dailies, weeklies and monthlies, and indeed in the Festival's catalogues and leaflets. The very title of the book is the same as the twelve pages' supplement to *The Times*, and the most colourful picture of the Archangel Jibril had already appeared in *The Illustrated London News*.

There is no space for more than a brief comment on two contributions, the first and the last, both by Jews. The first is by the editor who carries on here as elsewhere his campaign of denegration, depreciation and adulteration, now with the additional aid of pictures. These are often used as pegs on which to hang tendentious remarks, so much so that there is sometimes no obvious relation between the picture and its caption. Many scholars will question a caption which states that under the Umayyads the character of Islamic civilization 'became less Arab and more Persian and Byzantine' without a definition of 'civilization'. Others will no doubt dislike the new term *Pax Mongolica* and the assertion that it was an 'improvement' on the old order under the Abbasid caliphate. Others still will detect the sustained insinuation regarding Saladin. 'Significantly', we are told, 'he was not an Arab'. The writer of this must know that there was no significance at all to his contemporaries whether the Muslim hero was Kurd, Arab, Persian or Turk. If there is any significance now it is in the mind of a writer who has a contemporary political aim to serve.

The worst evidence of his political Zionist bias is displayed in a caption on page 100 concerning a black and white picture of the Old City of Jerusalem spread on the following two pages, the only one in the book to occupy so much space. Its source is given as 'Georg Gerster, *Magnum*' without any further identification. The name is that of a well known photographic agency with a Jewish representative in London. However the ultimate source of the aerial picture taken after the Israeli occupation in 1967 can hardly be in doubt. The caption reads: 'standing out clearly is the Ḥaram (Temple Mount) ...' The truncated name is of course al-Ḥaram ash-Sharīf. The name in bracket has been introduced since the Israeli occupation. It cannot be used as an explanatory name of the third holy place in Islam. Here again the editor of a book on Islam must know that all the Israeli administrative and legislative measures to alter the character of Jerusalem were, by six UN resolutions (two by the General Assembly and four by the Security Council) declared invalid and illegal.

Hence the reckless and highly irresponsible adoption of the Israeli name by a writer who is silent at the same time on the destruction by Israel of the Maghāribah quarter that stood on inalienable *waqf* land close to the walls of al-Ḥaram ash-Sharīf, and dedicated by al Malik al-Afḍal, son of Saladin. He is also silent on the usurpation by Israel of Islamic *waqf* land at the doorstep of al-Aqṣā Mosque, hallowed by the Prophet's *Isrāʾ* (Nocturnal Journey) to Jerusalem.[34] Instead the writer implies that the usurped area is part of the Jewish quarter 'nearest the Temple'. This 'historian' turned propagandist does not wish to remember that the Temple was destroyed by Titus in 70 AD. Of course the most revealing in a biased writer are just those incidental admissions which are incompatible with the essence of the subject in hand like the use of 'significantly' and 'the Temple' above.

The other article to be noted very briefly is a jumpy and shallow patchwork on 'Islam Today', and a veritable parody of this title. The bias of its writer is so transparent and his hostility to the subject is so fanatical that he disqualified himself for serious consideration except to indicate a few of his typical distortions, omissions and naïvity concerning admissible historical evidence. Two Muslim divines in the nineteenth century were accused in their lifetime of unbelief but were rehabilitated and became recognized as leaders of modern Islamic thought. Is a Jew, with pronounced animosity towards the Arabs and Islam, qualified to pronounce on their religious beliefs? Is he a credible witness on the subject of 'Islam Today' when he stresses this point beyond reason and omits all mention of the disestablishment of Islam as the state religion in Turkey? Is he not extremely naïve to deduce from a love song by a contemporary Syrian poet far-reaching political and cultural conclusions and to apply them not only to the whole Arab world but also to the whole Muslim world? Is Sixth Form affected rhetoric or absurd hyperbole a substitute for solid evidence?[35]

V

The historians and pseudo-historians whose inadequacies and prejudices were discussed above are behind the times. They are still like their predecessors Eurocentric in their view of Islam and the Arabs. They still obstinately refuse to respond to the post-war movement for the revision of conventional history with a view to purging it of national, racial and other bias and thereby promoting international and human understanding. In a way this obstinacy is a legacy of the mentality of the colonial period which is still discernible in those well-meaning Englishmen who advise or defend the Arabs in the spirit of the old pro-consuls. They do not seem to observe the contrast between their patronizing defence and the advocacy of Israel by other Englishmen, Jews as well as Gentiles. Like all good advocates they put forward the Israeli case as Israel would put it, not as they themselves prefer it to be.

There is, however, no advocacy of the Arabs among the Orientalists, patronizing or otherwise. The examples of blind bias that some of the living Orientalists show, even more than their predecessors, are a discredit to themselves and to their academic pretensions. Some of them have made matters worse by extending and intensifying the old prejudices against Islam to the modern Arabs. This is particularly true of writers with a Zionist bent. The danger in this development is that the general public in the West take Arabs and Muslims as almost synonymous. So the problem is still much as it was in medieval times. There is, however, a promising sign. The Christian missionaries have mellowed their hostility to Islam, and many of them show human sympathy with the plight of the Palestinian Arabs. No evidence of such sentiment is to be found among the Orientalists, even the Arabist, as their complete silence amply testifies.

This section will be focused on the evidence of hatred and prejudice in the writings of Orientalists and pseudo-Orientalists on contemporary Arab and Islamic affairs. But since the field is so wide and the output is so voluminous it must suffice to give samples from the writing of only four. The first is the present professor of Arabic at Cambridge who neglects to write on his speciality but finds time to publish adverse comments on Arab politics. He wrote what is quoted below after relinquishing the chair of Arabic at London and before occupying that at Cambridge, but he wrote often as Director of the Middle East Centre at this University. One of his letters is a defence of the British colonial measures in Aden against what he calls 'criminals' and what the British authorities themselves call 'suspects'. Deploring the then imminent British withdrawal he ascribed it, at least in part, to propaganda emanating from the 'Egyptian invaders', or the 'Egyptian occupiers of Yemen' or 'Egyptian colonialism'.

He who allowed himself to write such drivel must have known that the Egyptians were in the Yemen not as invaders or occupiers or colonizers, but at the invitation of the Republic which overthrew the Monarchy. He boasts in the same letter that he photographed a tribesman who allegedly had been tortured by Egyptian intelligence. One would have thought that a professor of Arabic might have found more profitable employment photographing Arabic documents. What business had he to take sides in an inter-Arab dispute, or even to defend British colonial methods? But the newspaper in which his letter appeared administered an apt rebuke to him in this brief remark: Egyptian methods in the Yemen did not justify similar British methods in Aden.[36]

Later in the same year the same writer was again in Aden and accompanied the High Commissioner on a short visit to the Islands of Kuria Muria (on what business?) He adduced flimsy evidence that the Islands belonged not to Aden about to be independent but to the Sultan of Muscat still dependent upon Britain. Two obviously British justifications are suggested: the Islands may be useful to an enemy planning a naval attack on Muscat, and the Sultanate's 'economic potentialities and advantages not found in the former British protectorates'. As to the Russian fishing vessels in the area the professor of Arabic turned political journalist wondered whether there was a 'political aspect' to their presence. And he did not forget his vendetta against Egypt even in this context. He complains that its propaganda against colonialism did not square with its 'cruel colonial war in the Yemen'.[37] The fundamental difference must have escaped him: the one colonialism was foreign and real and the other 'colonialism' Arab and imaginary. Here again what business has an English professor of Arabic in colonial propaganda, be it Arab or British?

Nor was Nāṣir spared a virulent attack, even on the occasion of his death. As if the writer who had himself reviled Islam cared about it being allegedly undermined by Nāṣir. His defeat in 1967 is celebrated with such gusto to the extent of claiming that Yemeni tribesmen greeted it with jubilation and also 'many' Arab governments who considered Nāṣir more of a threat to themselves than Israel was. There were indications, the writer adds maliciously, that Nāṣir was willing to ditch the Palestine cause if it suited his selfish interests. He credits Nāṣir with only one virtue 'political adroitness'.[38] What purpose was this useless journalese supposed to serve? It might have been of some use before the eclipse of British colonialism, but after the eclipse it sounds like pique at Nāṣir's contribution to that eclipse.

Equally useless journalese, if not always so crude, is the political output of the second writer singled out for consideration. He was professor of Near and Middle East History (a new euphemism for the Arabs and Islam) in London before personal circumstances made him transfer to Princeton. Quite apart from teaching he exercised, while at the School of Oriental and African Studies, considerable influence on new appointments and internally on promotions. One protégé was imported from the Hebrew University and another from Indiana University, both for political reasons. Both proved, in different ways, disappointing to their patron.

From Princeton, as previously from London, political opinions continued to be published. Although a prolific writer, nothing he published after his very short and not entirely original doctorate thesis[39] approached its standards in scholarship. Before and since he devoted considerable attention to contemporary politics, his principal works on the Arabs and Islam duplicate each other to a greater or lesser extent and reproduce practically the same substance recast in different moulds again and again. That may bring in material reward but no academic honours. Consider this advertisement: 'Ideas, Men and Events in the Middle East' as the sub-title of a composite book on 'Islam in History', reprinting what has already been published, sometimes more than once. The title itself is misleading, considering the heterogeneous and disjointed contents.

The writer's power of exposition is aided by a lucid English style, and both serve to conceal the defects in handling and marshalling of the evidence. He has an odd habit of citing obscure references when none is required but neglecting to document the most controversial statements. His pages are often decorated with foreign words and phrases, and the less he knows a language the more he is inclined to show that he does. His popularization is rendered rather attractive by bald assertions and clever comments, generally embellished with catchy phrases, apt metaphors and not infrequently rash irony.

In the last twenty years or so he published several contributions on the political problems of the hour. For example in the aftermath of Suez he made a radio broadcast against the general repentent call in Britain to 'come to terms with Arab nationalism'. The counter idea of the broadcast was that Arab nationalism itself must come to terms with Britain and the West. The broadcast contained a great deal of hazardous speculation, forecasts and some super-cilious preaching centred on the only definite recommendation: whatever happens leave Israel in possession of all the loot, which implied the injunction: take no account of the rights of the Palestine Arabs. There is a streak of vanity in the whole piece signified by the statement that 'our' part in the affair must be negative, i.e. doing nothing.[40]

That is one of two principal themes that run through most of the writer's political output, the other being speculation on the prospects of communism in the Arab world. As has been seen above this second theme was introduced most inappropriately even while writing on the *legacy* of Islam. All such writings are of course more reliable evidence of the writer's political convictions than of his trustworthiness as a scholar. They merely show that his heart is where his head ought to be. A writer so hard set in his opinions may be an excellent advocate but he can only be a bad judge. Occupying an academic post he might have preferred history or its near relative – truth. In one of his composite works repeating what was published before, the writer complained of the wide-spread ill-feeling against Israel in the Arab world. A reviewer spotted the bias in this complaint and wrote: 'He does less than justice to the truly dominant element, that is, the strength of the emotion aroused throughout the Arab world by the forcible establishment and subsequent conduct of the state of Israel in territory hitherto unquestionably and for many centuries Arab and very conscious of its Arabism.'[41]

A great deal of this writer's contributions on these lines is of course journalese speculation. Thus in 1971, following the signing of the Soviet–Egyptian treaty, he wrote an article that sought to show that Egypt had virtually become a Russian satellite and that under its terms armed Russian intervention was likely to force Egyptian compliance with Russian wishes. Scarcely a year after this assessment Egypt asked all the Russian military and other advisers to leave and they did so without public objection. Nor was there any objection when the treaty itself was abrogated. Instead of being sobered by the fact that his forecasts were so speedily proved false by events the same writer came with even bolder and wilder speculation concerning American and Russian policies, invariably representing the Arabs as the villains and Israel as the repository of all virtue.

As an over-confident partisan the writer's eloquence is nowhere more revealing of its weakness than in the attack on Sadat. We are told that America was 'unlikely' to waste much time on him as 'unstable and insecure'. Israel was equally unlikely to trust 'a self-declared collaborator with the Nazis' whose public utterances 'echo the tones of European-style racial anti-semitism'. Furthermore we are assured that 'the Egyptians were in no position to attempt a serious armed crossing of the Suez Canal eastwards'.[42]

For a professional journalist such vituperations and ventures in the unknown are a necessary occupational hazard, but he knows and the world knows that what forecasts he makes are ephemeral and more often than not turn out to be false. Why should an academic so rashly follow the same path into an over-cultivated field with so dim prospects of success? The writer concerned is apparently compelled by his Zionist commitment to run the risk. He obviously does so irrespective of appearing over-confident and presuming to possess special powers of prescience. Surely such dismal record of failed assessments and false forecasts might have deterred a lesser fanatic.

But he quickly returned to the charge with increased fury. In an article that cunningly panders to American national vanity he attacked this time a resolution, and its sponsors, passed by the United Nations General Assembly in October 1976 which declared Zionism, to be as practised in Israel, 'a form of racism and racial discrimination'. The title of the article, 'The Anti-Zionist Resolution', is itself partisan and controversial.[43] With a smoke-screen of scholarship the article is essentially an apology for Zionism. It uses the familiar excuses of the apologist who claims that the other side is equally if not more at fault. Thus the Mufti of Jerusalem was 'Hitler's coadjutor'; 'Nazis and other criminals (what court convicted them?) found haven in Arab countries.' Saudi Arabia refused *agrément* to a British ambassador who was a Jew. And so on.

Much of the article is an attack on Russia who is accused of having promoted the resolution. 'The speed', we are told, 'with which the passage of the resolution was announced by the Soviet information media, in contrast to their usual slowness, is instructive.' So indeed is the speed with which the article appeared in a well known American quarterly in the same month of October when the resolution was passed. Considering the fact that quarterlies of this calibre take months, sometimes years, to consider, place and then publish articles, it is a legitimate suspicion in this case of the influence of some American intelligence or political agency.

The two other writers that remain to be considered in this section are not Orientalists but on the fringe of British Orientalism. Both lecture on the politics of the 'Middle East' and both come originally from it. The one is Greek who was brought up among the Arabs in Egypt and Palestine, and the other is a Jew from Baghdad who also grew up among the Arabs. Both write on contemporary Arab politics and both dabble in modern Arab history, displaying various degrees of prejudice and animosity.

As stated above the Greek was imported to join in the campaign conducted from the School of Oriental and African Studies against the Arabs then led surreptitiously and skilfully by the then professor of Near and Middle East History. The story of the Jew is really that of one book: he was a student at St. Antony's College, Oxford in the early fifties and offered for the doctorate a thesis that was rejected by the then doyen of British Orientalists. An influential patron found for the student employment at the London School of Economics, and from such a respectable address the thesis, probably revised, was published in 1955. Since then its author did little more than search very diligently and persistently for scraps of evidence to prove it right and his tutor and all other like-minded scholars wrong.

But to start with the Greek. His patron was an editor of a series on the modern history of the Middle East, and in that capacity asked his protégé to contribute a volume on Egypt. The result was disastrous. The editor, with singular irresponsibility, neglected to edit the text, and the author, unequal to the task, produced a work in strangulated English for 'the general reader', very dull and full of factual mistakes. Any well-read peruser of its pages will readily feel that he had read the same thing elsewhere, more accurately presented and more elegantly expressed.[44]

Nor is his writing on politics more impressive. His opinions are often expressed with immoderate vehemence. A reviewer in a leading British journal wrote what very nearly reflects my own view of a short book entitled *Conflict in the Middle East*. He said the book was 'a venture into journalism'; much of it reads like 'an extended newspaper editorial', the author was 'uncertain whether a phenomenon is superficial or fundamental', but was prepared 'to risk his judgment being overtaken by events'.[45] Very much like his patron!

I would add that the book is not so much on *the* conflict (i.e. between the Arabs and Israel) as on inter-Arab political differences. The author judges these subjectively and harshly making little or no allowance for the fact that much of the seeds of conflict was sown by the West. Furthermore he seems to imply that the Palestinians deserve the injustice they suffered and still suffer because of what he terms their impractical political aims. Accidentally I came across an apt retort: an irate reader, possibly a student, wrote on the title page of the copy of the book in the Library of the SOAS these words: 'conflict in the head of' followed by an arrow pointing to the name of the author!

The other writer is considerably more aggressive in adulterating recent Arab history and more rancorous in his attitude to the Arabs in general. Almost all his writing since leaving Oxford is some extension or diversification of what he wrote there on the Sykes-Picot agreement of 1916 which was published under an ambitious and cumbersome title.[46] Written before the official British records for the period were open for public inspection, the book was based on tendentious selection of material, mainly from printed books. The aim was to stress an untenable proposition that the agreement was not as many British politicians and its Arab victims saw it, as contrary to previous British promises to the Arabs but as a 'responsible' settlement of the fate of the Arab provinces of the Ottoman Empire (i.e. by partition between Britain and France!). And yet the book very strangely contains neither the text nor the map of the agreement.

Two examples of biased citation of witnesses are typical: Rashīd Riḍā is quoted against the Sharif of Mecca when he was in political conflict with him in 1921, not when he was an enthusiastic supporter in 1916. Edouard Brémond, completely out of sympathy with the Arab Revolt, is quoted on the strength of its army and not the British director of intelligence who received regular reports from British officers with that army.

When the British records were opened for inspection it was immediately established that the British authorities in London and Cairo were against divulging the terms of the agreement to the Arabs as harmful to British interests. Still the same author persisted in his original assertion and continued to search for fugitive suggestions that the agreement was good for the Arabs and even that some of them accepted it. Nor was this obstinacy mellowed by the startling revelation that the British High Commissioner in Cairo, in answer to an enquiry from the Sharif of Mecca, denied the very existence of the agreement and that the telling of this lie was approved by the Foreign Office in London.[47]

Despite this and much else the same author persisted in his devious methods and continued to produce dubious results. A collection of articles he wrote over a period of twenty years, in design one-sided and in spirit polemical, no apparatus of footnotes safely tucked away at the end of the book can disguise its similarity to the Nazi textbook *Der Weg zum Reich* which included little that was inaccurate yet by selection, suppression and presentation it created a false historical picture.[48] Nor is this author courteous to predecessors he does not agree with. He seems, however, to agree with me in a peculiar way. I was the first to question the competence of Ronald Storrs in Arabic and to point out, *inter alia*, that the Arabic word for 'protectorate' which he claimed to have coined and took the trouble to have printed in Arabic characters in his memoirs was misspelled. Eight years later the idea and the example were adopted without acknowledgment by a hitherto only discourteous writer. But he was taken to task by a critic for omitting to mention one of my works, and I made a mild protest about the plagiarism.[49]

To conclude this section. It is obvious from the evidence cited above that the subjects of Islam and the Arabs as written and taught by Orientalists and the new breed of teachers of politics lag far behind the need of a changed world for which they are still the trainers of teachers, diplomatists, missionaries and businessmen. In content and in tone the writing and teaching is still largely anti-Islam and anti-Arab, particularly so regarding contemporary affairs. Those who graduate at the hands of Orientalists thus indoctrinated and who come into contact with Arabs and Muslims in the course of their business or duty often find it imperative to form a fresh point of view and even new vocabulary in order to express their relationship in a realistic manner different from that which they learned in the books of the Orientalists. This is one of their colossal failures.

NOTES

1. W. Montgomery Watt, *Muḥammad: Prophet and Statesman* (Oxford, 1961), pp. 15, 39, 112. See the review of this book by A. L. Tibawi in *The Islamic Quarterly*, vol. 6, 3–4, 1961, pp. 127–28.
2. Kenneth Cragg, *The Dome and the Rock* (SPCK, 1968) is reviewed by A. L. Tibawi in *The Islamic Quarterly*, vol. 12, 1–2 1968, p. 120.
3. Bernard Lewis, *The Arabs in History* (London, 1968 ed.) pp. 38–9.
4. *Historians of the Middle East*, edited by Bernard Lewis and P. M. Holt (OUP, 1962) pp. 2, 11.
5. *The Cambridge History of Islam*, edited by P. M. Holt, Ann K. S. Lambton and Bernard Lewis (Cambridge, 1970), vol. I, p. XI (Introduction by P. M. Holt).
6. Book review by C. E. Bosworth in *The Islamic Quarterly*, vol. 18, 1–2, 1974, p. 49.
7. J. D. Latham's articles in the *I. Q.* on archery and Andalusian and North African subjects are largely derivative, with no original ideas, from previous contributions by Arab, Spanish and French authors. His craving for recognition took him to an Islamic conference in London and persuaded an Islamic fortnightly to publish what amounted to an apology for English Orientalists. See Latham's text and a reply by A. L. Tibawi in *Impact International* for 22 June, and 27 July, 1973.
8. (a) John Wansbrough, *Quranic Studies: Sources and Methods of Scriptural Interpretation* (OUP, 1977).
   (b) Patricia Crone and Michael Cook, *Hagarism: The Making of the Islamic World* (CUP, 1977).
9. A. F. L. Beeston, *The Arabic Language Today* (London, 1970) and *Written Arabic* (CUP, 1968).
10. R. B. Serjeant, *Prose and Poetry from Hadramawt* (London, 1951). The full English title is 'South Arabic Poetry I Prose and Poetry from Hadramawt', dated London, 1951. On the other side of the book the full Arabic title is '*Mukhtārāt min al-Adab al-ʻAmmi al-Ḥaḍrami: Ashʻār wa-maqāmat wa-khaṭab*', dated London, 1950. How confused and confusing! (No other volume was published).
11. See the introduction written by R. B. Serjeant to A. J. Arberry (ed.) *Religion in the Middle East* (Cambridge, 1969), vol. II, p. 7.
12. In an article in the *Bulletin of the School of Oriental and African Studies*, vol. 41 Pt. I, 1978, p. 2.
13. T. M. Johnstone, *Eastern Arabian Dialect Studies* (OUP 1967).
14. See my first *Critique* (1964), pp. 17–18 (re J. N. D. Anderson).
15. N. J. Coulson, *A History of Islamic Law* (Edinburgh, 1964).
16. K. Cragg, *The Call of the Minaret* (New York, 1956) p. 17.
17. *The Middle East Forum*, vol. 48, 1972, pp. 135–42; also in *The Islamic Quarterly*, vol. 17, 1973 pp. 92–100.
18. A. L. Tibawi, *Arabic and Islamic Themes* (London, 1976), p. XIV (in the Introduction) and specific examples pp. 377, 379–87 (reproducing reviews of books by M. Maoz, P. J. Vatikiotis, K. S. Salibi and D. Hopwood).
19. F. Rosenthal in B. Lewis and P. M. Holt (eds), *Historians of the Middle East*, p. 35–6; cf. Critique, p. 11.
20. The article is by Bernard Lewis (*The Cambridge History of Islam*, vol. I, ch. 3). See my assessment of the treatment of al-Maʼmūn and Saladin in *Arabic and Islamic Themes*, pp. 297–98.

21. The decree is mentioned by Bernard Lewis in *The Emergence of Modern Turkey* (OUP, 1961) p. 114. One of my attempts to discover its location was published in *The Royal Central Asian Journal*, vol. 55, 3 1968, pp. 333–34 (Book review).

22. Ibn Hishām, *As-Sīrah an Nabawiyyah*, ed. by Mustafa Saqqa *et al* (Cairo, 2nd ed., 1375/1955), vol. I, pp. 501–504. The text refers to the document as Kītāb or Ṣaḥifah.

23. R. B. Serjeant, 'The Sunnah Jāmi'ah etc,' in the Bulletin of the School of Oriental and African Studies', vol. 41, Pt. I, 1978, pp. 1–42.

24. *The Legacy of Islam*, edited by Joseph Schacht with C. E. Bosworth, (Oxford, The Clarendon Press, 1974): article by Georges C. Anawati, pp.350–91.

25. *The Legacy of Islam*, article by Bernard Lewis, pp. 156–209.

26. See the article by P. M. Holt in vol. I, pp. 324–93, and A. L. Tibawi's review in *The Islamic Quarterly*, vol. 17, 1–2, 1973, pp. 92–100. The last three questions are discussed in greater detail by A. L. Tibawi's *Anglo-Arab Relations and the Question of Palestine 1914–1921* (London, 1977) pp. 464–66; 179–86; 278.

27. Muḥammad Kurd 'Ali, *al-Islām wal-Ḥaḍārah al-'Arabiyyah*, vol. I, first published in 1933, see the introduction to the third edition (Cairo, 1968). See also *al-Mudhakkirāt* (The Memoirs), Damascus (1367/1948), vol. I, pp. 186, 216 and vol.IV, pp. 1241–42.

28. 'Abbās Maḥmūd al-'Aqqād, *Ḥaqā'iq al-Islām wa-Abāṭīlu Khuṣūmihi* (Cairo, 1376/1957; 2nd ed. 1382/1962), pp. 178–79.

29. See 'Ibn Isḥāq's Sīrah: A Critique of Alfred Guillaume's English translation' by A. L. Tibawi in *The Islamic Quarterly*, vol. 3, 3, 1956–7, pp. 196–214.

30. *A Chronicle of Damascus 1389–1397* by Ibn Ṣaṣra, edited by W. M. Brinner, (The University of California, 1963), vol. II (Arabic text), p. 148, vol. I (English translation), p. 200. While looking for the word I saw by chance (p. 155) Ḥassān's famous line in his panegyric to the princes of Bani Ghassān with '*bi-Jilliqin*' whereas both grammar and scansion demand '*bi-Jilliqa*' (Jilliq is one of the names of Damascus).

31. See letter from Alfred Guillaume in *The Times*, 29 January 1952, p. 8, col. 5.

32. *Bulletin of the School of Oriental and African Studies*, vol. 25, pt 2, 1962, pp. 210f. Article by Zvi Keren. Letter signed D. M. Johnson on behalf of the Editorial board (chairman Bernard Lewis).

33. The first assertion was by Jacob Gerwitz of the Board of Deputies of British Jews, and the second by Donald Watts of the London School of Economics and Political Science, and both quoted in an article by John Smalldon published in *The Sunday Telegraph* on 4 April 1976.

34. Full details in A. L. Tibawi, *The Islamic Pious Foundations in Jerusalem: Origins, History and Usurpation by Israel* (London, 1978).

35. *The World of Islam* (Thames and Hudson: London, 1976). The first article discussed above is by Bernard Lewis, and the thirteenth and last noted above is by Elie Kedourie.

36. Letter in *The Observer*, 29 January 1967 from R. B. Serjeant.

37. Letter in *The Times*, 27 December 1967.

38. An assessment in *Asian Affairs*, n. s. vol. 2, pt. I, February 1971, p. 21.

39. See the opinion of H. A. R. Gibb (the tutor of the author) in the *Bulletin of the School of Oriental and African Studies*, vol. 10, 1940–1942, p. 797: Bernard Lewis, *The Origins of Isma'ilism* (114 pages).

40. *The Listener*, 27 November 1958, pp. 863–864.

41. *Asian Affairs* (1973), pp. 352–53 (Review by Stephen H. Longrigg).

42. Three articles by Bernard Lewis in *The Times*, 8 October 1971 and 20–21 September 1972.

43. *Foreign Affairs*, vol. 55, 1 October 1976, pp. 54–64.

44. See the two reviews by A. L. Tibawi, pointing out numerous factual mistakes and technical defects, of P. J. Vatikiotis, *The Modern History of Egypt*, published in *The*

Islamic Quarterly, vol. 13, 1, 1969, pp. 50–52, and in *Asian Affairs*, n. s. vol. I, 1, 1970, pp. 78–80.

45. *International Affairs*, vol. 48, 2, 1972, pp. 341–42, review by Peter Mansfield.

46. Elie Kedourie, *England and the Middle East: The Destruction of the Ottoman Empire, 1914–1921* (London, 1956).

47. cf. A. L. Tibawi, *Anglo-Arab Relations and the Question of Palestine 1914–1921*, p. 278.

48. Full review with more specific details by A. L. Tibawi in *The Middle East Journal*, vol. 21, I, 1971, p. 108.

49. A. L. Tibawi, *A Modern History of Syria including Lebanon and Palestine* (London, 1969) p. 220 (Storrs); *The Middle East Journal*, winter, 1978, p. 140 (critic); A. L. Tibawi, *Anglo-Arab Relations and the Questions of Palestine*, p. 514.

20

ON THE ORIENTALISTS AGAIN

A. L. Tibawi

In his comments on Donald P. Little's article 'Three Arab Critiques of Orient-alism', A. L. Tibawi questions Little's competence to comment on the subject; suggests that a more rigorous analysis of the arguments put forward is required; and wonders at the inconsistency of his conclusions. American orientalists, he adds, the heirs of a humane and liberal tradition, should feel ashamed of their failure to protest against the policy pursued by their government with regard to the Palestine question.

I have seen Professor Donald Little's article, 'Three Arab Critiques of Orient-alism,' in *The Muslim World* (LXIX [1979], 110–31) through the courtesy of one of the editors who also invited my comments. There is little to add to what I wrote nearly twenty years ago[1] or to what I have just written.[2] The article in question is obviously a much belated response to my first contribution. It had just missed taking account of the second. All I propose to say is merely expansion of the marginal notes I jotted down while perusing the article.

But first of all, I am rather uncertain with what authority the writer speaks. I gather his initial training was in English, but later received 'Orientalist' in-struction from Gustave von Grunebaum. He is professor of Islamic history and Arabic at McGill University. With all due respect, he does not seem to have established himself as an authority in these fields. I know of no works by him on

A. L. Tibawi, 'On the Orientalists Again', *The Muslim World*, 70, 1, 1980, pp. 56–61.

the classical Islamic and Arabic disciplines. Nor does he seem to be more qualified in the other main subject of the present discussion – modern Arab history and Arab nationalism. The only work I know by him, and indeed the only work he himself cites, is a short treatise he wrote for his doctorate on Mamluk historiography covering a period of three years, about the end of the seventh/thirteenth century, which was published in 1970.

Furthermore, the article itself does not indicate that its writer has made any special study of the works of the Orientalists I singled out for detailed criticism. More surprising still, there is little evidence that he familiarized himself with the contents of my own works, the warrant for venturing to criticize the works of others. Thus I am puzzled by his description of my book on modern Syria as 'a general history' (p. 112), the accusation that I 'confuse' Islam with 'Arabness' (p. 123) and the unjust censure of my alleged 'aggressive defensiveness towards Western scholarship' (p. 123).

A less intrepid writer might have been deterred by these limitations. I wonder if he is aware that they imposed on him a method of treatment which is at times too simplistic and borders on the journalese. He gives very brief and inadequate summaries of my arguments, without any of the supporting evidence, interspersed with his own opinions and embroidered with rhetorical questions and exclamation marks. He scratches some surface, but leaves the core hardly touched. Surely, detailed and documented discussion calls for much more rigorous analysis, and cannot be disposed of by the passing of summary judgment.

I will now go into details. Gibb's hackneyed dictum with which the article begins has long lost its validity, if only because of works by publicists like Husri and Razzaz. Gibb himself recognized its diminishing validity twice in the sixties when he and I discussed my first *Critique* of the Orientalists, and later my study of the transition from Islam to Arab nationalism.[3] On the latter occasion I suggested that the most perceptive people in any culture are often incapable of interpreting it to themselves or to those outside it. He did not disagree, nor did he reply when I asked him who was, in his opinion, an acceptable exponent of English culture at the time.

Of the English Orientalists, Gibb and Arberry were life-long friends. Both were aware that I had reservations concerning their respective understanding of Islam. With the third member of the trio, Guillaume, I could not establish a *rapport*. Right from the beginning of our acquaintance, I felt he had deep-rooted hostility to Islam. Open disagreement was on the vital question of the life of the Prophet. He was working on it when I first met him.

He set out to 'reconstruct' Ibn Isḥāq's text from the text of his scribe Ibn Hishām, and to produce an English translation thereof, with the aim of superseding the German translation by Weil published in 1864. I have shown by detailed comparison that the 'construction' often amounted to dismemberment and adulteration of both Ibn Hishām and Ibn Isḥāq. One of Guillaume's many blunders occurs on the very first page. The first line of a translation purported to be of Ibn Isḥāq begins thus: 'Abū Muḥammad 'Abdul Malik Ibn Hishām the

Grammarian said: This is the book of the biography of the apostle of God.' Another amusing blunder is due to defective logic and insufficient command of Arabic: 'Zaid Ibn Arqam said: I was an orphan child of 'Abdullah Ibn Rawāḥa, and he took me with him on this expedition.' How the son of Arqam was also the son of Rawāḥa, or how a child bereft of his father could go with his father on an expedition, are questions Guillaume the orientalist neither asked nor answered.

More serious were the subtle twists to which he subjected the narrative in order to pander to religious prejudices from which Weil was free. I have shown that in accuracy and understanding of the Arabic the latter was superior to Guillaume. Here is a small example with special significance. Weil translated *jahūl* correctly as *unwissend*, but Guillaume, from malice or sheer stupidity, translated it as 'barbarous,' and that was with reference to Muḥammad.[4]

The first evidence of Guillaume's hostility to his subject is clear from a note on the first page which insists that any tradition preceded by the verb *za'ama* must be either doubtful or simply a lie. I covered three printed pages with evidence to prove him wrong. In the standard dictionaries the word means 'he said or reported or thought,' and is also used of a report which may be right or wrong. More relevant to the *Sīra* is the use of the word in connection with a report that lacks the usual chain of transmitters. Hence its occurrence must be taken as a sign of *pious caution*, and not necessarily doubt, still less falsehood. I concluded the critique of Guillaume's translation by stating that it was unacceptable as a reliable reproduction of the received Arabic text.[5]

Soon after Guillaume's death, I received permission to publish Arberry's and Gibb's opinions on my criticism. Arberry had written: 'This is a substantial contribution to scholarship. It is hard-hitting, but I can see no fault in it. I think you should publish.' More reserved, as usual, Gibb's words were as follows: 'On the point of Guillaume's performance you are on the whole just, but harshly just on the point of his intentions.'

My *Critique* of the English-speaking Orientalists, however, did disturb both Gibb and Arberry, I sensed. As doyen of the establishment Gibb referred to it only once, in a laconic and rather enigmatic way. But Arberry was more forthcoming. He recognized that the story I told was 'sad but unfortunately true.' I always regarded him more 'Muslim' than Gibb. His attitude became clear when he invited me to lecture on the subject to the staff and students at the Middle East Centre in Cambridge immediately after the publication of the *Critique*.

Thus, far from being aggrieved by it, the two leading English Orientalists accepted it, implicitly or explicitly, as justified. It seems to me that Professor Little ought to have little cause to come out twenty years later with a blatant and unreasoned tirade. Producing no concrete evidence to back any of his opinions he voices strong objections to my documented criticism of certain idols he seems to regard as gods. He defends, among others, Guillaume, von Grunebaum and Montgomery Watt. I have just shown, in brief, the work of the first. I will now turn to the other two.

I knew von Grunebaum fairly well and was always amused by observing his arrogant assurance. We had the last tête-à-tête in Philadelphia in 1961 at the Conference of American Orientalists. I wrote my last assessment of one of his contributions just before his death, and it was published soon afterwards. It was concerned with his article, 'The Sources of Islamic Civilization.' I opened by paying tribute to his erudition and originality and excused his skepticism as legitimate in one who is outside the circle of believers. But I recorded that a *Christian* Arab scholar, the late Professor Nabih Faris, had blamed von Grunebaum for want of sympathetic understanding of Islam and for a 'subtle hostility to everything Muslim.'[7] I myself rejected the assumption of his article that the existence of parallels in Islamic civilization with other civilizations is valid proof of borrowing.

I added a complaint about his English, befogged by the excessive use of polysyllabic vocabulary and obscured by Germanic density. The sentences are inordinately long and the pronouns are often confused. Nor is the display of linguistic versatility or the array of incidental details conducive to easy comprehension. The cumulative effect of these adornments detracts rather than enhances the value of the product. This article is really a number of isolated glimpses, not a consistent whole, very quaint but unconvincing. Had the writer applied his skills to a few specific subjects and restricted himself to direct evidence, the outcome might have been more instructive.

My acquaintance with Montgomery Watt is slight, but I studied all his works on Islam and reviewed a number of them. As a typical example, I quote here from my assessment of his portrait of Muḥammad as a prophet and statesman. It simplified and popularized the author's earlier and more scholarly volumes. Almost every Orientalist has at one time or another tried his hand on the life of Muḥammad, but down to our own time their approach and its outcome continue to be colored with prejudice and hostility. Often enough, the Orientalists sat in judgment on Muhammad and Islam according to standards that ill befit his time and environment. Often enough they lingered on inevitable human contradictions in order to discredit the man and his cause.

Montgomery Watt's contributions 'had been remarkable for attempting to redress the balance. His command of the facts and his often imaginative interpretation are admirable. But his treatment of Muḥammad the statesman is more acceptable to Muslim opinion than that of Muḥammad the prophet.' For while his prophethood and sincerity are recognized, it is asserted in the same breath that he was 'aware' of Jewish and Biblical traditions. This is an ill-disguised resurrection of the hoary story of the alleged Judaeo-Christian 'origins' of Islam. That it is in conflict with the Qur'ān, or that its propagation in these 'liberal' times is offensive to the believers does not seem to have troubled the mind of the writer. He cannot be accused of ignorance of the Qur'ān or of Islamic sentiment. It is therefore inexplicable why he tried to ride two horses at the same time.[8]

The above must suffice to show that even the 'moderate' Orientalists are still shackled by a legacy of medieval prejudices. If it is still asked why I denounce Bernard Lewis as a biased writer on the Arabs and Islam and as a Zionist fanatic, and his protégé Vatikiotis as a pseudo-Orientalist and a blind Arabophobe, I would point out the evidence.[9]

It remains to consider one or two stray ideas advanced in the rather disjointed final parts of Professor Little's article. In this part he retreats from a number of positions he held at the beginning. He came round to the idea that, after all, Orientalists are not gods but fallible mortals. He accepts one of the indictments of their methods in my first *Critique*, and states that in 'a misguided attempt' to communicate they do 're-think' and 're-formulate' Islam, not in its own terms but in their own. He excuses this questionable scholarship on curious grounds: he hopes that as a result of my protests and the protests of others, 'a more measured tone' (no more!) in Orientalism may develop. However, he makes this development dependent on the acceptance of the idea that all knowledge is 'tentative' and subject to revision.

But he produces no evidence whatsoever that the Orientalists are prepared to revise their methods or ideas along these lines. The evidence that I cited in the *Second Critique* (p. 43) points to the contrary. The Orientalists failed to take any notice of the revision in the teaching and writing of world history after the Second World War. They failed to respond to the meaning of the changed relationship between their countries and former dependencies. With a few honorable exceptions, I found the professional Orientalists still distort and misrepresent Islam, and a new breed of pseudo-Orientalists are extending the distortion and misrepresentation to the Arabs.

Another idea is put forward in the article as an apology for Orientalism: the existence of a number of Arab scholars who accept, and themselves use, the Western approach to the Arabs and Islam. It is for the persons named (p. 124) to agree or disagree with what the writer says about them. I would only remind him that encounters between different cultures did and do produce alienated individuals, denationalized and deculturalized, who try to live in two worlds at the same time but are at peace in neither. Some of the persons named do not write in Arabic, others avoid speaking it, and some are 'neutral' or 'silent' on Arab or Islamic questions.

I had such unhappy results of Western education in mind when I deprecated in the first *Critique* the want of moral responsibility in Western teachers who, consciously or unconsciously, indoctrinate their immature and defenseless Arab or Muslim students. The matter is concerned with the content and 'tone' of what is taught and published by the Orientalists, charged as it still is with prejudice and hostility. Such is the tenor of an anguished letter I recently received from a Sudanese girl of noble family whose misfortune placed her under English tutors she regards as hostile to her faith and nation. I always advised that such students must receive thorough grounding in their tradition in their own countries before they are sent to any Western institution.

Before concluding, I must repudiate the imputation that I regard the treatment of the Arabs and Islam by Western scholars with 'deep bitterness and resentment' (p. 12). Neither sentiment is conducive to clear thinking. What I really feel is disappointment and disenchantment with those of them who claim, nay boast, to be heirs of a humane and liberal tradition, and yet fail to live up to its standards. I have in mind the callous indifference with which the so-called Arabists and Islamists among the Orientalists, the purveyors of 'amity of hate,' viewed and continue to view the colossal injustice and human misery inflicted on the whole of the Palestine Arab nation. Not a word of protest was uttered, even on humanitarian grounds! The American Orientalists in particular – and Professor Little declares himself as one of them – ought to be ashamed of their silence while their government persists in sustaining the injustice with money, arms and diplomacy.

Notes

1. 'English-Speaking Orientalists: A Critique of Their Approach to Islam and Arab Nationalism,' published in *The Muslim World*, LIII (1963), 185–204 and 298–313, and in *The Islamic Quarterly*, VII, 3–4 (1964), 23–45 and 73–88. Also published as a monograph by Luzac & Co. Ltd. (London) for the Islamic Cultural Centre, 1384/1964.
2. 'Second Critique of English-Speaking Orientalists and Their Approach to Islam and the Arabs,' published in a special issue of *The Islamic Quarterly*, XXIII, 1 (1979), 3–54, and also as a separate monograph published by the Islamic Cultural Centre (London), 1399/1979.
3. A. J. Arberry, ed., *Religion in the Middle East*, II (Cambridge: At the University Press, 1969), chapter 23, 'The Cultural Aspect,' 545–604, republished in my book, *Arabic and Islamic Themes* (London: Luzac and Co., Ltd., 1976), pp. 99–153 under the new title, 'From Islam to Arab Nationalism.'
4. Fowler's *Modern English Usage* clearly states that this adjective always 'implies contempt and moral condemnation.'
5. 'Ibn Ishāq's Sirah (Biography of Muhammad): A Critique of Guillaume's English Translation,' published in *The Islamic Quarterly*, III, 3, (1956), 96–214, and republished in my *Arabic and Islamic Themes*. pp. 25–52.
6. In *The Cambridge History of Islam* (Cambridge: At the University Press, 1970), II, 469–510. See my review of the volume including von Grunebaum's article in *Middle East Forum*, XVIII (1972), 135–42, and in *The Islamic Quarterly*, XVII (1972), 92–100.
7. *The Middle East Journal*, XIX (1965), 105–7 in a review of von Grunebaum's *Modern Islam: the Search for Cultural Identity*.
8. See my review of *Muhammad: Prophet and Statesman* in *The Islamic Quarterly*, VI (1961), 127–28.
9. *Second Critique*, pp. 10, 16–17, 20–21, 28–29, 31–34 (Lewis), and pp. 34–35, 39 (Vatikiotis).

PART X
EDWARD SAID'S *ORIENTALISM*:
REVIEWS AND REVIEW ARTICLES

Edward Said's *Orientalism* made a considerable impression on the academic world. In the period immediately following its publication, at least sixty reviews and review articles appeared in Britain and America (see Lata Mani and Ruth Frankenberg, 'Orientalism', *Economy and Society*, 14, 2, 1985). A representative sample might include Stuart Schaar's 'Orientalism at the Service of Imperialism', David Kopf's 'Hermeneutics versus History', M. Richardson's 'Enough Said', Sadik Jalal al-'Azm's 'Orientalism and Orientalism in Reverse', Ernest J. Wilson III's 'Orientalism: A Black Perspective' and Bernard Lewis's 'The Question of Orientalism'.

21

ORIENTALISM AT THE SERVICE
OF IMPERIALISM

Stuart Schaar

In 'Orientalism at the Service of Imperialism', Stuart Schaar – a professor of history at the Brooklyn College of the City University of New York – whilst admitting that in recent years decolonisation and the growth of the left have done much to transform 'classical' orientalism, argues that in North America much of the academic mainstream remains unaffected. In Iranian studies in particular, he asserts, orientalist attitudes of the most extreme kind continue to find expression.

In this brilliant and bold book, Edward Said criticises cultural imperialism and contributes in a major way to the process of decolonisation. Its appearance provides an appropriate occasion to discuss the nature of western scholarship on the Orient, especially the Muslim East, since the eighteenth century, and to analyse the interaction between American hegemony and western scholarship on the Third World. Finally, it offers a timely chance to survey, however briefly, contributions of western liberal scholarship to our understanding of contemporary Iran.

Adopting, and refining, Antonio Gramsci's idea of hegemonic culture[1] and Michel Foucault's notion of discourse,[2] Said argues that Orientalism is more than a field of study in the western world. In his view it is a 'corporate institution' (p. 13) encompassing a set of generalisations, structures, relationships,

Stuart Schaar, 'Orientalism at the Service of Imperialism', *Race and Class*, 21, 1, 1979, pp. 67–80.

texts, the whole forming a 'discourse', which defines the Orient and Orientals for the West. The function of Orientalism is '. . . to understand, in some cases to control, manipulate, even incorporate, what is a manifestly different world'. (p. 12)

THE ORIENTALIST DISCOURSE

By the nineteenth century, Orientalist discourse had become set, and its stereotypes disseminated throughout western culture: Orientalists had developed a consensus. Since this consensus was congruent with the interests of those in power, Orientalist ideas freely permeated aesthetic, economic, historical and political texts. Orientalism became an integral part of western culture.

Already, by the eighteenth century, certain Orientalists like Abraham-Hyacinthe Anquetil-Duperron and Sir William Jones had captured contemporary imagination by introducing an exotic new world – the Orient – to the West. The eccentric Anquetil translated into French *Avesta* texts (the sacred books of Persian Zoroastrianism) and the *Upanishads* (Hindu Vedic treatises on the nature of man and the universe). His translations jolted old beliefs and revealed to Europe the existence of ancient cosmogonical traditions beyond the Mediterranean basin. Their existence forced the questioning of the Bible's uniqueness and set in motion modern biblical criticism culminating in secular interpretations of religious texts. Jones, on the other hand, was a legal scholar. He founded the Asiatic Society of Bengal in 1784, and also worked as an official of the British East India Company; he felt absolutely no conflict of interest in serving imperialism and set the pattern which later Orientalists and area studies experts emulated. 'Whereas Anquetil opened large vistas,' Said writes, 'Jones closed them down, codifying, tabulating, comparing.' (p. 77)

The British in India and Napoleon in Egypt, recognising the potential in employing Orientalists like Jones for their empire-building, linked the Orientalist intellectual tradition with outright political domination. Napoleon, after gaining his knowledge of the Orient from careful reading of Orientalist texts, set out to conquer the East in 1798. He took with him a score of scholars whose product, 23 fat volumes of Egyptology, was meant to

> . . . restore a region from its present barbarism to its former classical greatness; to instruct (for its own benefit) the Orient in the ways of the modern West; to subordinate or underplay military power in order to aggrandize the project of glorious knowledge acquired in the process of political domination of the Orient; to formulate the Orient, to give it shape, identity, definition with full recognition of its place in memory, its importance to imperial strategy, and its 'natural' role as an appendage to Europe; to dignify all the knowledge collected during colonial occupation with the title 'contribution to modern learning' when the natives had neither been consulted nor treated as anything except as pretexts for a text whose usefulness was not to the natives; to feel oneself as a European in

command, almost at will, of Oriental history, time, and geography; to institute new areas of specialization; to establish new disciplines; to divide, deploy, schematize, tabulate, index, and record everything in sight (and out of sight); to make out of every observable detail a generalization and out of every generalization an immutable law about the Oriental nature, temperament, mentality, custom, or type; and, above all, to transmute living reality into the stuff of texts, to possess (or think one possesses) actuality mainly because nothing in the Orient seems to resist one's powers ... (p.86)

Following the model set by Jones and Napoleon's academicians, nineteenth-century Orientalists translated and anthologised texts; compiled dictionaries and encyclopaedias, and developed the field of philology. They compartmentalised knowledge in order to dominate it. They also modernised their fields by secularising their studies, revising their methodology in keeping with new scientific rigour, and restructuring their thought on a new rational basis (p. 122). Silvestre de Sacy and Ernest Renan from France and Edward William Lane of Britain were the most influential of the nineteenth-century Orientalists. Said reviews and assesses their contributions.

Their work made Orientalism effective and congruent with the interests and political concerns of imperialist-oriented rulers. Old stereotypes were retained, but the updating and systematisation of data and analysis enhanced the authority of Orientalist analysis which posited eastern inferiority, western superiority, eastern decadence, western vibrance, etc. In such ways, Orientalism revived, restructured and made more timely, helped prepare the way for further imperial control of the East. Simultaneously Orientalist discourse permeated western culture, providing themes, stereotypes and even texts for figures such as Flaubert, de Nerval, Lamartine, T. E. Lawrence, Burton and Chateaubriand.

US IMPERIALISM AND THE NEW SCHOOLS OF ORIENTALISM

By 1918 cracks had begun to appear in the structures which supported Orientalism: after the war the victorious English and French faced major crises at home and abroad. The legacy of war, the Bolshevik revolution and the rise of fascism, began to shake confidence in capitalism and bourgeois democracy. Cultural and economic crises further reduced European smugness concerning their received traditions, institutions, values and mores. Orientalism, as part of the hegemonic culture, was on trial. Widespread colonial revolts, from Tunisia to India, added significantly to the indictment. And though England and France took control of the 'fertile crescent', their new mandates provoked immediate resistance. North of the crescent, the Turks ejected their would-be conquerors. Mass demonstrations in Persia in favour of constitutionalism had prevented the British from establishing a protectorate there, so they turned instead to Reza Khan and helped him consolidate his power and do their bidding. But even the pawn could not be controlled, since British power looked weak from the Persian plateau. Consequently Reza Khan tried to ally Persia with fascist Germany whose ideology closely resembled his own. By 1941 the British sent him packing, but it was already clear that nationalism could threaten imperialism.

These triple strains (expansion of the imperial system, widespread colonial revolts and internal crisis) deeply marked Orientalism in the inter-war period. In the 1920s England and France needed added trained Orientalists to serve in their new Middle East mandates: two of the best of such scholars were the Frenchman Louis Massignon (d. 1962) and the Englishman Sir Hamilton A. R. Gibb (d. 1971) whose careers were rooted in ambivalence and doubts about their own culture. This produced a degree of humility in them which their predecessors lacked, and made it possible for them to approach the 'Islamicate' humanely, with openness. Yet the inherited weight of Orientalism, which shaped them fundamentally, twisted their perceptions. Although the inter-war years produced startling cultural transformations in other fields of knowledge, Orientalism, feeling the simultaneous strains of expansion and decline, remained wedded to its stodginess and insularity.

Said chose well in singling out Massignon and Gibb to illustrate transformations in Orientalism before and after the Second World War. Their lives reflected two major poles of change – decolonisation and the rise of the American empire[3] – that marked the period. After 1945 European Orientalism declined since, without formal empire, the Orientalist had little except the scholarly function. The shift was therefore to the new US imperium. Massignon and Gibb responded differently to colonialism and decolonisation, but both contributed to shaping the new directions of change. Gibb moved to the United States and helped organise the institutional basis of US cultural imperialism, while Massignon, the maverick, joined the struggle for decolonisation and set the stage for the development of revisionism[4] in French Islamic studies.

Said is one of the rare critics to appreciate fully Massignon's genius and great literary talents. He also admits Massignon's crucial role in Orientalism and acknowledges his seminal connection to the 'French Islamology' revisionist schools represented in the work of Jacques Berque, Maxime Rodinson, Yves Lacoste and Roger Arnaldez (pp. 265–66). But Said stops there, without assessing the long-term significance of Massignon's impact on revisionism.

Massignon, as a convert from atheism to mystical Catholicism, and as a talented poet, brought to his studies and activism the zeal of a convert and the romantic idealism of a poetical mystic. They totally coloured his perceptions of the Islamicate and especially his views of his hero, Mansur al-Hallaj (d. AD 922), the sufi (mystic) martyr on whom he reflected all of his life.

There was also another side to Massignon which Said recognises, but does not fully explore. In his later years, Massignon became an outspoken critic of French colonialism. His gradual political awakening began when he established close contacts with Algerian migrant workers whom he taught in special courses, beginning in the late 1920s and 1930s. These contacts and his intense asceticism raised his social consciousness. Increasingly, he supported anti-colonial causes (such as the rights of Palestinian, Madagascan and North African nationalism, etc.) and militated for social justice. Christian non-violence led him to stage recurrent fasts in order to protest French colonial policy and violence. He wrote polemics in the popular press; on a few occasions, when he spoke in favour of Algerian independence or participated in demonstrations, the police or *pieds noirs* pummelled him.

Said questions his motives (p. 270); they were deeply religious, archaic, pro-Semitic, anti-Aryan and moral, rather than political. Therefore his understanding of events rarely coincided with the analysis of those on whose behalf he militated. But, unquestionably, he hated injustice, could not be corrupted and disdained politicians, imperial administrators and scholars who treated people as objects and pawns.[5]

In a negative sense, he perpetuated Orientalism and its prejudices through the quality of his scholarship. He was so good at what he did that, even if one disagreed with his premises, the arguments and the discourse were original. His insights and the wide range of his concerns and knowledge, combined with his personal example of activism in a society where professors were supposed to stay ensconced in their ivory towers or else serve the state, contributed to revisionism in French scholarship about the Orient. And, by standing outside of the Orientalist institutional structures and condemning official apologists who ran them, Massignon demonstrated that they and their institutions could be bypassed or rendered irrelevant by those wishing to gain knowledge of the Orient.

Jacques Berque, one of the leaders of the French cultural decolonisation movement, whom Said praises, acknowledged his debt to Massignon in the 'Foreword' to his ground-breaking book, *The Arabs* (New York, 1964) in the following way

> I could never have achieved this interpretation had I not enjoyed the benefit of that of the late Louis Massignon. That admirable *sheikh* would have recognised where I have followed him, or contradicted him, or both at once. In all these cases, I am completely in his debt. (p. 18)[6]

Said has not recognised the full significance of this revisionism. If he had drawn out of Gramsci's notion of hegemonic culture the rich consequences inherent in the concept, he might have left us with some hope for change. For Gramsci there was a dynamic relationship between culture, politics and mass organisation, and he believed that to overcome bourgeois cultural hegemony, the left had to create mass political institutions which would generate their own ideas and analysis.[7]

In the French school of revisionism, people like Berque, Vincent Monteil, Samir Amin and Abdallah Laroui, a combination of non-marxists, marxists, and *marxisants*, have developed their analysis within the framework of French and Third World educational and research institutions which have legitimised and encouraged their scholarship. As Gramsci might have predicted, the transformation in French educational institutions since at least May 1968, and the development of new research centres in Africa and the Middle East, coupled with the marked increase in the left's influence and base of support in France and some ex-French colonies has provided a fertile environment in which new schools of thought concerning the Middle East and North Africa have been able to develop and converge with innovating scholarship in sub-Saharan African, Latin American and Asian studies. The French government's quest for bilateral alliances with radical Muslim oil-producing states and their desire to demonstrate their independence of US analysis and policies, has probably made the French ruling classes amenable to the new trends. In such a setting, new ideas and analysis are emerging as alternatives to classical Orientalism.

Decolonisation and the growth of the left in western Europe is changing the nature of discourse about the Third World. Anglo-Saxon research and writing on the Middle East and North Africa has begun to reflect this new shift.[8] In the US some Middle East scholars have recently formed regional study groups organised as the American Middle East Studies Seminar (AMESS). They are concerned with (1) the involvement of professors in policy 'formulation and implementation'; (2) the sources of funding for Middle East Studies; (3) 'the structure, membership and ideological orientations of' the mainstream professional organisation, the Middle East Studies Association of North America (MESA); and (4) the narrow ideological and methodological limits of the field.[9] In addition, MERIP *Reports*, *Review of Iranian political economy and history*, *Review of Middle East Studies* and the British journal *Khamsin* present alternative analysis of the culture and political economy of the Middle East and North Africa. Nevertheless, the mainstream of the American scholarly establishment has largely remained untouched by these developments.

MIDDLE EAST SOCIAL STUDIES

As the major post-war imperial power and the major source of neo-colonial control, the US had embarked on a crash programme to train area experts. These were supposed to service and rationalise the new empire and enable the US to compete favourably with the Soviet Union in the cold war. Funds for establishing area studies came from government agencies, foundations, universities, corporations and neo-colonial rulers who benefited from their connections with the US. America's needs were immediate, and the tradition was almost non-existent. But by importing European Orientalists, US Middle East social studies was stamped with the dogmas of Orientalism which Said has summarised as follows

1 [There is an] ... absolute and systematic difference between the the West, which is rational, developed, humane, superior, and the Orient, which is aberrant, underdeveloped, inferior ...

2 abstractions about the Orient ... are always preferable to direct evidence drawn from modern Oriental realities ...

3 the Orient is eternal, uniform, and incapable of defining itself; therefore it is assumed that a highly generalised and systematic vocabulary for describing the Orient from a Western standpoint is inevitable and even scientifically 'objective.'

4 ... the Orient is at bottom something either to be feared ... or to be controlled ... (pp. 300–301)

The 'old world' scholars moved to the new centre of Orientalism. Gibb came to Harvard to head the Center for Middle East Studies. Gustave Von Grunebaum helped establish the equivalent in Los Angeles. More recently, Bernard Lewis joined Princeton's Oriental Studies Program. Much of the US empire was informal, neo-colonial, in flux and therefore did not provide a stable base on which to build programmes; the new scholars were trained to deny the existence of the very empire that they served. Training proved to be superficial and most of the experts turned out to be only reflections of the shadows of the great Orientalists of the past. US Middle East area studies has had all the faults of classical Orientalism without any of its strengths, i.e. depth, stability and language ability. Lacking the long traditions which developed under the French and British imperial systems, the methods, opinions and sources of funding of the new area specialists are unstable. As arrivistes, they lack consistency and clarity of purpose. Their lack of competency, which Binder, a past-president of MESA,[10] himself underlines[11] adds to their personal insecurity, which in turn reinforces their opportunism.

Many of them are rationalisers and justifiers of US government policies in the Middle East;[12] others cater to the neo-colonial clients of the US in Middle Eastern and North African states; in both cases they reap material rewards, and compete to sell themselves to the highest bidders.

US POLITICAL ANALYSIS ON IRAN

Iranian studies illustrates my point. Two of the best known experts who have written the basic works on contemporary Iran, Marvin Zonis of the University of Chicago and James A. Bill of the University of Texas, typify post-war Iranian studies in the US. Their work also reflects the broader trends in US Middle East Social studies. Despite their recognising, as trained students of Iranian politics, the regime's corruption and tyranny, they can still write of royalty in glowing terms. Zonis (1971):

> ... none of these interviews would have been carried out in the absence of official cooperation and royal assent. His Imperial Majesty, Mohammed Reza Shah Pahlavi, Shahnshah, made that available with speed and kingly grace. His willingness to welcome foreign scholars is both courageous and laudable.[13]

Bill (1975):

> ... Empress Farah ... is a woman of deep intelligence and is genuinely concerned for her people. After a decade of championing humanitarian causes, the empress now addresses herself to the social and political problems of Iran. In 1970 she headed 26 different groups and organizations designed to solve social problems and to alleviate human suffering ... Unlike many members of the elite who are motivated solely by political opportunism and personal ambition, Empress Farah struggles to organize programs and policies that will benefit the Iranian people as a whole.[14]

Both Bill and Zonis have also stressed the good state of the Iranian polity, economy and society under the Shah's regime. They have mostly hedged these statements with the general reminder that, of course, Iran faced major problems, but the assessment has nevertheless left a positive image about Iranian conditions under the Shah. Both displayed confidence in the Shah's commitment to 'meaningful change and reform', and sought to discredit or dismiss his critics. Bill, for example, wrote the following in 1974:

> It would be a serious mistake to underestimate the importance and effect of the Shah-sponsored reforms. It is also a mistake to question the king's commitment and dedication to these programs. His own statements and activities clearly reveal that he is well aware of the challenges of modernization, and that he has decided to make a serious effort to confront that challenge.[15]

Likewise, Zonis reached similar conclusions a year later:

> ... the monarch's control over the internal situation is at its zenith. It is undoubtedly true that no Iranian ruler however exercised as much power or commanded as responsive a political system as does Mohammed Reza Pahlavi in 1974, 'urban guerillas' and censorious foreign critics notwithstanding ... the genius of the shah and his political elite plus oil revenues and good fortune are responsible for the enviable present situation of the regime.[16]

The context in which these statements were written is important. Iranian opposition groups in the US had been organising for years against the Shah's regime to expose the Pahlavi's tyranny and corruption, influence western public opinion and weaken US support for the Shah's regime. They asked people to boycott the galas staged by the Shah to impress a gullible world; they opposed people lending their names and reputations on his behalf. Simple statements like the ones quoted above from Bill and Zonis undermined such campaigns, and contributed to the attempt in the US to discredit the Iranian opposition.

Both authors have condemned terrorism and external critics of the old regime without explaining that the armed struggle began in response to mass killings, arrests and torture. At best, they refer to the repression of 'terrorism', in tones that give their readers the impression that the Shah's police were doing a good job.[17] Nowhere in their work have they attempted to catalogue or document the systematic use of torture, or the role of SAVAK (the secret police) in kidnapping, torturing and killing. Likewise, though Bill goes as far as labelling Iran a client state of the US,[18] in line with realpolitik analysis, neither he nor Zonis systematically analyses the nature of Iranian dependency on the US and attempts to draw inferences. Sometime in late 1978, however, as the revolution appeared on the verge of victory, Zonis became overtly critical of the Shah's regime, began praising the opposition and advocated the termination of US support for the Shah.

Zonis and Bill are worthy successors to an earlier generation of cold war US scholarship. Thus the same *Professor Leonard Binder* (see p. 74), in his 1964 book *Iran*,[19] dealt with the monarchy critically and recognised some of its shortcomings. He nevertheless concluded his book with the following plea:

> ... one would like to look forward simply to the establishment of a government with which Iranians might identify themselves ... but I believe that there is more chance of achieving such a highly desirable end through the patient working of the present system than by violently overthrowing it ... It may not be encouraging for those who seek reform to hear that they ought to continue as they have, nor would I suggest that the present transitional system is the best for Iran or that corrupt government policies are the best.[20]

Professor Binder was telling the Iranian people to be patient in the face of tyranny. Fifteen years passed under that so-called 'transitional regime'. By 1979 untold thousands had died, many had disappeared, were tortured and maimed, not as a result of revolution, but because of the Shah's police state policies.

Underlying Binder's analysis are a set of suppositions that distort history. He writes (pp. 61–2):

> Here is a nation Iran that has not ruled itself in historical times, that has had an alien religion imposed upon it, that has twisted that religion in order to cheat its Arab tormenters, that can boast no military hero, that is beset by the superstitions of its dervishes, that has been deprived by its poets and mystics of all will to change its fate, a nation where no patriot is untainted by self-seeking, where every public figure is identified by the foreign power he is said to serve, and where no one speaks the truth.

His reference to Islam as an 'alien religion imposed upon' the Iranians may be in harmony with the Pahlavi dynasty's studied subversion of Islam, but in dismissing the Iranian people's most cherished heritage, it constitutes an assault on their culture. Likewise, Binder implies that Iranians have always been acted on and never have shaped their own destiny; this ahistorical statement thereby dismisses as unreal the Iranian opposition's constitutional movement which has developed since 1905. Similarly, Prime Minister Mossadegh's two-year regime

(1951–3) holds no significance for Binder. As troublesome is his anti-Arab bias when he argues that the early Arab conquerors were 'tormentors' of the Persians. We know that in the complex relations between Persians and Arabs after the Muslim conquest of Iran (Khurasan), their interests often coincided and produced harmony. Binder, however, has injected this anti-Arab bias into the distant past.

Another scholar of Iran is R. M. Savory, Professor at the University of Toronto. In recent years he has authored an *Encyclopaedia of Islam* article on Iranian history (1973)[21] as well as a 1972 assessment of Iran in the 1960s for MESA's *International Journal of Middle East Studies* (IJMES).[22] A critical examination of his scholarship will show, however, how he has misled readers by omitting crucial data. For example, the CIA's involvement in the events surrounding Mohammed Mossadegh's ousting as Prime Minister of Iran in 1953 is well known – witness the assessment made by E. A. Bayne, a former US official in Iran:

> The Central Intelligence, well equipped with funds, entered the picture in earnest and a plot began to form with General Zahedi as its executive focus … By mid-summer … the Shah issued a *firman* dismissing Mossadegh, and appointed Zahedi as Premier. Mossadegh refused to accept the order, and Iran was momentarily without effective government authority. As much to dramatize the constitutional issue as to preserve the person of the monarch – there being no heir – the Shah was advised to leave the country, which he did.[23]

Yet, unbelievably, Savory has completely omitted any mention in his encyclopaedia article of the CIA's by then well-publicised and authenticated involvement in the planning for Mossadegh's overthrow and instead blamed the Tudeh (Iranian Communist) Party for provoking a general's coup. He wrote:

> On 13 August the shah issued a *farman* dismissing Musaddik and appointing General Zahidi Prime Minister. Musaddik refused to take cognisance of the *farman*, and the shah temporarily left the country. On … 19 August 1953 Zahidi suppressed the Tudeh mobs over which Musaddik no longer had any control, and succeeded in establishing himself in Tehran.[24]

And the editors of this, the leading Orientalist encyclopaedia (Van Donzal, Lewis, Pellat) are, in approving this article, implicated in such a major omission – if only by default.

In his 1972 IJMES article, after condemning Mossadegh for being a 'dictator' and a tool of the Tudeh Party, Savory wrote:

> The Persian monarchy … in 1953 successfully resisted a far more dangerous threat – subversion by totalitarian forces. The warmth and spontaneity of the Shah's welcome by the people when he returned to Iran

on 22 August 1953 seems to have astonished many foreign observers and commentators, but should not have occasioned any surprise to the student of Persian history.[25]

And the editor of IJMES, Stanford Shaw, Professor of Ottoman history at the University of California (Los Angeles), not only published Savory's article, but also repeated its biases and claims. Shaw wrote:

> Dr Savory describes how the opposition to the Shah today, led by a segment of the Persian intelligentsia, particularly Persian students outside the country, is based largely on the same romantic views of contemporary Iran which led Mohammed Mossadiq and others in the Iranian national movement to disrupt reform and so join the opposition led by the great landowners, the *ulama*, and others who successfully frustrated reform until the Shah himself took the lead in the famous 'white revolution'. Dr Savory points out how the Shah has gained the support of the mass of the people benefiting from his reforms, particularly the peasants, and also the army and the younger civil servants.[26]

Neither of them admitted to the heroic struggle of the *ulama* against the Shah's tyranny; instead they denigrated religious figures in the same way that Binder did in the quotation above. They also failed to mention the participation of the *bazaaris* in the long struggle that preceded the revolution. Neither did they mention in a positive way the abnegation of the Iranian left in leading an armed struggle against one of the world's most repressive regimes. Rather, Savory viewed their struggle as treason against the 'best of all possible rulers', the Shah of Iran.

OLD ORIENTALISM AND NEW DIRECTIONS

This necessarily brief review of American political analysis on Iran typifies the state of Middle Eastern area studies. In comparison to the old Orientalists like Massignon and Gibb, today's area experts have little substance and vision. There are exceptions, but they only prove the general rule. The old timers were products of a clearly-defined imperial age, replete with carefully-drawn structures, lines of authority and institutions. The new products of Third World area studies in North America live in an equally intense imperial age, but one with informal structures and insecure foundations, facing challenges and revolutionary pressures. Their insecurity, opportunism and shallowness reflects the condition of contemporary imperialism.

Edward Said has clarified how Orientalists and Middle East area experts have served the empire. It now remains for others working in Middle East studies who agree with his analysis and are distressed by the condition of the field, the 'discourse', the 'hegemonic culture', to pick up the challenge and do something about it. Said tells us that we need new ways of looking at the Middle East and he calls for the application of class analysis, comparative research and global perspectives to all people living in differentiated states of change. He condemns the tendency to compartmentalise the Middle East as a world apart, in need of different categories of analysis than any other part of the world. One can only agree. There are buried treasures there for the progressive scholar, both north and south. For example, in one of his passing remarks (p. 279) Said suggests 'that the history of Islam might be more intelligible for its resistance, political and non-political, to colonialism'. Using that as an organising theme one would like to see in future issues of *Race & Class* some discussion on the insurrectionary tradition in modern Islam. The aim would be to examine dynamics *within* the Islamicate that once gave it strength, and may act as the basis for transformation in the future. Historical studies become increasingly important because progressive transformations, if they are to succeed, need to be congruent with inherited traditions. The progressive forces within Islam have always been there. The problem is to flush them out from behind the veil of Orientalist obscurity.

NOTES

1. The ideas received by the ruling classes and transmitted through control of the media, education, religious institutions etc.
2. A tradition, produced by an accumulation of texts backed up by expertise, authority, institutions, etc., which carries sufficient weight to define the substance of new texts so that individual creativity may contribute to the formation of the texts, but is not responsible for them.
3. See John Campbell, 'The Middle East: the burdens of empire', *Foreign Affairs* (vol. 57, no. 3, 1979), 613–32, for a rare admission by the former director of studies at the New York Council on Foreign Relations, of the existence and importance of the American empire.
4. The word revisionism is here used in the sense to which it is applied to the revisionist historians of the cold war, such as Kolko and Alperovitz, who sought to redress traditional right-wing bias in American historiography.
5. See Vincent Monteil, 'Introduction', in Louis Massignon, *Parole donnée* (Paris 1962), pp. 7–47.
6. Jacques Berque, *Dépossession du monde* (Paris, 1964).
7. Antonio Gramsci, *Selections from the prison notebooks*, edited and translated by Quintin Hoare and Geoffrey Nowell Smith (New York 1971), and Perry Anderson, *Considerations on western marxism* (London, 1976), pp. 30–32 and 45.
8. As indicators see Roger Owen, 'Studying Islamic history', *Journal of Interdisciplinary History* (IV, 2, Autumn, 1973), 287–90; Edmund Burke, III, 'Towards a history of the maghreb', *Middle East Studies* (vol. II, no. 3, October 1975), pp. 315–17; and Bryan Turner, *Marx and the End of Orientalism* (London, 1979). Books by Talal Asad, Peter Gran, Mahmoud Hussein and Samir Radwan represent major revisionist contributions.
9. See AMESS, *New directions in Middle East studies newsletter* (vol. I, no. 1, Winter, 1978), p. 1.
10. Of the search for new sources of funding – which raises important questions of control and influence over Middle East studies – Binder wrote bluntly '. . . temptations will be great for this is the way we make our living, build our empires, and serve our ego needs'. Leonard Binder, 'Area studies: a critical reassessment', in *The Study of the Middle East: research and scholarship in the humanities and social sciences* (New York, 1976), p. 4.

11. Ibid., pp. 5–6.
12. Ibid., pp. 1–2.
13. Marvin Zonis, *The Political elite of Iran* (Princeton, 1971), p. ix.
14. James A. Bill, 'The patterns of elite politics in Iran', in George Lenczowski (ed.), *Political elites in the Middle East* (Washington, DC, 1975), p. 24.
15. James A. Bill and Carl Leiden, *The Middle East: politics and power* (Boston, 1974), p. 143.
16. Marvin Zonis. 'The Political elite of Iran: a second stratum?' in Frank Tachau (ed.), *Political elites and political development in the Middle East* (New York, 1975), pp. 212–213.
17. Bill and Leiden, op. cit., p. 139 and Zonis in Tachau, p. 208.
18. Bill and Leiden, op. cit., p. 202
19. Leonard Binder. *Iran: political development in a changing society* (Berkeley, 1962), pp. 61–2.
20. Ibid., p. 349.
21. R. M. Savory, 'Iran: history', in E. Van Donzal, B. Lewis and Ch. Pellat (eds.), *The Encyclopaedia of Islam*. New Edition, vol IV, fasc. 61–62 (Leiden, 1973), pp. 33–43.
22. 'The principle of homeostasis considered in relation to political events in Iran in the 1960s'. *International Journal of Middle East Studies (IJMES)* (vol. 3, 1972), 282–302.
23. E. A. Bayne, *Persian kingship in transition: conversations with a monarch whose office is traditional and whose goal is modernization* (N. Y., 1968). p. 161.
24. Savory, *Encyclopaedia*, p. 41.
25. Savory, *IJMES*, p. 286.
26. Stanford Shaw, *IJMES* (vol. 3, 1972), pp. 241–42.

22

HERMENEUTICS VERSUS HISTORY

David Kopf

In 'Hermeneutics versus History', David Kopf – Professor of history at the University of Minnesota – adopts a somewhat different approach to that of Schaar, arguing that Said's account of orientalism lacks historical precision. In particular, he suggests that Said misunderstands the nature of British orientalism in India. Far from promoting a Euro-centric view, British orientalism in the early nineteenth century contributed to the modernisation of Hindu culture, the reconstruction of the Hindu religion and the emergence of an Indian national consciousness.

> Much of the personal investment in this study derives from my awareness of being an 'Oriental' as a child growing up in two British colonies. All of my education, in these colonies (Palestine and Egypt) and in the United States, has been Western, and yet that deep early awareness has persisted. In many ways my study of Orientalism has been an attempt to inventory the traces upon me, the Oriental subject, of the culture whose domination has been so powerful a factor in the life of all Orientals.[1]

With this brief but revealing personal statement, Edward Said, sympathetic spokesman of West Asian Islam and devastating critic of Western imperialism in the Orient, joins the host of members of the third world intelligentsia in search of their roots who have spoken on intercivilizational encounter. To be sure, Said, as a sophisticated and eloquent literary critic, employs the

David Kopf, 'Hermeneutics versus History', *Journal of Asian Studies*, 39, 3, 1980, pp. 495–506.

'instruments of historical, humanistic and cultural research' but 'in none of that, however,' says he, 'have I ever lost hold of the cultural reality of, the personal involvement in having been constituted as "an Oriental"'.[2]

Said's anger at having been placed, as an 'Oriental,' in the network of Western myths and illusions created out of the East, to satisfy Western psychocultural needs, is a disturbing reminder that we dare not remain oblivious to the deep-rooted problem of identity among the intelligentsia of the third world (or of minorities and women). Often, out of our own overriding concern with the materialist conception of history, we refuse to accept the reality of marginal men and women who suffer from the consequences of their unenviable role as intermediaries between their own economically less developed and exploited communities and the intrusive imperialist West.

Said's *Orientalism* seems to be of the same genre as *The Discovery of India* by Jawaharlal Nehru, the *Autobiography of an Unknown Indian* by Nirad Chaudhuri, *The Second Sex* by Simone de Beauvoir, and even *Soul On Ice* by a young Eldridge Cleaver. For the most part, these books were not intended as scholarship, but rather to express a passionate rage at having been raped and humiliated by imperialist armies, white bigots, and male chauvinists. Most books of this sort accentuate the painful ambivalence between attraction for the despised dominant culture and rejection of the author's own degrading situation. In the process of responding to the power differential that separates the world of their origins from the world of their professions, the members of an intelligentsia become polarized into two camps – xenophile and xenophobe, herodian and zealot, Westernizer and nativist. An intelligentsia is always a result of intercivilizational encounter because, as Toynbee accurately pointed out many years ago, it arises 'in any community that is attempting to solve the problem of adapting its life to ... an exotic civilization to which it has been forcibly annexed or freely converted.'[3] I should add, in light of Said's monolithic treatment of Orientalism, that representatives of the colonial elite also develop their own ambivalence about, and polarized response to, subordinate Oriental cultures. At first I was puzzled by Said's failure to treat the bitter 1830s conflict – known historiographically as the Orientalist-Anglicist controversy – among the British in India over cultural attitudes and policies, for it had revolutionary consequences that shaped the cultural self-image of the Hindu intelligentsia.

Sooner or later, many writers from subordinated cultures or groups sublimate their rage into ideologies of restructuring or revitalizing their own ignored cultures. Elise Boulding, for example, opens *The Underside of History* by lashing out at William McNeil with righteous indignation for having mentioned women twice in a thousand pages of his *Rise of the West*, then offers what is to my knowledge the first world history of women.[4] Nehru's marvelously fresh vision of the Indian past, a gem of renaissance historical writing published as *The Discovery of India*, was written while Nehru was serving a jail sentence as a nationalist, and was dedicated 'to my colleagues and co-prisoners in the Ahmadnagar Fort Prison camp.' This is not to say that either Boulding or Nehru lacks bitterness and rage; but unlike Said, neither merely indulges in a dialectic of 'them and us.' Nehru the nationalist and politician would have agreed with many of Said's conclusions about the destructive impact of the West. But Nehru was also a builder of a new Asia, and not simply a destroyer of myths and illusions: 'Politics and elections were day-to-day affairs when we grew excited over trumpery matters. But if we were going to build the house of India's future, strong and secure and beautiful, we would have to dig deep for the foundations.'[5]

This is where Said's concept of Orientalism ought to be contrasted with the term as it was understood by the intelligentsia of other Asian societies, including India. Such a contrast reveals major differences. Nehru and other Indian writers were in fact impressed with the Orientalists they knew of, whose contributions they used freely as building blocks in their own reconstruction of history. It seems equally true from discussions with colleagues in China and Japan scholarship that Said's notion of Orientalism does not necessarily fit the historical situation in those areas, either. Said's most amply documented scholarship deals with Islamic Orientalism in West Asia (Eurocentrically referred to in the book as the 'Middle East'). About Islam in Pakistan, India, modern Bangladesh, Malaysia, Indonesia, or even Turkey, we learn next to nothing; nor does Said claim to focus much attention on these areas.

The problem, however, is not simply one of overgeneralizing from a limited area of study. Unfortunately, Said is not really talking about Orientalism as it existed in concrete historical reality: as an ideology, a movement, and a set of social institutions. For him it is an idea, a construct, almost always sinister, with its own 'history and a tradition of thought, imagery, and vocabulary.' It is a discourse, à la Michel Foucault. Said writes: 'Indeed, my real argument is that Orientalism is – and does not simply represent – a considerable dimension of modern political-intellectual culture, and as such has less to do with the Orient than it does with our world.'[6] Though the definition is broad and the promised undertaking ambitious; though the book is rich in biographical details of eminent Western imperialists; and though it does probe deeply into the consciousness of the imperialist mentality, *Orientalism* lacks historical precision, comprehensiveness, and subtlety. It is not unique among the writings of Asian intellectuals groping for a grand synthesis of East and West in order to resolve their identity crises. For example, the Bengali reformer Keshub Chandra Sen exposed the myths and illusions of Western imperialism, militarism, and nationalism in the 1870s, and proceeded to found the New Dispensation, a universal religion which he hoped would end what he regarded as the absurd sectarian differences between East and West. Rabindranath Tagore, Asia's first Nobel Prize winner in literature (1913), wrote one of the most devastating attacks in the English language on the sources of Western nationalism (1915), and then went on to establish Visva Bharati University (1921), an institution designed to bring Western and Eastern scholars together for the purpose of harmonizing religious and philosophical differences. Said's contribution, in this sense, complements these earlier critiques of the West.

But once more – and I cannot stress this enough – there are vast differences in approach and in program between Said and the renaissant Indian intelligentsia. The Bengali intellectual Rammohun Roy, for example, invented the notion of the Oriental Christ, a person whose nature, he believed, had been distorted by 'idolatrous' medieval Europeans. Protap Chandra Mazumdar, who helped to organize the first World Parliament of Religions (1893), actually wrote a book on the *Oriental Christ* (1883), in which he tried to prove that Europeans had taken Jesus 'completely out of historical and cultural context.'[7] On the other hand, Rammohun and Protap Chandra were also members of the Brahmo Samaj, a Hindu socio-religious reform movement which adopted humanistic ideas and ideals from the West to revitalize their own society and culture.

Vivekananda, who established the modern Ramakrishna Mission, with its impressive social service agencies and educational programs, consistently exposed the hypocrisy underlying Western attitudes to Oriental religions like Hinduism. Over seventy years before Said's *Orientalism*, Vivekananda wrote:

> Let me tell you that neither are we 'devils,' as the missionaries tell the world we are, nor are they 'angels,' as they claim to be. The less the missionaries talk of immorality, infanticide, and the evils of the Hindu marriage system, the better for them. . . . If, foreign friends, you come with genuine sympathy to help and not to destroy, god-speed to you. But if by abuses incessantly hurled against the head of a prostrate race in season and out of season, you mean only the triumphant assertion of the moral superiority of your own nation, let me tell you plainly, if such a comparison be instituted with any amount of justice, the Hindu will be found a head and shoulders above all other nations in the world as a moral race.[8]

Vivekananda's response to the West, and the *raison d'être* for his cultural regeneration program, were always framed in defiant nationalist terms. Other members of the intelligentsia, especially Brahmos, shifted ideologically between nationalism and universalism. In 1905, during the Swadeshi movement in Bengal, the Brahmo leader Rabindranath Tagore joined other nationalists in condemning Curzon's imperialist policies and applauded the burning of English goods on the streets of Calcutta. But two years later, in his most powerful novel, *Gora*, he deplored nationalism and imperialism as two heads on the same monster created by the modern West. Throughout most of the book, the hero Gora, a violently anti-Western Hindu nationalist, lashes out at all the malicious falsehoods and stereotypes fabricated by Europeans – rather as Said does. Then, in the final pages, after burying himself deeper and deeper in Hindu militancy, Gora learns from the man he had believed to be his father that he is not genetically a Hindu after all, but the son of an Irishman killed in the Indian

Mutiny. (Gora in Bengali means 'fair skinned.') His first response placed him in the limbo of an ambiguous identity: 'The foundations upon which from childhood all his life had been raised had suddenly crumbled into dust . . . He had no mother, no father, no country, no nationality, no lineage, no God even . . .'[9] But the book ends with a transformation, as Gora begins to accept the wider identity of universal humanism. He says: 'Today I am free . . . today I am really an Indian. In me there is no longer any opposition between Hindu, Muslim, and Christian. Today every caste in India is my caste, the food of all is my food.'[10]

In light of this expression of Tagore's own increasing need to accept the wider identity of universal humanism, the following passage at the very end of Said's book is most interesting:

> . . . we should remember that the study of man in society is based on concrete human history and experience, not on donnish abstractions, or in obscure laws or arbitrary systems. . . . The goal of Orientalizing the Orient again and again is to be avoided, with consequences that cannot help but refine knowledge and reduce the scholar's conceit. Without 'the Orient' there would be scholars, critics, intellectuals, human beings, for whom the racial, ethnic, and national distinctions were less important than the common enterprise of promoting human community.[11]

If this is indeed where Said's quest for identity is taking him, then his contemptuous treatment of Western nonsense about the non-West has a positive and hopeful purpose. If we can somehow overlook his unfortunate choice of the term 'Orientalism' to represent a sewer category for all the intellectual rubbish Westerners have exercised in the global marketplace of ideas, then surely the book has considerable merit. Indeed, Said's provocative style may be the only effective way to demonstrate that a persisting and pervasive inability to see Asian civilizations without racial bias and cultural distortion is as much a result of the grandiose paradigms created by sophisticated Western scholars and thinkers as of Western images of 'Asiaticks' found in newspapers and films.

The causal relation between the rise of mass journalism and Rudyard Kipling's popularity is well known. Said's critique of Karl Marx's 'Oriental' mode of production, though not original, is highly effective in assaulting influential non knowledge about Asiatick political economy.[12] Nor do the methodologies of social scientists necessarily transcend the limitations of the older dismal stereotypes of Orientals. Said is quite right, I believe, in accusing Max Weber and a host of other sociologists and anthropologists of perpetuating the myth 'that there was a sort of ontological difference between Eastern and Western economic (as well as religious) "mentalities."'[13] Said also delves into the neglected question of the alleged dichotomy between Oriental and Western sexuality. Says Said: 'Why the Orient seems still to suggest not only fecundity but sexual promise (and threat), untiring sensuality, unlimited desire, deep generative energies, is something on which one could speculate. . . .'[14] Without belaboring the point, anyone trying to teach Asian history to American students in a reasonably objective way – as part of human history – knows that he or she must face a welter of distorted ideas about the East.

My most serious reservation about Said's book, one to which I have already alluded, is that by making Orientalism the villian of the play, Said has confused key issues by distorting historical reality. The reader should be warned that this is not a work of historical scholarship. Though it is fashionable in some quarters to equate textual analysis with historical writing (a new moment of Eurocentricism), historians know that there is no substitute for the hard work of discovering and ordering the data of past human experience. Perhaps Said tried to include too long a span of years in such a brief book. Telescoping historical periods with hasty descriptions is always misleading. I do not mean to be naive when I say that a primary responsibility of the historian is to allow the past to speak for itself. I do not mean to imply that we should refrain from analyzing past events, nor do I mean to suggest that it is always possible to reconstruct the past as it was. Yet Said's procedure of dropping names, dates, and anecdotes to support a method which is profoundly structural and synchronic is diametrically opposed to history.

Orientalism as history exists and has existed outside of Said's personal conception of it. Historical Orientalism had a concrete reality, was complex, internally diverse, changed over time, and was never monolithic. It was quite independent of Said's 'discourse'; its focus and expression varied with time and with place. It was certainly not a unified set of propositions, universally accepted by all Westerners involved in Oriental administration and scholarship, whose progressive refinement was inseparable from the Western powers' gradual acquisition of much of the world's real estate.

What was historical Orientalism? Let us take the case of India. Not only was modern Orientalism born in Calcutta in 1784, with the establishment of the Asiatic Society of Bengal, but Indian cultural policy was conducted from 1772 to 1830 by a civil service elite known historiographically as the British Orientalists. No one would deny Said's contention that Orientalism was politically motivated and was an outgrowth of the British colonialist experience. Governor-General Warren Hastings, who started Orientalist activities in India and established the Asiatic Society, would have agreed with Said on this point. But Hastings articulated another purpose to justify the Society: 'Every accumulation of knowledge and especially such as is obtained by social communication with the people over whom we exercise a dominion founded on the right of conquest, is useful to the state: it is the gain of humanity.'[15]

The British Orientalists in India constituted a definite group of acculturated civil, military, and judicial officials (and some missionaries) created by Hastings in the 1770s as part of a new administrative and cultural policy. Hastings's purpose was to combat the cultural arrogance and general incompetence of Company officials who had served in India from the time of Clive (1750s) by inculcating a new set of values. Hastings aimed at establishing an Orientalized service elite competent in Indian languages and responsive to Indian traditions.

By the time the Asiatic Society of Bengal was founded and the eminent William Jones was chosen as its first president, Hastings's vision of an acculturated service elite had to some extent been realized. Britishers in South Asia were acquiring a curiosity about the whole range and substance of what has subsequently been called Indian civilization. There is little doubt that this transformation played a major role in reshaping the self-image of later civil servants by making them increasingly conscious of their professional and civic responsibilities.

I first encountered British Orientalism in India when, in the late 1950s, I began seriously researching the origins of the Bengal, Hindu, or Indian cultural renaissance. 'Renaissance' has referred to, among other things, Bengal's contribution to a modernized India, the earliest modernization of a vernacular language and literature, the emergence of a historical consciousness, the search for a new identity in the modern world, and the reconstruction of Hindu tradition to suit modern needs. 'Renaissance' has also been identified with social reform and religious reformation, cultural and political nationalism, asceticism and the spirit of capitalism, and with such intellectual currents as rationalism, scientism, and secularism.

When I sought the origins of the Bengal Renaissance twenty years ago, the most troubling paradox I had to confront was how an Indian modernistic movement could possibly be nurtured by, or flourish under, Western colonialism. I am sure Said would also question this. How could India achieve any lasting benefits from a foreign ruler who deprived it of political and economic autonomy? I discovered, much to my amazement, the contrary proposition that the Bengal Renaissance and Indian national awakening would have been inconceivable without the British colonial experience. The Bengal Renaissance emerged from the encounter with representatives of the dominant British elite. Now, after having studied comparable movements in Asia, Africa, and the United States, I am convinced that the social process of renaissance constitutes a new sense of identity among representatives of an exploited ethnic group, religious community, culture, or sex; and that the new consciousness emerges as a salvationist ideology among the intelligentsia of the penalized group, who act as brokers or intermediaries to representatives of the dominant or colonialist power.

It is almost a truism to declare that the great majority of nations in the world today owe their existence to liberation struggles against foreign tyranny and oppression. From the birth of a German national awakening against Napoleonic rule early in the nineteenth century to the subsequent multiple struggles in Europe and the third world, the process has been repeated. As American black advocates and feminists know all too clearly, the tyranny of dominance can go on for centuries without change. Movements dedicated to human rights or national awakening are not inevitable, and are certainly not possible without a very decisive change in the consciousness of those who suffer. Exploitation and

the awareness of being exploited are two different things: creating this awareness is often called 'consciousness raising.' And consciousness raising is precisely what the Bengal Renaissance and other renaissances are fundamentally
about. The educated few become aware of their disadvantage in the context of
Western dominance or of the dominance of whites or males, invent ideological
blueprints to revitalize their communities, and form associations and institutions to rid their cultures of abuses and shortcomings. If successful, renaissances
provide new sociocultural relationships, institutions, and values which are in
harmony with the requirements and functions of modernism.

Because renaissances are transformations of existing cultural patterns, particular traditions become modernized rather than Westernized. This process,
which is as subtle as it is complex, has been greatly misunderstood by observers
who mistakenly equate modernization with Westernization. Guy Métraux, in
the introduction to a volume of readings on *The New Asia*, had this to say about
this dubious equation:

> When Asian countries 'adopted' Western techniques and ideas, they did
> not entirely relinquish their ways. There was superimposition of institu-
> tions, various forms of syncretism, new attitudes arising side by side with
> ancient modes of thought. But whatever the fullness of change that took
> place or its pace, Asian societies have created, or are creating a way of life
> that enables them to participate fully in a modern world community.[16]

When I accepted this position, I could no longer feel comfortable with the
Westernized historiography of the Bengal Renaissance. The Westernizing
historians tended to ignore the Asiatic Society of Bengal and the College of
Fort William as institutions promoting cultural change because both were
Orientalist in inspiration. Instead, such historians emphasized the contribution
of Anglophile individuals and associations. It is not uncommon, for example, to
trace the genesis of the Bengal Renaissance to Derozio at Hindu College and
the Young Bengal movement; to Macaulay and his famous Minute of 1835;
to Bentinck, alleged hero of social reform; and to Alexander Duff, ardent
Westernizing missionary. Even the image of Rammohun Roy was reshaped to
make him appear an advocate of English language, education, and philosophy.
Many historians remained oblivious to the fact that Rammohun made use of
Orientalist scholarship, personally accessible to him, to rethink the Vedanta
and Hindu philosophical tradition. I still find it disconcerting that many
researchers have ignored connections between the Hindu modernizing efforts
of Debendranath, Keshub, Dayanand, Vivekananda, Rabindranath, and
Gandhi, on the one hand, and early Orientalist scholarship on the other.

British Orientalism gave birth to the Bengal Renaissance because it helped
Indians to find an indigenous identity in the modern world. This was obviously
not the intent of colonialists like Hastings, or like Wellesley, who founded the
College of Fort William in 1800. Their purpose was to convert an expatriate
class of Company officials into an Indianized, linguistically competent service

elite who would be increasingly effective in their professional and public responsibilities. Without Orientalist cultural policy, we would not have had the significant contributions to the fields of Indian philology, archeology, and history of such eminent scholars as William Jones, H. T. Colebrooke, Charles Wilkins, H. H. Wilson, and James Prinsep. But even more important was the Orientalist gift to the Bengal Renaissance and to Indian national awakening. Nirad Chaudhuri, though overstating the case with his customary excess, did see this gift clearly when he wrote:

> Historically, European oriental research rendered a service to Indian and Asiatic nationalities which no native could ever have given. ... The resuscitation of their past fired the imagination of the Hindus and made them conscious of a heritage of their very own which they could pit not only against the Muslims but also against that of the more virile English. Psychologically, the Indian people crossed the line which divides primitive peoples from civilized peoples.[17]

Though Orientalists were, at first, primarily concerned with the classical tradition, in the course of the nineteenth century they did provide Hindus with a systematic chronological view of their own past for the first time. Texts, heroes, and institutions were no longer relegated to the oblivion of sacred timelessness, but were given places in the annals of recorded civilization. That the Vedas were the scriptures of the Aryans, and that the Upanishads preceded the Vedanta were the discoveries of the British Orientalists. The knowledge that Buddha was once a human being as well as Sankara, that the Mauryas ruled a vast empire, and that classical civilization reached its peak under the Guptas were also significant accomplishments of Orientalist scholarship. The work of integrating a vast collection of myths, beliefs, rituals, and laws into a coherent religion, and of shaping an amorphous heritage into a rational faith known now as "Hinduism" were endeavors initiated by Orientalists. Though we are inclined to take for granted the herculean achievements of past generations, we should consider Nirad Chaudhuri's comment on pre-Orientalist Hinduism:

> In the eighteenth century, on the eve of the establishment of British rule, the Hindus had no recollection of their real past, nor any idea of the true character of the classical Sanscritic civilization. Their Hinduism was a broken-up and simplefied version of the Hinduism of ancient India. It was unorganized in space and unsupported in time. Its quality was neutral where it was not purely negative.[18]

The British Orientalist influence on the Bengal Renaissance was not simply academic or intellectual; it was also very practical. Because these men were primarily public officials rather than scholars, they went far beyond deliberating on history, philology, or archaeology at the Asiatic Society. They were men of social action working to modernize Hindu culture from within. Though Westernizers have repeatedly applauded the victory of Macaulay over the

Orientalists in 1835 as a starting point for the idea of progress in India, the facts speak otherwise. The Orientalist impact on Indian modernity was as creative as it was various:

> The Orientalists bear little resemblance to the dismal image that has been theirs since the Victorian era. The Orientalists served as avenues linking the regional elite with the dynamic civilization of contemporary Europe. They contributed to the formation of a new Indian middle class and assisted in the professionalization of the Bengali intelligentsia. They started schools, systematized languages, brought printing and publishing to India, and encouraged the proliferation of books, journals, newspapers, and other media of communication. Their output was urban and secular. They built the first modern scientific laboratories in India and taught European medicine. They were neither static classicists nor averse to the idea of progress; and they both historicized the Indian past and stimulated a consciousness of history in the Indian intellectual. ...[19]

In the 1830s, the Orientalists found their modernizing program challenged by an alternative cultural policy advocated by such dedicated Westernizers as Thomas B. Macaulay. Known as the Anglicists because they repudiated all Oriental languages in favor of English as the intellectual, commercial, and administrative lingua franca for India, these Britishers were as contemptuous of Asian religions and cultures as they were of the Orientalists who defended them. Curiously enough, the early generations of Anglicists were liberal on domestic issues in Great Britain, but conservative in their intolerance for all things Oriental. It is also curious to me that Said completely ignores this very group of proto-imperialists who were anti-Orientalist. It is *their* ideology and not that of the Orientalists which Said reviews in his work.

Take, for example, Charles Grant, civil servant and later East India Company official who opposed the Orientalism of Warren Hastings. He believed that Indian civilization was barbaric because its religion was degrading, and that it was both dangerous and a violation of the Christian spirit even to tolerate such a culture. In 1804, he denounced the College of Fort William, established four years earlier to serve as an Orientalist training center for civil servants. He feared that the kind of flirtation with Orientalism encouraged under Warren Hastings and the College of Fort William might lead to the 'Indianization' of British youth. They might undergo an 'assimilation to Eastern opinions' instead of 'retaining all the distinctions of our national principles, characters and usages.'[20]

Parliament reviewed the Charter of the East India Company in 1813, and debated whether missionaries should be allowed to preach the gospel in India. The Evangelical party, which defended the right of missionaries to preach freely among Hindus and Muslims, was consistently anti-Orientalist, or anti-Oriental, or both. Typical of the Evangelicals was William Wilberforce, who was a member of at least seventy philanthropic organizations primarily devoted to fighting moral corruption in England. In June 1813, in his famous speech before Parliament on the missionary question, Wilberforce argued that: 'The Hindu divinities were absolute monsters of lust, injustice, wickedness, and cruelty. In short, their religious system is one grand abomination.'[21]

In 1819, the year that James Mill was hired as Assistant Examiner of Correspondence at the India House, his *History of British India* first became available in India. Though this book had enormous influence in shaping precisely the images of the Orient Said writes about, Said makes no mention of it. Mill was anti-Orientalist and anti-Oriental. He attacked Voltaire and other *philosophes* for their 'silly, sentimental' infatuation with Oriental despotism, and dared to deflate the exalted image of William Jones in England.[22] But Orientalists in India questioned Mill's qualifications to write a history of India. Mill had never been to India, knew no Indian languages, and had relied on secondary sources to support his sweeping generalizations. If Said wishes to know where the low esteem of Orientals indeed originated, he should look to passages such as the following by Mill:

> Even in manners, and in the leading parts of the moral character, the lines of resemblance (between Indians and Chinese) are strong. Both nations are to nearly an equal degree tainted with the vices of insincerity; dissembling, treacherous, mendacious, to an excess which surpasses even the unusual measure of uncultivated society. Both are disposed to excessive exaggeration with regard to everything related to themselves. Both are cowardly and unfeeling. Both are to the highest degree conceited of themselves, and full of affected contempt for others. Both are in a physical sense, disgustingly unclean in their persons and houses.[23]

Gradually, the Westernizers got the upper hand in directing cultural policy in India. In 1835, Governor-General Bentinck's support of Macaulay's Minute on Education signalled the end of official patronage for Orientalism. There is one single reference to Macaulay's Minute in Said, but not in the historical context of the Anglicist-Orientalist controversy.

In his Minute, Macaulay ridiculed the Indian vernaculars as 'poor and rude.'[24] Oriental classical languages seemed especially inferior to Macaulay, since 'a single shelf of a good European library was worth the whole native literature of India and Arabia.'[25] Besides insulting South Asians themselves with such remarks, Macaulay angered the Orientalists, who had devoted decades of hard work to modernizing Indian languages. The part of the Minute which angered the Asians most is the often-quoted passage:

> It is I believe no exaggeration to say, that all the historical information which has been collected to form all the books written in the Sanskrit language is less valuable than what may be found in the most paltry abridgements used at preparatory schools in England. In every branch of physical or social philosophy, the relative position of the nations is nearly the same.[26]

What was the Orientalist response? When W. H. Macnaughten heard that Bentinck had supported Macaulay, he sent a vigorous reply to the Governor-General on behalf of the Orientalists. He began by questioning the qualifications of the men who were responsible for the resolution. 'I have heard gentlemen,' he wrote, 'who confessing without any pretensions to Oriental erudition, are in the habit of declaring their belief that the cherished Literature of one hundred millions of people is an unmixed mess of falsehood and absurdity.' He went on to say that 'if we wish to enlighten the great mass of the people of India we must use as our instruments the Languages of India ... our object is to impart ideas, not words. ...'[27] H. H. Wilson, then at Oxford University, and one of the greatest Orientalists along with William Jones and Max Müller, responded:

> Neither Lord William, nor Mr. Trevelyan know what they are doing ... Upon its [Sanskrit's] cultivation depends the means of native dialects to embody European learning and science. It is a visionary absurdity to think of making English the language of India. It should be extensively studied, no doubt, but the improvement of the native dialects enriching them with Sanskrit terms for English ideas must be continued and to effect this, Sanskrit must be cultivated as well as English.[28]

Between 1829 and 1835, the effects of Bentinck's support of Macaulayism greatly reduced the dynamism generated by two generations of Orientalist institutional growth and development. Under Bentinck's administration, the College of Fort William was dismantled, the Asiatic Society experienced grave financial difficulties, the Calcutta Madrassa and Sanskrit College came precariously close to extinction, the Calcutta School and School Book Societies were rendered impotent, and Serampore College anglicized its curriculum and so lost its attractiveness to Indians.[29]

Macaulayism had the immediate impact of splitting the loyalties of the Hindu intelligentsia into two opposite camps. Calcutta intellectuals, who for decades had responded sympathetically to the culture of the European (as they were themselves bolstered by Indian ideas), now faced new assumptions: that patterns of reform meant Westernization, and that Oriental civilizations were static and worthless. The intelligentsia were compelled to confront a crisis of identity. The Young Bengal movement drifted into a cultural limbo between their heritage, which they repudiated, and the English Utopia across the seas, to which they could never belong. Most of the intelligentsia, however, responded to the crisis by identifying with the Orientalist-reconstructed image of Hinduism, which they romanticized as apologists.

Because Said never explored, in the context of intercivilizational encounter between the Europeans and the Asian intelligentsia, issues like those examined above, he has misunderstood the nature and function of Orientalism – certainly in South Asia. Orientalism was the polar opposite of Eurocentric imperialism as viewed by the Asians themselves. Though the British Orientalist movement died during the Bentinck administration, its primary contribution of a revitalized Hindu cultural tradition and historical past lived on in the self-image of the South Asian intelligentsia. If Orientalism was merely the equivalent of imperialism, then how do we account for the increasingly nostalgic view of the Orientalists nurtured by later generations of Hindu intelligentsia? On 6 January 1862, for example, Girish Chandra Ghose, a leading Calcutta journalist, wrote:

> There are those among us who look upon this state of things [the growing feeling of Anglo-Saxon racial superiority among the British] with surprise. They call to mind the generation of Englishmen who, in past years, walked among our fathers without betraying the least symptoms of hatred. . . . They call to mind . . . Jones, Colebrooke, Wilson . . . and ask how it is that the successors of such men be so unsympathetic.
>
> As regards Indian literature . . . history, antiquities, the present race of Anglo-Indians [the British in India] . . . are lamentably ignorant. . . . Jones, Colebrooke, Wilson . . . respected our fathers and looked upon us hopefully at least with melancholy interest, as you would look on the heir of a ruined noble. But to the great unwashed abroad today, we are simply niggers – without a past, perhaps, without a future. They do not choose to know us.[30]

NOTES

1. Edward W. Said, *Orientalism* (New York: Pantheon Books, 1978), p. 25.
2. Ibid.
3. Arnold Toynbee, 'The Disintegration of Civilizations,' *A Study of History* (1939; rpt. New York: Oxford Univ. Press, 1962), 5: 154.
4. Elise Boulding, *The Underside of History* (Boulder, Colo.: Westview Press, 1976), p. 4.
5. Jawaharlal Nehru, *The Discovery of India* (1946; rpt. New York: Anchor Books, 1960), p. 28.
6. Said, p. 12.
7. P. D. Mazumdar, *The Oriental Christ* (Boston: George H. Ellis, 1883), p. 18.
8. Swami Vivekananda, quoted in D. Kopf, *British Orientalism and the Bengal Renaissance* (Berkeley: Univ. of California Press, 1969), p. 128.
9. Rabindranath Tagore, quoted in D. Kopf, *The Brahmo Samaj and the Shaping of the Modern Indian Mind* (Princeton: Princeton Univ. Press, 1979), p. 297.
10. Ibid.
11. Said, pp. 327–28.
12. Ibid., p. 153.
13. Ibid., p. 259.
14. Ibid., p. 188.
15. Letter from Hastings to N. Smith, 4 October 1784, quoted in S. K. Das, *Bangla Gadyasahityer Itihas* (Calcutta: Mitralay, 1963), p. 52.
16. Guy S. Métraux, 'Preface,' *The New Asia: Readings in the History of Mankind*, ed. Métraux (New York: New American Library, 1965), p. x.
17. Chaudhuri, quoted in Kopf, *British Orientalism*, p. 12.
18. Ibid.
19. Ibid., p. 275.

20. Extract from Public Letter to Bengal, 23 May 1798, quoted in Ainslie T. Embree, *Charles Grant and British Rule in India* (New York: Columbia Univ. Press, 1962), p. 190.
21. Great Britain, *Hansard's Parliamentary Debates* 26 (22 June 1813): 164.
22. See Kopf, *British Orientalism*, pp. 236–41.
23. James Mill, *History of British India*, 4th ed. (London: James Madden and Co., 1840), 2: 135.
24. Minute by Macaulay, quoted in Kopf, *British Orientalism*, p. 248.
25. Ibid., p. 249.
26. Ibid., p. 248.
27. Macnaughton, quoted in ibid., p. 250.
28. Wilson, quoted in ibid., p. 242.
29. Ibid., p. 241.
30. 'They Hate Us Youth,' in M. M. Ghose ed., *Selections from the Writings of Girish Chandra Ghose* (Calcutta: India Daily News Press, 1912), p. 434.

23

ENOUGH SAID

Michael Richardson

In 'Enough Said', Michael Richardson, an anthropologist attached to the School of Oriental and African Studies, London, finds Said's interpretation of orientalism 'manifestly idealist'. Moreover, in judging the work of the orientalist, Said may be accused of engaging in a power relationship similar to the one he accuses the orientalists of constructing. In denying the possibility of reciprocity between subject and object, Said effectively makes it impossible for the object to develop alternative models – an impossible conclusion.

In the past decade the question of representation in anthropological discourse has become a central theme, given particular focus by the debate associated with the volume *Writing Culture*.[1] This debate has tended to be limited to the actual process of writing ethnographies, something that has deflected debate away from a more general consideration of the perceptual framework of the ethnographic encounter and the way in which anthropological images are created and sustained.

The more general context of representation has been raised by Edward Said's controversial study *Orientalism*,[2] in which a consideration of how the West has conceptualized the Near East is used for a more general analysis of the way in which representation has been used by European consciousness in relation to its 'Other'. His central concern appears to have been to examine the consequences

Michael Richardson, 'Enough Said', *Anthropology Today*, 6, 4, August 1990, pp. 16–19.

that follow from what he gives early in the book as a definition of Orientalism as 'a Western style for dominating, restructuring and having authority over the Orient'.[3] As a Palestinian working within the Western intellectual tradition (he had published two books of literary criticism before *Orientalism* in 1978) he feels a personal stake in these issues, and he writes with a passion and urgency which give to his book some vitality and which have helped it to be widely influential.

Anthropological images of the Orient are largely absent from Said's account. It would, however, be naive to believe that anthropology is, or can be, exempted from the wider implications of his critique. Indeed, since anthropology is founded on a methodological separation between self and other, it could be said that anthropology would deny its own legitimacy if it were to accept the basis of Said's argument, even though some anthropologists, notably Ronald Inden,[4] have tried to revise their own work to take account of the implications that Said's study raises for anthropology. The success of such endeavours is open to question. It would today, more than a decade after publication of the original work, perhaps be more fruitful to question Said's own methodological assumptions and try to consider the extent to which his critique advances our understanding of the way in which we establish images and representations of other people, thereby enabling us to conceive the relationship between ourselves and the 'Other' in different terms, and to what extent it simply adds one more level of mystification to what is already a difficult terrain to survey. Does his critique do any more, in other words, than address itself to European masochism and guilt?

Said's approach is manifestly idealist. Situating his critique in the realm of ideas divorced from concrete relations of living, he is able to present us with a very convincing argument against the deleterious effects of a particular way of perceiving the Orient. Said insists that such perception was false; it was created in the European mind almost without reference to what the Orient was really like. One of Said's disciples, Christopher Miller, places the issue squarely in these terms: ... perception is determined by Orientalism rather than Orientalism being determined by perception.'[5] This statement, an idealist statement par excellence, sums up accurately, I believe, the impulse underlying not only Said's own approach, but also those who have followed him. It emphasizes the extent to which the 'real' Orient was irrelevant to the thrust of the movement to create a composite fictional character for the Orient. The images constituting this character were the products of who knows what perversity of mind (and Said shows curiously little interest in understanding *why* such images were created, beyond making a banal equation with imperialism) and are completely devoid of reality: 'The exteriority of the representation is always governed by some version of the truism that if the Orient could represent itself, it would; since it cannot, the representation does the job, for the West, and faute de mieux, for the poor Orient. "Sie können sich nicht vertreten, sie müssen vertreten werden", as Marx wrote ...'.[6] This passage is highly significant in relation to the work as a whole and we will return to consider it in more detail. For now we will look at some of the implications that arise from the apparent 'fictionality' of the Oriental construct.

The problem that arises here is that if such representations are false then there has at least to be the possibility of a representation that is 'true'. Towards the end of the book, Said appears to recognize this problem. He writes: 'I would not have written a book of this sort if I did not believe that there is a scholarship that is not as corrupt, or at least as blind to human reality, as the kind I have been mainly depicting'.[7] He is even able to give us an example: 'the anthropology of Clifford Geertz, whose interest in Islam is discrete and concrete enough to be animated by the specific societies and problems studied and not by the rituals, preconceptions, and doctrines of Orientalism'.[8] Yet, five years later, we find that the work of Geertz has been miraculously transformed into being simply 'standard disciplinary rationalizations and self-congratulatory clichés ...'.[9] We are given no indication of what might have caused this extraordinary transformation.

That Said feels under no compunction to justify his change of opinion here is indicative of his methodological approach. As he felt no necessity to explain what it was specifically that made the work of Geertz admirable in the first place so, it appears, he is not called upon to explain a radical change of opinion. In 1978 he had been seeking to place himself within 'Western' discourse, almost in the role of a radical reformer. By 1983, he is clearly seeking to orient his critique differently, seeking to find a place within a 'space' of anti-imperialist studies, in which the work of Geertz does not fit. This much is apparent in his article 'Orientalism Revisited?' in which he plays down the originality of his own study, to place it in a line of anti-colonialist writers who seem to have nothing but this, and the fact that Said approves them, in common.[10] What he is keen to establish is a catch-all critique providing the means to dispose of what he finds objectionable and to praise whatever he approves. This is exactly the power relation that he accuses the Orientalists of constructing in relation to the Orient. Unlike the Orient itself, however, contemporary Orientalists have the power to answer back, and not surprisingly they have not hesitated to do so. Said's pathetic response to some of these counterblasts indicates the weakness of his position, which he is incapable of defending, except by constantly shifting his ground.[11]

The more substantial question raised (or, one could equally argue, hidden) by Said's critique is the nature of reciprocity between subject and object. In this respect the extent that Said has adequately represented what the Orientalists themselves have said is largely irrelevant. His argument rather stands or falls on his denial of such a reciprocal relationship. Orientalism was imposed upon the Orient: it was a European project, more or less consciously elaborated, in which Orientalists were nothing but passive pawns. Whether or not Orientalist representations were accurate or not thereby becomes somewhat irrelevant.

The problem here is that if reciprocity between subject and object is impossible then, by the same token, the object cannot challenge the subject by developing alternative models. In fact, since the object has no real existence, being only a conceptualization of the subject's mind, it can never be a question of the former acting upon the latter. However, this just will not do, as Said has to recognize in the conclusion to his book, since to leave the matter there would be to freeze the relation in empty space. There could be no way of ever changing it. The only way out of the impasse is for the subject to develop representations of the object that would represent the object more faithfully. Given the extent of Said's critique, however, it is difficult to see how this can ever possibly occur. The best that can be achieved is that the representation should concur with Said's own understanding. But then by what right can Said stand as a representative of the Orient? He is consequently forced into a position that relies on precisely the same discourse that he is criticizing. Whether or not the 'Orientalists' are guilty of the central charge that Said makes against them, of believing that the Orient 'cannot represent itself, it must be represented' (and it cannot be said that he proves his case on this point) it would certainly appear that Said himself believes it; indeed such a belief is inscribed at the heart of his project. Furthermore, his own critique relies on just as much mis-representation of Orientalists as he accuses them of making in their representa-tions of the Orient. In Said's terms, in fact, his own conceptualization of 'Orientalists' is as pure an example of 'Orientalism' as one could wish for!

At this point, a consideration of the relation of reciprocity to representation is called for. We have already noted the use made by Said of Marx's phrase 'they cannot represent themselves; they must be represented'. This phrase is also used as an epigraph to the book and is clearly one of its central themes. Yet if we refer to the context in which Marx himself made this comment, we find that the implications for Marx are radically different from those that Said seeks to establish. Given the importance this phrase has for Said it is perhaps useful here to give the context of Marx's own argument.

Marx was considering not the Orient but the peasantry. He was concerned with understanding a concrete historical context: the failure of the revolution of 1848 and in this specific quotation he was looking at the relation of the peasantry to the Bonapartist party. He wrote: 'Insofar as these small peasant proprietors are merely connected on a local basis, and the identity of their interests fails to produce a feeling of community, national links, or a political organization, they do not form a class. They are therefore incapable of asserting their class interests in their own name, whether through a parliament or through a convention. They cannot represent themselves; they must be represented. Their representative must appear simultaneously as their master, as an author-ity over them, an unrestricted government power that protects them from the other classes and sends them rain and sunshine from above'.[12] If there are implications in this for the Orienttalist debate, they are certainly not the ones that Said himself takes up. What will be immediately apparent here is that for

Marx this relation is *dynamic*: the peasantry are not acted upon but rather actively seek such representation and use it for their own purposes. The relation between the Bonapartist party and the conservative peasantry is thus reciprocal: they need each other. It goes without saying that the idealist conclusion that Said draws here 'if the Orient could represent itself, it would; since it cannot, the representation does the job ...' would be wholly foreign to Marx. Indeed it reveals a curious naivety on the part of Said as to how people actually perceive images. Does he really believe that anyone actually thinks that images of the Orient are commensurate with what the Orient is actually like? Indeed it is arguable that it is only academic literary critics (whose work is by definition concerned primarily with representation) who would mistake a representation for the thing it represented.

Said would, however, wish to extend such a critique further to dissolve the subject/object relation altogether, something that is not unique to him but is rather a post-modernist stance. It certainly cuts to the heart of the anthropological project, since a relation of self to other is fundamental in anthropology and it is difficult to see how anthropology can possibly take form unless it engages with the complex dialectical relation between distanciation and familiarity that the subject/object relation implies. If at its root this relation is unable to entertain the possibility of reciprocity, then anthropology must resign itself to producing images that bear no relation to the object of study. Worse, such images could only function ideologically and involve falsification in a power context.

However, in this context Said fails to justify, or even argue, the presupposition that enables him to establish the monolithic nature of the object of his study: the European subject that has created Orientalism. What is the nature of this subject: Where did it originate? And how and why? Such 'willed, human work' as he calls it can hardly be born from empty space. Given the nature of his critique, it would seem incumbent upon him to at least address these issues. The fact that he does not do so emphasizes even more the 'Orientalist' nature of his own project: Orientalism is a given to be analysed; as such it becomes Said's own 'Other'. Thus, within his own work, the self/other relation remains intact.

Even if we allow for the possibility of the dissolving of the self/other relation, it must still be asked whether this can be done except by means of a tautological sleight of hand. He has certainly not taken on board the philosophical underpinning of this relation, which is contained in Hegel's anthropology and most notably in his treatment of the relation of master and slave,[13] for in Hegel's terms what is fundamental is reciprocity. In fact, it is more than reciprocal, it is symbiotic: the reality of the slave is the master; the reality of the master is the slave. Neither are free agents: each needs the other to complete his relation to the world. But this separation is also necessary for any sort of lucidity; without it undifferentiation and entropy take over. But in Hegel's terms, the differentiation between master and slave is, at root, illusory: it is the interplay of the relation, not its fixity, that is of importance. In Hegel's terms, then, Orientalism could be changed only by the Orient itself acting upon the relation. The Orient would have to recognize itself, something that Said refuses to accept. However, if the relation remains static then Orientalism will not, indeed cannot, change its ideological character. In this respect a critique such as Said's, acting solely on the form by which the subject master asserts its ascendancy, can change only the form and not the substance of such domination. Indeed it must become subsumed within the dominant subject; it must of necessity become part of the dominating ideology. In this respect Simon Leys was not merely being malicious when he wrote acidly: '*Orientalism* could obviously have been written by no one but a Palestinian scholar with a huge chip on his shoulder and a very dim understanding of the European academic tradition'.[14]

The deleterious consequences that Said's critique can have can be shown by a consideration of Johannes Fabian's *Time and the Other*.[15] Fabian takes up Said's critique almost wholesale and tries to apply it directly to the anthropological discipline as a whole. Virtually all of the reservations we have made concerning Said could be applied equally to *Time and the Other*, except that Fabian has made the critique even more vague by focusing not upon a definable group of people that could be called Orientalists but by taking up the question of how a perceptual category (time) and a particular sense (sight) have been utilized ideologically by the West, particularly in anthropology, against its Other.

As with Said there would be much value in such a critique if it focused on the ideological aspects involved in this relation. Unfortunately, again like Said, Fabian displaces the ideological aspects to locate the critique in the methodological categories themselves. This again conflates representation with the essence of what it represents and refuses to countenance the possibility that people are capable of making such a distinction. The weakness is especially evident in his treatment of time. Fabian writes as though historians, for instance, believe that time and history are the same thing, something that only a very naive historian would believe. Historical methodology, indeed, is acutely aware of the fact that history is a construction made *through* time and can never be commensurate with it. But what is curious here is the determination Fabian displays in seeking to establish a duality between an accursed Western idea of linear time and the 'Other's' cyclical concept. In philosophical terms this distinction is not a new one, going back to Vico and before. What is new is the virulent quality that now attaches to linear time itself rather than the perception of it. Yet though people may perceive time in different ways, the fact is that the defining characteristic of time is that it passes. This passing must necessarily occur in a linear way and the procedure ought surely not to be to make a linear/cyclical dichotomy but to understand how linear and cyclical qualities of time respond to each other. In the West it is true that ideologically a conception of the linear time has been established to provide a basis for Western hegemony. Again, however, this needs to be considered in its concrete historical circumstances, not detached from those circumstances and presented as though the concept of linear time itself was responsible for such distortion.

This argument can be developed more forcibly still if we consider Fabian's critique of the visual, which assumes almost apocalyptic proportions; and perhaps we may give an appropriately puritan response: 'If thine eye offend thee, pluck it out'. Having enumerated what he sees as the evil consequences of a hierarchy of the senses which places vision at the top, he is unable to think outside this framework, but rather emphasizes it so that vision gains an almost Luciferian quality. No matter: like a man confronted on the path by a cobra but prepared against all eventualities, Fabian has a mongoose in his knapsack in the shape of sound which he invokes for its 'dependable' qualities against the iniquitous vision. Insofar as he places such trust in the sense of hearing, however, it seems strange that he should use the visual form of a book to argue his point: to be consistent with his argument one would have thought he should have issued his critique on audio cassette. What does not seem to occur to Fabian is that the separation of the senses in this way is characteristic of the Cartesian thinking that he is supposedly criticizing. It is not that sight is in some way a hegemonic sense; if it has taken such a form it is because it has been isolated intellectually in Western discourse. In this respect again Fabian simply confounds his own supposed argument and shows how far it is rooted in the very discourse it is purportedly criticizing. Addressing a different, but contiguous, question, Eric Wolf has written: '... instead of assuming transgenerational continuity, institutional stability, and normative consensus, we must treat these as problems. We need to understand such characteristics historically to note the conditions for their emergence, maintenance, and abrogation. Rather than thinking of social alignments as self-determining, moreover, we need – from the start of our enquiries – to visualize them in their multiple external conditions'.[16] This is doubtless too much trouble for someone like Fabian, who prefers to establish spurious oppositions (coevalness vs allochronism; orality vs visualism) that deflect such questions.

Both Said and Fabian are, of course, part of the groundswell of contemporary criticism that takes refuge in the so-called 'post-modern condition', founded in a dubious Nietzschean subjectivism. Said dutifully quotes Nietzsche in defining truth as a 'mobile army of metaphors', but refuses to recognize the problematic that Nietzsche himself recognized in such a definition. How rarely do we hear Nietzsche's own corollary to this statement: 'The falseness of a judgement is to us not an objection to a judgement; it is here perhaps that our language sounds strangest. The question is to what extent it is life-advancing, life-preserving, species-preserving, perhaps even species-breeding. ...'[17] Furthermore, Nietzsche recognized that truth and falsehood existed in dialogic relation to each other. If one accepts that truth is nothing but a 'mobile army of metaphors' then one must, as Nietzsche recognized, establish a centring position that enables the relative value of a particular 'lie' to be qualitativized. Both Said and Fabian, in common with post-modernism in general, fall into the trap of all subjectivism and conflate general and specific critiques in a way that de-legitimizes both. The direction of the 'deconstructive' impulse in contemporary criticism is not negation but rather its subversion, to the extent that genuine negation becomes impossible.

In his *La Conquête de l'Amérique*, Tzvetan Todorov has attempted a critique that has some similarities with Said's, but in the opposite direction. He has considered the conquest of Mexico not in the terms we know so well, in which the double violence (Aztec and Spaniard) still has power to shock, but in terms of human sympathy: '"To ignore history", as the adage goes, is to risk repeating it, but it is not through knowing history that we know what to do. We are both like and not like the Conquistadores; their example is instructive, but we can never be sure that we would *not* behave like them, or that we are not in the process of imitating them as we adapt to new circumstances. But their history can be exemplary for us because it allows us to reflect on ourselves, to discover resemblances: once more the knowledge of self passes through that of the other'.[18] It is surely in this affirmation that anthropology ought to base itself. In considering one of the Conquistadores, Cabeza de Vaca, Todorov notes that he had 'reached equally a neutral point, not because he was indifferent to the two cultures, but because he was able to experience both internally; for him there was no longer a "they" around him. Without becoming an Indian, he had ceased to be completely Spanish'.[19] This flow of an individual between cultures constitutes the ambivalence of the anthropological experience, a relation that is never simple and never easy. But within this relation a dialogue is possible between cultures in which, as Todorov suggests, 'no-one has the last word, where none of the voices reduces the other to a simple object and in which neither takes advantage of his exteriority in relation to the other'.[20] But it is also the reality of the Western conquest that has established the possibility for such dialogue and communication. It is in the recognition of this fact that anthropological knowledge needs to be founded.

For anthropology, the critiques of Said and Fabian bring attention to our need to remain alert to our own social context. In addition to the usually assigned moral requirements towards the society one is studying, one also needs to be aware both of the institutional framework in which one is working and also of one's subservience to one's own culture. This is so no matter how strong the affinity anthropologists may feel with the people studied: if it weren't they would not return to write up their ethnographies. While we need to be aware also of the danger of turning the 'Other' into an ill-defined universal, we need at the same time to be conscious of the contrary danger of relativizing the 'Other' to the extent that the context of the ethnographic encounter in time and space is lost, and both observer and observed are reduced to a common denominator in which it becomes increasingly difficult to extricate one from the other.

In this context the very real problems of representation that undoubtedly need to be addressed are in danger of being subsumed by following the spurious direction in which Said has led the debate. Perception is not determined by Orientalism, or by anything else. It is of course true that our perceptions of the part of the world we have named as the Orient are conditioned by the representations that scholars and artists have established of that part of the world. We need to understand how such representations have functioned in practice and in this respect Said has provided some valuable raw material for a genuine consideration of what he convinces is a specific ideological construction that can be called 'Orientalism'. Such an ideology has determined nothing, however, and it is surely a dangerous illusion to believe that it ever has done.

NOTES

This is a substantially revised version of an article that appeared originally in French in GRADHIVA 5 (1988) under the title 'Orientalisme et négritude. De la réciprocity en anthropologie'.

1. Clifford, James & George E. Marcus. 1986. *Writing Culture: the poetics and politics of ethnography.* Berkeley: U. of California P.
2. Said, Edward, W. 1978 *Orientalism.* New York: Pantheon, This book was published as a Penguin paperback in 1985 and has been or will be translated into French, German, Arabic, Dutch, Polish, Turkish, Japanese, Serbo-Croat, Catalan, Portuguese, Iranian, Italian, Spanish and Greek.
3. *Orientalism,* p. 3.
4. Inden, Robert. 1986 Orientalist Constructions of India. *Modern Asian Studies.* 20(3) p. 401/46.
5. Miller, Christopher. 1985. *Blank Darkness: Africanist Discourse in French.* Chicago: U. of Chicago P. p. 15
6. *Orientalism,* p. 21.
7. *ibid.,* p. 326.
8. *ibid.,* p. 326.
9. Said, Edward W. 1985. 'Orientalism Revisited' in *Europe and its Other* (ed. F. Barker) (1985) Colchester: U. of Essex.
10. see *ibid.,* p. 214/5.
11. see for example Said's response to Bernard Lewis in the *New York Review of Books* 12 August 1982.
12. Marx, *Eighteenth Brumaire of Louis Bonaparte* in *Selected Works,* p. 122.
13. Hegel, *Phenomenology of the Spirit* p. 111/19 (1977) OUP.
14. Leys, Simon. 1988. *The Burning Forest.* London: Paladin p. 96.
15. Fabian, Johannes. 1983. *Time and the Other: How anthropology makes its Object.* New York: Columbia U. P.
16. Wolf, Eric. 1982. *Europe and the People Without History.* Berkeley: U. of California P., p. 387.
17. Nietzsche *Beyond Good and Evil* p. 17 (1975) Harmondsworth: Penguin.
18. Todorov, Tzvetan. 1982. *La Conquête de l'Amérique: La question de l'autre.* Paris: Seuil p. 257/8.
19. *ibid.,* p. 253.
20. *ibid.,* p. 253.

24

ORIENTALISM AND
ORIENTALISM IN REVERSE

Sadik Jalal al-'Azm

In part I of his review article 'Orientalism and Orientalism in Reverse', Sadik Jalal al-'Azm – a student of Arab culture, educated at Yale – notes Said's tendency to essentialise the occident, in much the same way that he accuses the orientalists of essentialising the orient; his frequent inclination to display a 'strong and unwarranted general anti-scientific bias'; and his fascination with verbal, textual and linguistic forms. In part II he suggests that Said's method might equally well be applied to the Arab discourse about the West which, in his view, shows signs of a sort of 'orientalism in reverse'.

PART I. ORIENTALISM

In his sharply debated book,[1] Edward Said introduces us to the subject of 'Orientalism' through a broadly historical perspective which situates Europe's interest in the Orient within the context of the general historical expansion of modern bourgeois Europe outside its traditional confines and at the expense of the rest of the world in the form of its subjugation, pillage, and exploitation. In this sense Orientalism may be seen as a complex and growing phenomenon deriving from the overall historical trend of modern European expansion and involving: a whole set of progressively expanding institutions, a created and cumulative body of theory and practice, a suitable ideological superstructure with an apparatus of complicated assumptions, beliefs, images,

---

Sadik Jalal al-'Azm, 'Orientalism and Orientalism in Reverse', *Khamsin*, 8, 1981, pp. 5–26.

literary productions, and rationalisations (not to mention the underlying foundation of commercial, economic and strategic vital interests). I shall call this phenomenon *Institutional Orientalism*.

Edward Said also deals with orientalism in the more restricted sense of a developing tradition of disciplined learning whose main function is to 'scientifically research' the Orient. Naturally, this *Cultural-Academic Orientalism* makes all the usual pious claims about its 'disinterested pursuit of the truth' concerning the Orient, and its efforts to apply impartial scientific methods and value-free techniques in studying the peoples, cultures, religions, and languages of the Orient. The bulk of Edward's book is not unexpectedly devoted to Cultural-Academic Orientalism in an attempt to expose the ties which wed it to Institutional Orientalism.

In this way Said deflates the self-righteous claims of Cultural-Academic Orientalism to such traits as scholarly independence, scientific detachment, political objectivity etc. It should be made clear, however, that the author at no point seeks to belittle the genuine scholarly achievements, scientific discoveries, and creative contributions made by orientalists and orientalism over the years, particularly at the technical level of accomplishment.[2] His main concern is to convey the message that the overall image of the Orient constructed by Cultural-Academic Orientalism, from the viewpoint of its own technical achievements and scientific contributions to the field, is shot through and through with racist assumptions, barely camouflaged mercenary interests, reductionistic explanations and anti-human prejudices. It can easily be shown that this image, when properly scrutinised, can hardly be the product of genuinely objective scientific investigation and detached scholarly discipline.

Critique of Orientalism

One of the most vicious aspects of this image, as carefully pointed out by Said, is the deep rooted belief – shared by Cultural-Academic and Institutional Orientalism – that a fundamental ontological difference exists between the essential natures of the Orient and Occident, to the decisive advantage of the latter. Western societies, cultures, languages and mentalities are supposed to be essentially and inherently superior to the Eastern ones. In Edward Said's words, 'the essense of Orientalism is the ineradicable distinction between Western superiority and Oriental inferiority ...'[3] According to this reading of Said's initial thesis, Orientalism (both in its institutional and cultural-academic forms) can hardly be said to have existed, as a structured phenomenon and organised movement, prior to the rise, consolidation and expansion of modern bourgeois Europe. Accordingly, the author at one point dates the rise of Academic Orientalism with the European Renaissance.[4] But unfortunately the stylist and polemicist in Edward Said very often runs away with the systematic thinker. As a result he does not consistently adhere to the above approach either in dating the phenomenon of Orientalism or in interpreting its historical origins and ascent.

In an act of retrospective historical projection we find Said tracing the origins of Orientalism all the way back to Homer, Aeschylus, Euripides and Dante.[5] In other words, Orientalism is not really a thoroughly modern phenomenon, as we thought earlier, but is the natural product of an ancient and almost irresistible European bent of mind to misrepresent the realities of other cultures, peoples, and their languages, in favour of Occidental self-affirmation, domination and ascendency. Here the author seems to be saying that the 'European mind', from Homer to Karl Marx and A. H. R. Gibb, is inherently bent on distorting all human realities other than its own and for the sake of its own aggrandisement.

It seems to me that this manner of construing the origins of Orientalism simply lends strength to the essentialistic categories of 'Orient' and 'Occident', representing the ineradicable distinction between East and West, which Edward's book is ostensibly set on demolishing. Similarly, it lends the ontological distinction of Europe versus Asia, so characteristic of Orientalism, the kind of credibility and respectability normally associated with continuity, persistence, pervasiveness and distant historical roots. This sort of credibility and respectability is, of course, misplaced and undeserved. For Orientalism, like so many other characteristically modern European phenomena and movements (notably nationalism), is a genuinely recent creation – the product of modern European history – seeking to acquire legitimacy, credibility and support by claiming ancient roots and classical origins for itself. Certainly Homer, Euripides, Dante, St. Thomas and all the other authorities that one may care to mention held the more or less standard distorted views prevalent in their milieu about other cultures and peoples. However, it is equally certain that the two forms of Orientalism built their relatively modern repertoires of systematic conventional wisdom by calling upon the views and biases of such prestigious figures as well as by drawing on ancient myth, legend, imagery, folklore and plain prejudice. Although much of this is well documented (directly and indirectly) in Said's book, still his work remains dominated by a unilinear conception of 'Orientalism' as somehow flowing straight through from Homer to Grunebaum. Furthermore, this unilinear, almost essentialistic, presentation of the origins and development of Orientalism renders a great disservice to the vital concerns of Edward's book, namely, preparing the ground for approaching the difficult question of 'how one can study other cultures and peoples from a libertarian, or nonrepressive and nonmanipulative, perspective,'[6] and for eliminating, in the name of a common humanity, both 'Orient' and 'Occident' as ontological categories and classificatory concepts bearing the marks of racial superiority and inferiority. It seems to me that as a logical consequence of Said's tendency to view the origins and development of Orientalism in terms of such unilinear constancy, the task of combating and transcending its essentialistic categories, in the name of this common humanity, is made all the more difficult.

Another important result of this approach bears on Said's interpretation of the relationship supposedly holding between Cultural-Academic Orientalism as representation and disciplined learning on the one hand, and Institutional

Orientalism as expansionary movement and socio-economic force on the other. In other words, when Said is leaning heavily on his unilinear conception of 'Orientalism' he produces a picture which says that this cultural apparatus known as 'Orientalism' is the real source of the West's political interest in the Orient, ie, that it is the real source of modern Institutional Orientalism. Thus, for him European and later on American political interest in the Orient was really created by the sort of Western cultural tradition known as Orientalism.[7] Furthermore, according to one of his renderings, Orientalism is a distribution of the awareness that the world is made up of two unequal halves – Orient and Occident – into aesthetic, scholarly, economic, sociological, historical and philosophical texts. This awareness not only created a whole series of Occidental 'interests' (political, economic, strategic etc) in the Orient, but also helped to maintain them.[8] Hence for Said the relationship between Academic Orientalism as a cultural apparatus and Institutional Orientalism as economic interest and political force is seen in terms of a *'preposterous* transition' from 'a merely textual apprehension, formulation or definition of the Orient to the putting of all this into practice in the Orient ...'[9] According to this interpretation Said's phrase 'Orientalism overrode the Orient'[10] could mean only that the Institutional Orientalism which invaded and subjugated the East was really the legitimate child and product of that other kind of Orientalism, so intrinsic, it seems, to the minds, texts, aesthetics, representations, lore and imagery of Westerners as far back as Homer, Aeschylus and Euripides! To understand properly the subjugation of the East in modern times, Said keeps referring us back to earlier times when the Orient was no more than an awareness, a word, a representation, a piece of learning to the Occident:[11]

> What we must reckon with is a large and slow process of appropriation by which Europe, or the European awareness of the Orient, transformed itself from being textual and contemplative into being administrative, economic, and even military.[12]

Therefore Edward Said sees the 'Suez Canal idea' much more as 'the logical conclusion of Orientalist thought and effort'[13] than as the result of Franco-British imperial interests and rivalries (although he does not ignore the latter).

One cannot escape the impression that for Said somehow the emergence of such observers, administrators and invaders of the Orient as Napoleon, Cromer and Balfour was made inevitable by 'Orientalism' and that the political orientations, careers and ambitions of these figures are better understood by reference to d'Herbelot and Dante than to more immediately relevant and mundane interests. Accordingly, it is hardly surprising to see Said, when touching on the role of the European Powers in deciding the history of the Near Orient in the early twentieth century, select for prominent notice the 'peculiar, epistemological framework through which the Powers saw the Orient',[14] which was built by the long tradition of Orientalism. He then affirms that the Powers acted on the Orient the way they did because of that peculiar epistemological framework. Presumably, had the long tradition of Cultural-Academic Orientalism fashioned a less peculiar, more sympathetic and truthful epistemological framework, then the Powers would have acted on the Orient more charitably and viewed it in a more favourable light!

Raw Reality and Its Representations

When Said is thinking and writing along these lines, it is hard to escape the strong impression that for him representations, images, words, metaphors, idioms, styles, universes of discourse, political ambiances, cultural sensitivities, highly mediated pieces of knowledge, extremely rarefied truths are, if not the very stuff of reality, then certainly much more important and informative substitutes for raw reality itself. If Academic Orientalism transmutes the reality of the Orient into the stuff of texts (as he says on page 86), then it would seem that Said sublimates the earthly realities of the Occident's interaction with the Orient into the etherial stuff of the spirit. One detects, therefore, a strong and unwarranted general anti-scientific bias in his book. This fact comes out most clearly in his constant inveighing against Cultural-Academic Orientalism for having categorised, classified, tabulated, codified, indexed, schematised, reduced, dissected the Orient (and hence for having distorted its reality and disfigured its particular mode of being) as if such operations were somehow evil in themselves and unfit for the proper understanding of human societies, cultures, languages etc.

Yet Said himself admits readily that it is impossible for a culture, be it Eastern or Western or South American, to grasp much about the reality of another, alien culture without resort to categorisation, classification, schematisation and reduction with the necessarily accompanying distortions and misrepresentations. If, as Said insists, the unfamiliar, exotic and alien is always apprehended, domesticated, assimilated and represented in terms of the already familiar, then such distortions and misrepresentations become inevitable. For Said:

> ... cultures have always been inclined to impose complete transformations on other cultures, receiving these other cultures not as they are but as, for the benefit of the receiver, they ought to be.[15]

He even finds 'nothing especially controversial or reprehensible' about the domestication of an exotic and alien culture in the terms of reference of another culture, because 'such domestications of the exotic take place between all cultures, certainly between all men.'[16] In fact Said elevates this to a general principle which emanates from 'the nature of the human mind' and which invariably governs the dynamics of the reception of one culture by another. Thus, 'all cultures impose corrections upon raw reality, changing it from free-floating objects into units of knowledge', because 'it is perfectly natural for the human mind to resist the assault on it of untreated strangeness'.[17]

In fact, at one point Said goes so far as to deny entirely the possibility of attaining 'objective truth' about other cultures, especially if they seem exotic, alien and strange. The only means for approaching and receiving them are those of reduction, representation and schematisation with all the attending distortions and falsifications which such operations imply and impose. According to Said:

> ... the real issue is whether indeed there can be a true representation of anything, or whether any and all representations, because they *are* representations, are embedded first in the language and then in the culture, institutions, and political ambience of the representer. If the latter alternative is the correct one (as I believe it is), then we must be prepared to accept the fact that a representation is *eo ipso* implicated, intertwined, embedded, interwoven with a great many other things besides the 'truth', which is itself a representation.[18]

If, as the author keeps repeating (by way of censure and castigation), the Orient studied by Orientalism is no more than an image and a representation in the mind and culture of the Occident (the representer in this case) then it is also true that the Occident in doing so is behaving perfectly naturally and in accordance with the general rule – as stated by Said himself – governing the dynamics of the reception of one culture by another. Accordingly the Occident in trying to deal (via its Orientalism) with the raw reality of the Orient does what all cultures do under the circumstances, namely:

1 domesticate the alien and represent it through its own familiar terms and frames of reference;
2 impose on the Orient those 'complete transformations' which Edward Said says cultures are prone to effect on each other so as to receive the strange, not as it is but as it ought to be, for the benefit of the receiver;
3 impose upon the raw reality of the Orient the necessary corrections needed to change it 'from free-floating objects into units of knowledge'; and
4 follow the natural bent of the human mind in resisting 'the assault on it of untreated strangeness'.

The Representation of Islam by the West

One of the examples given by Said is of particular interest:

> The reception of Islam in the West is a perfect case in point, and has been admirably studied by Norman Daniel. One constraint acting upon Christian thinkers who tried to understand Islam was an analogical one; since Christ is the basis of Christian faith, it was assumed – quite incorrectly – that Mohammed was to Islam as Christ was to Christianity. Hence the polemic name 'Mohammedanism' given to Islam, and the automatic epithet 'imposter' applied to Mohammed. Out of such and many other misconceptions 'there formed a circle which was never broken by imaginative exteriorisation ... The Christian concept of Islam was integral and self-sufficient'; Islam became an image – the word is Daniel's but it seems

to me to have remarkable implications for Orientalism in general – whose function was not so much to represent Islam in itself as to represent it for the medieval Christian.[19]

The significance of the above argument lies in the fact that Said nowhere carries it to its logical conclusion in the light of what he had stated to be generally true about the reductive dynamics of the reception of one culture by another. As he knows very well, the reception of Christianity by Islam in the East differs little from the account given above. To make this point I shall present the gist of the above quoted passage with the following alterations:

> One constraint acting upon Muslim thinkers who tried to understand Christianity was an analogical one; since Mohammed was no more than the Messenger of God it was assumed – quite incorrectly – that Christ was to Christianity as Mohammed was to Islam, namely, a plain Messenger of God or ordinary prophet. Hence the polemics against His incarnation, sonship, divinity, crucifixion, resurrection, and the automatic epithet of 'forgers' applied to the first guardians of the Holy Scriptures. Out of such and many other conceptions 'there formed a circle which was never broken by imaginative exteriorisation ... the Muslim concept of Christianity was integral and self-sufficient.' Christianity became an image – the word is Daniel's but it seems to me to have remarkable implications for how one culture receives another in general – whose function was not so much to represent Christianity in itself as to represent it for the medieval Muslim.

In the light of these critical remarks it should become clear: (a) why Said deals so harshly with Marx's attempts to understand and interpret Oriental societies; (b) why he deals so much more kindly with the Macdonald-Gibb view of Islam; and (c) why he deals so charitably and sympathetically with the mystico-theosophical extrapolations bred by Massignon's brand of Orientalism.

Said criticises and exposes the falsity of the sort of declarative assertions made by the Macdonald-Gibb variety of Orientalism about Islam and the Muslims. He attacks them for being abstract, metaphysical and untrue. Here is a sample of such assertions:

1 'It is plain, I think, and admitted that the conception of the Unseen is much more immediate and real to the Oriental than to the western peoples.'
2 'The essential difference in the Oriental mind is not credulity as to unseen things, but inability to construe a system as to seen things.'
3 'The difference in the Oriental is not essentially religiosity, but the lack of the sense of law.[20] For him, there is no immovable order of nature.'
4 'It is evident that anything is possible to the Oriental. The supernatural is so near that it may touch him at any moment.'
5 'Until recently, the ordinary Muslim citizen and cultivator had no political interests or functions, and no literature of easy access except religious

literature, had no festivals and no communal life except in connection with religion, saw little or nothing of the outside world except through religious glasses. *To him, in consequence, religion meant everything.*[21]

The trouble with such affirmations does not lie only in their falsity, abstractness and metaphysical character. Certainly neither Macdonald nor Gibb were simple victims when making these declarations of the 'epistemological framework' built by the traditions of Orientalism, as Said intimates. In fact one can argue convincingly that in a certain very significant sense:

1 it is true that in general the Unseen is much more immediate and real to the common citizens of Cairo and Damascus than it is to the present inhabitants of New York and Paris;
2 it is true that religion 'means everything' to the life of Morocan peasants in a way which must remain incomprehensible to present day American farmers;
3 it is true that the idea of an independent inviolable lawful order of nature is in many respects much more real, concrete and firmly established to the minds of the students of Moscow University than it is to the minds of the students of al-Azhar University (or any other university in the Muslim world for that matter).

What Edward fails to bring out is the fact that the affirmations of the Macdonald-Gibb brand of Orientalism are really declarative only in a very narrow sense. They masquerade as fully and genuinely declarative statements of permanent fact only to conceal a set of broad directives and instructions on how Occidentals should go about dealing with and handling the Orient and the Orientals, here and now. These directives are necessarily of a general nature and hence require a variety of 'operational definitions' to turn them into useful practical steps taken by such an assorted lot as Western missionaries, teachers, administrators, businessmen, army officers, diplomats, intelligence experts, politicians, policy-makers etc. For example, such people are guided by these implicit directives and instructions to allow for and take advantage of the fact that religious beliefs, tribal loyalties, theological explanations and so on still play a much more decisive role in the life of contemporary Oriental societies than they do in modern Western ones.

The very limitation of the declarative scope of the Macdonald-Gibb type of affirmations betrays not only their practical function and immediate relevance to actual situations, but also the profoundly ahistorical frame of mind and thought out of which they emanate. They pretend that the Unseen was always (and always will be) more immediate and real to the Orientals than to the Western peoples past, present and future. Similarly, they pretend that the idea of an independent lawful order of nature was always and will for ever be more real, concrete and firmly established to the Occidental's mind and life than it could ever be in the consciousness of Oriental human beings. The simple historical fact that at one time, say before the break-up of Christendom, the Unseen was as immediate and real to Occidentals, is not permitted to disturb the seemingly Olympian factual serenity of the Macdonald-Gibb pseudo-declaratives.

If one could speak of a hero when dealing with a book such as *Orientalism*, then Massignon emerges as the most favoured candidate for that role. This towering French Orientalist is praised for having surpassed all others in the almost impossible task of genuinely and sympathetically understanding Oriental Muslim culture, religion and mentality. Due to his profound humanism and compassion, Massignon, we are told, accomplished the feat of identifying with the 'vital forces' informing Eastern culture and of grasping its 'spiritual dimension' as no one else did before or since him in the West.[22]

But, in the final analysis, is not Massignon's presumed identification with the 'vital forces' and 'spiritual dimension' of Eastern culture simply a personalised, idealised and reiterated version of the classical Orientalist representation of an Orient 'overvalued for its pantheism, spirituality, longevity and primitivity',[23] a representation which Said has debunked so masterfully? Furthermore, we infer from the discussion of the meaning and importance of Massignon's work that he nowhere abandoned the cardinal assumption (and original sin, according to Said) of all Orientalism, namely, the insistence on the essentialistic separation of the world into two halves: an Orient and an Occident, each with its inherently different nature and traits. It is evident, then, that with Massignon, as with the work of any other Orientalist attacked by Said, Orient and Occident remain fundamental ontological categories and classificatory schemes with all their attending implications and applications.

We learn from Said's book: (a) that Massignon's Orient is completely consonant with the world of the Seven Sleepers and the Abrahamanic prayers;[24] (b) that 'his repeated efforts to understand and report on the Palestine conflict, for all their profound humanism, never really got past the quarrel between Isaac and Ishmael';[25] (c) that for him the essence of the difference between East and West is between modernity and ancient tradition;[26] (d) that in his view the Islamic Orient is always spiritual, Semitic, tribalistic, radically monotheistic and not Aryan;[27] (e) that he was widely sought after as an expert on Islamic matters by colonial administrators;[28] and (f) that he was of the conviction that it was France's obligation to associate itself with the Muslims' desire to defend their traditional culture, the rule of their dynastic life and the patrimony of believers.[29]

Now, the question to which I have no ready answer is, how can the most acute and versatile contemporary critic of Orientalism praise so highly an Orientalist who obviously subscribes to the entire apparatus of Orientalism's discredited dogmas?

Karl Marx and the Orient

The picture which emerges in Said's book concerning Marx's attitude towards the East runs more or less as follows:[30] Through his analyses of British rule in India, Marx arrived at 'the notion of an Asiatic economic system' (ie, the famous

Asiatic mode of production) which acted as the solid foundation for a sort of political rule known as 'Oriental despotism'. At first, the violent destruction and transformation of India's traditional social organisation appalled Marx and shocked him as a human being and thinker. His humanity was moved, and sympathy engaged, by the human miseries and suffering attendant upon such a process of transformation. At this stage of his development Marx still identified with downtrodden Asia and sensed some fellowship with its wretched masses. But then Marx fell under the sway of Orientalist learning, and the picture quickly changed. The labels of Orientalism, its vocabulary, abstractions and definitions came to dominate his mind and emotions.

According to Said, Marx – who initially recognised the individuality of Asia – became the captive of that formidable censor created by the vocabulary, learning and lore of Orientalism. He cites what supposedly happened to Marx's thought as an instance of how 'non-Orientalist's human engagements are dissolved [and] then usurped by Orientalist generalisations'. The initial sympathy and gush of sentiment experienced by Marx disappeared as he encountered the unshakable definitions built up by Orientalist science and supported by the Oriental lore that was supposed to be appropriate to it. Briefly, the case of Marx shows how 'an experience was dislodged by a dictionary definition'.[31]

This is how Said sees the metamorphosis which led Marx to the view (highly objectionable to Said) that Britain was making possible a real social revolution in India, by acting as the unconscious tool of history in bringing about that revolution. In this instance Britain is viewed by Marx as acting simultaneously as an agency of destruction and regeneration in Asia. Said unambiguously traces this mature view of Marx to Orientalism's pseudo-learning and fancies about the East, especially in its 19th century messianic and romantic variety. For him Marx forms no exception to all the Europeans who dealt with the East in terms of Orientalism's basic category of the inequality between East and West. Furthermore, he declares flatly that Marx's economic analyses of Asia are perfectly suited to a standard Orientalist undertaking.

I think that this account of Marx's views and analyses of highly complex historical processes and situations is a travesty. Undoubtedly, Marx, like any other creative genius, was greatly influenced by the lexicographical learning, dictionary definitions, abstractions, representations, generalisations and linguistic norms prevalent in his time and milieu. But only Said's excessive fascination with the verbal, textual and linguistic could lead him to portray Marx's mind as somehow usurped and taken over (against his better judgement and nobler sentiments) by the vocabulary, lexicography and dictionary definitions of the Orientalist tradition in the West! With Said one stands at times on the verge of regression into belief in the magical efficacy of words.

Marx's manner of analysing British rule in India in terms of an unconscious tool of history – which is making possible a real social revolution by destroying the old India and laying the foundations of a new order – cannot be ascribed under any circumstances to the usurpation of Marx's mind by conventional

Orientalistic verbiage. Marx's explanation (regardless of whether one agrees or disagrees with it) testifies to his theoretical consistency in general, and to his keen realism in analysing specific historical situations. This is evident from the fact that Marx always tended to explain historical processes in terms of social agencies, economic struggles, political movements, and great personalities which simultaneously played the role of destroyers and creators. These were often cast by him in the guise of 'unconscious tools' of a history unfolding itself in stages and sometimes in inscrutable and unpredictable ways. There is nothing specific to either Asia or the Orient in Marx's broad theoretical interpretations of the past, present and future. On this score his sources are thoroughly 'European' in reference and owe nothing to Orientalist learning. One only needs to recall those vivid passages in the *Communist Manifesto* where Marx portrays the modern European bourgeoisie in the double role of destroyer and creator: destroyer of the old inherited Europe, maker of its liberal present and usher of its proletarian future. Like the European capitalist class, British rule in India was its own grave-digger. There is nothing particularly 'Orientalistic' about this explanation. Furthermore, Marx's call for revolution in Asia is more historically realistic and promising than any noble sentiments that he could have lavished on necessarily vanishing socio-economic formations.

I shall cite another example related neither to Orientalism nor to Asia or the realm of politics. This is how Marx described the dual role of usurer's capital in the destruction of 'small-peasant and small-burgher-production' and in the making of modern industrial Europe.[32] On the one hand:

> [T]his usurer's capital impoverishes the mode of production, paralyses the productive forces instead of developing them ... It does not alter the mode of production, but attaches itself firmly to it like a parasite and makes it wretched. It sucks out its blood, enervates it and compels reproduction to proceed under ever more pitiable conditions. Hence the popular hatred against usurers ...

On the other hand:

> Usury, in contradistinction to consuming wealth, is historically important, inasmuch as it is in itself a process generating capital ... Usury is a powerful lever in developing the preconditions for industrial capital in so far as it plays the following double role, first, building up, in general, an independent money wealth alongside that of the merchant, and, secondly, appropriating the conditions of labour, that is, ruining the owners of the old conditions of labour.

Said's accusation that Marx subscribed to the basic Orientalist idea of the superiority of the West over the East seems to derive plausibility only from the ambiguity underlying his own discussion of this matter. That 19th century Europe was superior to Asia and much of the rest of the world in terms of productive capacities, social organisation, historical ascendency, military might and scientific and technological development is indisputable as a contingent historical fact. Orientalism, with its ahistorical bourgeois bent of mind, did its best to eternalise this mutable fact, to turn it into a permanent reality past, present and future. Hence Orientalism's essentialistic ontology of East and West. Marx, like anyone else, knew of the superiority of modern Europe over the Orient. But to accuse a radically historicist thinker such as Marx of turning this contingent fact into a necessary reality for all time is simply absurd. The fact that he utilised terms related to or derived from the Orientalist tradition does not turn him into a partisan of the essentialistic ontology of East and West any more than his constant use of such pejorative epithets as 'nigger' and 'Jew' (to describe foes, class enemies, despised persons, and so on) could turn him into a systematic racist and antisemite. No doubt, the typical messianic romantic vision was an essential part of Marx's historicism. But Said errs greatly in attributing this vision to the later influence of Orientalism. For the messianic and romantic aspect of Marx's interpretation of human history was with him from the beginning, and it encompassed the West long before he extended it to the East.

Orientalism and Dependency

I would like to end this section of my critique by drawing attention to a rather curious view and an enigmatic passage which occur towards the end of Said's book and right after his sharp critique of the contemporary Area Study Programmes which have come to replace the traditional departments and disciplines of Orientalism in Western universties and particularly in the United States of America. Said makes the following observation and judgement:

> The Arab World today is an intellectual, political, and cultural satellite of the United States. This is not in itself something to be lamented; the specific form of the satellite relationship, however, is.[33]

If I understand this passage correctly. Said finds the intellectual, political and cultural dependence of the Arab world on the United States quite acceptable; what he deplores is only the manner in which this dependence manifests itself at present. There are basically two standpoints from which we can view this position. The first emanates from a 'soft' and liberal interpretation of the meaning and implications of dependence; while the second flows from a 'hard' and genuinely radical understanding of the nature and consequences of this relationship.

According to the 'soft' interpretation Said seems to be: (a) simply taking note of the well-known fact of the superiority and supremacy of the United States *vis à vis* its satellites; and (b) hoping that, given greater American comprehension and appreciation of the realities of the Arab world, the lamentable aspects of the satellite relationship can be ameliorated. Such a development would greatly enhance the chances of greater political maturity, cultural independence and intellectual originality in the Arab world. In other words, the objective is not for the Arab world to shake off its dependence altogether, but to alter and improve its circumstances, terms and *modus operandi*, in the direction of a more genuinely equal and balanced relationship. As a result Said blames the United States – and not the satellite – for an unsatisfactory and deplorable condition relating to 'the specific form of the satellite relationship'. More precisely, he blames the American Middle-East experts who advise the policy-makers because neither of these two have succeeded in freeing themselves from the system of ideological fictions created by Orientalism. He even warns these experts and their masters that unless they look at the Arab world more realistically and try to understand it without the abstractions and fanciful constructions of Orientalism, America's investment in the Middle East will have no solid foundation on which to lean. He says:

> The system of ideological fictions I have been calling Orientalism has serious implications not only because it is intellectually discreditable. For the United States today is heavily invested in the Middle East, more heavily than anywhere else on earth: the Middle East experts who advise policymakers are imbued with Orientalism almost to a person. Most of this investment, appropriately enough, is built on foundations of sand, since the experts instruct policy on the basis of such marketable abstractions as political elites, modernization, and stability, most of which are simply the old Orientalist stereotypes dressed up in policy jargon, and most of which have been completely inadequate to describe what took place recently in Lebanon or earlier in the Palestinian popular resistance to Israel.[34]

All in all, Said's position here departs little from the conventional wisdom of the liberal establishments of the West in general and of the United States in particular.

The 'hard' and radical interpretation of the meaning and consequences of dependence has been developed and widely publicised by such scholars and social thinkers as Paul Baran, Andre Gunder Frank, Pierre Jalée, Claude Julien, Samir Amin and Arghiri Emmanuel. According to their account, dependence is structurally incapable of generating any sort of ties save those of the intensified exploitation, pillage and subjugation of the satellite by the centre.

According to this view, Said's vague thoughts on the subject can only foster additional illusions concerning the nature of the satellite relationship and generate dangerously false expectations about its possible implications and actual applications. The essence of the illusion lies in Said's perilous assumption that the lamentable aspects and manifestations of the satellite relationship can be satisfactorily reformed and improved to the ultimate benefit of both the Arab world and the heavy American investment in the Middle East. For the radical view of dependence holds that the satellite relationship leads to the further development of the already profound underdevelopment of the satellite itself. Hence its inevitable conclusion that salvation for the Arab world will remain an unattainable goal until the relationship of dependence is definitively and unambiguously smashed. From this also derives its inevitable criticism of Said for ending his book on a distinctly classical Orientalist note:

1 by not finding the satellite relationship between East (the Middle East) and West (America) lamentable as such;
2 by giving good advice to American policymakers and their Middle East experts on how to strengthen the basis of their investment in the area and on how to ameliorate the conditions of 'the specific satellite relationship', by ridding themselves of misleading Orientalist fictions and illusions; and
3 by forgetting that should American experts and their masters listen to his advice the Orient will find an even more formidable enemy in American imperialism than it already has.

PART II. ORIENTALISM IN REVERSE

One of the most prominent and interesting accomplishments of Said's book, as mentioned before, is its laying bare Orientalism's persistent belief that there exists a radical ontological difference between the natures of the Orient and the Occident – that is, between the essential natures of Eastern and Western societies, cultures and peoples. This ontological difference entails immediately an epistemological one which holds that the sort of conceptual instruments, scientific categories, sociological concepts, political descriptions and ideological distinctions employed to understand and deal with Western societies remain, in principle, irrelevant and inapplicable to Eastern ones. This epistemological assumption is epitomised in H. A. R. Gibb's statement to the effect that applying 'the psychology and mechanics of Western political institutions to Asian or Arab situations is pure Walt Disney.'[35] It is also shown in Bernard Lewis' declared belief that 'recourse to the language of left-wing and right-wing, progressive and conservative, and the rest of the Western terminology . . . in explaining Muslim political phenomena is about as accurate and as enlightening as an account of a cricket match by a baseball correspondent.'[36] In other words, the vast and readily discernible differences between Islamic societies and cultures on the one hand, and European ones on the other, are neither a matter of complex processes in the historical evolution of humanity nor a matter of empirical facts to be acknowledged and dealt with accordingly. They are, in addition to all that, a matter of emanations from a certain enduring Oriental (or Islamic) cultural, psychic or racial essence, as the case may be, bearing identifiable fundamental unchanging attributes. This ahistorical, anti-human and even anti-historical 'Orientalist' doctrine, I shall call *Ontological Orientalism*.

Obviously, Ontological Orientalism is thoroughly ideological and metaphysical in the most pejorative senses of these terms. Furthermore, Said spared no effort in his book to expose this fact.

Ontological Orientalism is the foundation of the image created by modern Europe of the Orient. As Said has shown, this image makes more genuine

and instructive revelations about certain European states of affairs, particularly about expansionary projects and imperial designs, than it does
about its supposed object. But nonetheless this image has left its profound
imprint on the Orient's modern and contemporary consciousness of itself.
Hence Said's important warning to the subjects and victims of Orientalism
against the dangers and temptations of applying the readily available structures, styles and ontological biases of Orientalism upon themselves and
upon others.

I would like to contend that such applications, not only did take place but are
continuing on a fairly wide scale. Furthermore, falling in the temptations
against which Said has warned engenders what may be called *Orientalism in
Reverse*.

In what follows, I shall discuss this contention in terms of a specific instance
of this reversed Orientalism, namely *Ontological* Orientalism in Reverse, as I
propose to call it.

To explain, I shall refer to two instances: the first drawn from the well-known
phenomenon of secular Arab nationalism, the second from the recent movement of Islamic revival.

Arab Nationalism and Orientalism in Reverse

A prominent man of thought and politics in Syria published about two years
ago a series of articles in which he proposed to study certain 'basic' words in
the Arabic language as a means to attaining 'genuine knowledge' of some of
the essential characteristics of the primordial 'Arab mentality' underlying
those very words.[37] Upon noting that the word for 'man' in Arabic (*insân*),
implies 'companionship', 'sociability', 'friendliness', and 'familiarity' (*anisa,
uns, anîs*, etc), he triumphantly concluded that the implicit view held by the
'primordial Arab mind' says that man has a natural tendency to live with other
men, or, as he himself explained, 'the primordial Arab mind innately possesses
the philosophical idea that man is by nature a social being.' Then our author
made the following telling comparison:

> The philosophy of Hobbes is based on his famous saying that 'every man is
> a wolf unto other men', while, on the contrary, the inner philosophy
> implicit in the word *insân* preaches that 'every man is a brother unto other
> men'.

I submit that this piece of so-called analysis and comparison contains, in a
highly condensed form, the entire apparatus of metaphysical abstractions and
ideological mystifications so characteristic of Ontological Orientalism and so
deftly and justly denounced in Said's book. The only new element is the fact that
the Orientalist essentialistic ontology has been reversed to favour one specific
people of the Orient.

It should be evident that one of the significant features of Ontological
Orientalism in Reverse is the typical Orientalist obsession with language, texts,

philology and allied subjects. It simply imitates the great Orientalist masters – a poor imitation at that – when it seeks to unravel the secrets of the primordial Arab 'mind', 'psyche' or 'character' in and through words. In other terms, it has obediently and uncritically adopted what Said pejoratively called the Orientalists' 'textual'[38] attitude to reality. In the above instance of so-called analysis and comparison that I have cited, one can easily see the panglossian and even quixotic character of the attempt to capture something about such a complex historical phenomenon as the cultural, mental and psychic life of the Arabs, past and present, by literally applying what has been learned from Orientalist books and philological analyses.

This reversed Orientalism sins doubly because it tries to capture the essence of the 'Arab mind' by learning how to analyse Arabic words and texts from the words and texts of the master Orientalists. Like a platonic work of art, its textual attitude becomes twice removed from the original reality.

Thus Orientalism in Reverse presents us with variations on Renan's racist theme as derived from his philological analyses and linguistic speculations. But the novel element is the conclusion of Orientalism in Reverse that comparative philological and linguistic studies prove the ontological superiority of the Oriental mind (the 'Arab mind' in this case) over the Occidental one. For, have we not shown that the sublime idea of the 'brotherhood of man' is innate and original to the 'primordial Arab mind,' while Hobbes' base idea of 'the war of all against all' is innate and original to the 'primordial European mind'?

In classical Orientalist fashion, the essence of the 'Arab mind' is explored by an Arab thinker through language only and in hermetic seclusion from such unwelcome intrusions as socio-economic infrastructures, politics, historical change, class conflicts, revolutions and so on. This primordial Arab 'mind', 'psyche' or 'essence', is supposed to reveal its potency, genius and distinguishing characteristics through the flux of historical events and the accidents of time, without either history or time ever biting into its intrinsic nature. Conversely, the series of events, circumstances and accidents forming the history of such a people as the Arabs can never be genuinely understood from this point of view, without reduction, through a series of mediations and steps, to the primary manifestations of the original unchanging nature of the Arab 'mind', 'psyche' or 'essence'.

Here I shall cite another example. Said points out correctly that:

> The exaggerated value heaped upon Arabic as a language permits the Orientalist to make the language equivalent to mind, society, history, and nature. For the Orientalist the language *speaks* the Arab Oriental, not vice versa.[39]

Orientalism in Reverse follows suit – not only faithfully but also more recklessly and crudely. Thus, another Syrian author wrote the following on the unique status of the Arabic language and the wonders it reveals about the 'primitivity' of the Arab and his language:

After having studied the vocal characteristics of every letter of the Arabic language I proceeded to apply their emotional and sensory connotations to the meanings of the words starting with those letters, or at times ending with them, by means of statistical tables drawn from the dictionaries of the Arabic language. After carefully examining the marvellous results yielded by this study it appeared to me that the originality of the Arabic language transcends the limits of human potentialities. I thought then, that no logical and reasonable explanation of this miracle of a language can be supplied except in terms of the category of the primitivity of the Arab and his language.[40]

The crucial conclusion of this line of reasoning runs as follows:

Thus, Arabic letters become transformed from mere vocal containers filled with human sensations and emotions to the quintessence of the Arab, of his *'asabiya*, spirit and even of the constituents of his nationality.[41]

In perfect Renanian fashion this notion of the primitivily of the Arab and his language is made to define a primary human type with its inimitable essentialistic traits out of which more specific forms of behaviour necessarily flow. This is very explicitly and roughly – hence candidly and honestly – stated by still another Syrian ideologue in the following manner: 'The essence of the Arab nation enjoys certain absolute and essential characteristics which are: theism, spiritualism, idealism, humanism and civilisationism.'[42]

Not unexpectedly it follows that this absolute essence of the Arab nation is also the implicit bearer of a civilising mission affecting the whole world. Given the decline of the West at the end of the twentieth century the Orient is supposed to rise under the leadership of the Arab nation and under the banner of its *mission civilisatrice* to guide humanity out of the state of decadence to which Western leadership has brought it. For, the 'western essence' produced such unmistakable signs of decadence as: 'mechanism, darwinism, freudianism, marxism, malthusianism, secularism, realism, positivism, existentialism, phenomenalism, pragmatism, machiavellism, liberalism and imperialism', all of which are worldly doctrines manifesting 'a purely materialist essence.'[43]

In contrast, 'The human universe' (i.e., man, humanity, the world, life, civilisation) is today awaiting its appointed encounter with 'the nation bearing that mission and chosen to lead it out of its impasse'. Furthermore: 'No matter how tragic the condition of the Arab nation may be at present there is not a shred of doubt that this nation alone is the promised and awaited one, because it alone acquired perfectly, ages ago, all the ideal constituents, characteristics and features of a nation. Accordingly, it has come to possess, in a uniquely deep-rooted manner, all the various ideal human traits, excellences and virtues which render it capable and deserving of carrying out the lofty mission for which it was chosen ...'.[44]

I turn now to the second instance illustrating what has been defined as Ontological Orientalism in Reverse.

Islamic Revivalism and Orientalism in Reverse

Under the impact of the Iranian revolutionary process, a revisionist Arab line of political thought has surfaced. Its prominent protagonists are drawn, in the main, from the ranks of the left: former radicals, excommunists, unorthodox marxists and disillusioned nationalists of one sort or another. This nebulous political line found an enthusiastic response among a number of distinguished Arab intellectuals and writers, such as the poet Adonis, the progressive thinker Anwar 'Abd al Malek and the young and talented Lebanese critic Ilias Khoury. I would add also that its partisans proved themselves quite prolific, utilising various forums in Lebanon and Western Europe to make their views, analyses and ideas known to the reading public. Their central thesis may be summarised as follows: The national salvation so eagerly sought by the Arabs since the Napoleonic occupation of Egypt is to be found neither in secular nationalism (be it radical, conservative or liberal) nor in revolutionary communism, socialism or what have you, but in a return to the authenticity of what they call 'popular political Islam'. For purposes of distinctness I shall refer to this novel approach as the *Islamanic trend*.

I do not wish to dispute the above thesis of the Islamanics in this presentation. Instead, I would like to point out that the analyses, beliefs and ideas produced by the Islamanic trend in defense of its central thesis simply reproduce the whole discredited apparatus of classical Orientalist doctrine concerning the difference between East and West, Islam and Europe. This reiteration occurs at both the ontological and epistemological levels, only reversed to favour Islam and the East in its implicit and explicit value judgements.

A prominent feature in the political literature produced by the Islamanic trend is its insistence on replacing the familiar opposition of national liberation against imperialist domination by the more reactionary opposition of East against West.[45] In the West, the historical process may be moved by economic interests, class struggles and socio-political forces. But in the East the 'prime mover' of history is Islam, according to a recent declaration by Adonis.[46]

Adonis explains himself by openly admitting that in studying Arab society and its internal struggles:

> I have attributed primacy to the ideological-religious factor because in Arab society, which is built completely on the basis of religion, the modes and means of production did not develop in a manner leading to the rise of class consciousness. The religious factor remains its prime mover. Consequently, its movement cannot be explained by means of such categories as class, class consciousness, economics, let alone economism. This means that the struggle within Arab society has been in the main of an ideological-religious nature.[47]

Adonis' sweeping conclusion is naturally enough, to 'do away with class struggle, oil and economics,'[48] in order to arrive at a proper understanding of Oriental (Muslim, Arab, Iranian) social dynamics.

In other words: ideas, beliefs, philosophical systems and ideological super-structures are sufficient to explain the 'laws of motion' of Oriental societies and cultures. Thus, an enthusiastic Islamanic announced that 'the Iranian Revolu-tion reveals to us with the greatest emphasis ... that the laws of evolution, struggle and unity in our countries and the Orient are other than and different from those of Europe and the West.'[49] A third Islamanic assured us that 'all this permits Khomeini to translate his simple Islamic ideas into a socio-political earthquake which the most perfect and sophisticated theoretical/philosophical systems failed to detonate.'[50] Accordingly, the latest advice of the Islamanics to the Arab Left is to rearrange their priorities in such a way as to stand them on their head: 'to give ultimate importance to the cultural and ideological factors which move the masses and to proceed to reformulate scientific, economic and social truths on this basis'.[51]

According to an Orientalist such as H. A. R. Gibb (and others) this stable, unique, self-identical Islamic totality regulates the detailed workings of all human, cultural, social and economic phenomena subsumed under it. Further-more, its coherence, placidity and inner strength are primarily imperilled by such foreign intrusions as class struggles, economic interests, secular nationalist movements, democratic ideas, 'Westernised' intellectuals, communist parties, etc. So, it is hardly surprising to see Adonis doing two things:

First, opposing 'nationalism, secularism, socialism, marxism, communism and capitalism'[52] à la Gibb et al., on account of the Western source of these ideas and their corrosive influence on the inner structures of Islam which keep it oriental.[53]

Secondly, interpreting the Iranian Revolution in terms of a simple emphatic formula: 'Islam is simply Islam', 'regardless and in spite of politics, the class struggle, oil and economics.' Here, Adonis is presenting as ultimate wisdom the barren tautology of Ontological Orientalism, so well brought out in Said's critique: 'The Orient is the Orient'. 'Islam is Islam'; and, following the illustrious footsteps of such Ontological Orientalists as Renan, Macdonald, Von Grunebaum and Bernard Lewis, Adonis and the other Islamanics imagine that they can comprehend its essence in isolation from the economics, sociol-ogy, oil and politics of the Islamic peoples. As a result they are anxious to secure Islam's Orientalist ontological status not only as the 'prime mover' of Islamic history, but also as the alpha and omega of the 'Islamic Orient'. In the Islamic world nothing really counts save Islam.

It is noteworthy that the favourite metaphor of the Islamanics is derived from the basically fixed, unprogressive, uninnovative cyclic movement of the oceans. Islam, they say, is once again in high tide after the low ebb of past generations and even centuries. I submit that this Islamanic view of Islam is in essence, and in the light of its logical consequences, no different from the metaphysical preachings of Ontological Orientalism. In other words, Islam is paraded before us in much the same way as H. A. R. Gibb saw it, as a monolithic unique Oriental totality ineradicably distinct in its essential nature from Europe, the West and the rest of humanity.

Thus, in classical Orientalist fashion, (reversed, however) Adonis affirms condescendingly that the peculiar characteristic of the Western essence is 'technologism and not originality'. He then proceeds to enumerate the major features distinguishing Western thought on account of that inherent trait. According to him these are: system, order, method and symmetry. On the other hand, 'the peculiarity of the Orient', for him, 'lies in originality' and this is why its nature cannot be captured except through, 'the prophetic, the visionary, the magical, the miraculous, the infinite, the inner, the beyond, the fanciful, the ecstatic' etc.[54]

Accordingly, it should come as no surprise if the revolutionary struggles and sacrifices of the Iranian people amount, in the eyes of the Islamanics, to no more than either 'a return of Islam' (the high tide metaphor) or to a manifestation of the innate Islamic opposition to non-Islamic peoples and influences (the East–West contradiction) as Bernard Lewis will have us believe.[55] Similarly, the Islamanics would seem to be in full accord with Morroe Berger's conclusion that 'for modern Islam neither capitalism nor socialism is an adequate rubric.'[56] But why? The reason, as pointed out by Said, is that according to Ontological Orientalism (both in its reversed and original versions) it really makes no sense to talk about classical, medieval or modern Islam; because Islam is always Islam. Islam can withdraw, return, be in low ebb or high tide, but not much more than that. And since so-called 'Modern Islam', according to Ontological Orientalism Reversed, is really no more than a reasserted version of the old Islam, Adonis finds no embarrassment in advising the Iranian revolution about its present and future problems in the following archaic and theological jargon.

> It is self-evident that the politics of prophecy laid the foundations for a new life and a new order. It is also self-evident that the politics of the *imâmate* or *wilâya* is correct guidance by the politics of prophecy, or rather it is the same as the politics of prophecy by inspiration and without full identification. For, every *imâmate* or *wilâya* belongs to a particular age, and every age has its particular problems. Thus, the importance of the politics of the *imâmate* and even its legitimacy lie in the extent to which it is capable of *ijtihâd* to comprehend the change of modes and the newly arising realities under the correct guidance of the politics of prophecy.[57]

Similarly, is it not this kind of conservative 'Orientalistic' logic which underlies the recent Iranian debate on whether the 'Islamic Republic' may be described as democratic? The official Islamic line, which prevailed, argued that 'Islam' can not accept any additional qualifiers since it cannot be but Islam. In other terms, just as it makes no sense to speak about classical, medieval or modern Islam – considering that Islam is always Islam – similarly, it makes no sense to talk about an Islamic republic being democratic, considering that the Islamic republic is always Islamic and cannot be anything else. Hence, Khomeini's statement in one of his many interviews about the Islamic republic: 'The term *Islam* needs no adjective, such as *democratic*, to be attributed to it ... The term *Islam* is perfect, and having to put another word right next to it is, indeed, a source of sorrow.'[58]

Ontological Orientalism in Reverse is, in the end, no less reactionary, mystifying, ahistorical and anti-human than Ontological Orientalism proper.

NOTES

1. *Orientalism*, Pantheon Books, New York, 1978.
2. Said recounts the achievements of Academic Orientalism on p96.
3. *Orientalism*, p42.
4. *Ibid*, p50.
5. *Ibid*, pp 56, 62, 68.
6. *Ibid*, p24.
7. *Ibid*, p12.
8. *Ibid*.
9. *Ibid*, p96.
10. *Ibid*.
11. *Ibid*, pp202–203.
12. *Ibid*, p210.
13. *Ibid*, p91.
14. *Ibid*, p221.
15. *Ibid*, p67.
16. *Ibid*, p60.
17. *Ibid*, p67.
18. *Ibid*, p272.
19. *Ibid*, p60.
20. In other words, a natural order governed by invariable laws.
21. *Ibid*, pp276–279. (Emphasis added by Edward Said.)
22. *Ibid*, pp265–270.
23. *Ibid*, p150.
24. *Ibid*, p267.
25. *Ibid*, p270.
26. *Ibid*, p369.
27. *Ibid*, p271.
28. *Ibid*, p210.
29. *Ibid*, p271.
30. *Ibid*, pp153–156.
31. *Ibid*, p155.
32. *Capital*, vol III, Chapter 36.
33. *Orientalism*, p322.
34. *Ibid*, p321.
35. *Ibid*, p107.
36. *Ibid*, p318.
37. Georges Saddikni, 'Man, Reason and Synonyms', *al-Ma'rifa*, Damascus, October 1978, pp7–17. Mr Saddikni was until very recently a member of the Ba'th Party's National (pan-Arab) Command and head of its Bureau for Cultural Affairs. He was Syria's Minister of Information for many years.
38. *Orientalism*, p92.
39. *Ibid*, p321.

40. Hasan Abbas, 'The Arabic Letters and the Six Senses', *al-Ma'rifa*, October, 1978, pp140–141.
41. *Ibid*, p143.
42. Isma'il 'Arafi, *Qital al-'Arab al-Qawmi*, published by the Ministry of Culture and National Guidance, Damascus, 1977, p70.
43. *Ibid*, p145.
44. *Ibid*, pp147–148.
45. Anwar 'Abd al-Malek re-emphasised recently his conviction that the main feature of our times is the continuing 'civilisational confrontation between the Orient and the Occident'. (*Arab Studies Quarterly*, vol 1, no. 3, Summer 1979, p180).
46. 'Islam and Political Islam', *An-Nahar Arabe et Internationale* Paris, January 22, 1979, p64. Republished in *Mawâqif*, Beirut, no. 34, Winter 1979, pp149–160.
47. *Mawâqif*, No. 34, p155.
48. *Ibid*, p152.
49. Walid Nuwayhed, *al-Safîr*, daily newspaper, Beirut, December 19, 1979, Editorial page.
50. Suhail Kash, *al-Safîr*, January 3, 1979.
51. Sa'd Mehio, *al-Safîr*, January 20, 1979.
52. *Mawâqif*, no. 34, pp147–48.
53. *Orientalism*, p263.
54. *Mawâqif*, no. 36, Winter 1980, pp150–153.
55. *Orientalism*, p107.
56. *Ibid*, p108.
57. *An-Nahar Arabe et Internationale*, Paris, February 26, 1979, p24. See also *Mawâqif*, 34, p158.
58. *Al-Safîr*, October 10, 1979.

25

ORIENTALISM: A BLACK PERSPECTIVE

Ernest J. Wilson III

Whereas Sadik Jalal al-'Azm looks at orientalism from an Arab point of view, Ernest J. Wilson III, a member of the Political Science Department at the University of Michigan, looks at it from the perspective of a black American. Black people in America, he suggests, suffer from a kind of 'internal orientalism', in which they are described as the 'other'. Intellectuals and political leaders of the Afro-American community should challenge the orientalist paradigm, and 'explore the creation of new world-views that would operate from within a Third World perspective'.

Domination, like liberation, tends to be a total phenomenon. It cannot easily be restricted to the political, cultural or economic. When social groups seek to dominate others they have historically done so through every institution and social process at their disposal. Some efforts are conscious and carefully crafted strategies of domination. Others, especially after the initial forceful establishment of control, come to be automatic and unconscious. Similarly, when people struggle against domination and for liberation, one of the conclusions quickly forced upon them is that their movement must encompass the breadth and width of a people's life. If it is to be far-reaching in its scope and lasting in its effect then a liberation movement must insinuate itself into all human

Ernest J. Wilson III, 'Orientalism: A Black Perspective', *Journal of Palestine Studies*, 10, 2, winter 1981, pp. 59–69.

relationships, not merely between oppressor and oppressed, but between man and woman, parent and child, religious teacher and follower. Each of these fundamental relationships must be touched and transformed by the movement, since the character of the social domination is there and must be altered.

Certainly, the evidence of African liberation in Algeria or Mozambique points to the ubiquity of change. Thus, when the struggle breaks out in earnest, it will be fought in the realm of ideas, in the media as well as in the trenches. In turn, the struggle will be resisted by those who hold power using prisons, union busting and truncheons as well as the more subtle forms of control, including cooption, all the way through changing college curriculae and admissions procedures. As the struggle mounts, more and more of the oppressed come to recognize its totality, and to learn the 'there is no refuge except in purposeful action.' Actions, perceptions and feelings that once seemed merely personal and idiosyncratic now appear political, closely interconnected with and reflecting the character of the society.

The actual interconnectedness of things, despite the artificial barriers of convention, is perhaps a useful point of departure to consider the recent efforts by Black Americans and Palestinians to establish contact with one another, and to reflect further on the totality of anti-colonial struggles in an interdependent world.

The political importance of barriers of social convention must be considered when we examine the bitter and antagonistic establishment response that greeted the early attempts at Afro-American/Palestinian bridge building. The vitriol in the press cannot be understood only in terms of what was or was not accomplished during these few and limited sessions, for little concrete was, in fact, accomplished. No wars were declared or ended, there was no massive shift of political coalition, and millions of dollars did not trade hands – the usual topics that invite such intense scrutiny. Rather, these counterattacks were a response to threats to the old, established ways of defining and dividing and ruling the world. Such contacts challenged the dominant Euro-centric, racist vision of what the world must be.

I contend that the campaign launched against these two coloured, colonial peoples was spurred because two unpredictable and volatile forces were breaking down old walls of containment and were cautiously seeking out an alliance. The old categories of 'domestic' and 'international' were challenged. The most 'irrational' and potentially dangerous force within the belly of capitalism's bastion – Blacks – was sending powerful signals to the great unstable, 'irrational' and unpredictable force *beyond* the bastion's walls – the Palestinians – in that most explosive of regions, the Middle East. Of course, the Russians are more powerful and more of a threat to America's leaders, but they are a threat that is known, stable and predictable. US unions are perhaps more powerful domestically than Blacks, with their occasional spasms of protectionism and occasional anti-capital postures; but they are also more stable and less threatening than Blacks. Thus, it was the image of domestic 'savages,' looters from the South Bronx and Black radicals finding common cause with the 'murderers and terrorists' of Munich and the bombers of oil pipelines that prompted such racist responses. *That* was the genie let out of the bottle that the media sought to crush; that was the demon that demanded exorcism.

This first step toward greater communication and the possibility of cooperation should be seen as part of a larger effort on the part of both Blacks and Palestinians to reach out into the wider world. One of the characteristics of being dominated is that the daily struggle to survive is so terribly demanding that one has time for little else. The next meal, or outfoxing the landlord or the butcher takes priority over manoeuvres on the international stage. Yet lately in the Black American community there has been a much greater outward movement. American Blacks are now reaching out to understand how other areas and issues in this increasingly interdependent world may affect the material and political interests of the Black community: issues from energy to Afghanistan, SALT II and the threatened resumption of the Cold War. The 'Euro-Arab Dialogue' is but one example of the worldwide outreach efforts of the Palestinians. These parallel – though by no means identical – movements would eventually intersect; the question was one of timing and context.

The mutual benefits of such a meeting are clear. There would be quite simply one additional force, one new international pressure group, that could be brought to bear, however obliquely, against conservative and *status quo* forces internationally, and especially in capitalism's bastion, the United States of America. Ironically perhaps, the greatest model of the successful use of such international and domestic alliances is the 30-year-old success story of the Israeli-US Jewish alliance. The fear on the part of this Israeli-US Jewish alliance is clear – that the US political and economic support for Israel will be weakened, and perhaps an anti-Jewish backlash will be stirred up in the US. But the palpable aversion to the American Black/Palestinian talks goes much deeper into both the psyche of non-Jewish White America, and into the material interest of America's ruling circles.

It is useful to recall the tremendous fear in American political and economic ruling élites when the Black revolt of the 1960's began to smash headlong into the conduct of the undeclared war in Vietnam. Would it be possible to fight two wars simultaneously? Here, we aren't talking about Vietnam on one hand and the War on Poverty on the other (although trying to fight those two wars did lead to the inflationary stagnation that is torturing America today). Rather, it was the undeclared war of the FBI, the CIA, and local law enforcement agencies against Black radical groups like the Black Panthers and the Student Non-violent Coordinating Committee (SNCC) that preoccupied the powers that be, and with good cause. Therefore, the threat to the present conduct of foreign and domestic policy priorities and the underlying structural features of the US that they reflect is not an alliance between Operation PUSH and the PLO. It is the fear that these contacts may presage further, more radical contacts in the 1980's which could coincide with Black domestic rebellion, with possible White and Black guerrilla conflicts, at the same time that the Middle East situation is deteriorating from internal pressures and possible threats from the USSR moving onto the world market to meet COMECON oil needs. In the middle of this potential Middle East conflagration stands the PLO just as the 'Negro problem' stands at the centre of US desires to 'reindustrialize' without provoking domestic revolt. There is, therefore, every good reason on the part of the American establishment to accomplish its two major imperatives in the rest of this century – a private sector-led, supply-side, de-regulated strategy of monopoly capitalist 'reindustrialization' domestically, with the pacification of the oil lands around the Gulf internationally – without creating a Palestinian-Afro-American alliance, and without producing changes that will lead them both to rise up in revolt.

Yet in retrospect what is most remarkable about the modest Afro-American openings to the East is not that they took place but that they did not occur sooner, and are not happening with even greater frequency. To understand why they have not, it is useful to consider the recent work of an Arab-American author who, with a steady and unflinching eye, dissects the single cloth of Western domination in the area of the world that they call the Orient. Edward Said's work *Orientalism* (New York: Pantheon Books, 1978) is useful for what it can tell us about the history of the region that concerns us here. But it is ultimately more useful for what it can tell us about how dominant cultures come to capture, de-nature, and assimilate other cultures. Said, through massive documentation, shows us precisely how ideologies and research institutions and assorted partial truths are erected on the sure base of economic and political domination. Yet so sure is his grasp of the facts of domination that his narrative rarely – one is tempted to say never – permits a flash of anti-colonial or anti-imperialist resistance to show, nor strategies of liberation to shine through this great grey Orientalist wall of world domination.

Edward Said's purpose in *Orientalism* is to demonstrate the way in which a distinct 'vocabulary and imagery' (p. 68) is employed by Western observers of the East, and how these constitute a veritable structure of knowledge and perception, collectively sustained and transmitted by universities, research institutes, and official pronouncements of governments and the popular press. Western perceptions of the 'real world' must pass through this ensemble which thereby shapes 'reality' for the viewer. The structure of beliefs and values is what is called Orientalism. Orientalism is the way Westerners learn about the Orient; it is a set of categories, of questions and implied answers which are based more upon the political and social needs of the West, than upon the underlying realities of Eastern peoples (Arabs, Indians, etc.).

The main 'dogmas of Orientalism' guide Westerners' study of the Eastern civilizations, and provide the general axioms which shape subsequent specific conclusions about concrete phenomena and events. Said offers his list of what the principal dogmas are:

1. 'Absolute and systematic difference between the West and the Orient.' The West is rational, developed, humane, superior, while the Orient is aberrant, undeveloped, inferior.
2. Abstractions about the Orient are always preferable to direct evidence drawn from modern Oriental realities.
3. 'The Orient is eternal, uniform, and incapable of defining itself' (or speaking for itself: it must be interpreted).
4. The Orient is to be feared ('Yellow Peril', 'Mongol hordes') or to be controlled (pp. 300–301).

These principles are, in turn, promulgated and reproduced from generation to generation through means as diverse as travelogues written by 'apolitical humanist' wanderers, by leaders of military expeditions, and by 'objective' scientists from Western countries. Eventually, Orientalism as a form of domination and a way of discourse takes on a life of its own, gaining a certain degree of intellectual autonomy but still serving the same purposes.

But ultimately, all the general principles and their specific applications are sustained and propped up through raw power. Orientalism, after all is said and done, is 'fundamentally a political doctrine' (p. 204). It facilitates the daily business of one group dominating another. The Orientalist then mixes the fact of domination with the fact of differences and concludes that all aspects of the culture are inferior.

To the Afro-American audience all of this should sound very familiar, for we are very much at home on such ground. The Black community has been subjected to a kind of *internal* Orientalism. Its members too have been defined as 'The Other,' to be feared and controlled; the dark, exotic native son viewed as the near mirror image of civilized and respectable white people. The concerns and apprehensions of the dominant society are projected upon Black society. Black Americans too, in the view of the oppressor, have their common appointed spokesmen and their annointed leaders. And like Orientalism as described by Said, the white study of the 'Negro Problem,' especially prior to the militance of the 1960's, tended to ignore the ever-present anti-imperialist or radical nationalist movements of Black history, at the same time that the white-controlled state apparatus repressed these same movements.

What Said has contributed therefore is a very useful guide to what Langston Hughes called, in his book of the same title, the 'ways of white folks.' He has focused on their external predations on other cultures of coloured peoples, just as Hughes in his short stories examined their predations on domestic people and cultures of colour. Although he does not do so as self-consciously as a Fanon, for example, he shows the reader from Latin America or Africa or Afro-America the outline of his or her own domination. His analytical categories, and especially his linking of political and economic domination – in a word, imperialism – on the one hand, and the intellectual life of the dominant culture on the other, are applicable beyond the Middle East. Some of its worldwide applicability comes from what is one of the most novel and interesting features of the work – its nearly exclusive focus on the mores and internal meanings of Euro-American culture, and not on the impact of that cultural domination on the subject peoples. This was the terrain that Said chose to map, and it is indeed a relatively uncharted one. Still, it is a peculiarly undialectical exploration, which often leaves the reader with little feel for the reality behind the stereotype, and which also tends to reproduce the Orientalist's own exclusive focus upon the dominant culture with little examination of the reactions to and attacks upon Orientalism by the dominated.

A consequence of Dr. Said's tight focus on the oppressor rather than on the oppressed is that by the end of the book the possibilities for change seem remote indeed. He cites only a handful of examples of those who, like himself, managed to break through the bonds of Orientalism to strike out on a new road of liberated scholarship. One wonders if there were so few efforts at cultural as well as political liberation from Western domination. Of course there were [others], but because of his stated objectives Said did not include them. [Not] to do so is perfectly legitimate, but leaves the reader with little vision of a reconstructed future vision of a truly liberated society.

Here too one is reminded of Afro-American efforts in the late 1950's and 1960's to criticize the prevailing biases of white scholarship, to criticize it from within, and then simultaneously search for ways to set up parallel Black institutions, as with Black Studies programmes. One wonders if this is happening today in the Middle East. One remembers too the resolute and vicious resistance by Whites to the entire Black Studies movement. Especially singled out for crude denunciations and sarcasm in the popular press were efforts by Blacks to insist upon their own historical ties to Africa as well as certain political objectives that they shared. These same forces hounded people like Malcolm X and Stokely Carmichael for the same reasons. For Afro-Americans to insist upon their Africanness threatened the psychological categories, as well as the political interests, of many Whites in America.

All of this suggests that not only do dominant cultures try to maintain the integrity of their world-view and their political control by crafting and recrafting modes of knowing other cultures, but they will respond with special alacrity and concern when heretofore self-contained and 'orientalized' groups try to reach out to make contact with one another. We might postulate three levels at which challenges to Orientalism operate, especially if we conceive Orientalism to be another word for an organizing paradigm.

First, intellectuals and political leaders could challenge the sub-categories that operate within the orientalist paradigm, but without challenging the logic of Orientalism as such. Next, challenges could be made against the very notion of the entire paradigm and its principal dogmas as the once-dominated seek to destroy it and replace it with a view of the world that reflects their own unique structural position and cultural heritage. Finally, a special kind of challenge is launched against the West when separate 'Orientalisms' – in this case the world-view 'containing' Arabs and that 'containing' American Blacks – are shattered and the once divided and conquered peoples reach out to explore potential political alliances as well as explore the creation of new world-views that would operate from within a Third World perspective. The dictum 'Divide and Conquer' is reversed: Unite and Conquer.

This latter challenge to Western domination occurred when American Blacks and the PLO began their discussions. It challenged many of the prevailing categories carefully constructed by the United States' domestic and international versions of Orientalism.

However, negative visions of what must be destroyed are not sufficient to build a more humane and democratic world order. The dominated of the world, whether in the Middle East, North America, Africa or elsewhere must fashion a consistent set of goals and a set of strategies and tactics to get there. The foundation for such a change has been laid down, for example, in the discussions originating within the Third World which led to demands on the industrialized 'Northern' countries to create a New International Economic Order (NIEO). One task before American Blacks is to explore the implications of an NIEO for their own efforts for liberation within the US, and to examine more seriously and consistently the role that international alliances may play in future Black liberation movements, movements which may be the best hope for a more humane and democratic America. To such an effort, Blacks may bring what the Black intellectual and activist W. E. B. DuBois called the problem of the veil. Black Americans, he argued, viewed the world about them as through a veil, with two hearts and through two separate but intertwined visions – one Black, the other American and white. He saw this as an ever-present and painful dilemma which afflicted the Black man in America. The double vision of DuBois may have transformative power, as leaders like Martin Luther King have long recognized. In foreign affairs as in domestic, Blacks must try to turn this vision to an advantage.

Turning the 'two-ness' DuBois described into an advantage and using its insights to transform US foreign policy means that Blacks must draw from their painful and unique view from the bottom of American society, a structural position whose resultant ideologies have also been heavily informed by an African cultural heritage. This unique vantage point should make Afro-American political leaders and intellectuals sensitive to two issues. The first, through shared cultural norms and racial oppression, is a sensitivity to African demands and needs. The second is a general sensitivity to demands from the oppressed of the world, from the Palestinians to sovereign Third World nations seeking international justice. Armed with such a vision a new Black leadership could transform the current world view of American foreign policy away from its myopic focus on the 'Soviet Menace' and other East-West issues, to place North-South issues centrally on the agenda. This is of course, what Andy Young tried to do during his tenure at the United Nations. Such a vision would also call for a more democratic foreign policy, insisting that 'foreign' policy not be seen as foreign to the bread-and-butter issues of the average American Black or White, but central to them.

Such a redefinition will only come about, however, through linking this outward-looking vision with the requirements for social change within the United States. In other words, it must be rooted initially in the domestic needs of the Black poor and working class in this country. To construct such an international vision means that the phenomenon of domestic domination/liberation remains at the centre of the analysis. What must be analysed in detail is whether, in fact, it is possible for the United States to adapt itself to the rapid changes in today's international arena without fundamentally altering the condition of Black oppression. These are international adaptations which will be attitudinal and cognitive, as well as material. The question of whether America can be truly great if its Black citizens are suffering from oppression has been posed throughout Black history in this country, and most recently during the conjuncture of the war in Vietnam and Black domestic rebellion. The answer given then was no. Much of the current stagflation and loss of international prestige experienced by the US results from trying to ignore this domestic contradiction throughout the Johnson war years. The problems that Black Americans face are not problems susceptible to easy solutions at the margin. They are structural problems that can only be met with structural solutions. This means big political and economic changes in everything from sectoral balances to the regional distribution of firms to the labour intensiveness of American industry. This will require something that America has thus far refused to develop – a national industrial policy consciously and democratically arrived at and implemented. The political volatility and the growing economic marginalization of Black people in America will render all efforts at 'reindustrialization' extremely problematic. Yet some form of structural readjustment is absolutely imperative if America as a whole is to be able to grow in tomorrow's more highly competitive, more mercantilist and more politicized world. This brief discussion of the position of the Black masses in US adjustments to a changing international order is meant to be suggestive of the kinds of issues that need to be addressed throughout the 1980's.

As history may put Afro-Americans at centre stage in the coming decade as the US is forced to adapt rapidly to a new international environment of many other powerful actors, so history puts the usual burden on the Afro-American intellectual. For it is the intellectuals among the community who must begin to reconstruct a vision of a unified world-view in which the dialectic between America's standing in the world on the one hand, and the position of Black Americans domestically is systematically explored. How is the internal dialectic between Afro-American domination and Afro-American liberation influenced by the new environment?

Afro-American intellectuals must renounce the carrots and sticks of mere 'professionalization' through an uncritical integration into the ranks of socially certified status categories of lawyers, economists and other purveyors of publicly acceptable data bits. Not to do so is to accept the position of 'native informer' (Said's term) or of intellectual irrelevance. It is absurd for Black intellectuals to buy into artificial disciplinary boundaries at a time when daily events come more and more to challenge their analytic validity. One good example of reactionary efforts to delimit critical Black inquiry are the moves underway around the country intellectually to gut Black Studies departments. Here again Said's notion of Orientalism is useful. What we are seeing in the US is what Said has described for Oriental Studies in the US and elsewhere, to wit, the dominant social system forcing its constituent parts to conform to prevailing economic and political norms by changing institutions responsible for the production, dissemination and evaluation of knowledge. First there are pressures to separate African from Afro-American subject matter. Then there are efforts to quash the idea that Afro-American studies should share methodological and normative orientations with Third World studies, whether Chicano, Native American or Arab. This is not to say that Black Studies cannot be strengthened through greater focus. The question is what shall be the issue that informs the focus: Afro-Americans (or Africans or Arabs) as a strictly American social pathology, or as human actors on a world stage seeking liberation? In a period of growing class formation in the Black community, Black activists and intellectuals must struggle to sustain a liberationist, 'anti-Orientalism' perspective.

If we can retain the focus on *domination/liberation set within a rapidly changing international context*, we will have made an important contribution to the future of critical Black studies and critical thinking in general. This will mean a hard-headed examination of many questions which now deserve more attention than they have been given in the past. Again, a good starting point to the programme of the NIEO. We can ask, what will be the impact on Black economic and political conditions of the United States acceding to Third World NIEO demands? Will there be a short-term, medium-term or long-term improvement in economic conditions, or will Black economic status decline? Will political conditions improve? How will monetary and foreign aid reforms demanded by Third World countries affect Black domination/liberation in the US? It appears initially that there are a number of political gains and economic losses which work in opposite directions here. For example, Black support of a more just price for raw materials, and occasional Third World diplomatic support of Black domestic demands, cannot hide the fact that Blacks are especially hit by higher oil prices. Jobs lost through foreign trade tend to be among workers with the least skills, lowest education and little mobility, characteristics which most of the Black workforce share. Yet there are other benefits, including the creation of jobs in other sectors. Are these jobs Blacks can get? This raises the inevitable political economic question as to whether the economy must get worse for Blacks in America before things can be improved politically. Or can there be a variable sum game wherein Black conditions improve along with movement towards an NIEO? My suspicion is that this is the case. The point is, however, that these are questions that demand very serious investigation, and they cannot be sidestepped or simply assumed.

These then are the kinds of questions which are rightfully forced upon the Afro-American leadership once the barriers between them and the outside world are chipped away through actions such as reaching out to explore the Palestinian issue independently. A kind of restraining 'Orientalism' has prevented Palestinians and Afro-Americans from even considering reaching out to one another, just as a kind of domestic Orientalism has failed to prompt Blacks in greater number to consider the impact of the wider world system on Black efforts at liberation within the US. Several trends are likely to erode such barriers. Firstly, the objective fact of growing US reliance on imports and on exports for jobs and profits is bringing this fact home to all Americans. This awareness is prompted, of course, by the recent supply interruptions and price hikes on imported oil.

The second factor is heightened international conflicts over trade, investment and strategic relations between North and South, East and West, and among Western nations. This will no doubt impinge more and more on everyone's consciousness throughout the 1980's. Finally, the debilitating stagflation of the past seven years is likely to continue for at least the next seven. This will lead Black and White Americans alike to search for its world causes, and to examine the solutions that other countries, with other social systems, have tried to make work for them.

This leads us full circle back to our earlier discussion of Black American–Palestinian relations. Within the structuralist analysis given above, such relations are important to the degree that they provide one more wide window on the world for Black Americans to recognize the interrelationship of domestic and international factors from a progressive perspective. A better understanding of the Palestinian struggle provides an important example of another dominated people seeking not merely 'participation' but liberation through a reordering of the prevailing political relations, *using international as well as national strategies*. The 'Palestinian problem' is now before the entire world for resolution. It is not just a local struggle. The resolution of the Black liberation struggle will have international as well as local significance, not only for Blacks but for the United States as a whole, and hence the entire international community. The time has not yet come when Third World nations define it in their interest to support efforts at Black liberation because that liberation will prompt a more progressive US position on the New International Economic Order. But that time may still come.

The challenge to American Blacks is to create a new vision, a new paradigm, that recognizes not only the ties that bind us to the domestic structures that dominate, but also the ties that bind us to overseas political movements seeking liberation, and to the big international shifts that can make liberation possible. Conversely, Black intellectuals must also think through and clarify the impact that a successful Black liberation movement in the US would have on the possibilities for world peace.

26

THE QUESTION OF ORIENTALISM

Bernard Lewis

It was left to Bernard Lewis, professor of Near Eastern studies at Princeton and a leading orientalist, to launch a root and branch assault on Said's interpretation of orientalism. Said's account of the subject, Lewis argues, is not only seriously flawed from an academic point of view – it deals only with a small part of the Arab world, ignores German, Austrian and Russian orientalism, and frequently displays ignorance of historical fact – it also displays prejudice, bias and obsession.

Imagine a situation in which a group of patriots and radicals from Greece decides that the profession of classical studies is insulting to the great heritage of Hellas and that those engaged in these studies, known as classicists, are the latest manifestation of a deep and evil conspiracy, incubated for centuries, hatched in Western Europe, fledged in America, the purpose of which is to denigrate the Greek achievement and subjugate the Greek lands and peoples. In this perspective, the entire European tradition of classical studies – largely the creation of French romantics, British colonial governors (of Cyprus, of course), and poets, professors, and proconsuls from both countries – is a long-standing insult to the honor and integrity of Hellas and a threat to its future. The poison has spread from Europe to the United States, where the teaching of Greek history, language, and literature in the universities is dominated by the evil race of

Bernard Lewis, *Islam and the West* (Oxford University Press, 1993), ch. 6.

classicists – men and women who are not of Greek origin, who have no sympathy for Greek causes, and who, under a false mask of dispassionate scholarship, strive to keep the Greek people in a state of permanent subordination.

The time has come to save Greece from the classicists and bring the whole pernicious tradition of classical scholarship to an end. Only Greeks are truly able to teach and write on Greek history and culture from remote antiquity to the present day; only Greeks are genuinely competent to direct and conduct programs of academic studies in these fields. Some non-Greeks may be permitted to join in this great endeavor provided that they give convincing evidence of their competence, as, for example, by campaigning for the Greek cause in Cyprus, by demonstrating their ill will to the Turks, by offering a pinch of incense to the currently reigning Greek gods, and by adopting whatever may be the latest fashionable ideology in Greek intellectual circles.

Non-Greeks who will not or cannot meet these requirements are obviously hostile and therefore not equipped to teach Greek studies in a fair and reasonable manner. They must not be permitted to hide behind the mask of classicism but must be revealed for what they are – Turk-lovers, enemies and exploiters of the Greek people, and opponents of the Greek cause. Those already established in academic circles must be discredited by abuse and thus neutralized; at the same time steps must be taken to ensure Greek or pro-Greek control of university centers and departments of Greek studies and thus, by a kind of academic prophylaxis, prevent the emergence of any further classical scholars or scholarship. In the meantime the very name of classicist must be transformed into a term of abuse.

Stated in terms of classics and Greek, the picture is absurd. But if for classicist we substitute 'Orientalist,' with the appropriate accompanying changes, this amusing fantasy becomes an alarming reality. For some years now a hue and cry has been raised against Orientalists in American and to a lesser extent European universities, and the term 'Orientalism' has been emptied of its previous content and given an entirely new one – that of unsympathetic or hostile treatment of Oriental peoples. For that matter, even the terms 'unsympathetic' and 'hostile' have been redefined to mean not supportive of currently fashionable creeds or causes.

Take the case of V. S. Naipaul, author of a remarkable account of a tour of Muslim countries. Mr. Naipaul is not a professor but a novelist – one of the most gifted of our time. He is not a European, but a West Indian of East Indian origin. His book about modern Islam is not a work of scholarship and makes no pretense of being such. It is the result of close observation by a professional observer of the human predicament. It is occasionally mistaken, often devastatingly accurate, and above all compassionate. Mr. Naipaul has a keen eye for the absurdities of human behavior, in Muslim lands as elsewhere. At the same time he is moved by deep sympathy and understanding for both the anger and the suffering of the people whose absurdities he so faithfully depicts.

But such compassion is not a quality appreciated or even recognized by the grinders of political or ideological axes. Mr. Naipaul would not toe the line; he would not join in the praise of Islamic radical leaders and the abuse of those whom they oppose. Therefore, he is an Orientalist – a term applied to him even by brainwashed university students who ought to know better.

The ultimate absurdity was reached in a letter to the *New York Times*,[1] the writer of which is described as 'a doctoral candidate in history and Near East studies' at a major university. Writing in protest against a favorable reference to Lord Curzon and his book on Iran, the letter writer describes him as 'the very symbol of British Orientalist thinking' and observes that 'even in his own time [he] was considered by Iranian and Western democrats alike to have played a principal part in the tragic fate of the people of that country.' The writer of the letter then goes on to speak approvingly of E. G. Browne, whose *The Persian Revolution*, published in 1910, was 'a very different book.' In it 'he spoke ... of the accomplishments of the revolution' and revealed the sinister role of Lord Curzon.

There is no doubt about Lord Curzon's role as a doughty defender of British imperial interests or about Professor Browne's anti-imperialist and pro-Iranian stance. What is curious, to say the least, is that Lord Curzon, who in the course of a long and active political and imperial career rose to be viceroy of India and at a later date secretary of state for foreign affairs, is designated as 'the very symbol of British Orientalist thinking,' whereas E. G. Browne, professor of Arabic at Cambridge and one of the leading Orientalists of his day in England and indeed in Europe, is acclaimed for his presumed anti-Orientalism. Both the noble lord and the learned professor would surely have been surprised at these designations. To find a precedent for such high-handed treatment of language, one must go back to Humpty Dumpty, who, it will be recalled, when challenged on his use of 'glory' to mean 'a nice knock-down argument,' replied: 'When *I* use a word ... it means just what I choose it to mean, neither more nor less.' This use of the term Orientalism is clearly a perversion of language. It is, however, sadly accurate, since it reflects a by-now wide spread perversion of truth.

What, then, is Orientalism? What did the word mean before it was poisoned by the kind of intellectual pollution that in our time has made so many previously useful words unfit for use in rational discourse? In the past, Orientalism was used mainly in two senses. One is a school of painting – that of a group of artists, mostly from western Europe, who visited the Middle East and North Africa and depicted what they saw or imagined, sometimes in a rather romantic and extravagant manner, sometimes even pornographic. The second, and more common, meaning, unconnected with the first, has hitherto been a branch of scholarship. The word, and the academic discipline which it denotes, dates from the great expansion of scholarship in western Europe from the time of the Renaissance onward. There were Hellenists who studied Greek, Latinists who studied Latin, Hebraists who studied Hebrew; the first two groups were sometimes called classicists, the third Orientalists. In due course they turned their attention to other languages.

Basically these early scholars were philologists concerned with the recovery, study, publication, and interpretation of texts. This was the first and most essential task that had to be undertaken before the serious study of such other matters as philosophy, theology, literature, and history became possible. The term 'Orientalist' was nor at that time as vague and imprecise as it appears now. Since theology was considered unsuited to non-Christian religions, the term applied to only one discipline, philology. In the early stages there was only one region, that which we now call the Middle East – the only part of the Orient with which Europeans could claim any real acquaintance.

Since its earliest recorded history, Europe has been looking at its neighbors in the East sometimes with fear, sometimes with greed, sometimes with curiosity, and sometimes with disquiet. For centuries, indeed for millennia, relations between the two have shown a pattern of conquest and reconquest, attack and counterattack. The great kings of Persia threatened and invaded the cities of Greece; they were in turn conquered by Alexander. The Arabs wrested Syria and Palestine, Egypt and North Africa, Sicily, Spain, and Portugal from Christendom; they lost their European acquisitions to the Reconquest, but Muslim arms were able to save the rest from the counterattack of the Crusaders. The Tatars conquered Russia, and the Ottoman Turks took Constantinople from the Byzantines and twice advanced as far as Vienna before beginning the long retreat that politicians and, later, historians called 'the Eastern question.' And as the Arabs departed from southwestern Europe and the Tatars and Turks from eastern and southeastern Europe, they were followed by their triumphant former subjects, who now embarked on their own still-vaster expansion into the Asian and African homelands of their former conquerors.

The problems presented by Ottoman weakness and withdrawal were called 'the Eastern question' because for most Europeans the source of danger and invasion, from the first Persian vanguard to the last Ottoman rear guard, had been the area immediately to the east of Europe. This was *the* East, and no more specific definition was needed, since no other East was known. The Eastern question, in French *la question orientale*, was the question posed by Europe's immediate neighbor the Ottoman Empire, whether through the menace of its strength or, later, the temptation of its weakness. In French, as generally in European usage, the region to which the terms 'Orient' and 'Oriental' are applied begins in the eastern Mediterranean. In American usage the terms 'Orient' and 'Oriental' have come to be applied almost exclusively to far more distant regions, of which ancient and medieval Europe had very little knowledge or even awareness.

For the ancient Greeks, Asia meant the shore of the Aegean Sea opposite them. When they became aware of a more vast and remote Asia looming beyond, they named the immediate neighborhood Asia Minor. In the same way, when a greater, stranger, richer, and more distant East occupied the attention of Europeans, they began in time to speak of the old, familiar neighboring East by such terms as 'Near' and 'Middle,' to distinguish it from what lay beyond. The Portuguese and the Dutch, the English and the French followed one another around the Cape of Good Hope to the fabulous lands of India and Southeast Asia; some penetrated even as far as China and Japan. European merchants brought back goods that transformed the economy and the social habits of the West. Scholars and missionaries brought back texts that philologists examined with the self-same methods that they had developed for Latin and Greek, Hebrew and Arabic.

With the progress of both exploration and scholarship, the term 'Orientalist' became increasingly unsatisfactory. Students of the Orient were no longer engaged in a single discipline but were branching out into several others. At the same time the area that they were studying, the so-called Orient, was seen to extend far beyond the Middle Eastern lands on which European attention had hitherto been concentrated and to include the vast and remote civilizations of India and China. There was a growing tendency among scholars and in university departments concerned with these studies to use more precise labels. Scholars took to calling themselves philologists, historians etc., dealing with Oriental topics. And in relation to these topics they began to use such terms as 'Sinologist' and 'Indologist,' 'Iranist' and 'Arabist,' to give a closer and more specific definition to the area and topic of their study.

Incidentally, the last-named term, 'Arabist,' has also gone through a process of re-semanticization. In England, in the past, the word 'Arabist' was normally used in the same way as 'Iranist' or 'Hispanist' or 'Germanist' – to denote a scholar professionally concerned with the language, history, or culture of a particular land and people. In the United States, it has come to mean a specialist in dealings with Arabs, particularly in government and commerce. For some, though not all, it also means an advocate of Arab causes. This is another example of word pollution, which has deprived us of the use of a necessary term. The term 'Hispanist' does not mean an apologist for Central American tyrants or terrorists, an admirer of bullfighters, an observer or practitioner of Spanish affairs, or a purveyor of bananas. It means a scholar with a good knowledge of Spanish, specializing in some field of Spanish or Latin American history or culture. The word 'Arabist' ought to be used in the same way. This, however, is probably a lost cause, and some other term will have to be found. Some have even suggested the word 'Arabologist,' on the analogy of 'Sinologist,' 'Indologist,' and 'Turcologist.' This term might bring some gain in precision but also a considerable loss of elegance. A not unworthy group of scholars, engaged in the study of a truly great civilization, deserves a better label.

The term 'Orientalist' is by now also polluted beyond salvation, but this is less important in that the word had already lost its value and had been in fact abandoned by those who previously bore it. This abandonment was given formal expression at the Twenty-ninth International Congress of Orientalists, which met in Paris in the summer of 1973. This was the hundredth anniversary of the First International Congress of Orientalists convened in the same city, and it seemed a good occasion to reconsider the nature and functions of the congress. It soon became clear that there was a consensus in favor of dropping this label – some indeed wanted to go further and bring the series of congresses to an end on the grounds that the profession as such had ceased to exist and the congress had therefore outlived its purpose. The normal will to survive of institutions was strong enough to prevent the dissolution of the congress. The movement to abolish the term 'Orientalist' was, however, successful.

The attack came from two sides. On the one hand there were those who had hitherto been called Orientalists and who were increasingly dissatisfied with a term that indicated neither the discipline in which they were engaged nor the region with which they were concerned. They were reinforced by scholars from Asian countries who pointed to the absurdity of applying such a term as 'Orientalist' to an Indian studying the history or culture of India. They made the further point that the term was somehow insulting to Orientals in that it made them appear as the objects of study rather than as participants.

The strongest case for the retention of the old term was made by the Soviet delegation, led by the late Babajan Ghafurov, director of the Institute of Orientalism in Moscow and himself a Soviet Oriental from the republic of Tajikistan. This term, said Ghafurov, had served us well for more than a century. Why should we now abandon a word that conveniently designates the work we do and that was borne with pride by our teachers and their teachers for many generations back? Ghafurov was not entirely pleased with the comment of a British delegate who praised him for his able statement of the conservative point of view. In the vote, despite the support of the East European Orientalists who unanimously agreed with the Soviet delegate, Ghafurov was defeated, and the term 'Orientalist' was formally abolished. In its place the congress agreed to call itself the 'International Congress of Human Sciences in Asia and North Africa.'

The term 'Orientalist' was thus abolished by the accredited Orientalists, and thrown on the garbage heap of history. But garbage heaps are not safe places. The words 'Orientalist' and 'Orientalism,' discarded as useless by scholars, were retrieved and reconditioned for a different purpose, as terms of polemical abuse.

The attack on the Orientalists – more specifically on Western Arabists and Islamicists – was nor in fact new in the Muslim world. It had gone through several earlier phases, in which different interests and motives were at work. One of the first outbreaks in the postwar period had a curious origin. It was connected with the initiation of the second edition of *The Encyclopedia of Islam*, a major project of Orientalism in the field of Islamic studies. The first edition had been published simultaneously in three languages – English, French, and German – with the participation of scholars drawn from these and many other countries. It took almost thirty years and was completed in 1938. The second edition, begun in 1950, was published in English and French only and without a German member on the international editorial board.

The Muslim attack was launched from Karachi, the capital of the newly created Islamic republic of Pakistan, and concentrated on two points, the lack of a German edition and editor and the presence on the editorial board of a French Jew, the late E. Lévi-Provençal. The priority, indeed the presence, of the first complaint seemed a little odd for Karachi, and was clarified when in due course it emerged that the organizer of this particular agitation was a gentleman described as 'the *imam* of the congregation of German Muslims in West Pakistan,' with some assistance from a still unreconstructed German diplomat who had just been posted there, and had taken this task upon himself.[2]

The episode was of brief duration and aroused no echo or very little echo elsewhere in the Islamic world. Some other campaigns against Orientalists followed, most of them rather more local in their origin. Two themes predominated, the Islamic and the Arab. For some, who defined themselves and their adversaries exclusively in religious terms, Orientalism was a challenge to the Islamic faith. In the early 1960s a professor at Al-Azhar University in Egypt wrote a little tract on Orientalists and the evil things they do.[3] They consist, he said, mainly of missionaries whose aim is to undermine and ultimately destroy Islam in order to establish the paramountcy of the Christian religion. This applies to most of them, except for those who are Jews and whose purpose is equally nefarious. The author lists the Orientalists who are working against Islam and whose baneful influence must be countered. He provides a separate list of really insidious and dangerous scholars against whom particular caution is needed – those who make a specious parade of good will.

These lists include among others the name of the late Philip Hitti of Princeton. The author of the booklet describes him as follows:

> A Christian from Lebanon. ... One of the most disputatious of the enemies of Islam, who makes a pretense of defending Arab causes in America and is an unofficial adviser of the American State Department on Middle Eastern Affairs.
>
> He always tries to diminish the role of Islam in the creation of human civilization and is unwilling to ascribe any merit to the Muslims. ... His *History of the Arabs* is full of attacks on Islam and sneers at the Prophet. All of it is spite and venom and hatred. ...

The late Philip Hitti was a stalwart defender of Arab causes, and his *History* a hymn to Arab glory. This response to it must have come as a shock to him. Similar religious complaints about the Orientalist as missionary, as a sort of Christian fifth columnist, have also appeared in Pakistan and more recently in Iran.

Committed Muslim critics of Orientalism have an intelligible rationale when they view Christian and Jewish writers on Islam as engaged in religious polemic or conversion – indeed, granted their assumptions, their conclusions are virtually inescapable. In their view, the adherent of a religion is necessarily a defender of that religion, and an approach to another religion, by anyone but a prospective convert, can only be undertaken for defense or attack. Traditional Muslim scholars did not normally undertake the study of Christian or Jewish thought or history, and they could see no honorable reason why Christians or Jews should study Islam. Indeed, one of the prescriptions of the *dhimma*, the rules by which Christians and Jews were permitted to practice their religions under Muslim government, forbids them to teach the Qur'ān to their children. Medieval Christians had a similar view. When they began to study Islam and the Islamic scriptures, it was for the double purpose of dissuading Christians from conversion to Islam and persuading Muslims to adopt Christianity. This approach has long since been abandoned in the Christian world, except in a few outposts of religious zeal. It remained for much longer the prevailing perception of interdenominational relations in the Muslim world.

A different approach, expressed in a combination of nationalist and ideological terminology, is to be found among some Arab writers. Curiously, most of those involved are members of the Christian minorities in Arab countries and are themselves resident in Western Europe or the United States. A good example is an article by a Coptic sociologist living in Paris, Anouar Abdel-Malek, published in the UNESCO journal *Diogenes* in 1963, that is, a year or so after the publication of the Cairo pamphlet. In this article, entitled 'Orientalism in Crisis,' Dr. Abdel-Malek sets forth what became some of the major charges in the indictment of the Orientalists. They are 'Europocentric,' paying insufficient attention to the scholars, scholarship, methods, and achievements of the Afro-Asian world; they are obsessed with the past and do not show sufficient interest in the recent history of the 'Oriental' peoples (more recent critics complain of the exact opposite); they pay insufficient attention to the insights afforded by social science and particularly Marxist methodology.

Dr. Abdel-Malek's article is written with obvious emotion and is the expression of passionately held convictions. It remains, however, within the limits of scholarly debate and is obviously based on a careful, even if not sympathetic, study of Orientalist writings. He is even prepared to concede that Orientalism may not be inherently evil and that some Orientalists may themselves be victims.

A new theme was adumbrated in an article published in a Beirut magazine in June 1974 and written by a professor teaching in an American university. One or two quotations may illustrate the line:

> The Zionist scholarly hegemony in Arabic studies [in the United States] had a clear effect in controlling the publication of studies, periodicals, as well as professional associations. These [Zionist scholars] published a great number of books and studies which impress the uninitiated as being strictly scientific but which in fact distort Arab history and realities and are detrimental to the Arab struggle for liberation. They masquerade in scientific guise in order to dispatch spies and agents of American and Israeli security apparatuses, whose duty is to conduct field studies all over

the Arab states. ... These are astonishing facts of which Arab officials should keep track if they are to distinguish between legitimate and honest research conducted by some American professors on the one hand, and that conducted by students and professors motivated by American security and hegemony on the other. These officials should not allow Arab wealth to support American and Israeli interests. They should carefully and honestly scrutinize every appeal for material or for moral support. They should never allow Arab money to be used for weakening, defaming, or compromising the Arabs.[4]

This is a key text, which may help us considerably to understand the politics of academic development in Middle Eastern studies in the period that followed.

Another attack against 'the Orientalists' came from a group of Marxists. Their polemics reveal several oddities. One is the assumption that there is an Orientalist conception or line to which all Orientalists adhere – an illusion which even the most superficial acquaintance with the writings of Orientalists should suffice to dispel. Most of these critics are not themselves Orientalists. This does not mean that they reject the Orientalist doctrine or orthodoxy, which in fact does not exist; it means that they do not possess the Orientalist skills, which are exercised with little difference by both Marxist and non-Marxist Orientalists. Most serious Marxist writing on Middle Eastern history is the work either of Marxists who are themselves Orientalists, trained in the same methods and subject to the same disciplines as their non-Marxist colleagues, or of authors who rely on the writings of Orientalist scholars, both Marxist and non-Marxist, for the materials on which they base their analyses and conclusions.

A good example of this is Perry Anderson's perceptive book *The Lineages of the Absolutist State*. Though interesting and thoughtful, it bases its treatment of Middle Eastern and in general Islamic matters exclusively on secondary sources, on the works of the Orientalists. There is no other way – that is, unless of course the scholars are willing to take the trouble to acquire the necessary skills and read the primary sources in Arabic, Persian, Turkish, and other languages. But this, besides being difficult and time-consuming, would have the further disadvantage that the scholars themselves would then be exposed to the charge of Orientalism. Marxist scholars like Maxime Rodinson in France and I. P. Petrushevsky in Russia have made major contributions to Middle Eastern history which are recognized and accepted even by those who do not share their ideological commitments or political allegiances. They in turn, in their work, show far more respect for fellow Orientalists of other persuasions than for fellow Marxists with other conceptions of scholarship.

The main exponent of anti-Orientalism in the United States has for some time past been Edward Said, whose book *Orientalism*, first published in 1978, was heralded by a series of book reviews, articles, and public statements. This is a book with a thesis – that 'Orientalism derives from a particular closeness experienced between Britain and France and the Orient, which until the early nineteenth century had really meant only India and the Bible lands' (p. 4). To prove this point, Mr. Said makes a number of very arbitrary decisions. His Orient is reduced to the Middle East, and his Middle East to a part of the Arab world. By eliminating Turkish and Persian studies on the one hand and Semitic studies on the other, he isolates Arabic studies from both their historical and philological contexts. The dimensions of Orientalism in time, and space are similarly restricted.

To prove his thesis, Mr. Said rearranges both the geography and the history of Orientalism and, in particular, places the main development of Arabic studies in Britain and France and dates them after the British and French expansion in the Arab world. In fact, these studies were well established in Britain and France long before even the erroneously early date that he assigns to British and French expansion – and at no time before or after the imperial age did their contribution, in range, depth, or standard, match the achievement of the great centers of Oriental studies in Germany and neighboring countries. Indeed, any history or theory of Arabic studies in Europe without the Germans makes as much sense as would a history or theory of European music or philosophy with the same omission.

Mr. Said attempts to justify this procedure:

> I believe that the sheer quality, consistency, and mass of British, French, and American writing on the Orient lifts it above the doubtless crucial work done in Germany, Italy, Russia, and elsewhere. But I think it is also true that the major steps in Oriental scholarship were first taken in either Britain and France [sic], then elaborated upon by Germans. ... What German Oriental scholarship did was to refine and elaborate techniques whose application was to texts, myths, ideas, and languages almost literally gathered from the Orient by imperial Britain and France. (pp. 17–18, 19)

It is difficult to see what the last sentence means. Texts, in the sense of manuscripts and other written materials, were certainly acquired in the Middle East by Western visitors. But the collections in Germany, Austria, and elsewhere are no less important than those of 'imperial Britain and France.' How precisely does one 'gather' a language, literally or otherwise? The implication would seem to be that by learning Arabic, Englishmen and Frenchmen were committing some kind of offense. The Germans – accessories after the fact – could not begin to do their work of 'refinement and elaboration' on these languages until the British and the French had first seized them; the Arabs, from whom these languages were misappropriated, along with myths and ideas (whatever that may mean), were correspondingly deprived.

The whole passage is not merely false but absurd. It reveals a disquieting lack of knowledge of what scholars do and what scholarship is about. The reader's anxiety is not allayed by the frequent occurrence of stronger synonyms such as 'appropriate,' 'accumulate,' 'wrench,' 'ransack,' and even 'rape' to describe the growth of knowledge in the West about the East. For Mr. Said, it would seem, scholarship and science are commodities which exist in finite quantities; the West has grabbed an unfair share of these as well as other resources, leaving the East not only impoverished but also unscholarly and unscientific. Apart from embodying a hitherto unknown theory of knowledge, Mr. Said expresses a contempt for modern Arab scholarly achievement worse than anything that he attributes to his demonic Orientalists.

Anti-Orientalism is essentially an epistemology – concerned, in the words of the Oxford English Dictionary, with 'the theory or science of the method or grounds of knowledge.' In this sense it should deal with facts and not, so one would assume, with fantasy or invention. One of the most puzzling features of Mr. Said's *Orientalism* is precisely the idiosyncratic way, at once high-handed and inventive, in which he treats the facts on which it purports to be based. In his perception, the Orientalist was the agent and instrument of the imperialist, and his interest in knowledge was as a source of power. The Arabic scholar, along with the soldier, the trader, and the imperial civil servant, had a common purpose – to penetrate, subjugate, dominate, and exploit. To sustain this interpretation, Mr. Said presents a revisionist view of the growth of Arabic studies in Britain and France, the growth of British and French power in the Arab lands, and the connections between the two.

When I first read *Orientalism*, the narrative substratum – the numerous references and allusions to both sequences of events and the relationship among them – left me frankly mystified. Had Mr. Said devised one of those alternative universes beloved of science fiction writers? It seemed difficult at the time to find any other explanation of his maltreatment of several centuries of intellectual and general history. Some of the misstatements have no discernible polemic purpose and may be due to honest ignorance, as, for example, the belief that Muslim armies conquered Turkey before they conquered North Africa (p. 59). This would be rather like putting the English Civil War before the Norman Conquest. Although no doubt irrelevant to the main issue, this procedure would not inspire confidence in the writer's ability to evaluate work on English history. A similar approach, this time to comparative philology, is revealed in another passage in which the German philosopher Friedrich Schlegel is chided because even after 'he had practically renounced his Orientalism, he still held that Sanskrit and Persian on the one hand and Greek and German on the other had more affinities with each other than with the Semitic, Chinese, American or African languages' (p. 98).

Even more remarkable is Mr. Said's transmutation of events to fit his thesis: 'Britain and France dominated the Eastern Mediterranean from about the end of the seventeenth century on [*sic*]' (p. 17) – that is, when the Ottoman Turks who ruled the eastern Mediterranean were just leaving Austria and Hungary and when British and French merchants and travelers could visit the Arab lands only by permission of the sultan. The postdating of Arabic studies in England

and France and the relegation of German scholarship to a secondary role are equally necessary to Mr. Said's thesis – and equally false.

The mystery of Mr. Said's alternative universe was not solved for me until some years later when for the first time I read a remarkable book by a French scholar, Raymond Schwab, entitled *La Renaissance orientale*.[5] This book is not, as an unwary bibliographer might assume, a discussion of some revival of learning in the Far East. Schwab, a French poet and man of letters who died in 1956, uses the word 'Renaissance' in its original sense as a revival of learning in Europe. The Orient of which he speaks is primarily India, with some extension both east and west. In the Middle East he has little to say about the European study of Islam, but he does pay some attention to the exploration of the ancient Middle East, the excavation of its buried monuments, the decipherment of its forgotten scripts, and the recovery of its lost languages by Western scholars.

From the Middle East and more especially from Iran, Schwab's trail of discovery led toward India and ultimately beyond. His book deals with two major and related themes. The first is the process of discovery itself, and Schwab tells the fascinating story of how successive scholars – first Englishmen and Frenchmen who had unique opportunities to study India firsthand and then others, above all Germans, who devoted their lives to building up a new corpus of knowledge concerning the languages, cultures, and religions of India. The second, and in the context of his work the more important of the two themes, is the way in which this new material from India became part of the European intellectual tradition. Many fascinating connections emerged, among them Hindu pantheism and the German philosophers, Sanskrit philology and the Aryan myth, the impact of Buddhism on Emerson and Thoreau, and the Indian component in the Romantic revival. Schwab's immense literary erudition and profound cultural insight enabled him to illustrate with many examples how the texts, translations, and studies published by European Orientalists reached and influenced writers as diverse as Goethe, Lamartine, Vigny, Wagner, Whitman, and Tolstoy. The same European Indologists also had some impact in India, but that is another story.

Orientalism and the ensuing wave of anti-Orientalism are obviously deeply influenced by a reading of Schwab's book, which is frequently and admiringly cited. The otherwise mystifying schema of Arabic studies in the West as seen by Mr. Said becomes intelligible, though not of course acceptable, when one compares it with Schwab, whose framework has been taken over and applied to another region and another purpose.

This change of purpose, like any other such argument, is debatable, but the change of region reduces the argument to absurdity. Between the development of Indic and Islamic studies in Europe, there is a world of difference. India had never invaded or even remotely threatened any part of Europe. The Western study of India came at a relatively late stage, when Europe was powerful and expanding and a weakened India was falling under foreign control. The recovery of texts was indeed made possible by Europe's commercial and ultimately military expansion into South and Southeast Asia.

The study of Islam in Europe, in contrast, began in the High Middle Ages and was concerned not with a conquered but a conquering world. Insofar as Islamic studies in medieval Europe had a practical purpose, it was defensive and not aggressive: the defense of a beleaguered Christendom against the Saracen, the Turk, and the Tatar. In the age of European expansion from the sixteenth century onward, a practical interest in the Middle East would have been better served by paying attention not to Arabic, least of all to classical Arabic, but to Turkish, at that time the language of government in all Arab countries east of Morocco. Those historians who work in archives know that the letters received in London and Paris from the rulers of Algiers, Tunis, and Tripoli, not to speak of the eastern Mediterranean countries, were written not in Arabic but in Ottoman Turkish.

Although the relationship between Europe and the Islamic world was later transformed and in some measure even reversed, it remained profoundly different from the European relationship with India. The processes of discovery were entirely different in their circumstances, their chronological sequence, their geographical distribution in Europe, the attitudes that inspired them, and the results that they achieved. Anglo-French domination in the Fertile Crescent lasted for only a few decades, from the end of the First World War to the aftermath of the Second. Their domination in Arabia, Egypt, and North Africa lasted somewhat longer, but only in Aden and Algeria did foreign rule reach and exceed one hundred years. Even during their period of domination, British and French rule in many of the Arab lands was indirect, mediated through such devices as the mandate and the protectorate. Nowhere in the Arab world was there anything remotely resembling British rule in India in its extent, depth, duration, and enduring effects. Mr. Said, who believes that Egypt was 'annexed' by Britain (p. 35), presumes a similar process in the Arab world.

The theme of violent seizure and possession, with sexual overtones, recurs at several points in the book. 'What was important in the latter [sic] nineteenth century was not *whether* the West had penetrated and possessed the Orient, but rather *how* the British and French felt that they had done it' (p. 211). Or again: 'the space of weaker or underdeveloped regions like the Orient was viewed as something inviting French interest, penetration, insemination – in short, colonization ... French scholars, administrators, geographers, and commercial agents poured out their exuberant activity onto the fairly supine, feminine Orient' (pp. 219–20). The climax (so to speak) of these projected sexual fantasies occurs in Mr. Said's bravura piece, where he reads an elaborate, hostile, and wholly absurd interpretation into a lexical definition of an Arabic root which I quoted from the classical Arab dictionaries.[6]

The limitations of time, space, and content which Mr. Said imposes on his subject, though they constitute a serious distortion, are no doubt convenient and indeed necessary to his purpose. They are not, however, sufficient to accomplish it. Among the British and French Arabists and Islamicists who are the ostensible subject of his study, many leading figures are either not mentioned at all (Claude Cahen, E. Lévi-Provençal, Henri Corbin, Marius Canard, Charles Pellat, William and Georges Marçais, William Wright, all of whom made important contributions) or mentioned briefly in passing (R. A. Nicholson, Guy Le Strange, Sir Thomas Arnold, and E. G. Browne). Even for those whom he does cite, Mr. Said makes a remarkably arbitrary choice of works. His common practice indeed is to omit their major contributions to scholarship and instead fasten on minor or occasional writings.

All of this – the arbitrary rearrangement of the historical background and the capricious choice of countries, persons, and writings – still does not suffice for Mr. Said to prove his case, and he is obliged to resort to additional devices. One is the reinterpretation of the passages he cites to an extent out of all reasonable accord with their authors' manifest intentions. Another is to bring into the category of 'Orientalist' a whole series of writers – littérateurs like Chateaubriand and Nerval, imperial administrators like Lord Cromer, and others – whose works were no doubt relevant to the formation of Western cultural attitudes but who had nothing to do with the academic tradition of Orientalism which is Mr. Said's main target.

Even that is still not enough, and to make his point Mr. Said finds it necessary to launch a series of startling accusations. Thus in speaking of the late-eighteenth early-nineteenth-century French Orientalist Silvestre de Sacy, Mr. Said remarks that 'he ransacked the Oriental archives. ... What texts he isolated, he then brought back; he doctored them. ...' (p. 127). If these words bear any meaning at all it is that Sacy was somehow at fault in his access to these documents and then committed the crime of tampering with them. This outrageous libel on a great scholar is without a shred of truth.

Another, more general accusation against Orientalists is that their 'economic ideas never extended beyond asserting the Oriental's fundamental incapacity for trade, commerce, and economic rationality. In the Islamic field these clichés held good for literally hundreds of years – until Maxime Rodinson's important study *Islam and Capitalism* appeared in 1966' (p. 259). M. Rodinson himself would be the first to recognize the absurdity of this statement, the writer of which had obviously not taken the trouble to acquaint himself with the work of such earlier Orientalists as Adam Mez, J. H. Kramers, W. Björkman, V. Barthold, Thomas Arnold, and many others. All of them dealt with Muslim economic activities; Arnold was an Englishman. Rodinson, incidentally, makes the interesting observation that with some of Mr. Said's analyses and formulations carried to the limit, 'one falls into a doctrine altogether similar to the Zhdanovist theory of the two sciences.'[7]

The Germans are not the only scholars omitted from Mr. Said's survey. More remarkably, he has also omitted the Russians. Their contribution, though considerable, is less than that of the Germans or even of the British and the French. It could, however, have been very useful to him in another sense, in that

Soviet scholarship, particularly in its treatment of the Islamic and other non-European regions of the Soviet Union, comes closest – far more so than any of the British or French scholars whom he condemns – to precisely the kind of tendentious, denigratory writing that Mr. Said so much dislikes in others. Curiously, however, the Russians, even in their most abusive and contemptuous statements about Islam, enjoy total exemption from Mr. Said's strictures.

This omission can hardly be due to ignorance of Russian; such disabilities have not inhibited Mr. Said's treatment of other topics, and in any case summaries of relevant Soviet scholarly works are available in English and French. The political purposes of Mr. Said's book may provide the explanation. Said, it may be recalled, believed that South Yemen was 'the only genuinely radical people's democracy in the Middle East.'[8] A writer who is capable of taking this self-description at face value is likely to be willing to let Academician S. P. Tolstov, who saw Muḥammad as a shamanistic myth, and Professor E. A. Belayev, who described the Qur'ān as the ideological expression of a slave-owning ruling class, full of slave-owning mentality, slip by without even a slap on the wrist.

One final point, perhaps the most astonishing. Mr. Said's attitude to the Orient, Arab and other, as revealed in his book, is far more negative than that of the most arrogant European imperialist writers whom he condemns. Mr. Said speaks of 'books and journals in Arabic (and doubtless in Japanese, various Indian dialects and other Oriental languages). . . .' (p. 322). This contemptuous listing, and especially the assumption that what Indians speak and write are not languages but dialects, would be worthy of an early-nineteenth-century district commissioner.

Even more remarkable is Mr. Said's neglect – or perhaps ignorance – of Arab scholarship and other writings. 'No Arab or Islamic scholar can afford to ignore what goes on in scholarly journals, institutes, and universities in the United States and Europe; the converse is not true. For example, there is no major journal of Arab studies published in the Arab world today' (p. 323). The first statement is hardly a reproach; the rest is simply untrue. Mr. Said is apparently unaware of the enormous output of journals, monographs, editions, and other studies being published by universities, academies, learned societies, and other scholarly bodies in many different Arab countries.[9] He is apparently equally unaware of the large and growing literature of self-criticism produced by Arab authors who try to examine some of the failings and weaknesses of Arab society and culture and in so doing make, in a much more acute form, many of the observations for which Mr. Said attacks the Orientalists and for which he accuses them of racism, hostility, and a desire to dominate. He does not even seem to know the considerable body of writing by Arab authors on the subject of Orientalism; at least, he does not mention it.[10]

Despite a predominantly unfavorable response among reviewers in learned journals (with the curious exception of *The Journal of the American Oriental Society*, the house organ of American Orientalists), Said's *Orientalism* has had a considerable impact.

The success of this book and the ideas or, to be more precise, the attitudes that it expresses, in spite of its science fiction history and its lexical Humpty-Dumptyism, requires some explanation. One reason is certainly its anti-Westernism – the profound hostility to the West but more particularly the liberal and democratic West, since Germany is accorded a partial and Russia a total exemption. This responds well to the sentiments of those in the West, and especially in the United States, who condemn their country as the source of all the evil in the world as arrogantly and absurdly as their forbears acclaimed it as the source of all good. Similarly, the book appeals by its use of the ideas and still more of the language of currently fashionable literary, philosophical, and political theories. It meets the world's growing need for simplification by reducing all the complex national, cultural, religious, social, and economic problems of the Arab world to a single grievance directed against a small group of easily identified and immediately recognizable malefactors. There is, as anyone who has browsed in a college bookshop knows, a broad market for simplified versions of complex problems. Precisely this kind of simplification, so attractive to Western readers, has evoked the most serious critique of anti-Orientalism among Arab writers and thinkers who feel that the best interests of their society and the solving of its genuine problems cannot be served by the blurring of issues and the naming of scapegoats.

Some of those who have adopted anti-Orientalist philosophies have themselves been competent professional Orientalists with a mastery of the skills of their trade. But there have been others for whom the new epistemology was a welcome relief from drudgery, and some part of the book's attraction may be attributed to its harsh strictures on textual and philological scholarship. These bring reassurance and even encouragement to some who wish to make a career of studying the Orient but have either failed or not attempted to master its languages.

There are several major languages in the Middle Eastern area, and all of them are difficult. All but one – modern Turkish – are written in scripts other than the Latin script. All are shaped by cultural traditions different from those of Europe and North America. The study of these languages is an arduous task. To learn Arabic even adequately, let alone well, can take as much time and effort as to learn several European languages. Inevitably, therefore, the study of Arabic and other Middle Eastern languages has become a specialized field in itself. In the past, those who engaged in this field of specialization usually lacked either the time or the inclination to equip themselves in the social science or, to a lesser extent, the historical disciplines. Historians, whose work is mostly based on written evidence, have been more ready to learn languages and acquire as much of the philological technique as is necessary for understanding their sources. But social scientists from outside the area have not always troubled to learn its languages.

Naturally both groups, sociologists and philologists, have tended to decry what they do not possess. The hard-core philologist is an almost extinct species;

those who believe that social, economic, political, and even literary theory may not only inform but also replace the study of sources continue to flourish. One of them, in a recent review of a work on Middle Eastern history, spoke with contempt of Orientalists who try to understand the history of another civilization by 'the minute examination of difficult texts.' In addition to indicating a well-attested preference for the superficial examination of easy texts, the remark illustrates a profound need to which anti-Orientalism provides a welcome relief. According to a currently fashionable epistemological view, absolute truth is either nonexistent or unattainable. Therefore, truth doesn't matter; facts don't matter. All discourse is a manifestation of a power relationship, and all knowledge is slanted. Therefore, accuracy doesn't matter; evidence doesn't matter. All that matters is the attitude – the motives and purposes – of the user of knowledge, and this may be simply claimed for oneself or imputed to another. In imputing motives, the irrelevance of truth, facts, evidence, and even plausibility is a great help. The mere assertion suffices. The same rules apply to claiming a motive; goodwill can be established quickly and easily by appropriate political support. This is demonstrated *in Orientalism*, in which scholars whose methods and procedures are indistinguishable by any scholarly or methodological criterion are divided into sheep and goats according to their support or lack of support for Arab causes. Such support, especially when buttressed by approved literary or social theories, can more than compensate for any lack of linguistic or historical knowledge.

It does not seem to have occurred to those who hold such views that their attitudes are profoundly condescending to the Arabs and other non-Western peoples. Who, after all, would pretend that one could do serious scholarly work on France without French, on Germany without German, even on Sweden without Swedish? Or that the effort to learn these languages is commonly inspired by hostile motives?

The response to anti-Orientalism in the Arab world raises different and, in the last analysis, more interesting and more important questions.

Orientalists in Europe and America have dealt with all the cultures of Asia – China and Japan, India and Indonesia; and in the Middle East their studies are by no means limited to the Arabs but have included the Turks and Persians as well as the ancient cultures of the region. There is a radical, one might almost say a complete, difference in the attitudes of virtually all these other peoples toward the scholars who study them from outside. The Chinese, the Indians, and the rest are not always admiring of the Orientalists who deal with them, and are sometimes critical, on scholarly grounds, of their work. Sometimes they simply ignore them; sometimes they regard them with a kind of tolerant amusement; sometimes they accept them in the way that Greek scholars have accepted the Hellenists. The violent and vituperative attack on Orientalists is limited – apart from the Muslim reaction against the perceived threat from a rival faith – to one group and one group only among the peoples whom the Orientalists have studied, namely, the Arabs. This raises the interesting question of whether the Arabs differ significantly from other Asian and African peoples or whether the Arabic specialists differ in some significant way from other Orientalists.

Some help in answering this question may be found in another important fact – that this hostility to Orientalists is by no means universal or even dominant in Arab countries. Many of the Orientalists most violently attacked by the Saidian and related schools have taught generations of Arab students and have been translated and published in Arab countries.[11] Arab scholars working in the various fields with which the Orientalists have been concerned – history, literature, language, philosophy, and others – have made normal use of Orientalist publications. They have contributed extensively to Orientalist journals and have participated generally in Orientalist symposia, colloquia, and other international activities. Arab scholars have often differed from Orientalists in their findings and judgments, just as Arab scholars and Orientalist scholars have differed among themselves. These have, for the most part, been scholarly differences, not clashes of ethnic or ideological allegiances, and they have been discussed within the norms and courtesies of scholarly debate. The hue and cry against the Orientalists was raised not by scholarly colleagues interested in their work and competent to evaluate it but from quite other sources.

Significantly, the critique of the Orientalists has evoked a powerful and increasing countercritique from Arab writers. Although for the most part they share the disenchantment of the anti-Orientalists with Western civilization and their resentment at what the West has done in the Arab lands, these Arab writers are appalled by the smug, self-satisfied, and naively simplistic explanations that the critics offer of the disasters that the Arab world has suffered and the problems that it still faces. In a brilliant essay, the Egyptian philosopher Fu'ād Zakaria divides the anti-Orientalists into two main categories. The first school of criticism is religious and apologetic, a defense of the integrity and perfection of Islam against what they see as an attack by hostile forces, variously described as Christians, missionaries, Jews, Marxists, atheists, and the like, seeking to undermine and discredit Islam in order to impose their own beliefs. For the most part, these critics do not know the languages in which the Orientalists write and are therefore obliged to rely on quotations and a few translations. More important, they have no understanding whatever of the kind of modern critical scholarship of which Western Orientalism is a part and so are, for example, quite unaware that modern Western scholars are at least equally merciless in analyzing their own religious and cultural traditions.

The second group, according to Professor Zakaria, attack Orientalism from a political-cultural and not from a religious point of view. Indeed, the most vocal among them are not Muslims at all but are Christian or post-Christian expatriates living in Western Europe or the United States. They are perfectly familiar with modern Western secular civilization and its scholarly culture as well as its languages. Therefore, in this respect, they are able to wage war against the Orientalists with their own weapons. But they have a serious weakness – the poor knowledge that most of them possess of the classical Arab, Islamic civilization of which they claim to be the defenders. Here they are at a disadvantage not only as compared with the Muslim apologists but also as compared with the Orientalists themselves. If the defenders of Islam have a naive and essentialist view of the West about which they know so little, the Westernized defenders of the Arab political and cultural heritage have an equally naive and essentialist view of the realities of this heritage in the past and the predicament of its heirs at the present. The illusions offered by the anti-Orientalists can only worsen this predicament by delaying or impeding the cold, critical self-analysis that must procede any serious effort for improvement.

After examining the methods and modalities of anti-Orientalism in some detail, Professor Zakaria ends with a psychosocial analysis of the motives of both the Orientalists and their two types of opponent. In discussing those whom he calls the 'westernizing expatriates,' he suggests an interesting additional motive – the natural desire of the immigrant, in search of self-respect and the respect of his new compatriots, to maximize the achievements of his culture of origin and to minimize the differences that distinguish it from the culture of his new home.

This insight would appear to be confirmed by Mr. Said's assertion, in a PBS debate in 1977, that the fourteen-centuries-old Islamic tradition and civilization are no more meaningful for the Arab world today than are seventh-century events in Europe for an understanding of present-day America. Experts in Iraq and Iran thought otherwise. Only a few years later, in their war propaganda against each other, both countries daily evoked events and personalities of the seventh century, in the sure knowledge that they would be understood. One does not quite see American contenders for power making a point by a rapid allusion to the Anglo-Saxon heptarchy, the rise of the Carolingians, or the wars of the Lombards.

Professor Zakaria's concluding remarks are noteworthy:

> Orientalism is surely not without blemish, but the greater danger would be if we denied our faults merely because others speak of them for unobjective purposes. Our cultural task at this stage is to take the bull of backwardness by the horns and criticize ourselves before we criticize the image, even if it is deliberately distorted, that others make of us.[12]

The critique of Orientalism raises several genuine questions. A point made by several critics is that the guiding principle of these studies is expressed in the dictum 'knowledge is power' and that Orientalists were seeking knowledge of Oriental peoples in order to dominate them, most of them being directly or, as Abdel-Malek allows, objectively (in the Marxist sense) in the service of imperialism. No doubt there were some Orientalists who, objectively or subjectively, served or profited from imperial domination. But as an explanation of the Orientalist enterprise as a whole, it is absurdly inadequate. If the pursuit of power through knowledge is the only or even the prime motive, why did the study of Arabic and Islam begin in Europe centuries before the Muslim conquerors were driven from eastern and western European soil and the Europeans embarked on their counterattack? Why did these studies flourish in European countries that never had any share in the domination of the Arab world and yet made a contribution as great as the English and French – most scholars would say greater? And why did Western scholars devote so much effort to the decipherment and recovery of the monuments of ancient Middle Eastern civilization, long since forgotten in their own countries?

Another charge leveled against the Orientalists is that of bias against the peoples they study, even of a built-in hostility to them. No one would deny that scholars, like other human beings, are liable to some kind of bias, more often for, rather than against, the subject of their study. The significant difference is between those who recognize their bias and try to correct it and those who give it free rein. (Accusations of cultural bias and political ulterior motives might also gain somewhat in credibility if the accusers did not assume for themselves and accord to Marxist-Leninist scholarship a plenary indulgence.)

Beyond the question of bias there lies the larger epistemological problem of how far it is possible for scholars of one society to study and interpret the creations of another. The accusers complain of stereotypes and facile generalizations. Stereotyped prejudices certainly exist – not only of other cultures, in the Orient or elsewhere, but of other nations, races, churches, classes, professions, generations, and almost any other group one cares to mention within our own society. The Orientalists are not immune to these dangers; nor are their accusers. The former at least have the advantage of some concern for intellectual precision and discipline.

The most important question – least mentioned by the current wave of critics – is that of the scholarly merits, indeed the scholarly validity, of Orientalist findings. Prudently, the anti-Orientalists hardly touch on this question and indeed give very little attention to the scholarly writings of the scholars whose putative attitudes, motives, and purposes form the theme of their campaign. Scholarly criticism of Orientalist scholarship is a legitimate and indeed a necessary, inherent part of the process. Fortunately, it is going on all the time – not a criticism of Orientalism, which would be meaningless, but a criticism of the research and results of individual scholars or schools of scholars. The most rigorous and penetrating critique of Orientalist, as of any other, scholarship has always been and will remain that of their fellow scholars, especially, though not exclusively, those working in the same field.

Notes

1. *New York Times*, 20 December 1986.
2. Pakistan press, spring and summer 1955, especially editorial and news columns in *Morning News* (Karachi), 24 August 1955, and two letters by Sh. Inayatullah, protesting against this campaign, published in the *Pakistan Times*, 1 and 28 September 1955.

3. Muhammad al-Bahī, *Al-Mubashshirūn wa'l-Mustashriqūn wa-mawqifuhum min al-Islām* (Cairo, n.d. [ca. 1962]).

4. Ibrahim Abu-Lughod, 'Al-Saytara al-Ṣahyūniyya 'ala al-dirāsāt al-'arabryya fi Amrīkā,' *Al-Adab* 12, no. 6 (June 1974):5–6.

5. Raymond Schwab, *La Renaissance orientale* (Paris, 1950). An English translation, *The Oriental Renaissance: Europe's Rediscovery of India and the East, 1680–1880*, trans. Gene Patterson-Black and Victor Reinking (New York, 1984), is so inaccurate as to be unusable.

6. In a discussion of some Islamic terms for 'revolution,' I began the examination of each term – following a common Arab practice – with a brief look at the basic meanings of the Arabic root from which it was derived. One passage, introducing the term most widely used in modern Arabic, ran as follows: 'The root *th-w-r* in classical Arabic meant to rise up (e.g. of a camel), to be stirred or excited, and hence, especially in Maghribi usage, to rebel. It is often used in the context of establishing a petty, independent sovereignty; thus, for example, the so-called party kings who ruled in eleventh-century Spain after the breakup of the Caliphate of Cordova, are called *thawwār* (singular *thā'ir*). The noun *thawra* at first means excitement, as in the phrase, cited in the *Sihāh*, a standard medieval Arabic dictionary, *intazir ḥatta taskun hadhihi 'l-thawra*, wait until this excitement dies down – a very apt recommendation. The verb is used by al-Iji, in the form *thawarān* or *ithārat fitna*, stirring up sedition, as one of the dangers which should discourage a man from practising the duty of resistance to bad government. *Thawra* is the term used by Arabic writers in the nineteenth-century for the French Revolution, and by their successors for the approved revolutions, domestic and foreign, of our own time' ('Islamic Concepts of Revolution,' in *Revolution in the Middle East and Other Case Studies*, ed. P. J. Vatikiotis [London, 1972], pp. 38–39.)

   This definition, in both form and content, follows the standard classical Arabic dictionaries and would have been immediately recognized by anyone familiar with Arabic lexicography. The use of camel imagery in politics was as natural for the ancient Arabs as horse imagery for the Turks and ship imagery among the maritime peoples of the West.

   Said understood the passage differently: 'Lewis's association of *thawra* with a camel rising and generally with excitement (and not with a struggle on behalf of values) hints much more broadly than is usual for him that the Arab is scarcely more than a neurotic sexual being. Each of the words or phrases he uses to describe revolution is tinged with sexuality: *stirred, excited, rising up*. But for the most part it is a 'bad' sexuality he ascribes to the Arab. In the end, since Arabs are really not equipped for serious action, their sexual excitement is no more noble than a camel's rising up. Instead of revolution there is sedition, setting up a petty sovereignty, and more excitement, which is as much as saying that instead of copulation the Arab can only achieve foreplay, masturbation, coitus interruptus. These, I think, are Lewis's implications, no matter how innocent his air of learning, or parlorlike his language' (pp. 315–16). To which one can only reply in the words of the Duke of Wellington: 'If you can believe that, you can believe anything.'

7. Maxime Rodinson, *La fascination de l'Islam* (Paris, 1980), p. 14. The 'two sciences' of Zhdanov and his successors and imitators have been variously defined, according to the ideological alignments, the political purposes, and the social or even ethnic origins of the scientists.

8. *New York Times Book Review*, 31 October 1976.

9. Such as, for example, the *Review of the Arab Academy* (Damascus), *al-Abhāth* (Beirut), the *Review of Maghribi History* (Tunis), and the Bulletins of the Faculties of Arts and of Social Sciences of Cairo, Alexandria, Baghdad, and other universities.

10. For example, the writings of Tibawi and Khatibi, and Najib al-Aqiqi's three-volume Arabic work on Orientalism and Orientalists, surely the most comprehensive treatment of the subject in any language.

11. I may perhaps mention here that several of my own publications, including some to which the anti-Orientalists have taken the strongest exception, have been translated and published in the Arab world – in Egypt, Lebanon, Libya, Saudi Arabia, Algeria, and Iraq.

12. Fu'ād Zakaria, 'Naqd al-Istishrāq wa'azmat al-thaqāfa al-'Arabiyya al-mu'āṣira,' *Fikr* (Cairo) 10 (1986):33–75. An abridged French translation is included in a volume of Professor Zakariya's essays, entitled *Laicité ou Islamisme: les arabes à l'heure du choix* (Paris and Cairo, 1990), pp. 119–66. For other Arabic critiques of anti-Orientalism, see Ṣādiq al-'Aẓm, *Al-Istishrāq wa'l-istishrāq ma'kūsan* (Beirut, 1981), partial English version: 'Orientalism and Orientalism in Reverse,' *Khamsin* 8 (1981):5–26; Nadīm al-Bīṭār, *Ḥudūd al-Huwiyya al-Qawmiyya* (Beirut, 1982), chap. 6, pp. 153–96: 'Min al-istishrāq al-gharbï ilā 'istishrāq 'Arabi.' Some of these and others are discussed by Emmanuel Sivan in his *Interpretations of Islam: Past and Present* (Princeton, 1985), chap. 5, pp. 133–54: 'Edward Said and His Arab Reviewers.' Between 1987 and 1990, the Office of General Cultural Affairs of the Iraqi Ministry of Culture and Education published several volumes entitled *Orientalism*, containing articles and interviews in both Arabic and English. With the exception of Dr. Ṣādiq al-'Aẓm's essay, all of the above appeared after the original publication of this article.

PART XI
QUALIFICATIONS
AND ELABORATION

In the two decades following the publication of *Orientalism*, Edward Said's work spawned a series of studies in which academics, drawn from a variety of disciplines, reinterpreted their own subjects in the light of Said's conclusions, further elaborated his thesis or questioned its validity. In 1985 B. J. Moore-Gilbert – a student of Anglo-Indian literature – in *Kipling and 'Orientalism'*, considered the way English writers portrayed India, and the life of Anglo-Indians, in their works. In 1986 the anthropologist Ronald Inden, in 'Orientalist Constructions of India', attempted a critique of Indology, designed to reveal the impact on that subject of the 'orientalist discourse'. In 1991 Aijaz Ahmed – a social scientist and student of English literature – in 'Between Orientalism and Historicism', compared and contrasted the work of Edward Said in *Orientalism* (1978) with that of Ronald Inden in *Imagining India* (1990). In 1992 Billie Melman – a student of women's history – in *Women's Orients*, investigated the way in which Western women experienced life in the Middle East. In 1993, in an article entitled 'Deep Orientalism? Notes on Sanskrit and Power Beyond the Raj', published in Carol A. Breckenridge and Peter van der Veer (eds.), *Orientalism and the Postcolonial Predicament*, Sheldon Pollock – a student of Sanskrit and Indic studies – investigated the impact of orientalism on the national political culture of Germany in the second half of the nineteenth century and the first half of the twentieth. In 1914 Lisa Lowe – a student of comparative literature – in *Critical Terrains*, argued that it was necessary to 'revise and render more complex' the thesis that an 'ontology of Occident and Orient' appears in a consistent manner 'between all cultural and historical movements'. Finally, in 1995, in *Orientalism: History, Theory and the Arts*, John MacKenzie argued that Said's analysis of orientalism and European culture in the age of imperialism was fundamentally flawed, for 'both Self (Europe) and Other (the Orient) were locked in processes of mutual modification, sometimes slow but inexorable, sometimes running as fast as a recently unfrozen river'.

27

'GORGEOUS EAST' VERSUS 'LAND OF REGRETS'

B. J. Moore-Gilbert

In Kipling and 'Orientalism'*, B. J. Moore-Gilbert explains that a principal motive of Anglo-Indian literature was the correction of metropolitan misconception regarding life in India. This misconception was, so the Anglo–Indians believed, either the product of complete ignorance – it was generally agreed that the English people at home showed little or no interest in their empire abroad – or a product of the image of the 'gorgeous East', manufactured by such writers as Beckford, Moore, Southey and Scott.*

Such fanciful visions of life in the East did much to stimulate literary production in the subcontinent. The earliest novels which can properly be considered Anglo-Indian were premised upon the need to correct metropolitan misconceptions. In *Hartly House, Calcutta*, Sophia Goldborne's first letter home to Arabella begins thus: 'I have to inform you, that all the prejudices you have so long cherished . . . must be done away; and for this plain reason, that they are totally groundless.' (p. 1) So recurrent is the invocation of British ignorance that it may be seen as a formal structural characteristic; thus W. B. Hockley's decision to write *The English in India* for those who 'feel anxious to understand the mode of living at the presidencies of India' (vol. 1, p. 6), or the desire of the author of *The Bengalee* to bring Anglo-India 'to the better acquaintance of our fellow-countrymen in England.' (p. 5) G. O. Trevelyan's 'most earnest desire

B. J. Moore-Gilbert, *Kipling and 'Orientalism'* (London: Croom-Helm, 1986), pp. 31–5.

and most cherished ambition' was to build upon these foundations. ([*The competition Wallah,*] 1864, p. 5) The efforts of such writers had, however, done little to modify conventional metropolitan ideas by Kipling's time, according to the *Pioneer*. The paper was adamant even then that 'profound ignorance of Indian life and manners exists in England.' (24 Feb 1882, p. 2) In 1888 it attacked the romanticisation of India by Gautier and de Montepin (9 Jan, p. 5) and the *Gazette*, while acknowledging that *Nana Sahib* – in which Sarah Bernhardt was appearing in London – might be good drama, lamented that it was full of 'historical improbability.' (17 Jan 1884, p. 4) In H. S. Cunningham's *The Coeruleans* (1887), Masterly claims that his Indian province is regarded in England 'as only a far-off colonial detail ... as to which no human being in his London set could affect to possess the most rudimentary knowledge or to feel the very slightest concern.' (vol. 1, p. 12)

This sense of alienation seems paradoxical. Even by 1849, according to the author of *On the Deficiency of European Officers in the Army of India*, sufficiently close ties existed between the two cultures to prevent such a difference of perception: 'There is not a family of note, from the middle to the highest circles, which has not several blood relations or connexions, intimate friends or acquaintances, in the civil and military services of India.' (p. 61) But, as Edward Money complained just after the Mutiny in *The Wife and the Ward*, such links did little to abate 'this apathy, this ignorance on all Indian subjects; for how many thousands have family ties that interest them in these sunny lands, and yet truly how little is known in England of every-day life in India.' (p. 19)

By Kipling's time, moreover, improvements in communications, effected by the construction of the Suez canal, steamships and railways, had made India a fashionable destination for travellers. However, this traffic, in Anglo-Indian eyes, only served to consolidate traditional misconceptions. Its reviews of memoirs published as a result of cold-weather visits were usually scathing: one example is the *Pioneer*'s vituperative notice of Cuthbert Larking's *Bando-bast and Khabar* (25 Feb 1888, p. 2), the fruits of a seven month visit. The pernicious effects on the metropolitan imagination of what the *Pioneer* called 'that modern Goth the globe-trotter' (15 Mar 1888, p. 3) had long been lamented by literary figures. In 1828, for example, W. B. Hockley complained thus: 'Travellers may have imposed upon people, by describing India as the seat of innumerable pleasures and luxuries, but such is not the case.' [*The English in India,*] (vol. 1, p. vi) In 1856, the *Calcutta Review* asserted that 'the branch of literature most readily chosen by complete ignorance as least likely to involve failure or provide contempt should be the writing of Travels.' (Dec, p. 278) Amongst Kipling's contemporaries, H. S. Cunningham condemns Sir Theophilus Prance, in *The Coeruleans*, for his credulity about cold-weather travellers; and Sara Duncan's *Simple Adventures* summarised the feelings of most Anglo-Indians in her assertion that it 'may be set down as an axiom that the genus globe-trotter is unloved in Calcutta.' (p. 169) Kipling's writing, too, is contemptuous of such itinerants. In the figure of Jevon, in 'A Friend's Friend' [*Plain*

Tales from the Hills], the author presents the consequences of the insensitivity to which the 'travelling gentleman' was felt to be customarily liable; and in *From Sea to Sea*, Kipling is embarrassed to find himself, albeit temporarily, in the ranks of 'the globe-trotter – the man who "does" kingdoms in days and writes books upon them in weeks.' (vol. 1, p. 3) Similarly, it seems no coincidence that the man who does the Indian protagonist of 'Lispeth' (P.T.H.) such emotional violence should be a cold-weather visitor.

It is important to note that such hostility to metropolitan visitors – and the images of India they subsequently produced – involved the question of expertise as regards the representation of India. The *Gazette* makes this explicit in complaining that 'to the public mind, at home, the last eminent traveller, fresh from the Indian tour, is a more reliable authority than the last Anglo-Indian retired from the service.' (11 Feb 1885, p. 2) This conflict of perspectives often expresses itself in Anglo-Indian fiction by parody or inversion of the conventions of metropolitan travel writing. The journey to India is commonly presented as one of disillusion, in which the expectations of a young man leaving for his first appointment in India are compared ironically with the unglamorous actuality of the sub-continent. In the gap between idealisation and reality, the literary tradition locates the measure of Britain's confusion about its overseas dependency. This structure is often applied in tandem with the development of the protagonist to personal maturity. The manner in which he adjusts to the disappointment apparently inevitable upon arrival is thus an index of his potential not simply for self-fulfilment, but for imperial service. A striking illustration of this dual structure is provided by Captain Meadows Taylor's novel, *Tippoo Sultaun*. When Herbert Compton's regiment is unexpectedly ordered out to India, his conception of his future occupation is fantastical and vague. It consists of a 'feverish vision of palaces amidst gardens, where the graceful palm-trees and acacia waved over fountains which played unceasingly, and threw up a soft and almost noiseless spray into the air, and where he wandered amidst forms clad in such oriental garbs as his fancy supplied, gorgeous, and dazzling with gold and gems.' (vol. 1, p. 304) The first sight of Bombay promises to fulfil Compton's anticipations; but these are rapidly eroded, and by the end of the first night profound melancholy has settled upon the young officer and his comrades-in-arms. Actual experience of India soon dissolves their expectation of a 'Gorgeous East', 'which they discovered, with no small chagrin, existed only in their imaginations.' (vol .1, p. 320)

An analogous disillusionment is undergone by Adela Balfour in J. W. Kaye's *Long Engagements*. Her scandalous attachment to Danvers while her fiancé is away on the first Afghan campaign is viewed by Herbert Gray as partly a reaction to and consolation for her 'exaggerated expectations'; and, he concludes, the 'feeling on actual arrival in India was generally one of disappointment.' (pp. 104–5) The tedious environment of Mulkapore shatters Nora O'Neill's preconceptions in Mrs. Croker's *Pretty Miss Neville*: 'I expected to see gorgeously caparisoned elephants the only means of transit; and I was prepared to behold tigers sporting about the plains.' (p. 133) Auntie Vinnie suffers similarly in Sara Duncan's *Vernon's Aunt*: 'Bombay was a deep, keen and bitter disappointment to me.' (p. 26) Philip Ambrose's inability to reconcile his fantasy about the ease and brilliance of British existence in India with the rigorous demands actually made upon him is the source of much of the irony of Cunningham's *The Coeruleans* and leads finally to his tragic disgrace. G. O. Trevelyan summarises the effects of such experiences thus: 'A man gains more new ideas, or, which comes to the same, gets rid of more old ones, within his first month on Indian soil than during any equal period of his life.' (1864, p. 21)

Kipling uses the journey of disillusion to the same ends as his predecessors. Thus, in '"Yoked With An Unbeliever"' (P.T.H.), the Barron family do not possess even an elementary geographical sense of the empire. Phil's mother believes Darjeeling to be a '"port on the Bengal Ocean"' (p. 30) and Agnes, his fiancée, believes India is 'divided equally between jungle, tigers, cobras, cholera, and sepoys.' (p. 29) While the disappointment of Phil's expectations of India causes him no lasting grief, Kipling follows established precedent in emphasising the potentially tragic consequences of this disenchantment in other stories. Dicky Hatt of 'In the Pride of His Youth' (P.T.H.) also foolishly overestimates the glamours of Indian service. After a brief period of skimping, he anticipates that 'Mrs. Dicky Hatt was to come out, and the rest of life was to be a glorious golden mist.' (p. 174) Duncan Parenness has comparable ambitions which are likewise unfulfilled. Both descend into madness and despair. The most dramatic instance of disillusionment occurs in 'Thrown Away' (P.T.H.) in which the Boy eventually commits suicide.

Anglo-Indian fiction, then, evolved in some measure in response to an aggrieved belief that the nature of life in the sub-continent was little understood or cared about in Britain. It challenged the contributions made to metropolitan 'Orientalism' by both travel writing and fiction and in so doing helped to define the exiled community and its culture as distinct by perspective and preoccupation from its British equivalents. In place of the myth of the 'Gorgeous East', it sought to produce an alternative vision which was a good deal less glamorous and exciting. This is organised around a recurrent core of topics which form the staple of Anglo-Indian fiction's social commentary.

28

ORIENTALIST CONSTRUCTIONS
OF INDIA

Ronald Inden

In 'Orientalist Constructions of India' Ronald Inden, Professor of Indology at the University of Chicago, suggests that Western Indologists have in the past frequently produced an 'Indological' construction of India. In this construction, they have seen caste as India's essential institution, both the cause of its low level of political and economic development and a factor contributing to its repeated conquest by outsiders. In the following extracts – 'Opening Discussion' and 'The Hegemonic Account' – Inden describes the philosophical basis of his critique of Western Indology and explains how such a 'hegemonic' account of Indian history came to be created.

OPENING DISCUSSION

Now it is the interest of Spirit that *external* conditions should become *internal* ones; that the natural and the spiritual world should be recognized in the subjective aspect belonging to intelligence; by which process the unity of subjectivity and (positive) Being generally – or the Idealism of Existence – is established. This Idealism, then, is found in India, but only as an Idealism of imagination, without distinct conceptions; – one which does indeed free existence from Beginning and Matter (liberates it from temporal limitations and gross materiality), but changes everything into the merely Imaginative; for although the latter appears interwoven with definite conceptions and Thought presents itself as an occasional concomitant, this happens only through accidental combination. Since, however, it is the abstract and

Ronald Inden, 'Orientalist Constructions of India', *Modern Asian Studies*, 20, 3, 1986, pp. 401–3 and 416–21.

absolute Thought itself that enters into these dreams as their material, we
may say that Absolute Being is presented here as in the ecstatic state of a
dreaming condition (Hegel, *Philosophy of History*, p. 139).

This essay is critical of Indology and the related disciplines in the social sciences.
Its aim is to establish a space for the production of a new knowledge of South
Asia. The object of the critique is what I, following others, refer to as
'Orientalist discourse', and the accounts of India that it produced. It has
emerged out of work that I have been doing for the past decade on Hindu
states and rituals in 'early medieval' India. What I present here is to be seen as a
provisional part of a larger study of Hinduism and kingship which I hope to
complete soon. Although I write here from the standpoint of an Indologist,
historian, and anthropologist of India, the problems with which I deal here are
not confined to those disciplines. They are shared by scholars in the other
human sciences as well.

My concern in the 'deconstruction' that follows is not to compare the
'theories' or 'explanations' of these accounts with the 'facts' of Indian history.
On the contrary, I take the position that those facts themselves have been
produced by an 'episteme' (a way of knowing that implies a particular view of
existence) which I wish to criticize. The episteme at issue presupposes a
representational view of knowledge. It assumes that true knowledge merely
represents or mirrors a separate reality which the knower somehow transcends.
Adherence to this position has allowed the scholar to claim that his (rarely her)
knowledge is natural and objective and not a matter for political debate. It has
also operated to produce a hierarchic relationship between knower and known,
privileging the knowledge of the scientists and other experts and leaders who
make up the former while subjugating the knowledges of the people who
comprise the latter.

My own position relies on a reading of the works of thinkers as diverse as R.
G. Collingwood (post-Hegelian), Antonio Gramsci (post-Marxian), and Michel
Foucault (post-structuralist), and, indirectly, Jacques Derrida (deconstruction-
ist). It has also benefited a great deal from the writings of Anthony Giddens in
critical sociology on human agency, and of Roy Bhaskar on 'transcendental
realism' in the philosophy of science. It is my assumption that reality transcends
the knower. The knowledge of the knower is not a 'natural' representation of an
external reality. It is an artifical construct but one which actively participates
(especially when it comes to social knowledge) in producing and transforming
the world.

Two of the assumptions built into the 'episteme' of Indology are that the real
world (whether that is material and determinate or ideal and ineffable) consists
of essences and that that world is unitary. Entailed in these two assumptions is a
further assumption. It holds that there exists a 'human nature' which itself
consists of a unitary essence. It is also supposed that, at a lower level, each
culture or civilization embodies a similarly unitary essence. Since the unitary
essence of human nature is assumed to be most fully realized in the 'West', a

major difficulty (if not the fundamental one) that has confronted the scholar of non-Western Others has been how to reconcile the essence of the Other's civilization, with the Euro-American manifestation of human nature's unitary essence – rational, scientific thought and the institutions of liberal capitalism and democracy. Not infrequently this essence is substantialized and turned into an Agent (God, Reason, Western Man, the Market, the Welfare State, the Party) who is seen as using the people and institutions of the West as instruments and history is seen as teleogical: a hypostatized Agent is moving humanity towards its natural and spiritual (essential) end.

Indological discourse, I argue, holds (or simply assumes), that the essence of Indian civilization is just the opposite of the West's. It is the irrational (but rationalizable) institution of 'caste' and the Indological religion that accompanies it, Hinduism. Human agency in India is displaced by Indological discourse not onto a reified State or Market but onto a substantialized Caste. This has entailed several consequences for the Indological construction of India. It has necessitated the wholesale dismissal of Indian political institutions, and especially of kingship. To give this construct of India credibility, the depiction of Indian thought as inherently symbolic and mythical rather than rational and logical has also been required. Finally, it has been necessary for Brahmanism or Hinduism, the religion considered to be the justification of caste, to be characterized as essentially idealistic (i.e., apolitical).

Caste, conceived in this way as India's essential institution, has been both the cause and effect of India's low level of political and economic 'development' and of its repeated failure to prevent its conquest by outsiders. Given this, it was only 'natural' for European scholars, traders, and administrators to appropriate the power of Indians (not only the 'masses', but also the 'elite') to act for themselves. This they have done since the formation of Indological discourse made it possible. Despite India's acquisition of formal political independence, it has still not regained the power to know its own past and present apart from that discourse.

The fixation on caste as the essence of India has had still another effect. It has committed Indology, largely descended from British empiricism and utilitarianism, to a curious and contradictory mixture of societalism, in which Indian actions are attributed to social groups – caste, village, linguistic region, religion, and joint family – because there are no individuals in India, and individualism, in which Indians' acts are attributed to bad motives.

The purpose here is to produce a knowledge of India that helps restore that power, that focuses on the problematic of formulating and using a theory of human agency which avoids the pitfalls of the representational theory of knowledge. This will require that those of us in the discipline work free of the incoherent combination of societalism and individualism that prevails in the study of South Asia. It will also entail the abandonment of the substantialism and essentialism that have permitted the discipline of Indology and its affiliates in the social sciences to evade the issue of human agency.

[...]

THE HEGEMONIC ACCOUNT

Sir William Jones (1746–94) is usually the man who is credited with first suggesting that Persian and the European languages were related to one another and not descended from Hebrew. He was also the person largely responsible for founding, in 1784, the first Indological institution, the Asiatick Society of Bengal. If any one person can be named as the founder of Indology, it is certainly he.[1] Because he advocated the importance of studying Eastern languages and texts in India, he and some of his colleagues were dubbed 'Orientalists'. They were opposed by certain utilitarians, who came to be known as 'Anglicists' because they argued that Western knowledge in English should displace the Eastern. The most notable of these opponents was James Mill, whose *History of India* was, in large part, written as a refutation of some of Jones's ideas. The victory which Mill and his colleagues gained over the 'Orientalists' in shaping the policies of the East India Company had the effect (hardly surprising given the convergence of utilitarian thought with commercial and colonial objectives) of securing dominance for the utilitarian or positivist view both in government practice and in the fledgling discipline of Indology.

Every discipline has, within its particular historic formations, texts or accounts which can be dubbed 'hegemonic'. The idea of a text as 'hegemonic' that I use here is taken in large part from Gramsci, particularly in the sense that such a text is not concerned with narrow and internalist issues of the discipline itself but with the broader questions of India's place in the world and in history, issues in which those outside of the discipline, the active subjects of the world – business and government leaders – and the more passive subjects of the world's history, the populace at large, are interested. It is, furthermore, an account that is seen, during the period of its predominance, to exercise leadership in a field actively and positively and not one that is merely imposed on it. A hegemonic text is also totalizing – it provides an account of every aspect of Indian life. It accounts for all the elements that the relevant knowing public wants to know about.[2]

Certain accounts within the discipline of Indology or South Asian studies can be considered as exercising hegemony therein under various circumstances. Because hegemonic accounts have had to be comprehensive not only in their intended content but also in the audience they actually reach, they have tended to be accounts that are strong in all three of the aspects I have outlined above. They have been commentative as well as descriptive and explanatory or interpretive as well as commentative. Jones, in addition to being grouped with the losing Orientalists, failed to produce a single, comprehensive account of India. So his essays, well-written and rhetorically persuasive as many of them were, hardly constituted a hegemonic text. Here, too, Jones can be seen as losing out to Mill, for the latter's *History* was indeed a hegemonic account.

Throughout the nineteenth century, Mill's *History* remained the hegemonic textbook of Indian history. Later Indologists have either (wittingly or unwittingly) reiterated his construct of India or they have (directly or indirectly) written their accounts as responses to it. To see both reiteration and response together in the same book, one has only to pick up a later edition of this work, the fifth, edited by the Sanskritist and Orientalist, Horace Hayman Wilson (1789–1860).[3] He attempted in his long qualifying notes, to 'claw back' this formative text to a more 'scholarly', removed position. Mill's text was not confined, however, to the studies of scholarly gentlemen. It was 'required reading' at Haileybury College, where, until 1855, civil servants of the East India Company were trained. It held sway within Indology, fending off the challenge posed to it by Mountstuart Elphinstone's unfinished *History of British Power in the East*, until 1904. That was the year in which Vincent Smith (1848–1920) published his *Early History of India* (Oxford University Press). Smith's book became the hegemonic secondary revision of 'ancient' and 'early medieval' history of India for the next fifty years. But Mill's work was not completely set aside even then. Smith himself included selections from it in his more comprehensive *Oxford History of India* in 1919.[4]

The utilitarians considered conduct that was 'reverential, ceremonial, status-ordered, as distinct from practical, calculating, "useful",' as 'non-rational'.[5] So Mill, unlike Renou, is quite blunt in his characterization of Hindu ceremonies. The rationalization for Hindu 'excess' woven into his text consists of Mill's placement of Hindu civilization at an earlier time and lower 'stage' of evolution, the 'barbaric', than some (e.g., Jones) thought:

> To the rude mind, no other rule suggests itself for paying court to the Divine, than that for paying court to the Human Majesty; and as among a barbarous people, the forms of address, of respect, and compliment, are generally multiplied into a great variety of grotesque and frivolous ceremonies, so it happens with regard to their religious service. An endless succession of observances, in compliment to the god, is supposed to afford him the most exquisite delight; while the common discharge of the beneficent duties of life is regarded as an object of comparative indifference. It is unnecessary to cite instances in support of a representation, of which the whole history of the religion of most nations is a continual proof (pp. 276–7).

As I have already indicated, not every Indologist has explicitly included secondary revisions in his account. Renou himself, although fully prepared to present the theories of others, remained rather skeptical of most such efforts, largely because he considered them too reductionist.[6] On the whole, he preferred to leave his reader face to face with his representation of the disorderly Indian mind and its products unrationalized. Renou's refusal to theorize does not mean, however, that he avoided the naturalist assumptions of these reductionist theories. Renou, like Mill, consistently depicted Hinduism as a religion that has been unable to transcend the false knowledge and inferior practices of 'primitivism'.[7] Furthermore, the very fact that he did not provide his own secondary revisions or challenge those of others had the effect of permitting the theories of others to hold sway in the discipline. The point that Lorenzen makes about the Orientalists who come after Mill applies also to Renou. He says that their works

> are characterized by a meticulous concern for accuracy, an exhaustive collection of all available facts, and an almost obsessive avoidance of systematic generalization and evaluation.

The difficulty with this profusion of positivist scholarship on the part of Indologists was, as Lorenzen correctly indicates, that

> Virtually none of them even tried to mount an effective counterattack against more popular imperialist interpretations of ancient Indian history and society.[8]

The result is that the curious reader has had to turn elsewhere, to the work of Mill, Smith, and others, to find those full 'interpretations', those texts which I refer to as secondary revisions. But this is, perhaps, beside the point, for the following reason. Renou, we have seen, attributed the same dreaming irrationality to the Indian mind that Mill and Hegel did. It is difficult, therefore, to see how a comprehensive interpretation written by Renou would have differed in its major presuppositions from the regnant views of the Indian Other.

The question I would pose, even at this juncture, is: whose thought is it that is dream-like in these commentative and explanatory texts, the Indians', to whom it is attributed, or the Indologists' themselves? It could well be that careful, empirical study of Indian texts and practices has indeed disclosed to us a culture whose bearers are lost in an irrational dream state. This is a difficult proposition to defend, however, because Europeans took dreaming irrationality as a distinctive trait of Indian thought *before* the field of Indological research was even established. I am not just referring to Hegel, with whose characterization I prefaced this paper. The portrayal of India as a land of fabulous wealth, of miracles, of wishes fulfilled, a Paradise of sensual pleasures and exotic philosophers, apparently constituted a reiterated theme in medieval thought. As Jacques Le Goff puts it, 'A poor and limited world formed for itself an extravagant combinatoric dream of disquieting juxtapositions and concatenations.'[9] I am claiming that it is wrong to see Indian thought as essentially dreamlike and to view Indian civilization as inherently irrational. So it would be equally wrong to suggest that dreams of India as an exotic land are an essential feature of an hypostatized West. The dream or image of the medieval European differed from that of the nineteenth-century scholar and imperialist. He did not see India as an *inferior* land of the *past*, but as a *superior* land of the *future*, a paradisiac kingdom ruled by a priest-king, Prester John, who might, it was hoped, come to save Christendom.[10] Even so, this prehistory of Indology should make one skeptical of any argument that Indology has only represented Indian thought to the European and American 'as it really is.'

Let me conclude this section with some comments on the relationship of Freud to Indology. The major reason for using Freud's theory of dream interpretation here is that his theory makes quite explicit the discursive principles that have, for the most part, remained implicit in the discipline of Indology. What makes this possible is the fact that both share the same presuppositions about the relationship of knowledge to reality. Both presuppose a duality of knower and known. Both assume that the discourse of the knower, that of the scientist, is a privileged discourse in relation to the knowledges of the known, the Other of the human scientist. For Freud that Other is an Other internal to the West, the neurotic person who is his 'patient'. The Other of the Indologist is an externalized Other, the civilization of India. For both the analyst and the philologist, however, the knowledges of those whom they studied were what Foucault refers to as 'subjugated knowledges'. These comprised, according to him:

> a whole set of knowledges that have been disqualified as inadequate to their task or insufficiently elaborated: naive knowledges located low down on the hierarchy, beneath the required level of cognition or scientificity.[11]

Freud privileged Western scientific rationality in the form of psychoanalysis (or the interpretation of dreams) in much the same way that the Indologist (Renou) privileged his variant of that rationality, philology. The knowing subject, the analyst or Sanskritist is rational, the persons who are the subjects of inquiry are, in relation to him, irrational. The knowledges of the latter are distorted representations of their own reality. They are knowledges that must be subjugated. They are knowledges that must be introduced, annotated, catalogued, broken up and analyzed in 'data bases', apportioned out in monographs, reports, gazetteers, anthologies, readers, and course syllabi. I shall return to this question of the dualism of knower and known in the Conclusion. Let me now, however, turn to a brief examination of the construction of India that appears in the hegemonic texts of Indological discourse.

NOTES

1. On Jones and the establishment of the Society, see the excellent study of S. N. Mukherjee, *Sir William Jones: A Study in Eighteenth-Century British Attitudes to India* (Cambridge: Cambridge University Press, 1968), pp. 80–90.
2. Chantal Mouffe, 'Hegemony and Ideology in Gramsci,' in *Gramsci and Marxist Theory*, ed. C. Mouffe (London: Routledge and Kegan Paul, 1979), pp. 168–204, esp. pp. 193–4.
3. (London: J. Madden; Piper, Stephenson and Spence, 1858).
4. A. L. Basham, 'James Mill, Mountstuart Elphinstone and the History of India.' in *Historians of India, Pakistan and Ceylon* (London: Oxford University Press, 1961), ed., C. H. Philips, pp. 217–29; and his, 'Modern Historians of Ancient India,' in the same volume, pp. 266–74.

5. J. W. Burrow, *Evolution and Society*, (Cambridge University Press, 1970), p. 2.
6. Renou, *Religions*, pp. 19–20, 47–8.
7. *Ibid.*, pp. 52–3, 109.
8. D. Lorenzen, 'Imperialism and the Historiography of Ancient India,' in *India – History and Thought: Essays in Honour of A. L. Basham*, ed. S. N. Mukherjee (Calcutta: Subarnarekha, 1982), p. 86.
9. Jacques Le Goff, 'The Medieval West and the Indian Ocean: An Oneiric Horizon,' in his *Time, Work, and Culture in the Middle Ages*, tr. A. Goldhammer (Chicago: University of Chicago Press, 1980), p. 197.
10. Heimo Rau, 'The Image of India in European Antiquity and the Middle Ages,' *India and the West: Proceedings of a Seminar Dedicated to the Memory of Hermann Goetz*, ed. Joachim Deppert (New Delhi: Manohar, 1983), pp. 205–6.
11. Michel Foucault, *Power/Knowledge: Selected Interviews and Other Writings, 1972–1977*, ed. Colin Gordon (New York: Pantheon Books, 1980), p. 82.

29

BETWEEN ORIENTALISM AND HISTORICISM

Aijaz Ahmad

In 'Between Orientalism and Historicism: Anthropological Knowledge of India' – a shorter version of a talk originally given at a Fellows' Seminar held at the Centre of Contemporary Studies, Nehru Memorial Museum and Library, New Delhi – Aijaz Ahmad, a senior fellow of the Indian Council for Social Science Research and a teacher of English, notes the non-disciplinary character of Edward Said's Orientalism *(and also of Ronald Inden's* Imagining India*), and the fact that the foregrounding of literature in* Orientalism *(and anthropology in* Imagining India*) facilitates a reading of history primarily from its system of representation, rather than from the history of material productions and appropriations – a shift from the political economy of production to the cultural complexes of representation that raises the question of the postmodernist forms of knowledge.*

Much of the methodological difficulty of Said's Orientalism, *Aijaz Ahmad concludes, resides in the fact that (1) Said tries to occupy theoretical positions which are mutually contradictory; (2) defines his object of knowledge, orientalism, in ways which are mutually incompatible; and (3) disables himself from acquiring a coherent anti-imperialist position by adopting an attitude towards Marxism so antagonistic as to be virtually hysterical.*

Aijaz Ahmad, 'Between Orientalism and Historicism', *Studies in History*, 7, 1, n.s., 1991, sections 2–5.

II

There had already been, well before the advent of Edward Said's book, a great many critiques, both large and small, in areas as diverse as Literature and History, Economics and Anthropology, of the tie between imperialist forms of cultural domination on the one hand, colonial conquest and imperialist pillage on the other. The striking novelty of *Orientalism* resided, thus, not in its thematics but in its scope, procedure and basic thesis – not simply its range of borrowing from the constituted academic disciplines but, far more crucially, its explicit invocation of Foucault, its declaration that the object of his study, namely Orientalism, was a *discourse* and its insistence that this was the constitutive discourse of Western civilisation as such, both chronologically, in the sense that we find it there already in the oldest European textualities, and also civilisationally, since it is by defining the 'Orient' as the dangerous, inferiorised civilisational Other that Europe has defined itself. I shall return to Said's uses of Foucault in a moment, but it is worth noting that in its narrative method as well as its choice of the main texts, Said's procedures are radically anti-Comparative Literature and literary history. For, it is the proposition of this other tradition that (*a*) there *is* a unified European/Western identity which is at the *origin* of history and has *shaped* this history through its *thought*; (*b*) this seamless and unified history of European identity and thought runs from Ancient Greece to our own time, through a specific set of beliefs and values which remain eternally the same, only getting more dense, and getting expressed on ever larger scales through more and more elaborate forms; and (*c*) that this history is immanent, and therefore available to reconstruction through the canon of its *great books*. Said subscribes to the *structure* of this idealist metaphysic so rampant in conventional literary history, even though he attaches altogether different valuation to a great many of the *great books*. He duplicates, in other words, all those procedures even as he debunks the very tradition from which he has borrowed the procedure. Not only that! What he posits *against* what he debunks are the values, precisely, which he has learned from that very tradition: tolerance, universality, non-racialistic pluralism, liberalism, humanism, sympathetic participation in the emotional *experience* of the Other, etc. This too is radically anti-Foucaultian, in the sense that Foucault was quite possibly the most rigidly anti-Humanist writer of our time. Many of the book's theoretical, methodological and political incoherences come from this effort to simultaneously uphold the absolutely contrary traditions of Auerbachian High Humanism and Nietzchean anti-Humanism.

As if these contradictions were not enough, Said tries also to exploit three quite different definitions of 'Orientalism' which he offers in the very beginning of the book. In his own words, first:

> Anyone who teaches, writes about, or researches the Orient – and this
> applies whether the person is an anthropologist, sociologist, historian, or

philologist – either in its specific or in its general aspects – is an Orientalist, and what he or she does is Orientalism.

In this sense, then, Orientalism is an identifiable, interdisciplinary area of academic knowledge, though exceedingly sweeping in its breadth. But then, in the second definition, it becomes something much more than even that, far exceeding academic boundaries, and becomes at least a transhistorical mentality, in the widest sense of that term, if not altogether a full-scale epistemology:

> Orientalism is a style of thought based upon an ontological and epistemological distinction made between 'the Orient' and (most of the time) 'the Occident' . . . . *This* Orientalism can accomodate Aeschylus say, and Victor Hugo, Dante and Karl Marx.

We shall return to the difficulties of this particular inflation, but let me cite the third definition:

> Taking the late eighteenth century as a very roughly defined starting point Orientalism can be discussed and analyzed as the corporate institution for dealing with the Orient . . . in short, Orientalism as a Western style for dominating, restructuring, and having authority over the Orient.

These three definitions come on two consecutive pages (2, 3), and Aeschylus and Dante are in fact mentioned as examples of the Orientalist 'style of thought' five lines before the eighteenth century is identified, in the third definition, as the 'roughly defined starting point'. The third definition, meanwhile, is immediately followed by the first of the many extensive references to Foucault as the conceptual mentor:

> I have found it useful here to employ Michel Foucault's notion of a discourse, as described by him in *The Archeology of Knowledge* and in *Discipline and Punish*, to identify Orientalism. My contention is that without examining Orientalism as a discourse one cannot possibly understand the enormously systematic discipline by which European culture was able to manage – and even produce – the Orient politically, sociologically, militarily, ideologically, scientifically, and imaginatively during the post-Enlightenment period.

The mention of the eighteenth century and the 'post-Enlightenment period' places one kind of emphasis, the mention of Aeschylus another kind, which itself goes back to the opening paragraph where we had been told, in the very third sentence, that 'The Orient was almost a European invention, and had been since antiquity a place of romance . . . .' Nor is this issue of periodisation a minor matter. On pp. 56–57, we get this crucial statement:

> Consider first the demarcation between Orient and West. It already seems bold by the time of the *Iliad*. Two of the most profoundly influential qualities associated with the East appear in Aeschylus' *The Persians*, the

earliest Athenian play extant, and in *The Bachae* of Euripedes, the last one extant . . . . What matters here is that Asia speaks through and by virtue of the European imagination, which is depicted as victorious over Asia, the hostile 'other' world beyond the seas. To Asia are given the feeling of emptiness, loss, and disaster that seem thereafter to reward Oriental challenges to the West; and also the lament that in some glorious past Asia fared better . . . .Two aspects of the Orient that set it off from the West in this pair of plays will remain essential motifs of European imaginative geography. A line is drawn between two continents. Europe is powerful and articulate; Asia is defeated and distant. Aeschylus *represents* Asia . . . . It is Europe that articulates the Orient; this articulation is the prerogative. not of a puppet master, but of a genuine creator, whose life-giving power represents, animates, constitutes the otherwise silent and dangerous space beyond familiar boundaries . . . .

The Orientalist discourse has already been set in motion, then, in the earliest of the Athenian tragedies, not in general but in the specific regularities which shall henceforth determine its structure: Asia's loss, Europe's victory, Asia's muteness, Europe's mastery of discourse; Asia's inability to represent itself, Europe's will to represent it in accordance with its own authority. The terms are set, and there is little that later centuries will contribute to the *essential* structure, though they will doubtless proliferate the discourse in enormous quantities. As Said puts it on p. 62: 'It is as if, having once settled on the Orient as a locale suitable for incarnating the infinite in a finite shape, Europe could not stop the practice'. And: 'Only the source of these rather narcissistic Western ideas about the Orient changed in time, not their character'.

Now, if all of this is true, then in what sense could one take the eighteenth century 'as a roughly defined starting point'? In other words, one does not really know whether Orientalist discourse begins in the post-Enlightment period or at the dawn of European civilisation, whether in the period of the battle of Plassey or in the period of the battle of Troy. This, then, raises the question of the relationship between Orientalism and colonialism. In one sort of reading, where post-Enlightenment Europe is emphasised, Orientalism appears to be an ideological corollory of colonialism. But so insistent is Said on identifying its origins in European Antiquity and its increasing elaboration throughout the European Middle Ages that it seems to be the *constituting element*, trans-historically, of what he calls 'the Eurpean imagination', so that colonialism begins to appear as a product, indeed the realisation of the project already inherent in Orientalism.

But *why* has Europe needed to constitute – 'produce' is Said's stark word – the Orient as 'that hostile *other* world'; to 'animate', as he puts it, 'the otherwise silent and dangerous space' as 'one of its deepest and most recurring images of the Other' (p. 1). Well, because, 'European culture gained in strength and identity by setting itself off against the Orient as a sort of surrogate and even underground self.' (p. 3) There are many passages of this kind, and Said borrows his language from so many different kinds of conceptual frameworks and intellectual disciplines that one is simply bewildered. There is, for example, enough existentialism in Said's language, derived from identifiable chapters of Sartre's *Being and Nothingness*, which stands in a peculiar relation with Derridean ideas of Identity and Difference, all of which is mobilised to posit in some places that the West has *needed* to constitute the Orient as its Other in order to constitute itself and its own subject – position; this idea of constituing Identity through Difference points, again, not to the realm of political economy, in which colonisation may be seen as a process of capitalist accumulation, but to a neccessity which arises within discourse and has always been there at the origin of discourse, so that not only is the modern Orientalist presumably already there in Dante and Euripedes but modern imperialism itself appears to be an effect that arises, as if naturally, from the necessary practices of discourse. That is one sort of difficulty. But there is another one as well, namely that the matter of Identity-through-Difference doubtless points to the primacy of representation over all other human activities, but why must representation also *inferiorise* the Other? Said again offers greatly diverse ideas, so that in quite a few places this inferiorisation is shown to be a result of imperialism and colonialism in the sense in which most of us would understand these words, but in another set of formulations, which draw their vocabulary from psycho-analysis, the West' seems to have suffered something resembling ego-anxiety whereby the ego constitutes its own coherence through aggressive objectifica-tion of the Other, so that what Said calls Orientalism comes to resemble what Lacanian Freudianism would designate as the phallic Imaginary.

But let us return to the three definitions, especially the intermediate one which defines Orientalism as 'a style of thought based upon an ontological and epistemological distinction between "the Orient" and (most of the time) the Occident'. There are two aspects of it which are very striking. One is Said's own way of constantly speaking of Europe, or the West, as a selfidentical, fixed being which has always possessed an essence and a project, an imagination and a will; and of the 'Orient' as its object, textually, militarily etc. He speaks of the West, or Europe, as the one which produces the knowledge, the East as the object of that knowledge. He seems to posit, in other words, stable subject – object identities, as well as ontological and epistemological distinctions between the two. In what sense, then, Said himself is *not* an Orientalist, or, at least, as Sadek-al-Azm puts it, an Orientalist-in-reverse? Said quite justifiably accuses the Orientalist for essentialising the Orient, but his own processes of essentialising 'the West' are equally remarkable. The second striking feature of this definition is that it identifies the *West* as that peculiar historical agent which constitutes itself by constituting the Other as inferior and dangerous. This was not, one should have thought, a European peculiarity. Assertions of those sorts of distinctions between Orient and Occident, East and West, is by no means a trait of the European alone; any number of Muslims do it, and when Ayatullah Khomeini does it he does so hardly from an orientalist position; and in our own case of course, Hindu spirituality is always posited against Western materialism, not to speak of Muslim barbarity. Nor is it possible to read our own old *kavyas* and *Dharmshastras* without noticing the way *dasyus*, *shudras* and women are constantly turned into dangerous and inferiorsed Others. This is not a merely polemical matter. The relationship between the Brahminical and the Islamic High textualities, the Orientalist knowledges of these textualities, and there modern reproductions in Western as well as non-Western countries, is such a wilderness of mirrors, in which reflections are refracted in such diverse ways, that we need the most incisive of operations, the most delicate of dialectics, to disaggregate these densities.

III

One of the theoretical difficulties in Said's work is that he has never been able to work out his relationship with the two slightly older intellectuals of his generation, Foucault and Derrida, whose work has influenced him the most. The matter of Derrida, I shall here ignore, but his relationship with Foucault shall bear some remarks,[1] since so much in the book is owed to Foucault and because this clarification bears directly upon the matter of periodisation, which is of some interest to historians.

Now, Foucault doubtless knows how to be allusive, delights in destabilising the questions, but underneath all his multiple enunciations, one knows exactly what his agreements and disagreements with Marxism actually are. His first and irreconcilable difference is that he locates Marx firmly within the boundaries of what he calls the 'Western episteme'; in its epistemic construction, he says, the thought of Marx is framed entirely by the discourse of Political Economy as this discourse is assembled within that logocentric episteme.[2] From this purported philosophical difference, then, follows, his equally clear disagreement with Marx on the issue of the principle that might govern historical narrativisation; he radically denies that narratives of history, can be assembled at the twin sites of the state and economic production, which he deems to be the exclusive originating sites of Marx's historical narrative. I shall not here examine these propositions of Foucault, because I am at the moment interested only in how Foucault resurfaces in a distorted form in Said's thought. For, after disagreeing with Marx on these fundamental premises, Foucault then goes on to specify both the spatial limits and the temporal constitution of the episteme he is engaged in. He insists that it is a *Western* episteme; about the rest of humanity he makes no claims of knowledge. Second, he locates the constitution of this episteme, historically, in the processes that range from roughly the sixteenth century to the eighteenth. Foucault always sidesteps Marxist terminology, but he knows what he is talking about, namely that emergence of bourgeois society which spans from primary accumulation upto the first Industrial Revolution. With the exception of *Histoire de la follie*, which he finished before fully working out his philosophical system in what became *The Archeology of Knowledge* and *The Order of Things* – with the exception of that one book, all the narratives he assembled later – the institutions of schooling and incarceration, the formation of the medical gaze and technologies of the body, the Prospectus of modern sexualities – all begin in that crucible of bourgeois beginnings. And, the episteme is Western *because* it is located in a transition which occurred in Europe.

The difficulty is that Said reduces Foucault to a *terminology*, i.e., discourse, regularity, representation, epistemic difference, etc., but he refuses to accept the consequences of Foucault's own mapping of history. For, the idea that there could be *a* discourse – that is to say, an epistemic construction – spanning both the pre-capitalist and the capitalist periods is not only an un-Marxist but also a radically un-Foucaultian idea. In the one instance, late in life and much after *Orientalism*, when Foucault tried to write a *History of Sexuality*, he could find no straightforward line of progression from Antiquity to the modern discourse; the work of course remained unfinished owing to his untimely death, but it was also perhaps unfinishable. In all the work that he did finish, Foucault never speaks narratively or theoretically of a full-fledged discourse prior to the 16th century because what he calls 'discourse' presumes the inert but enabling presence of modern state forms, modern institutional grids, objectified economic productions, modern forms of rationalised planning. Said's idea that the ideology of modern imperialist Eurocentrism is already inscribed in the ritual theatre of Greek tragedy, that Dante's *Christian* judgement on Muhammed as a heretic deserving of Hell's ninth circle can be joined to the repugnant representation of Arabs on modern American TV, or that Marx's passage on the role of British colonialism in India can be seamlessly integrated into the transhistorical Orientalist discourse, and even that there could be a *singular* discourse traversing all history and all European textualities – are all ideas which are ahistorical not only in the ordinary sense but also specifically anti-Foucaultian in a methodological sense. I do not normally agree with a great deal that I find in Foucault, but I must recognise that Foucault was by and large careful in his procedures. It is not for nothing that Foucault never constructed the history of any discourse on the basis of master texts; Freud's psychoanalytic procedure has no privilege in Foucault's thought over the country priest who supervises the Catholic girl's confession. He always distinguishes *discourse* from canonical tradition, from mentality, from institution. His philosophical distinction between *discursive* regularity and *personal* statement, his historiographic preoccupation with specifying the *form* and *boundary* of discourse, his obdurate refusal to collapse one discourse into another – the discourse of incarceration into the discourse of sexuality, for example – are fundamental to his thought, and the prolixity of his prose stands in direct contrast to the austerity of his boundaries. Said observes none of those austerities.

IV

Riven between his anti-Westernist passion and his Foucaultian allegiance, Said wavers widely on the key question of what kind of discourse Orientalism *is* i.e., whether it is a system of mere representations in the post-modernist sense attached to it in the respective positions of Foucault and Derrida, or a system of *mis*representations wilfully produced by the so-called 'West' in the pursuit of power and eventually colonial occupation. Both these positions have their own advantages, and Said characteristically tries to exploit both. At one point (p. 272) Said says that the difference between representations and *mis*representations is a matter only of degree. What Said offers here is of course the Nietzschean idea that representation is always already a misrepresentation, and he quotes Nietzsche directly to that effect, on p. 203 ('truths are illusions . . .' etc). But he also seems to suggest that the difference really does not matter. This is of course a very peculiar position for a political writer to take. For, the issue of 'representation' has been central to collective living for more centuries than one can count, as for example in the idea that only men should represent women, or that only the older can represent the younger, or that only the upper caste can be represented in the village assembly. In another range of meanings – who does the King represent? – the Mughals, for example, answered by invoking, exactly like the medieval European monarchs, the idea of the Divine Rights of Kinghship; the King was the *Zill-e-Subhani*, Shadow of God on Earth. Modern polities begin when such arbitrary notions of representation are challenged and proper forms of representation demanded, so that the issue of who has the right to represent whom is neither a textual question nor one that arose only between the European and the non-European – nor has the question yet been settled, even in the larger areas of class, gender or nation. And, of course, anyone who has ever participated in a trade union, a political party, any collective enterprise of any substantial magnitude, *knows* that the difference between representation and misrepresentation is always very great, as does any historian, though in less visceral ways, who has ever looked for empirically determinable facts. It is a peculiarity of the post-modernist mind that it elides these densities of historical experience into a purely *textual* notion of 'representation'. But all these dimensions we shall here ignore, because what Said is talking about is, precisely, textuality.

In the Foucaultian definitions, representations cannot be referred back to any truth outside or beyond themselves, nor to the intentionality of the representer, because the structure of the representation is already inscribed *in* and always regulated *by* the Power of discourse. Representation corresponds thus not to an external object, a truth, a subjectivity, a purpose, a project, but to the discursive regularity only. You cannot ask, for example, whether H. A. R. Gibb's interpretation – that is to say, representation – of Al-Mavardi's text is accurate or not, because that would be to presume that a criterion of truth actually exists, which Foucault denies. You refer the representation, instead, not to the truth of that which is represented but to the *effect* of truth produced by the representation itself; you refer Gibb's interpretation, therefore, not to Al-Mavardi's statements which it claims to represent, but to the Orientalist discourse which Gibb reproduces and to the *effect* of Gibb's own reading. This is very convenient for Said, for the following reason.

The archive of Western knowledges can now be treated as an autonomous archive *constituted* by the Orientalist discourse, with the consequence that (*a*) any statement within this archive which is not an Orientalist statement can be breezily consigned to irrelevance, and (*b*) the autonomous archive thus constructed would now be studied in terms of its own properties and regularities, for a better representation of this very archive for Western readers, with scant scrutiny of that which is represented in it or of the extremely complex meanings and significances that this archive has had for audiences and intelligentsias in Asia and Africa. This is what Said relentlessly does. His ideal reader is the Western reader, and the Western textualities Said examines literally by the hundreds. The non-Western reader is simply not addressed, because that would bring up the question of what the structure of the histories of Asian and African countries have been; in what way the European representation does or does not correspond to the non-European empirical fact; what consequences, if any, those very textualities have actually had in these other circumstances; and how the numerous social strata among the colonised people have responded, if they needed to respond, to that archive. I might add that this refusal to engage with the actual history of the non-West also serves, for Said and for Colonial Discourse Analysis generally, a cultural nationalist purpose in a very paradoxical way. Let me illustrate this again with the example of Gibb, to whom *Orientalism* administers an extensive and well-deserved dressing-down (leading to thirty-four index entries), but without any discussion of what the relationship might be between Gibb's scholarship and interpretation ('representation') of Arab – Islamic canonicities on the one hand, and, on the other, the content of those canonicities in their own time as well as their contemporary uses in the political and juridic discourses of Islamic fundamentalism today. In other words, a unitary object called 'Islam' is cited as the object of Orientalist representation, Gibb is taken to task for his highhanded and condescending representations, but no mention is made of the fact that the theocratic absolutism of Mulla Al-Mavardi, Ibn-e-Tamiyya or Al-Ghazali – the sort of 'high textuality' which is (mis)represented in Arabist Orientalism – reflects the monarchical absolutism of the medieval Islamic Caliphate, hence constituting structurally a twin of European medievality, and that it is precisely this theocratic absolutism which is routinely invoked today by the whole range of Islamic revolutionaries, from the Irani clerisy to the Arab Akhwan-al-Muslimun to Pakistan's Jama'at-e-Islami. Facts of that nature – disagreeable facts about our own past and present practices – are eluded altogether. Thus, this high modernism of discursive theories, which speaks only of the representation but never of the objects represented, serves to conceal what cultural nationalism would like to conceal and leaves the door open for an unexamined indigenist rage against foreigners *because* they are foreigners. One is now free to heap abuse on William Jones, Colebrook, Renan, Gibb and others, but one need not look at the monarchist absolutism of medieval Islamic jurisprudence, the politics of caste and gender in Hindu Smriti literature, or the many fundamentalisms and revivalisms of today in South and West Asia. I shall speak at some length of the indigenist and obscurantist possibilities inherent in Saidian perspectives when I get to the matter of Ronald Inden.

V

There are many other aspects of Said's work which deserve the closest scrutiny, but those shall have to be addressed elsewhere. Meanwhile, there are certain disjunctures between his work and the great many texts which have been produced directly under his influence, which are also worthy of some brief summation. One such disjunction simply is that although the main passion which had animated Said's own writing was directly political – for all its heady errors, *Orientalism* had been Said's way of negotiating his location in America and returning to a political present – most of the work that has followed in his footsteps displays, by contrast, no such political urgency and engagement, is usually quite academic, far more tame, quite well-behaved, colourless and even at times, spineless. This is no fault of his, but such are the ways of incorporation. In any case, his work has been read mainly in the direction of treating what he calls 'Orientalism' as a system of *mis*representations. This has led, then, to work in essentially three directions.

The first, as I indicated earlier, is in the direction of writing an even more elaborate history of colonial misrepresentations and impositions. If Said has written about Kipling, one can write about Forster; if he has analysed ten travel narratives, one can analyse a hundred; if he has mentioned two eighteenth century romances, one can write a dissertation on a hundred minor fictions of the same period. Most of this work is not very interesting, but a surprising amount is really good and it does help revise the prevailing notions of the cultural canon in the metropolitan countries, though, as one can see readily, the essential function of this kind of reading is to enlighten the *metropolitan* reader, in the name of course of the colonial subject. The category of 'Colonial Discourse Analysis', interdisciplinary in aspirations but usually dominated by teachers of English, has arisen in this space. Aside from the *quality* of the work thus produced, which is and perhaps has to be inevitably uneven, sometimes even highly faddish, two tendencies can be remarked in this kind of work quite frequently. One is that the colonial process seems to be analysed not as a *process* at all but as a discrete *object*, unrelated to the pasts, in the plural, both of England and India; and largely unrelated also to the ongoing processes of class formation and gender construction in both the colonising and the colonised formation. That what got said by some of the British about the *dangers* of education for the generality of Bengalis might have been said at the same time, and equally vociferously, by the same class of Englishmen about the dangers of education for the British working classes as well; or that a knowledge of English was perhaps as central to the self-organisation of the emergent class of the Calcutta-based rentier bourgeoisie – part landed, part urban and commer-cial – as it was to the cultural visions of a Macaulay; or that the religious indoctrination which was imparted, through the agency of Bunyan and Milton, to the Indian child in the colonial classroom was modelled upon the exact and prior indoctrination (through those same texts) of the Englishwoman in the parlour of her home, through that same method of recitation which was later to be adopted in the classroom, both in India and England – of all such overlaps between histories of the colony and histories of class and gender – and also the histories of the colony and the colonising country – most of the texts of 'Colonial Discourse Analysis' tend to be almost wilfully ignorant. And, I say 'wilfully' because that controlling image of a unified West and a unified Orient, always external to each other and locked in mortal conflict of possession and subordination since the beginning of time, simply does not permit a sustained engagement with the category especially of class but of gender as well, except superficially.

The other aspect of the Saidian pressure on the so-called 'Colonial Discourse Analysis', which then largely converges with the Subalternist pressure, is that it radically transforms the status of the research archive assembled during the colonial period under British administration and mostly by English writers. One way of putting it might be that if that British knowledge had once been a realm of sacred truth for historians like Jadunath Sarkar, these Saidian and Subalternist pressures are fast transforming that same archive into a realm of pure untruth, distortion etc., so that, for example, Professor Inden explicitly, and Professor Partha Chatterjee in a more nuanced way, can begin to argue that caste in Indian society is simply a fabrication of the British Census and Population Survey. What is lost sight of in this kind of reading is that that archive is a collection neither of truths nor untruths, that it is simply a vast historical resource for helping us understand our own past, and that we need to approach that archive now with the same kind of scepticism, respect and scholarly care, subjecting it to that same objective scrutiny, that we shall reserve, let us say, for Abul Fazl's *Akbarnama* or the Puranic sources. After all, one does not have to *believe* in the Puranic genealogies in order to use them for historical reconstruction or to acknowledge that their construction may indeed correspond to some realities of their time. Not does one have to defend the absolutist atrocities of medieval monarchs to make a sound judgement about the events of Babar's time, based upon the available record. What Saidian kind of denunciation does is to make the colonial archive radically unavailable for the same kind of judicious judgement, critical and uncollaborative but also respectful of its sources.

The corollary of that uncritical contempt for the British archive is the pressure to over-valorise indigenous practices and textualities – regardless of locations in formations of class, caste, gender, state structure, structure of Belief. This, too, fits. For, Said had also argued that 'the West', starting with the Athenians, has also taken away the right of the Orient to represent itself. So, there has also been an emphasis on self – representation of the Orient, now reborn as the Third World. In the field of literature, then, a new category – Third World Literature –

which is published in the Western languages, by the Western publishing houses, interpreted by scholars located in Western countries, even written often enough by writers choosing to live in the West – has come into being. About this issue I have written extensively elsewhere. So I need not go into that.[3] What is remarkable, however, is that the propositions of *Orientalism* have also helped refurbish, in those aspects of Social Science which overlap with History, quite conservative, rightwing versions of a certain kind of indigenism under the label of authenticity and agency of the Third World historical subject. Admittedly, these indigenist pressures are coming from a great many directions, mainly from the more obscurantist versions of the bourgeois social sciences produced within India; the Saidian pressure, and more obliquely thus far the Subalternist one, have been only contributing factors, and that too only in certain radicalist tendencies.[4] It is also the case, however, that if the Western archive has done nothing but silence, misrepresent and fabricate false images of non-Western cultures, the task, necessarily, is to restore the authenticity of those cultures through their own practices, rituals and representations. Moreover, if issues of class and gender are not constitutive of our societies, if these societies are constituted *only* by colonialism and *not* by structures of domination and subordination which chronologically predate the advent of colonialism, however they may have been transformed by the colonial intervention, then *any* ritual or representation, drawn from any cluster of practices, so long as these are indigenous and uncontaminated by foreign contact, would represent our collective authenticity. In this harder version of indigenism, the modern Indian cannot represent India because of being already polluted by foreign contaminations; only the pre-modern, preferrably the pre-Muslim, Indian can be 'authentic'.[5] This is where Anthropology of the most obscurantist kind can have its day.

NOTES

1. For a scrupulous examination of Said's misuse of Foucault, though with very different emphasis, see 'On *Orientalism*' in James Clifford's *The Predicament of Culture*, Harvard, 1988.
2. I attach the word 'logocentric' to what Foucault calls 'the Western episteme' not in order to confuse Foucault's thought with Derrida's but because Foucault has always insisted, since his very first major work. *Histoire de la Follie*, that binary constructions are the specific attribute of this episteme and that it is the fundamental binary of rational/irrational which constitutes it.
3. See my 'Jameson's Rhetoric of Otherness and the "National Allegory"', in *Social Text*, no. 17 (Fall 1978, New York); '"Third World Literature" and the Nationalist Ideology', in *Journal of Arts and Ideas*, nos. 17–18 (June 1989, New Delhi), and more recently, 'Salman Rushdie's *SHAME*: "Floating Upward"', Occasional Paper, Second Series, Number XXXIV, Centre for Contemporary Studies, Nehru Memorial Museum and Library, New Delhi. See also my forthcoming Occasional Paper, from the same source, entitled 'Disciplinary English: Theory, Third Worldism, and Literary Study in India'.
4. If the evolving trajectory of Professor Partha Chatterjee's work, or the essay 'Subaltern as Perspective' by Professor Veena Das, which closes Volume VI of *Subaltern Studies* (1989) is any indication, this indigenist component in the Subalternist Project may well increase.

5. The bad faith and the comprador character of these indigenisms is witnessed in the fact that they bank so heavily upon the more bourgeois kinds of Western social science. Witness, for example, the use of the most Right-Wing version of psychoanalysis in the constructions of Ashis Nandy.

30

HUMANISING THE ARABS

Billie Melman

In her study of the relations of Western women with the orient, the relations of the 'other within' with the 'other without', Billie Melman – a student of women's history – concludes that Europe's representation of the orient was not uniform; that there existed a plurality of notions and images of the 'other'; that the discourse about things oriental was polyphonic; and that European experience of the eastern Mediterranean was heterogeneous, and not merely political. Where a patriarchal elite may well have attempted to impose a cultural and political hegemony, women travellers – many of whom remained in the Middle East for long periods – offered alternative views, different from, and more complex than, the orientalist topos. Contact frequently led, not to 'cultural smugness', but to an identification with the other that cut across the barriers of culture, religion and ethnicity.

The following extract, from the chapter entitled 'An "Orientalist" Couple: Anne Blunt, Wilfred Scawen Blunt and the Pilgrimage to Najd', is of particular interest, as it illustrates clearly the tensions that exist between orientalist authority and the individual gendered experience; canonicity and writing against canonical texts; feminine identity and the identity of the explorer; and the work of the professional orientalist and the amateur.

In the *Authentic Arabian Horse* she [Lady Blunt] 'graduates' or progresses from the hyperbole which characterises the early writings to a more balanced attitude

Billie Melman, *Women's Orients* (Macmillan, 1992), pp. 301–3.

and critical observation. More significant even, the book suggests that between the early encounters with nomad life and her death, Lady Blunt had conceptualised her impressions of and views on, 'authenticity' and cross-cultural relations. We should not be misled by the title of the book. The history of the thoroughbred Arabian is also a history of the authentic Arab. Analogy between an aboriginal group, preserving the notion of a 'primitive' life and a 'pure' species, both representing Nature, rather than civilisation, is transparent and runs through the book. The Arabian is a standard among horses as the Arab is an ideal type among oriental people. But more importantly even, the *Authentic Arabian Horse* is about the exchange of information between cultures; about the ways in which knowledge in the West about the Middle East is processed and about the relation between cross-cultural observation and power. We seem, Lady Anne argues, to know a lot about Arabians (and Arabs) but our knowledge is in fact limited and derives from outside sources, in the West and the Middle East itself:

> In the Western *outside world* the origin of the horse of Arabia has been and remains a subject of controversy, both as to where he came from and as to how he got his type. No such doubt exists in the *inside world*, which considers its possession of the Arabian horse is as ancient as the creation. Now the views of both outside worlds, Eastern and Western – and therefore the views of the great majority – have been expressed freely and abundantly, in countless volumes, in many languages, at first in manuscripts and later in print, while the *unwritten views of the restricted world* have remained almost inaccessible. For apart from the fact that the Nomad [sic] world is unable to produce a written record of its mood and thought, the chances of intimate intercourse with it by word of mouth are made difficult not for outsiders, even for those of the neighbouring Arabic-speaking regions.[1]

The passage deserves attention for three reasons. First is the location or relative position of the ethnographer/historian and his or her subject or interest. At the centre of the optical field is not the metropolitan society, nor even the familiar urbanised Orient, but the desert. The West is relegated to the periphery of the vision: it is the 'outside', a remarkable departure from the ethnocentric discourse on the Middle East. The second trait that marks off the text from standard writing is the distinction between literate and non-literate societies with an oral culture. The spoken word, both the conversation of contemporary Bedouins and the ancient lore preserved in Arabic poetry from before the *hajra* (notably in the Qasida or formal Arabic odes), is as important as written authorities.[2] Third and last is the association between political power and the collection of information. Nomad societies are 'minorities'. They are pressed by the politically superior West and those parts of the Middle East which had already been westernised, and were now exposed to processes of modernisation. And there is not a shadow of a doubt where the sympathies of the writer lie, nor where is the place and task of the ethnographer:

> my object is to present the case of the minority after giving a short survey of that of the majority; showing the gulf between the outer and inner circles, for it has been my good fortune to spend many years in intimate converse with members of those very horse-breeding tribes.[3]

'Converse' is the key-word. It denotes a system of communication in which two reciprocating parties exchange information. The nomad is not merely an object, but an active participant in a dialogue between cultures. Elsewhere, in a reference to Charles Doughty's remarks on the dangers to a nomadic culture in the urbanised and westernised Hijaz, Blunt again emphasises the need for faithful documentation of a disappearing minority. The duty of the sympathetic Westerner is to

> present the case of the seldom-heard voice from within before it shall have been finally stifled by the growing pressure from without, as might well happen even as a more or less immediate consequence of the appalling upheaval of 1914.[4]

This was, I guess, written in 1916, certainly after the outbreak of the First World War, possibly, even probably, towards the end of Lady Anne's life (the extracts are titled 'Lady Anne Blunt's Last Words'), before the outbreak of the Arab Rebellion. And in the jingoist atmosphere of 1915 and 1916 criticism, even in the private, on the purpose and nature of the war, was daring and certainly not very common.

As with the writings on the landscape of the Nafud and Jabal Shammar, so with the notes on the Shammar themselves, Lady Blunt self-consciously adopts an approach that may best be described as unromantic. She is at pains to de-romanticise *Western and Oriental* notions about Arabians and Arabs. Her criticism then is directed both at the Western audience and unauthentic Eastern people. Romance, she argues, is alien to the nature of the Arabs and their view of the world and life. The Bedouins are materialists. Spiritualism, pietism and a propensity to fantasy and 'romance' characterise the Islamised towns of the peninsula and of the Middle East at large. And spiritualism and romantic escapism also characterise the modern West. The gist of the distinction between, on the one hand a materialist nomad people and on the other a romantic urban culture, means the disseverance of the former from Islam. Lady Blunt, it seems, admires the Shammar not because they are Muslims but because they have preserved the pagan culture of the era before the *hajra* and the Islamisation of the Middle East. Unlike Blunt she was not attracted to Muslim religion. And in contradistinction to him she does not seem to appreciate the materialist aspects of that religion which appealed to the Darwinist in Blunt.

Notes

1. Judith Baroness Wentworth, *The Authentic Arabian Horse* (1942), pp. 311–12.
2. Ibid., Chapter VI, 'The Golden Horsemen of Arabia', pp. 109–41, for her knowledge of the written sources.
3. Ibid., p. 312.
4. Ibid.

31

INDOLOGY, POWER, AND THE CASE OF GERMANY

Sheldon Pollock

As Sheldon Pollock, professor of Sanskrit and Indic studies at the University of Chicago, shows in his article 'Deep Orientalism? Notes on Sanskrit and Power beyond the Raj', orientalism, as a discourse of power, may be directed not only outwards, towards a distant people, state or culture, but also inwards, towards a part of the national political culture that produced it. The particular instance that Sheldon Pollock cites in his article is that of Germany, where, he concludes, in the nineteenth and twentieth centuries, German Indology helped lay the ideological foundations of national socialism.

The early history of Indology is constituted out of a network of factors, economic, social, political, and cultural, that make any generalization about it at the same time simplification. With that caution understood, I think we can broadly identify three constituents in early Indian studies as especially important for their historical effectiveness and continuing vitality. These are British colonialism, Christian evangelism (and its flip side, theosophy and related irrationalisms), and German romanticism-Wissenschaft.

In the West, Sanskrit studies from the beginning developed from the impetus provided by one or another of these constituents. The earliest grammars of the language, for example, are the work of German and Austrian missionaries of the seventeenth and eighteen centuries (Hanxleden, Paulinus; Roth 1988);

Sheldon Pollock, 'Deep Orientalism? Notes on Sanskrit and Power beyond the Raj,' in Carol A. Breckenridge and Peter van der Veer, *Orientalism and the Postcolonial Predicament* (Philadelphia: University of Pennsylvania Press, 1993), pp. 80–96.

many of the first Sanskrit manuscripts in Europe were collected by French missionaries, some of the first attempts at Sanskrit editing and publishing are those of the British Baptists at Serampore in Bengal (e.g., Carey and Marshman 1806–10). One of the first Europeans to learn Sanskrit well enough to make use of it was – obligatory reference – William Jones, supreme court judge under the East India Company (1785; Cannon 1970: 646, 666, 682ff.), whose principal motive, like that of another important early Sanskritist, Colebrook, was the administration of law in British India. One of the critical moments in the academicization of Sanskrit studies was the encounter in Paris (1803–04) of the dominant character in German romanticism, Friedrich von Schlegel, with Alexander Hamilton of the East India Company (Rocher 1968). From Hamilton Schlegel learned enough Sanskrit (*Über die Sprache und Weisheit der Indier*, 1808; Oppenberg 1965) to encourage his brother, August Wilhelm, to learn more, and it was A. W. von Schlegel who went on to hold the first chair for Sanskrit in Germany, at the University in Bonn (1818).

All of this history is certainly well known. I review it here to disentangle the three principal components so that, by arranging them side by side in their bare outline, we can appreciate more fully the fact that it was particular institutions of European power, the church, the corporation, the university, that created and later sponsored Indology; that, however we may wish to characterize the ends of these various institutions, it was their ends that Indology was invented to serve.

The principal target of the orientalist critique in South Asia has been the intimate and often complicated tie, sometimes the crudely heavy link, between Indology and British colonialism, and we now possess sharp analyses of some of its most subtle forms (for instance, Cohn 1987).[1] Some of the postulates in this critique about precolonial power, and the more complex and challenging issue of a postcolonial 'European epistemological hegemony,' I will discuss below. But the creation of Indological knowledge and its function in colonial domination need no elaboration here.

The various forms of cultural and spiritual domination represented by missionary Indology do not require special comment here either, although its cognate phenomenon, nineteenth-century theosophy and its wide range of modern-day incarnations, merit discussion within an orientalist analysis. It would be worth examining how these representations, especially in their highly commodified, scientistically packaged, and aggressively marketed contemporary forms, continue to nourish one of the most venerable orientalist constructions, the fantasy of a uniquely religion-obsessed India (and a uniquely transcendent Indian wisdom), and how this fantasy in turn continuously reproduces itself in contemporary scholarship, given the institutional monopolization of Indian studies by the 'history of religions,' and presents one of the most serious obstacles to the creation of a critical Indology.

The third major component of Indology, my oddly hyphenated German romanticism-Wissenschaft, is less easily accommodated within an explanatory framework of colonial instrumentality and thus not accidentally was the one major form that Said left unaccounted for in his analysis.[2] Trying to conceptualize in larger terms the meanings and functions of German orientalism invites us to think differently, or at least more expansively, about orientalism in general. It directs our attention momentarily away from the periphery to the national political culture and the relationship of knowledge and power at the core – directs us, potentially, toward forms of internal colonialism, and certainly toward the domestic politics of scholarship.

No serious encounter with orientalism as it relates to traditional India can avoid the case of Germany. There are two reasons that are immediately obvious, because of their very materiality: the size of the investment on the part of the German state in Indological studies throughout the nineteenth and the first half of the twentieth centuries (without this involving, it bears repeating, any direct colonial instrumentality) and the volume of the production of German orientalist knowledge. On both counts Germany almost certainly surpassed all the rest of Europe and America combined.[3]

In dissecting what accordingly has to be seen as the dominant form of Indianist orientalism, both in sheer quantity and in intellectual influence, two components seem worth isolating: the German romantic quest for identity and what was eventually to become one of its vehicles, the emerging vision of *Wissenschaft*.

The romantic search for self-definition (beginning in the early nineteenth century but with impulses continuing halfway into the twentieth, and perhaps beyond) comprised initially a complex confrontation with, on the one hand, Latin-Christian Europe, and on the other, the universalizing Enlightenment project of humanism. The discovery of Sanskrit was one of the crucial components in this search. As a British historian put it in 1879: 'Not in a merely scientific or literary point of view, but in one strictly practical, the world is not the same world as it was when men had not yet dreamed of the kindred between Sanscrit, Greek, and English' – and, he should have added, German.[4] As is manifest in the responses of the first Germans to learn the language (Friedrich von Schlegel and Othmar Frank, among others), Sanskrit was thought to give evidence of a historical culture, and spiritual and ultimately racial consanguinity, for Germans independent of, and far more ancient than, Latin or Christian culture.

This romantic dream seems to have sharpened into the vision of an Indo-Germanic *Geisteswelt* only gradually. The principal German cultural dichotomy in the early nineteenth century had juxtaposed Germania and Rome. This came to be replaced by the antithesis and finally essentialized dichotomy between 'Indo-German' and 'Semite.' Indo-German, acccording to one of the best short accounts, was largely a *Kontrastbegriff*, called into being by the social and economic emancipation of Jews in the course of the century (von See 1970). But what made it possible to construct and consolidate this dichotomy, in addition to an 'orientilizing' epistemology, was 'orientalist' knowledge itself.

The discourse on Aryanism that this orientalist knowledge generated was, to a degree not often realized, available to the Germans already largely formulated for them at the hands of British scholarship by the middle of the nineteenth century. This discourse included a generous selection of what were to become the topoi of 1930s Germany: the celebration of Aryan superiority; the willingness to recognize racial kinship between European and Indian coupled with a readiness to establish (where this was politically useful) and explain (with the commonplaces that recur in 1933) the degeneracy of the South Asian Aryans; the politically driven disputes on the original homeland; even proposals for a eugenics program in India (calling for a revivification through racial planning of the debilitated South Asian Aryan stock). It might even be said that Aryanism was one conceptual building block in the totalizing projects of a good deal of nineteenth-century British work on India (H. S. Maine, J. W. Jackson, F. Max Mueller – a list easily extended)[5]

In the German instance, however, orientalism as a complex of knowledge-power has to be seen as vectored not outward to the Orient but inward to Europe itself, to constructing the conception of a historical German essence and to defining Germany's place in Europe's destiny. If the 'German problem' is a problem of identity, and 'the German figure of totalitarianism' racism (Lacoue-Labarthe and Nancy 1990: 296), the discourse of Aryanism and, consequently, the orientalism on which it rested was empowered to play a role in Germany it never could play in England.

There is no need to trace further here the beginnings in the nineteenth century of the orientalist creation of Indo-German as counteridentity to Semite, still less the general place of India in the rise of German romanticism, for a good deal of work has already been done on those topics (e.g., Schwab 1950: 74ff.; Willson 1964; Stern 1961: 3–94; Römer 1985: 62ff.) What I want to focus on instead is the end point of the process, by which I mean not so much its chronological end but its consummation, in the period of National Socialism. In this culminating instance, I think two things happen: First, there come to be merged what hitherto seemed by and large discrete components of German orientalism, romanticism and Wissenschaft. Second, 'orientalist' knowledge becomes part of the official worldview of a newly imagined empire, and in this German allomorph of British imperialism – the attempt to colonize Europe, and Germany itself, from within – orientalism has its special function to discharge.[6]

With some exceptions (the Göttingen orientalist, though not Indologist, Paul de Lagarde in the last third of the nineteenth century, for instance), the emerging vision of science/scholarship, *Wissenschaft*, seemed to be a current running parallel to and rarely intersecting with the quasi-mystical nativism of romanticism; indeed, this disjunction seems somehow prefigured already in the characters and careers of those fellow Sanskrit students in Paris in 1815, the romantic A. W. von Schlegel and the scientist Franz Bopp (the latter of whom in 1816 was the first systematically to demonstrate the cognate relationship between India and European languages).[7] And I suggest it was precisely a new interpenetration of 'science' and nativism that in the 1930s endowed German Indology with its specific power and significance. Indeed, the conjunction in NS Indology of cultural-nationalist primitivism and high intellectual technology presents an instance at the level of the academy of a much broader phenomenon fundamental to National Socialist culture, which a recent scholar has appositely characterized as 'reactionary modernism.'[8]

The characteristics of this 'science' merit historical analysis no less than the constructions of romanticism. An inventory of the epistemological instruments of *Indologie* would include, besides Bopp's comparative linguistics, other nineteenth-century intellectual technologies developed for the human sciences, such as the text-criticism of Wolf and Lachmann, the philology of Böckh, and the historiography of Ranke. What above all interests me here, however, is the general conceptual framework within which these components combine to operate. Part of this framework consists in the claim of objectivity, of 'value-free scholarship,' which seems to have been more vigorously asserted the deeper the crisis of European culture grew.

I want to look very briefly at one of the more forceful and historically significant apologies for such scholarship, the programmatic lecture 'Wissenschaft als Beruf' (Science/Scholarship as Vocation/Profession) that Max Weber delivered before students of the University of Munich only months before his death. There is nothing in itself 'orientalist' about this defense, which was made by a political economist and meant to apply broadly to the human sciences. But it is worth singling out by way of preface to a discussion of National Socialist Indological scholarship partly because of its historical location – it was presented in late 1918 or the beginning of 1919, the liminal moment in modern German history;[9] partly because it gives lucid expression to a set of beliefs about scholarship and to a justification of method that seem to infuse the scholarship of the period, including academic Indology; and partly because of what may be a deep and enduring self-deception. I think it is all-important to try to understand the set of presuppositions that sustained belief in the possibility of producing 'serious scholarly work,' which viewed itself as utterly distinct from other modes of state discourse such as propaganda, directly under the aegis of the swastika. In a way, Weber's lecture, intended as an attack on the politicization of scholarship, and indeed, viewed with suspicion and hostility especially by conservatives,[10] may help us grasp one basic ideological precondition for the intersection of scholarship and state power, at the very moment when that intersection was about to become interpenetration.

What for Weber were the 'least problematic' issues of scholarship need no problematizing here. It is irrelevant for understanding much NS-era Indology to question the formal and positivistic ideals of scholarship (consistency, noncontradiction, evidence, argument, philological and historical precision), for they were also accepted as ideals generally by NS scholars. Nor is there anything very troubling about Weber's claim that, given the fundamental undecidability of competing value systems, scholarship should attempt to remain value-neutral. What is surprising is his reluctance to extend this relativism to 'science' itself, to its descriptions, representations, constructions. We are presented at once with a conception of the 'political,' as open advocacy of partisanship, that seems wilfully shallow, and with an unquestioned assumption that, despite the fundamentally political nature of social and cultural existence, including scholarly existence, the transcendence of political values really is possible. Weber demands, for example, of the students listening that they should just 'establish the facts.' He offers to prove 'in the works of our historians that, wherever the man of scholarship comes forth with his own value judgments, the full understanding of the facts ceases' (Weber 1984: 26). In all of this there is little acknowledgment that historical or cultural facts (Webber takes 'democracy,' that most ideologically protean entity, as his example) may not actually be lying about like so many brute existents waiting merely to be assembled, but are actually constituted as 'facts' by the prejudgments – by the values – of the historians and 'men of scholarship' themselves. Relentless in driving politics from the lecture room, Weber seems to have left it to rule untroubled in the study.

The objectivism Weber enshrines was no more questioned in Indology than it was in any other institutional scholarship in the Germany of the period. And what I am wondering is whether it is the putative separability of 'fact' from 'value,' to which Weber gives expression in his lecture, and consequently the decontextualization and dehistoricization of the scholarly act itself, the objectification of scholarship – and all in the interests of a depoliticization of scholarship in the face of war and revolution – that enabled some of the most politically deformed scholarship in history, including Indological history, to come into existence. I want at least to entertain this hypothesis when examining institutional Indology in Germany during the period of NS power, 1933–45, although the paradox of NS scholarship is more complicated: While denouncing a Weberian objectivism as alien to the spirit of scholarship meant to serve the new Germany,[11] the Indologists in fact believed that the scholarship they were producing to that end was scientific and objective. The NS Indologists, it seems, were Weberians in reverse: relentless in driving 'objectivism' from the classroom, they yet felt it had to rule, and could indeed rule, in the study.

EX ORIENTE NOX: INDOLOGY IN THE TOTAL STATE

Before the logical aporia of legitimacy, political systems have only a relatively limited repertory of methods of legitimation. Some political systems (certain once-existing 'socialist' systems, for example) employ myths of utopia, while fascist systems employ myths of origins (Lyotard 1987). The NS state sought legitimation in part by the myth of 'Aryan' origins. This, as we have seen, had been provided early in nineteenth-century Indian orientalism – a benchmark is Friedrich von Schlegel's identification (1819) of the 'Arier' as 'our Germanic ancestors, while they were still in Asia' (Sieferle 1987: 460). In the later NS search for authenticity, Sanskritists, like other intellectuals – 'experts in legitimation,' as Gramsci put it – did their part in extrapolating and deepening this discourse. They finally would heed the words of the nineteenth-century proto-fascist (and 'Wahldeutscher') Houston Stuart Chamberlain: 'Indology must help us to fix our sights more clearly on the goals of our culture. A great humanistic task has fallen to our lot to accomplish; and thereto is aryan India summoned.'

The myth of Aryan origins burst from the world of dream into that of reality when the process of what I suggest we think of as an internal colonization of Europe began to be, so to speak, shastrically codified, within two months of the National Socialists' capturing power (April 1933). The 'Law on the Reconstitution of the German Civil Service,' the 'Law on the Overcrowding of German Schools,' and a host of supplementary laws and codicils of that same month were the first in a decade dense with legal measures designed to exclude Jews and other minority communities from the apparatuses of power (including 'authoritative' power, the schools and universities), and to regulate a wide range of social, economic, and biological activities.

For some, linguistic activity should have been included. The Kiel (later Munich) Sanskrit and Iranist Hermann Güntert had already in 1932 expressed a view on the relationship of race and language consonant with such control, which he elaborated in a manifesto in 1938, 'New Times, New Goals,' when he became editor of the journal *Wörter und Sachen*.

> A man alien to a given ethnic and racial group does not become, simply because he speaks their language – one originally alien to him – and 'beholds the world' via the constructions of that language, a comrade of the folk [*Volksgenosse*], even if the language – which was originally alien – had been used already by his forebears. For far more potently, deterministically, unconsciously do primal dispositions and peculiarities of his inherited substance issue forth, whereas language is far more easily changed and transformed than those deep spiritual dispositions such as customs, notions of justice, Weltanschauung, and the general emotional life. Should those who are alien to the race have long-term influence, they would transform the language according to their own nature and try to adapt it as far as possible to their spiritual natures – that is to say, they would become pests upon, corrupters of this language. It is therefore perfectly clear: A people creates itself a language appropriate to it, and not vice versa! A people is the power that commands all the life of a language.[12]

The whole weight of these early laws rested on the concept 'Aryan' (or rather, somehow significantly, at first on its negation[13]): 'Beamte, die *nicht arischer* Abstammung sind, sind in den Ruhestand zu versetzen' ('Civil servants *not of aryan* descent are to be pensioned off'), '. . . die Zahl der *Nichtarier* [soll] ihren Anteil an der Gesamtbevölkerung des Reichs nicht übersteigen' ('The number of *non-aryans* [allowed into schools] [shall] not exceed their percentage among the general population of the empire') (Walk 1981: 12ff.).[14] It is not necessary to review here the long and rather complex prehistory of the term *Arier* – the essence is caught in the remark of Victor Klemperer, that '"aryan man" is rooted in philology, not natural science' (Klemperer [1947] 1987: 148)[15] – nor to analyze the justification of the category constructed by 'race-science,' which was the master conceptual scheme in operation here and which itself had significant orientalist dimensions.[16] The point I want to make has nothing whatever to do with historical truth or scientificity of terminology; it has to do with the mobilization of meaning for the purpose of domination as it is contextaully bound to Germany in the years 1933–45.

In this connection, two points are worth stressing. First, the concept of *Arier*, which was ambiguous to the scholarly mind and opaque to the popular, absurdly so for a juridical term, required substantial exegesis, as the initial supplementary decrees for the execution of the *Arierparagraph* make clear.[17] Second, to contribute uncritically to this exegesis was to justify what Löwith aptly terms 'political zoology' and to contribute to the marginalization, exclusion, dehumanization, and ultimately extermination of 'lesser' peoples in a manner congruent with, if exceeding, standard-issue colonialism. In this project, German Indology participated in some crucial ways. I want to explore a few of these, adopting Haug's formulation and asking how German Indologists *qua Indologists*, by means of their specific epistemological tools and sense of scholarly purpose as Indologists, helped to effect the 'fascisization' of Germany Indologically (cf. Haug 1989: 5).

Regarding the role of 'ideology' in the consolidation and execution of NS power, I will only allude here briefly to the ongoing debates on functionalist and 'idealist' explanations that have long been contending in the analysis of National Socialism (as indeed of other political formations). The importance and effectivity of the notional, of the intellectual and ideological and 'welt-anschaulich,' in addition to or even independent of the material, seem to have gained at least parity in current re-thinking in the historiography of the movement. This seems in part attributable to the fuller history of the Holocaust now available, since the extermination of the Jews would seem to pose a serious challenge to any purely functionalist explanation of National Socialism.[18] Yet, whatever the actual effectivty of the ideational dimension of National Socialism may have been, there is no doubt that the builders of the movement believed in the necessity of providing it with an intellectually convincing doctrine. And this was to become one that in the end relied, more than any other state doctrine in European history, on the putative results of scholarly – archaeological, philo-logical, anthropological, Indological – research.

I can examine here in some detail only a few examples of Indology as practiced in NS Germany; an exhaustive typology and analysis are premature. The range of contribution is wide and multifaceted (and bibliographically altogether unsystematized); the degree of candor and self-consciousness about congruence with state discourse differs markedly in these contributions; and the interpretation of most of them necessitates a confrontation with serious problems of scholarly method and purpose. Yet one thing that is uniform and clear about these texts is the set of basic 'orientalist' ideologemes they adopt – about an Aryan culture of the past, its survival into and meaning for the German present, the role and ability of Indology in capturing its nature, its superiority and the concomitant debasement of others – and the scholarly foundations with which these components are supplied.

The earliest Indological intervention after the National Socialists took power, within months of the law on the 'Reconstitution' of the civil service mentioned above, and a model for what was to come, is the programmatic article 'German Antiquity and the History of Aryan Thought' by Walther Wüst, Vedic specialist at the University of Munich, student of Wilhelm Geiger, successor to Hans Oertel, later rector of the university (Wüst 1934).[19] What the first adjective in the title means, says Wüst, everyone knows; the second one, however, is far less clear, although 'by reason of the laws of racial protection it has become more familiar than any other word in the German language.' To explicate it, Wüst brings to bear the full and ponderous apparatus of philological and historical Indology. Etymology, literary history, comparative religion, folklore, and archaeology are all summoned to testify that the ancient *āryas* of India were those who felt themselves to be the 'privileged, the legitimate' (Wüst's interpretation of *ārya*) because they established the superiority of their race, their culture, their religion, and their worldview in the course of struggle with host populations. The 'deep significance' and 'indestructible grandeur' attaching to the terms *Arier, arisch* have been preserved into the present thanks to tradition and racial memory (*Erberinnerung*). The *Ṛg Veda* as an Aryan text 'free of any taint of Semitic contact'; the 'almost Nordic zeal' that lies in the Buddhist conception of the *mārga*; the 'Indo-Germanic religion-force' of yoga; the sense of race and the 'conscious desire for racial protection'; the '*volksnahe* kingship' – such is the meaning of the Indo-Aryan past for the National Socialist present, a present that, for Wüst, could not be understood without this past.

The search for German identity and NS self-legitimation in the Aryan past found in Wüst's early essay is characteristic of a great deal of Indological work of the period; his article in fact is a catalog of commonplaces. But equally characteristic, and crucial for us to note, is the 'scholarly' dimension. Wüst repeatedly distances himself from amateurs, charlatans, and ignorant nonspecialists (*Sachunkundigen*) and invokes and exploits to a fault the standards of philological and historical scholarship. More than anything, it is this commitment to 'science' to substantiate the order of the state, and the vision that scholarship could gain access to a realm of objective truth independent of historical interests and values, that makes this orientalist scholarship so typical of the period and so disquieting.

Lest we isolate this scholarly activity from the world of concrete power, it is worth recounting a speech given by Wüst (in his capacity as [then] SS-Hauptsturmführer) on March 10, 1937, in the Hacker-Keller, Munich, before the commanders of the SS officer corps South and the SS subordinate commanders and regulars of the Munich garrison. In 'The Führer's Book "Mein Kampf" as a Mirror of the Aryan World-View' (1937), Wüst seeks to establish a general set of continuities between ancient Indian and contemporary German thought (or rather *Weltanschauung*, for which he offers a long etymological excursus).[20] After providing a catalog of what he takes to be basic 'Indo Aryan' representations (the world as ordered and 'bright', existence as growth, the eye as a microcosmic sun, god as the father, the law of fate, and the like), he argues that all of it is to be found in Hitler's *Mein Kampf*, a text that thus evinces a spiritual continuum stretching from the second millennium BC to the present. 'But we see these connections in their maturest state,' he adds, 'perhaps in personality. In this context, I would like to make reference to a particularly significant connection.' He proceeds to recount the Buddha's sermon on the Middle Way, the realization that fulfillment lay between self-indulgence and self-denial, and then proceeds to argue that

> this very closely correlates with an experience the Führer had during his Vienna period, when as part-time worker he came face to face with suffering, and went through the wretched dwellings of the workers and saw their want. There the Führer spoke the profound words: 'At that time I was warned not to choke on Theory nor to become shallow on Reality' ['Damals wurde ich gewarnt, entweder in der Theorie zu ersticken oder in der Wirklichkeit zu verflachen']. I know of no more striking example of this hereditary, long-term tradition than the ingenious synopsis contained in the brief words of the Führer and the longer confession of the great aryan personality of antiquity, the Buddha. There is only one explanation for this, and that is the basic explanation for components of the National-Socialist world-view – the circumstance, the basic fact of racial constitution. And thanks to fate, this was preserved through the millennia ... [through] the holy concept of ancestral heritage [*Ahnenerbe*]. (Wüst 1937: 17–18)[21]

Neither Wüst's improbable thesis, nor the spectacle of a professor of Sanskrit lecturing before members of the central apparatus of Nazi terror on Indo-European etymologies and Buddhist *sūtras* to prove the 'absolute fact' of the superiority of Aryan cosmology and its afterlife, should blind us to what is significant here: the propriety and need Wüst felt of legitimating the NS *Weltanschauung* by anchoring it in an ancient Indian *darśana*.

As an example of pedantic *wissenschaftliche* antiquarianism coupled with a primitivism and irrational cultural nostalgia that finds itself suddenly, incredibly, and perilously invited into the inner sanctum of political power, the work and career of Wüst may be extreme.[22] What is typical, however, is again the 'orientalist' character of his scholarship, in every essential dimension of the term, both as representing an ontological and epistemological division between an 'us' and some 'them', and as serving to sustain a structure of manifest domination.

A fuller account of the more notable expressions of NS Indology would include the work of Ludwig Alsdorf, Professor of Sanskrit and Jainology at Münster and Berlin (Alsdorf 1942 is a *Fachgeschichte* of Indology that gives unusually clear voice to its ethnic and national purposes);[23] Jakob Wilhelm Hauer, Professor of the History of Religions at Tübingen (Hauer 1934 argues that the *Bhagavad Gītā* is an 'Aryan' text; Hauer 1937 offers an assemblage of the principle NS themes on Indo-Aryan antiquity);[24] and Hermann Lommel, Professor of Sanskrit and Iranian at Frankfurt (Lommel 1939 makes the attempt to distill the 'authentic Aryan spirit' of the oldest cultural monuments to achieve an awareness of 'our own historically evolved and genetically [*blutmässig*] inherited way of being'; Lommel 1939 [!] is a disquisition on the Aryan god of war). Requiring more complex theorization are those texts – issuing on a flood after 1933 – that, without any overt commitment to National Socialism, fully embrace the terms of its discourse by their unchallenged participation in and acceptance of the *Fragestellungen*, the thematics, of NS Indology. An example of this more sophisticated orientalism is the work of Paul Thieme (1938), an analysis of the Sanskrit word *arya*, where at the end he adverts to the main point of his research: to go beyond India in order to catch the 'distant echo of Indo-germanic customs' (p. 168). Apparently arcane articles on such topics as 'Alt-indoarisch *matya*-, n. "Knüppel als bauerliches Werkzeug"' (Ernst Schneider, *WZKM* 47 [1940]: 267ff.) feed into, and were intended to feed into, a complex state doctrine of *Blut und Boden*, Indo-Germanic farmers versus nomadic Orientals, Nordic heroes versus Semitic traders, and so forth.

One focal point of Indological work during the NS period that merits more than the brief observations possible here was the question of the *Urheimat* (the original home of the Aryans). To a degree the Urheimat issue had always been a scholarly question prompted and driven by the ideological demands of the European polities in which this discourse originated. Yet no matter how squarely situated at the intersection of scholarship and politics the question shows itself to be, as in Germany in the 1930s, it has almost universally been debated with a breathtaking pretense of political detachment. The first major scholarly salvo of the 1930s was fired with the publication of *Germanen und Indogermanen ... Festschrift für Herman Hirt* (1936).[25] In his introduction, Helmuth Arntz, the editor, asserts the purely scholarly nature of their investigations: 'Much poison has been poured out, even upon our scholarship; much hate and bitterness does the world fling at the Third Reich, the new state we have finally built for ourselves. That our scholarship is no longer free, but muzzled and misused for propaganda purposes – that is the worst reproach. This Festschrift refutes that. Each of the participating scholars was free to say what he wishes; and the fact that high scholarship is a cultural factor of propagandistic value holds for other nations as well as ours' (p. viii).[26] The volume edited later that same year by the ethnologist of tribal South Asia, the Austrian W. Koppers, *Die Indogermanen- und Germanenfrage*, was meant to provide a counterweight to the *Hirt Festschrift*.[27] Also in 1936 (in what hardly seems an accidental *Stellungnahme*), the whole debate is deflated by the great Russian phonologist Trubetskoy. Speaking before the Cercle linguistique de Prague in December, he argued that there may never have taken place a 'Proto-Indo-Germanic language' diffusion carried by Indo-German groupings – in fact, there never may have existed a Proto-Indo-Germanic language – but only 'a gradual approximation of languages, the one to the other, through mutual borrowing over time.'[28] From among the complexities of NS analysis of the Urheimat question it is worth calling attention to the way the nineteenth-century view expressed by Schlegel was reversed: the original Indo-Europeans were now variously relocated in regions of the Greater German Reich; German thereby became the language of the core (*Binnensprache*), whereas Sanskrit was transformed into one of its peripheral, 'colonial' forms.[29]

Of course, more 'traditional' Indological work, of a text-critical, lexical, epigraphic, numismatic variety, was taking place during the period – the same sort of work produced, say, under the sign of nineteenth-century French orientalism for Arabic (of the genre wherein, given the context of NS deformities, some postwar historians like Rothfels were prepared to see an 'inner emigration' and a 'sort of opposition'). But such philological work, despite illusions as to its rocklike imperviousness to political-social life that are still widespread in the field, is an instrument of meaning – social, historical, ideological – and presupposes questions of such meaning whether these are articulated or not. And when such questions of meaning did find articulation in Germany in the years 1933–45, they seem to have been in the main purely 'orientalist' questions.[30]

I want to illustrate the typicality noted above in regard to Wüst's scholarship by a brief account of the final phase of orientalism in the NS period, the wartime program funded by the Imperial Ministry of Education called the 'War Effort of the Humanities' (*Kriegseinsatz der Geisteswissenschaften*, 1941–42).

The task of the 'War Effort' (or 'Aktion Ritterbusch' as it was sometimes called after the Kiel legal scholar who initiated the *Einsatz*), was to encourage scholars of the humanities 'to place in the foreground of their work the idea of a new European order.'[31] As part of this effort, and at the suggestion of the executive committee of the German Oriental Society,[32] a 'Working Session of German Orientalists and German Orientalist Archaeologists' was convened in Berlin in 1942. Ritterbusch's opening statement adequately conveys the self-understanding of much German scholarship of the period with respect to its relationship with state power:

> I do not have to emphasize again here how acutely aware the German humanities are of their political-historical responsibility, and how very much they wish to prove, through their own learning and initiative, that they are not only a great, indeed, critical power of our popular [*völkisch*] life, but that they wish to contribute to the formation of world-historical decisions and dispositions that are coming to maturity and being decided

upon in this war – to contribute and to partipate for the benefit of the people and the Führer and the historical mission of the Empire. (Schaeder 1944: 5)

What interests me particularly in this scholarly convention of orientalists contributing to the mission of empire is the contribution of Erich Frauwallner, Professor of Sanskrit at the University of Vienna, who is widely regarded as the preeminent authority on Indian philosophy of his generation (and member of the National Socialist German Workers Party [NSDAP] since 1932, when the party was still illegal in Austria). In his presentation, Frauwallner argued that the special meaning of Indian philosophy lay in its being 'a typical creation of an aryan people,' that its similarities with western philosophy derived from 'the same racially determined talent,' and that it was a principal scholarly task of Indology to demonstrate this fact. Reiterating an axiom of NS doctrine, that 'Wissenschaft in the strict sense of the word is something that could be created only by nordic Indo-Germans,' Frauwallner adds, 'From the agreement in scientific character of Indian and European philosophy, we can draw the further conclusion that philosophy as an attempt to explain the world according to scientific method is likewise a typical creation of the Aryan mind' (Frauwallner 1944; cf. 1939).

Indian knowledge, again, is meaningful to the degree that it assists in the self-revelation of 'Aryan' identity. The very raison d'être of Indology for Frauwallner, as it seems to have been for so many scholars of the period, is fundamentally conditioned by this racialism. The ideology of objective 'science,' moreover, not only governs Frauwallner's presentation; his whole purpose is to demonstrate that this science exists in a realm beyond ideology – that it is a fact of biology. What alone enables him to do this, I think, is 'orientalist' knowledge production.

I have observed often enough that all the Indologists cited above are 'serious' scholars; their work was argued out on sophisticated historical and philological grounds, not on the 'intuitive' principles of crude propagandists like the chief party idealogue Rosenberg (although no German Indologist ever felt the call to criticize Rosenberg, and some, like Alsdorf [1942: 86] cite him as authoritative). They are for the most part unimpeachable with respect to scholarly 'standards.' What is of the essence to see is that it is within the realm of Wissenschaft that this knowledge production is taking place, Wissenschaft that provided the warrant of objective truth that constituted it as scholarship.

To what degree this work was motivated by opportunism or cynicism it is not easy to discover. It may be pointed out, however, that German Indolog shows a support for National Socialism noteworthy among the humanities for its breadth.[33] In the early and important *Declaration of Allegiance ... to Adolph Hitler* (*Bekenntnis ... zu Adolph Hitler* [Dresden n.d. (November 11, 1993)]), the names of a good number of the most distinguished Indologists of the period are prominent (including Schubring, Sieg, Nobel, Hertel, F. Weller). Of the twenty-five or so Indology professors of the NS period (leaving aside Dozenten, etc.), perhaps a third were active participants in the party or the SS, according to documents preserved in the Berlin Document Center. (Some examples, from a first, incomplete census: Ludwig Alsdorf, NSDAP No. 2697931 [entry into party 1 August 1933]; Bernhard Breloer, NSDAP No. 5846531 [1 May 1937], SS-Unterscharführer, SS No. 230317 [26 June 1933]; Erich Frauwallner, NSDAP No. 1387121 [29 November 1932]; Jakob Wilhelm Hauer, SS-Under-sturmführer, SS No. 107179, NSDAP No. 50574 [1 May 1937]; Richard Schmidt, NSDAP No. 2492244 [1 June 1933], SS-Obersturmführer.[34]) No German Indologist made any public statement on the state appropriation of Indological learning – perhaps none could have made such a statement, since there was little discernible appreciation of the politics of interpretation. Apart from the Indologists victimized by the 'Aryan paragraphs' whether as Jews themselves or because they were married to Jews (including Bette Heimann [emigrated], Walter Neisser [suicide, 1941], Walter Ruben [emigrated], Isidore Scheftelowitz [emigrated], Richard Simon [died 1934], Moritz Spitzer [fate unknown], Otto Stein [died in Lódź/ Ghetto, 1942], Otto Strauss [died in flight in Holland, 1940], Heinrich Zimmer [emigrated]), none publicly opposed the regime, or left the country. As far as I can tell, only one, Heinrich Lüders, ran afoul of the NS state, being forced to take early retirement from his position at the University of Berlin in 1935.[35] Quite as important, to my knowledge no German – or indeed, any other – Indologist has undertaken an analysis of the field and the relationship of the questions of scholarship and the questions of state since the war. In the flood of work since the late 1960s on every conceivable dimension of scholarship in the National Socialist period, it is noteworthy that there has been no publication on the topic from within the Indological community (even on an autobiographical occasion; typical is the silence of von Glasenapp in *Meine Lebensreise* [1964]). I would also like to call attention to the substantial increase in the investment on the part of the NS state in Indology and 'Indo-Germanistik.' Both Himmler and Rosenberg sponsored institutes centrally concerned with 'Indo-Germanische Geistesgeschichte.'[36] There is preserved a planning memo on the postwar Institut für arische Geistesgeschichte approved by Hitler in 1940, in which Rosenberg wrote:

> The nineteenth century left behind extensive research on the history of the Indiens, Iranians, and Greeks, and their intellectual/cultural creations. With the exception of Greek literature, Indian and Iranian thought has not penetrated European consciousness very deeply. To strengthen this con-sciousness, [and] – given the collapse of the entire Palestinian [i.e., Jewish] tradition – to free a more ancient and far more venerable one from its concealment, is the critical *weltanschauliche* task of the Munich institute. Therefore it will also be its task, in addition to working up the important sources and presenting syntheses of them, to re-issue those works that are essential for National Socialist *Weltanschauung*, and for the development

of an intellectual tradition, e.g., L.v. Schroeder, *Indians Literatur und Kultur*,[37] Böthlingk [sic], *Indische Sprüche*. (Document reproduced in Poliakov and Wulf 1983: 133ff.)

Motives are not always easy to discern, no doubt. All we can know is that between this scholarship and basic ideologemes of the NS state there is distinct congruence; what we need to know is what made this congruence possible and how it worked. In German Indology of the NS era, a largely nonscholarly mystical nativism deriving ultimately from a mixture of romanticism and protonationalism merged with that objectivism of Wissenschaft earlier described, and together they fostered the ultimate 'orientalist' project, the legitimation of genocide. Whatever other enduring lessons this may teach us, it offers a superb illustration of the empirical fact that disinterested scholarship in the human sciences, like any other social act, takes place within the realm of interests; that its objectivity is bounded by subjectivity; and that the only form of it that can appear value-free is the one that conforms fully to the dominant ideology, which alone remains, in the absence of critique, invisible as ideology.

As one of its dominant forms, German Indology has to be accommodated in any adequate theorization of orientalism. But the German case also suggests that orientalism, thought of as knowledge serving to create and marginalize degraded communities – even members of one's own community – and thus to sustain relations of domination over them, reveals itself as a subset of ideological discourse as such.[38] If consideration of the British use of forms of orientalist knowledge for domination within India might help us theorize the German use of comparable forms for domination within Germany, the latter may help us theorize how Indian forms of knowledge serve in the exercise of domination in India – may suggest a sort of eastern orientalism, in the service of a precolonial colonialism. The self-representation of Indians no more escapes the realm of interests than the representations of their oppressors; and just as there have been other imperialisms than that forming the last stage of capitalism, so there may have been other 'orientalisms' to sustain them.

NOTES

1. The complexity of this tie may be illustrated by Warren Hastings's preface to the first English translation of a Sanskrit text, Wilkins's *Bhagavadgītā*:

   Every accumulation of knowledge, and especially such as it obtained by social communication with people over whom we exercise a dominion founded on the right of conquest, is useful to the state; it is the gain of humanity; in the specific instance which I have stated, it attracts and conciliates distant affections; it lessens the weight of the chain by which the natives are held in subjection; and it imprints on the hearts of our own countrymen the sense and obligation of benevolence. Even in England, this effect of it is greatly wanting. It is not very long since the inhabitants of India were considered by many as creatures scarce elevated above the degree of savage life; nor, I fear, is that prejudice yet wholly eradicated, though surely abated. Every instance which brings their real character home to observation will impress us with a more generous sense of feeling for their natural rights, and teach us to estimate them by the measure of our own. But such instances can only be obtained in their writings; and these will survive when the British dominion in India shall have long ceased to exist, and when the sources which it once yielded of wealth and power are lost to rememberance. (1785: 13)

A more exquisite expression of liberal imperialism would be hard to find.

2. As widely remarked, and acknowledged, 1985: 1.
3. See the table prepared by Rhys Davids, which shows for the year 1903 a total of 47 professors (26 of them full professors) for 'Aryan' orientalism in Germany (Rhys Davids, 1903–04, which he juxtaposes to the four professorships in England, the colonial metropole). For the years around 1933 that more centrally concern me in these 'Notes,' the *Minerva Jahrbuch* shows substantial programs in Indology at 13 German universities. The important question of the political economy of Indology in Germany in the period 1800–1945 awaits serious analysis.
4. Edward Augustus Freeman, 1879. A prescient document, widely disseminated in its reprinted form in the Harvard Classics, vol. 28.
5. Leopold 1974 provides a good survey. A number of these representations, in particular India as the cradle of Aryan civilization, have lived on in British (and Indian) discourse well into the twentieth century, often taking on a particularly local political inflection. Compare Annie Besant's remarks to the Indian National Congress in 1917: 'The Aryan emigrants, who spread over the lands of Europe, carried with them the seeds of liberty sown in their blood in their Asian cradleland. Western historians [I believe she is referring in the first instance to H. S. Maine] trace the self-rule of the Saxon villages to their earlier prototypes in the East and see the growth of English liberty as up-springing from the Aryan root of the free and self-contained village communities …'. This was recently cited by (then) Vice President R. Venkatraman of India in his Centenary address at the Adyar Library (1988: 198).
6. A third moment is worth noting: National Socialism made Germany safe again for the open expression of a racism that, while generally accepted in nineteenth-century European scholarship – and indeed, constitutive of orientalism – had largely been excluded from the scholarly sphere for half a century (cf. Laurens 1988; the new freedom to hate publicly is brought out clearly in an early tract on the 'worldview' of National Socialism by Karl Zimmerman (1933: 20–22). One might well speculate as to what degree other European scholarship would have differed had its political idiom permitted unconstrained public expression. For the notion of an 'inner colonization' of Europe, I now see that I have to some degree been anticipated by the fascism critique of Césaire and Fanon, who regarded it as European colonialism brought home (see most recently Young 1990: 8).
7. For the intellectual-historical appropriation of Bopp – who would certainly have resisted it – in the NS period, see Richard Harder 1942.
8. Jeffrey Herf 1984.
9. It is thus, ultimately, against the values of the November Revolution that Weber counterposes the values of value-free science; his earlier adumbrations of this topic ('On Objectivity,' etc.) thus may be thought to be superseded by his formulation here. A memorable eyewitness account of Weber's presentation and its backdrop can be found in Löwith 1986: 15–17.
10. Ringer 1969: 352ff.
11. The idea of an engaged, anti-objectivist Indology finds expression frequently in the period (e.g., in the introduction to Lommel 1935, or Güntert 1938, especially p. 11). Position papers on the question more broadly viewed were prepared by the Hauptamt Wissenschaft (e.g., 'Weltanschauung und Wissenschaft,' MA-608

[H.W. VortragsMsk 1938], 55672–99, in the archives of the Institut für Zeitgeschichte, Munich).

12. Güntert 1938: 6–7 (here and throughout the essay all translations are my own unless otherwise indicated); Güntert 1932, especially p. 115. The logical extrapolation of such a position is found in the demands raised by the German Student Union's campaign against 'Un-German Spirit' during their book burnings of April–May 1933 (e.g., No. 5: 'The Jew can only think jewishly. If he writes in German, he lies'; No. 7: 'We demand of the state censor that Jewish works be published only in Hebrew. If they be published in German, they should be characterized as translations' [document published in Poliakov and Wulf 1983: 117–18]). The control of language itself is an elementary form of social power, as will be apparent in the case of India.

13. I believe I now see why: '... racism always tends to function *in reverse* ... : the racial-cultural identity of the "true nationals" remains invisible, but it is inferred from (and assured by) its opposite, the alleged, quasi-hallucinatory visibility of the "false nationals": Jews, "wops," immigrants ...' (Balibar 1990: 285).

14. As of April, 1933, 800 professors (out of a total of 7,000) had lost their positions; 85 percent of these were Jews. By 1937, 1684 professors had been dismissed. The Jewish student population dropped from 4,382 in 1933 to 812 in 1938 and zero after November 1938. See Jurt 1991: 125.

15. On the whole question, see, most recently, Sieferle 1987, who is useful principally for his analysis of nineteenth-century theories of race but is otherwise insufficient and sometimes misleading. He also incomprehensibly ignores altogether the work of professional Indologists, Iranists, and Indo-Europeanists during the NS period on the question of 'Arier' (as on attitudes toward the Indian Freedom Movement).

16. There are two key figures here. The first is Egon Frhr. von Eickstedt, professor at Breslau. Much of his work focused on the racial history of South Asia: cf. *Rassenkunde und Rassengeschichte der Menschheit*, 1934 (note the encomium in Alsdorf 1942: 4) and the journal he founded in 1935, *Zeitschrift für Rassenkunde und ihre Nachbargebiete*, which carried substantial articles of his own and of others who worked in South Asia, e.g., Heine-Geldern. The second, better known, is Hans F. K. Günther, professor at Jena, later Berlin, who also had a basic subcontinental orientation: cf. especially *Die nordische Rasse bei den Indogermanen Asiens*, 1934, as well as his own journal, *Rasse*, 1934ff. A separate study could be devoted to the 'orientalist' dimension of 'race-science,' in particular its interpreting Indian 'caste law' as an expression of racial 'hygiene,' and adducing India as a warning of the dangers of the 'blood chaos' that National Socialism prevented at the eleventh hour (for both themes, see Günther 1936). The ratio *ārya* : *caṇḍāla* [outcaste, untouchable] :: German : Jew was made already by Nietzsche, cited in Alsdorf 1942: 85.

17. The first, in all its confusion, reads as follows: '"Aryan" (also known as Indo-Germans or Japhites) includes the three branches of the Caucasian (white) race; these may be divided into the western (European), i.e., the Germans, Romans, Greeks, Slavs, Latvians, Celts, Albanians, and the eastern (Asiatic) Aryans, i.e., the Indians (Hindus) and Iranians (Persians, Afghans, Armenians, Georgians, Kurds). "Non-aryans" are therefore 1) members of the two other races, namely, the Mongolian (yellow) and the Negro (black) races; 2) members of the two other branches of the Caucasian race, namely, the Semites (Jews, Arabs) and Hamites (Berbers). The Finns and Hungarians belong to the Mongolian race, but it is hardly the intention of this law to treat them as non-aryans' (cf. also Sieferle 1987: 461–62). The confusion in the popular mind, however, continued; see for example the article 'Nichtarisch oder Jüdisch?' in the anti-Semitic journal *Hammer* (No. 799/800 (1935), pp. 376–77), prompted by the 'Wehrgesetz' of 1935, which prohibited non-Aryans from joining the army (the author was worried about the potential exclusion of such 'loyal' and 'martial' non-Aryans as Finns, Hungarians, and 'Moors'). I have looked in vain for any detailed social-historical analysis of the

term 'Arier' in the NS period. (I would add that it appears incorrect to claim that 'Arier,' etc. had ceased to be meaningful on the juridical plane after 1935 [Sieferle 1987: 462], though the question requires specialist adjudication. Certainly the process of expropriating Jewish businesses, which begins in earnest after Crystal Night [November 9, 1938], was referred to as 'Arisierung,' and laws so formulated seem to have been passed as late as September 1941 [Walk 1981: 348]. Anyway, the terminology remained a potent racist shiboleth and constantly appears in official and private documents until the end of the regime.)

18. For an example of this recentering of the notional, see Tal 1980, and Lacoue-Labarthe and Nancy 1990.

19. This paper was later presented again as a speech before the German Academy at the University of Munich on December 6, 1939, and reprinted in Wüst 1942: 33ff. (the latter collection was favorably reviewed by Frauwallner [1943: 'Let us hope ... that (the book) has the desired effect in scholarly circles and wins as many adherents as possible']). Some scholars of the period do seem to raise the issue of the historical validity of the term 'arisch' as used in contemporary discourse (for instance Lommel 1934; Krahe 1935), but avoid, or cannot conceive of, any critique.

20. For the contemporary resonance of the term cf. Klemperer 1987: 151–57.

21. According to additional documents from the BDC, the speech was printed and distributed to the SS. Wüst was later to be named director of the SS's research institute 'Das "Ahnenerbe"' (Kater 1974).

22. Especially notable is his drive for institutional dominance in the Indological and Indo-European studies establishment. Wüst for instance got himself appointed – or appointed himself – to the editorship of a number of important journals in these fields including *Wörter und Sachen* (1938), *Wiener Zeitschrift für die Kunde des Morgenlandes* (1939), *Archiv für Religionswissenschaft* (1939). This is of a piece with his attempt to institutionalize and direct popular media coverage of scholarship in general through his short-lived 'Deutscher Wissenschaftlicher Dienst' (1940: cf. MA-116/18 HA Wiss. S. 75 in the archives of the Institut für Zeitgeschichte, Munich). His more practical contributions to the NS regime include consultation in the creation of 'scientific research institutes' exploiting Hungarian Jewish prisoners in concentration camps; see the memo from Himmler of May 26, 1944 reprinted in Poliakov and Wulf 1983: 319.

23. However we may wish to define 'the ideology of the Third Reich' – whether as *völkisch* doctrine or as the strategy of the state for world domination – in neither case would it be correct to say that Alsdorf made no 'concessions' to it (Bruhn et al. 1990: ix).

24. 'A product of the most serious scholarly research, which is meant to serve contemporary life as well,' Richard Schmidt 1939: 546.

25. (1936): *Germanen und Indogermanen: Volkstum, Sprache, Heimat, Kultur. Festschrift für Herman Hirt*, two volumes (with contributions by, among others, von Eickstedt, H. F. K. Günther, Hauer, Reche, and Dumézil, but also by Benveniste and Meillet).

26. Contrast Wilhelm Schmidt's claim (in Scherer 1968: 314) that 'East-thesis' submissions (placing the *Urheimat* in Asia or Russia, as opposed to Northern Europe) were rejected (p. 313).

27. Koppers et al. 1936. Cf. the review by Otto Reche ('Professor für Rassen-und Völkerkunde, Leipzig'): 'This entire edifice of notions is tied up with church dogma [Koppers, a priest, was affiliated with Societas verbi divini in Mödling] and thus assuredly in no way scholarship ...' (Reche 1940: 17).

28. 'The homeland, the race and the culture of a supposed Proto-Indo-German population have been discussed, but this is a population that may never have existed'; 'the only thing these people [i.e., speakers of IE] have in common is the fact that their languages belong to the same family ...' since '"Indo-Germanic" is

a purely linguistic notion' (1936: 81, 83; cf. Renfrew 1987: 108–9). Speaking of improbable coincidences and the politics of the *Urheitmatfrage*, I would call attention to the hypothesis recently presented, on the eve of continental unification in the European community, that lays 'less emphasis on specific ethnic groups and their supposed migrations,' and instead imagines peaceful Indo-European farmers spreading in a gradual, egalitarian, and what seems to be an ethnically almost homogeneous 'wave of advance' throughout Europe (Renfrew 1987: 288).

29. Schlegel's image did live on, however; the Münster Sanskritist Richard Schmidt could still speak, in a learned journal in 1939, of the ancient Indians as 'our ancestors' ('unsere Urahnen,' *Wiener Zeitschrift für die Kunde des Morgenlandes* 46: 157; cf. Schmidt 1939: 548, where he refers to Meister Eckhart and Saṅkara as 'race-comrades' [*Rassengenossen*]). The myth of origins still carries on a twilight career among adherents of the new 'conservatism,' especially on the French right. See especially Jean Haudry, 1981, along with the review that puts this work into perspective, Bernard Sargent 1982. (The intellectual wing of the French right involved here – G.R.E.C.E. *Nouvelle École*, Alain de Benoist – is situated by d'Appollonia 1983.)

30. In the most recent reconsideration of the German 'intellectual quest' for India, D. Rothermund asserts that 'In the Nazi period [German Indology] could survive by virtue of the esoteric character it had acquired ... This type of "inner emigration" was, in fact, the only saving grace for Indologists, because the tradition of the German quest for India was perverted at that time by being pressed into the service of Hitler's ill-conceived racial theory ...' (1986: 17). I see little evidence of this 'esoteric' dimension in the NS period, or of 'inner emigration,' nor is it in the least self-evident that the racial theory of the NS state constituted a 'perversion' of the romantic/idealist quest (rather than, say, its telos).

31. Losemann 1977: 108; see also Kater 1974: 193ff.

32. *See Zeitschrift der deutschen morgenländischen Gesellschaft* 96 (1942): 12ff. The process of *Gleichschaltung* in the German Oriental Society awaits study. It was only in 1938 that the organization actually passed a by-law whereby Orientals, Jews, and anyone else ineligible for 'imperial citizenship' were denied membership (*ZDMG* 94 [1940]: 7–8). As far as I know, no history of the DMG exists, and this is a real desideratum for the study of institutional orientalism, especially in the NS and postwar years. Worth noting is the reappearance in the society's postwar membership list of people like Wüst (*ZDMG* 100 [1950] 23), despite apparent 'deNazification' (cf. *ZDMG* 99 [1950]: 295).

33. At least in view of the generalizations of Kater 1983: 110.

34. This list could probably be expanded with further archival search, to include, for instance, the already mentioned Hermann Güntert, professor of Sanskrit and comparative philology, who according to Maas (1988: 279n.) was installed as a dean in Heidelberg (1933–37) by the 'political leadership' (this certainly harmonizes with the essay of his excerpted above, as does Wüst's approval of his editorship of *Wörter u. Sachen* from 1938 on. (Incidentally, locating the Indo-German 'Urheimat' in the east was not necessarily a sign of anti-Nazism, as Wolfgang Meid implies [1974: 520].) Also excluded are Indo-Europeanists strictly speaking, who merit a list of their own, starting with W. Porzig (dismissed from the University of Bern for Nazi activities already in the 1920s, he exchanged positions with Debrunner in Jena; he was banned from teaching after the war but rehabilitated in 1951 [Maas 1988: 270n.]).

35. The event that led to this awaits clarification, but for now consult with due caution Alsdorf 1960: 577 (and cf. Morgenroth 1978: 54–55). Lüders continued, however, to sit on the board of the DMG. It may be noted that the aged Geiger, according to personal papers consulted by Bechert, objected privately to the behavior of Wüst.

36. On the former, see Kater 1974; for the latter, see the documents reproduced in Poliakov and Wulf 1983: 133ff.
37. Von Schroeder, familiar to Indologists as the punctilious editor of the *Kāṭhaka-saṃhitā* and *Maitrāyaṇī Saṃhitā*, is also the author of the *The Culmination of the Aryan Mystery in Bayreuth* (Von Schroeder 1911) and of *Houston Stewart Chamberlain, A Life Sketch* (Von Schroeder 1918). His book on aryan religion (Von Schroeder 1914–16), above all the chapter entitled 'Die Arier,' is a summa of the racialist topoi that were to become staples of NS discourse.
38. In the sense of 'ideology' powerfully argued by Thompson 1984.

BIBLIOGRAPHY

Texts of the National Socialist Period

Alsdorf, Ludwig (1942), *Deutsch-Indische Geistesbeziehungen*, Heidelberg, Berlin, Magdeburg: Kurt Vowinckel Verlag, vol. 7 of *Indien Handbuch*, ed. Kurt Vowinckel.

Frauwallner, Erich (1944), 'Die Bedeutung der indischen Philosophie', in Schaeder 1944, pp. 158–69.

Günther, Hans, F.K. (1936), 'Indogermanentum und Germanentum, rassenkundlich betrachtet', in *Germanen und Indogermanen: Volkstum, Sprache, Heimat, Kultur*, Heidelberg: Winter, pp. 317–40.

Güntert, Hermann (1932), 'Deutscher Geist: Drei Vorträge', Buhl-Baden: Konkordia.

—— (1938), 'Neue Zeit – neues Ziel', *Wörter und Sachen* I, vol. 19, section I–II.

Harder, Richard (1942), 'Franz Bopp und die Indogermanistik', *Nationalsozialistische Monatshefte*, 13, pp. 751–61.

Hauer, J. Wilhelm (1934). *Eine indo-arische Metaphysik des Kampfes und der Tat: Die Bhagavad Gita in neuer Sicht*, Stuttgart: Kohlhammer.

—— (1937), *Glaubensgeschichte der Indogermanen*, vol. I, Stuttgart: Kohlhammer.

Koppers, Wilhelm et al. (eds) (1936), *Die Indogermanen und Germanenfrage: Neue Wege zu ihrer Lösung*, Salzburg: Anton Pustet, Institut für Völkerkunde an der Universität Wien.

Krahe, Hans (1935), 'Die alten Arier', *Geistige Arbeit*, 2, 23, p. 6.

Lommel, Hermann (1934), 'Von arischer Religion', *Geistige Arbeit*, 2, 23, pp. 5–6.

—— (1935), *Die Alten Arier: Von Art und Adel Ihrer Götter*, Frankfurt a. M.: Klostermann.

—— (1939), *Der Arische Kriegsgott*, Frankfurt a. M.: Klostermann.

Reche, Otto (1940), Review of Koppers et al. 1936, *Orientalistische Literaturzeitung*, 1/2, pp. 11–18.

Schaeder, Hans Heinrich, (ed.) (1944), *Der Orient in Deutscher Forschung*, Vorträge der Berliner Orientalistentagung, Herbst 1942. Leipzig: Harrossowitz.

Schmidt, Richard (1939), Review of Hauer 1937, *Orientalische Literaturzeitung*, 8/9, pp. 546–8.

Schroeder, Leopold von (1911), *Die Vollendung des arischen Mysteriums in Bayreuth*, Munich: Lehmann.

—— (1914–16), *Arische Religion*, Leipzig: Hässel.

—— (1918), *Housten Stewart Chamberlain: Ein Abriss seines Lebens auf Grund eigener Mitteilungen*, Munich: Lehmann.

Thieme, Paul (1938), *Der Fremdling im Rigweda*, Leipzig: Brockhaus.

Wüst, Walther (1934), 'Deutsche Früzeit und arische Geistesgeschichte', *Süddeutsche Monatshefte*, 31, 12, pp. 697–739.

—— (1937), 'Des Führers Buch "Mein Kampf" als Spiegel arischer Weltanschauung', typescript, Berlin Document Center.

—— (1942), *Indogermanisches Bekenntnis*, Berlin–Dahlem: Das Ahnenerbe.

Zimmerman, Karl (1933), *Die geistigen Grundlagen des Nationalsozialismus*, Leipzig: Quelle & Mayer (n.d.).

OTHER TEXTS

Alsdorf, Ludwig (1960), 'Die Indologie in Berlin von 1821–1945', *Studium berolinense*, Berlin: de Gruyter, pp. 567–80.

Balibar, Étienne (1990), 'Paradoxes of Universality', in David T. Goldberg, (ed.), *Anatomy of Racism*, Minneapolis: University of Minnesota Press, pp. 283–94.

Bruhn, Klaus et al. (1990), *Ludwig Alsdorf and Indian Studies*, Delhi: Motilal Banarsidass.

Cannon, Garland (1970), *The Letters of Sir William Jones*, Oxford: Clarendon Press.

Carey, William and Joshua Marshman (1806–10), *The Ramayana of Valmeeki* 3 vols, Serampore: Baptist Mission Press.

Cohn, Bernard S. (1987), *An Anthropologist among the Historians and Other Essays*, Delhi/New York: Oxford University Press.

Freeman, Edward Augustus (1879), 'Race and Language', in Freeman, *Historical Essays*, third series, London: Macmillan, pp. 173–226.

Haudry, Jean (1981), Les Indo-Européens, Paris: PUF, (Que sais-je?).

Haug, W. F. (ed.)(1989), *Deutsche Philosophen 1933*, Berlin: Argument, special edition 165.

Herf, Jeffrey (1984), *Reactionary Modernism*, Cambridge University Press.

Jurt, Joseph (1991), 'La Romanistique allemande sous le Troisième Reich: attentistes, résistants, émigrés', *Actes de la Recherche en Sciences Sociales*, 86/87, March, pp. 125–8.

Kater, Michael (1974), *Das 'Ahnenerbe' der SS 1933–1945*, Stuttgart: DVA.

Klemperer, Victor (1987), *LTI: Notizbuch eines Philologen*, Leipzig: Reclam (first published 1947).

Lacoue-Labarthe, Philippe and Jean-Luc Nancy (1990),'The Nazi Myth', *Critical Inquiry*, 16, 2, pp. 291–312.

Laurens, Henri (1988), 'Le Concept de race dans le *Journal Asiatique* du XIX siècle', *Journal Asiatique*, 276, pp. 371–81.

Leopold, Joan (1974), 'British Applications of the Aryan Theory of Race to India, 1850–1870', *English Historical Review*, 89, pp. 578–603.

Losemann, Volker (1977), *Nationalsozialismus und Antike*, Hamburg: Hoffmann & Campe.

Löwith, Karl (1986), *Mein Leben in Deutschland vor und nach 1933: Ein Bericht*, Stuttgart: Metzler.

Lyotard, Jean-François (1987), 'Notes on Legitimation', *Oxford Literary Review 9*, pp. 106–18.

Maas, Utz (1988), 'Die Entwicklung der deutschsprachigen Sprachwissenschaft von 1900 bis 1950', *Zeitschrift für Germanistische Linguistik*, 6, pp. 253–90.

Meid, Wolfgang (1974), 'Hermann Güntert: Leben und Werk', in *Antiquitatis Indogermanicae*, Innsbruck: Innsbrucker Beiträge zur Sprachwissenschaft.

Morgenroth, Wolfgang (1978), 'Sanskrit Studies in Berlin', in *Sanskrit Studies in the GDR*, Berlin: Humboldt University, Institute of Asian Sciences.

Oppenberg, Ursula (1965), *Quellenstudien zu Friedrich Schlegels Übersetzungen aus dem Sanskrit*, Marburg: Elwert, Marburger Beiträge zur Germanistik, p. 7.

Poliakov, Léon and Joseph Wulf (1983), *Das Dritte Reich und seine Denker*, Berlin: Ullstein (first published in 1959).

Renfrew, Colin (1987), *Archaeology and Language: The Puzzle of Indo-European Origins*, Cambridge University Press.

Rhys Davids, T. W. (1903–4), 'Oriental Studies in England and Abroad', *Proceedings of the British Academy*, pp. 183–97.

Ringer, Fritz (1969), *Decline of the German Mandarins*, Cambridge, MA: Harvard University Press.

Rocher, Rosane (1968), *Alexander Hamilton 1762–1824: A Chapter in the Early History of Sanskrit Philogy*, New Haven, CT: American Oriental Society.

Römer, Ruth (1985), *Sprachwissenschaft und Rassenideologie in Deutschland*, Munich: Fink.

Roth, Fr. Heinrich (1988), *The Sanskrit Grammar and Manuscripts of Fr. Heinrich Roth [1620–1668]*, ed. Arnulf Camps and Jean-Claude Muller, Leiden: J. R. Brill.

Rothermund, Dietmar (1986), *The German Intellectual Quest for India*, Delhi: Manohar.

Sargent, Bernard (1982), 'Penser – et mal penser – les Indo-Européens', *Annales: ESC*, 37, pp. 669–81.

Scherer, Anton (ed.) (1988), *Die Urheimat der Indogermanen*, Darmstadt: Wissenschaftliche Buchgesellschaft.

Schwab, Raymond (1950), *La Renaissance orientale*, Paris: Payot.

von See, Klaus (1970), *Deutsche Germanen-Ideologie* Frankfurt: Athenaum.

Sieferle, Rolf Peter (1987), 'Indien und die Arier in der Rassentheorie', *Zeitschrift für Kulturaustausch*, 37, pp. 444–67.

Stern, Fritz (1961), *The Politics of Cultural Despair: A Study in the Rise of the Germanic Ideology*, Berkeley: University of California Press.

Tal, Uriel (1981), 'On Structures of Political Theology and Myth in Germany prior to the Holocaust', in Yehuda Bauer and Nathan Rosenstreich, (eds), *The Holocaust as Historical Experience*, New York and London: Holmes and Meier, pp. 43–74.

Thompson, John B. (1984), *Studies in the Theory of Ideology*, Berkeley: University of California Press.

Venkatraman, R. (1988), Centenary address at Adyar Library. *Adyar Library Bulletin* 52.

Walk, Joseph (ed.) (1981), *Das Sonderrecht für die Juden im NS-Staat*, Heidelberg: Mueller.

Weber, Max (1984), *Wissenschaft als Beruf*, 7th edn, Berlin: Dunker und Humbolt.

Willson, A. Leslie (1964), *A Mythical Image: The Ideal of India in German Romanticism*, Durham, NC: Duke University Press.

Young, Robert (1990), *White Mythologies: Writing History and the West*, London: Routledge.

32

TURKISH EMBASSY LETTERS

Lisa Lowe

In an introduction to her account of Lady Mary Wortley Montagu's Turkish Embassy Letters *(1717–18), Lisa Lowe – associate professor of comparative literature at the University of California, San Diego – accepts that eighteenth-century portraits of the orient as exotic and uncivilised contributed to the ideology of orientalism. But the* Turkish Embassy Letters, *she argues, must be seen as the exception that proves the rule. For in her letters Lady Montagu explicitly challenges many received representations, particularly those concerning the role of women.*

Lady Mary Wortley Montagu's *Turkish Embassy Letters* (1717–1718) explicitly challenge the received representations of Turkish society furnished by the seventeenth-century travel writers who preceded her. Although she writes in that tradition of letters about traveling in Turkey, Montagu distinctly sets herself apart from that tradition by criticizing the representations of women, marriage, sexuality, and customs in the travel accounts of Robert Withers, George Sandys, John Covel, Jean Dumont, and Aaron Hill. In redressing many of what she insists are the misconceptions and inaccurate representations of Turkish women propagated by these male travel writers, Montagu reports how, as a woman, she is permitted greater access to Turkish female society, and claims that her difference from these earlier writers may in fact be due to her

Lisa Lowe, 'Travel Narratives and Orientalism: Montagu and Montesquieu', in L. Lowe, *Critical Terrains: French and British Orientalisms* (Ithaca: Cornell University Press, 1991), pp. 31–2.

being a woman. In this sense Montagu's position with regard to English travel writing is paradoxical, or multivalent, in a manner that the earlier travelers' accounts are not. On the one hand, some of her descriptions – written as they are from her position as wife of a British ambassador – resonate with traditional occidental imaginings of the Orient as exotic, ornate, and mysterious, imaginary qualities fundamental to eighteenth-century Anglo-Turkish relations. At the same time, unlike the male travel writers before her, she employs comparisons that generally liken the conditions, character, and opportunities of European women to those of Turkish women. Montagu's identification with Turkish female society invokes an emergent feminist discourse that speaks of common experiences among women of different societies; in addition, Montagu's identification with the wives and mistresses of Turkish dignitaries also makes use of the existing discourse of class distinction, and an established identify of aristocratic privilege across cultures. Montagu's representations of Turkey in the *Letters* thus employ both the rhetoric of identification, most frequently in her descriptions of Turkish court women, and the rhetoric of differentiation with regard to other aspects of Turkish society in general. Indeed, Montagu's observations often invoke the rhetoric of both similarity and difference; that is, in the very act of likening Turkish and English women, Montague relies on and reiterates an established cultural attitude that differentiates Orient and Occident, that constitutes them as opposites. The paradoxes of the British ambassador's wife's relation to Turkish women call our attention to the sense in which in the eighteenth century, English orientalism is not monochromatically figured through an opposition of Occident and Orient but figures itself through a variety of other differentiating discourses. The *Turkish Embassy Letters* provide a particular example of orientalist representations overlapping with rhetorics of gender and class, and of orientalism generated by differently gender-determined and class-determined positions.

33

HISTORY, THEORY AND THE ARTS

John MacKenzie

In his conclusion to Orientalism: History, Theory and the Arts, *John MacKenzie – a student of British imperial history and culture – condemns Said's analysis of East–West relations in the period of European imperialism root and branch. Said's analysis he finds to be 'rigidly binary' and 'unsustainable'. In reality, he concludes, orientalism was endlessly protean, as often consumed by admiration as by denigration and depreciation.*

In his Wellek Library Lectures in Critical Theory, published as *Musical Elaborations*, Edward Said has produced his most unequivocal statement of a hermetic and stereotypical Western culture, mutually essentialising both West and East:

> For in the encounter between the West and its various 'Others' ... there was often the tactic of drawing a defensive perimeter called 'the West' around anything done by individual nations or persons who constituted a self-appointed Western essence in themselves; this tactic protected against change and a supposed contamination brought forward threateningly by the very existence of the Other. In addition, such defensiveness permits a comforting retreat into an essentialised, basically unchanging Self. By the same token, there is a move to freeze the Other in a kind of basic objecthood.[1]

John MacKenzie, *Orientalism: History, Theory and the Arts* (Manchester University Press, 1995), pp. 208–15.

It is surprising that such a rigidly binary argument should have been made in a series of lectures about music, for the evidence of the arts suggests that the case is unsustainable. As the foregoing chapters have been relentlessly concerned to point out, the artistic record of imperial culture has in fact been one of constant change, instability, heterogeneity and sheer porousness. It is impossible to recognise either the 'essentialised, basically unchanging Self' or the freezing of 'the Other in a kind of basic objecthood'. The western arts in fact sought contamination at every turn, restlessly seeking renewal and reinvigoration through contacts with other traditions. And both Self and Other were locked into processes of mutual modification, sometimes slow but inexorable, sometimes running as fast as a recently unfrozen river.

Of course those other cultures were themselves highly heterogeneous. The approach to the eastern Other can only be fully understood through a recognition of the complexity of the range of Others which constituted at once both threat and potential liberation. Thus each of the European states, some only fully formed in the late nineteenth century, responded positively and negatively to each other, to the reinvocation of mythic pasts (Norse, Celtic, Germanic, for instance), to internal Others (including newly discovered and privileged folk traditions), to renewed cultural obsessions (medievalism and chivalry are good examples), as well as to other continents and their religious and artistic complexes. It is only when Orientalism is placed in this wider context that it begins to make sense as one of several cultural courts of appeal.

In art, it was used to recreate a feudal, chivalric, pre-industrial world of supposedly uncomplicated social relations, clear legal obligations and retributions, heroic connections with the environment, a supposedly appropriate separation of gender spheres, and enthusiasm for craft production. It also provided opportunities for the extension of techniques, the handling of bright light, powerful colours, abstract design, compositional rhythms and a sense of geographical space and meteorological extremes. In architecture, it offered fresh conjunctions, new syncretic approaches, the marriage of form to function, and a whole fresh language for the buildings designed for the rapidly growing leisure industry. In design, it produced new sensations over a whole range of artefacts, revolutionary approaches to ornament, different ways of handling space, colour, composition, texture, even a reversal of the 'scientific' developments of western art and design in perspective, optical adjustments and visual accuracy. In music, composers sought in the East an extension of instrumental language, different sonorities, new melodic possibilities and complex rhythmic patterns. In doing so, they attempted to establish both national and cosmopolitan styles. While in the theatre, character, spectacle, movement, design and fabric created a fresh visual and dramatic language, opportunities both for display and for satire, often a parodying of Self through the portrayal of the Other. In all these arts, the result was often the profound extension of mood and of psychological state, a dramatic liberation from existing conventions and constricting restraints; and in each of them the repeated appeal to a different cultural tradition infused radical movements more frequently than it propped up existing conservative ones.

Naturally, such appeals were frequently resisted and powerfully criticised. They were judged against other possible sources of inspiration, derived from the past, from previously obscured internal cultures, or from different intellectual movements. Orientalism was but one of a whole sequence of perceived or invented traditions invoked by the restless arts. As we saw particularly clearly in the music chapter, composers at different times turned to various eastern sources, as well as to many nearer home, such as Spain, Scotland, or the inspiration of the folk. In doing so, they were often seeking out a distinctive national style, pursuing a need to separate themselves from a dominant (usually German) tradition. But among these, the 'oriental obsession' was a continuing and constantly changing phenomenon, repeatedly adapted to the needs of the age and the yearning for innovation. Time and again, composers discovered their most distinctive voice through the handling of exotica. These were not passing fads, nor were they mere embellishments which ultimately left western forms unchanged. As we have seen, the capacity for assimilation often obscured the graft, but the resulting artistic organism was unquestionably new and different from that which had avoided all such contacts with the Other.

In music, as in the other arts, this process was rarely a matter of genuine representation; it seldom involved realistic facsimile. Sometimes it was concerned with stereotype and caricature, but in the majority of cases it was a matter of stimulation, extension, adaptation and absorption in the pursuit of a more or less syncretic form. Such a synthesis was indeed essential to the creative act. To be sure, it was invariably based upon perception rather than actuality, a constructed East rather than the real thing. As Oscar Wilde put it, long before Edward Said, 'the whole of Japan is a pure invention ... The Japanese people are ... simply a mode of style, an exquisite fancy of art.'[2] Yet this exquisite fancy was a mutually conceived invention. Ever since oriental carpets, ceramics and fabrics had begun to arrive in Europe (and indeed earlier in other parts of Asia) the needs of the market had produced their inevitable modifications. The interaction of European taste, demand, market forces and commodity production had operated through a process of natural selection to create an 'appropriate' East. Producer and consumer were wholly complicit in this process. This was equally true of those arts which did not involve moveable artefacts.

Yet even if the products and the visions or aural perceptions of eastern arts were thus devised and prefabricated rather than faithfully reproduced, none the less they represented characteristics, forms, techniques, moods, modes of thinking and feeling which were perceived to be radically divergent from – and therefore capable of transforming – those of Europe. However modified in production or refracted through a western prism, these traditions bore a shifting relationship to an underlying reality. If they had not existed, been progressively unveiled and absorbed, there can be little doubt that the development of the western arts and associated taste would have been different. What's more, the artistic characteristics of the various Easts were not devised in order to facilitate rule, but to encourage an invigorating contamination. And, as we have seen, the influence of those oriental arts was at its most radical at precisely the supposed high point of European imperialism in the late nineteenth and early twentieth centuries. Indeed, they were often embraced by artists, designers, musicians and other practitioners who were most out of sympathy with dominant political ideas. The coincidence of oriental interests and radical ideologies is striking in all the arts.

Thus, a fascination with Orientalism was as likely to be oppositional as consensual in relation to established power structures, a promoter of a ferment in ideas as in artistic innovation. This has continued to be so in the twentieth century in all those areas *not* covered in this book, radical religious movements, mysticism, philosophy, sexuality and the popular exploration of world music. Moreover, there has been a considerable degree of continuity in these processes. It is difficult to discover in any of the arts at whatever period sets of clearly delineated binary oppositions, sharp distinctions between the moral Self and the depraved Other. Rather has the whole experience been one of instabilities and fusions, attraction and repulsion, an awareness of characteristics to be peremptorily rejected as well as devoutly embraced. And of course the content and balance of this mixed bag of wished-for gems and undesirable rejects changed over time.

Many modern scholars have begun to recognise these shifting ambivalences in the wide range of texts, literary, religious and philosophical, topographical and administrative, historical and anthropological, through which the East has been explored by the West. But the arts reflect these dualities both more obviously and in some ways more profoundly. Above all, the arts reflect the genuine refreshment repeatedly secured from drinking at eastern wells. Moreover, interesting parallels – as well as intriguing differences – can be found among them. The shift in interest (though these concerns are also heavily interleaved from the late eighteenth century) from the Ottoman Empire and the Middle East first to South Asia and then to the Far East is common to all. In each case, the appeal to changing Easts was used to reassess, redefine and reinvent significant aspects of the western arts. The increasing accessibility of different areas of the East and of their respective arts led to a repeated dialectical restructuring of the trinity of language, form and mood.

In their introduction to *Exoticism in the Enlightenment* Rousseau and Porter have argued that analysing the exotic was a particularly exacting and invigorating challenge to eighteenth-century thinkers and artists, that to a certain extent reactions to the East have been in a downhill mode ever since, through the condescension of the Romantic era, the racial exclusiveness of the period of high imperialism, to the swings from overweening arrogance to the failure of confidence in the twentieth century.[3] But the evidence of the arts fails to confirm such a counter-progressive view. In the Enlightenment period, the arts of the

East were sampled, tasted and used as embellishments to create new moods. As I have argued in each of my chapters, exotic ideas certainly entered the bloodstream, but in a relatively weak solution.

Nevertheless, in the succeeding period concepts of the sublime and the picturesque, of more potent emotional responses and heightened sensibilities, of revolutionary potential and individual heroic action were all assumed to be readily discoverable in the East. In the Romantic era, the vision of an oriental court of appeal becomes a profoundly significant one. The Anglicists appeared to rubbish such an appeal to exotica, even – as Macaulay did – to attack the taste for eastern ceramics and other items of internal decoration. But none of the arts seems to have responded to the suggestion that the western drawbridge should be raised, or at least only lowered in order to facilitate the subduing of the outer world to western technology and cultural modes. On the contrary, before long the arts of eastern traditions were being used as a weapon to attack the productive processes of industrialism, its resultant social relations and its shoddy products. By the end of the century, perceptions of eastern artistic canons were being used to mount a full-scale radical assault on western conventions.

The radical inspiration of the late nineteenth and early twentieth centuries is also an experience shared across all the arts, with little suggestion of time-lags in their responses. The remarkable sequence of exhibitions through which the arts of other cultures were unveiled reflected not only the commodification and consumption of the world by the West, the continuing organisation of knowledge and taxonomising of cultures, but also the excitement of artists, designers, musicians and performers at discovering fresh extensions of language, form and mood, albeit complying with their own perceived needs for change. The climax of this came in the twenty-five years preceding the First World War, undoubtedly a period of great ferment, with Asia as a significant catalyst, throughout all of the arts surveyed in this book. And invariably artists developed a well-nigh reverential approach to those characteristics of oriental arts from which they believed the West could benefit. It is true that Japan figured prominently in this, but it was far from being a unique source of eastern inspiration.

What's more, aspects of popular culture were not behindhand. There can be little doubt that stereotype and caricature, racially conscious attitudes, and notions of moral, technical and political superiority were highly prevalent here. But none the less, the same feeling of instability, of fascinating cross-race contact in both sexual and cultural fields, of the need to negotiate the dilemmas and contradictions of power emerges from the theatrical record. It is true that the responses of critics and of elements of the audience, particularly in the gallery, may well have been very different, but even so it is abundantly apparent that what was presented could seem endlessly attractive, another side of Self waiting to be released from repression or financial and social constraint. Just such a sense of desirable new moods, opportunities and attractive stereotypes of ease and leisure or of fantasy and illusion were promoted by the Orientalism of seaside architecture – in pier, tower, ballroom or bandstand – or of the theatre

and the cinema. Aspects of art, design, music and drama undoubtedly perco-
lated down, and when they did so in the form of satire and parody, they were
fulfilling a long tradition of popular burlesque. Orientalism was but one vehicle,
albeit a particularly visible and exciting one, in which such parodies could be
conveyed. These burlesques are sometimes read in dismissive, even insulting
ways, but they always imply affectionate knowledge; generally they creatively
destabilise rather than destructively undermine.

In any case laughter is itself a highly unstable phenomenon. As the analysts of
humour have always pointed out, it is never far from tears. Its sympathetic
responses often emerge from a troubled sense of the nearness of the conditions
portrayed. This is surely true of all great art (and the popular is not excluded
from this category). Most art operates through opposites, laughter and tears,
triumph and tragedy, the profane and the spiritual, violence and peace, the
neurotic and the calm. It secures its elevating power through the exploration of
such dualities, the fundamental realities of human existence.

This is equally true of the Orientalist arts. No true art can ever be founded
upon a perpetual parade of cultural superiority, an outpouring of imperialist
(sexist/racist) bile, an earnest expectation of decline and destruction, though the
work of late twentieth-century scholars with particularly contemporary axes to
grind attempts to project such singleminded negatives. Nor are the majority of
consumers likely to purchase, look at or listen to that which they wholly
denigrate, or seek to dominate and destroy. That notions of superiority and
inferiority, racial feeling and pride can enter into the complex of sensations of
those who imbibe such art cannot be denied, given the intellectual climate of the
period, but the power of art comes from its capacity to disturb. Cultural cross-
referencing, a sense of lost ideals, an appreciation of the beauty of a pre-
industrial craftsmanship, a perception of a pure and vibrant landscape, an
awareness of more unbuttoned approaches to life and colour, unfettered
responses to the human personality, emotional, sexual, languorous, violent
or ecstatic, can all coexist with value-laden and ethnocentric cultural and racial
ideals.

The modern critique of Orientalism has generally committed that most
fundamental of historical sins, the reading back of contemporary attitudes
and prejudices into historical periods. The word 'barbaric' has been read in its
modern one-dimensional meaning rather than in its nineteenth-century complexity, with its suggestions of the sublime, lack of restraint, an attractive
colourful and dramatic approach, liberating new sensations on a grand scale. It
was this kind of response which was expected of many Orientalist paintings,
musical expression and dramatic performance. Appropriately contextualised
readings substitute highly desirable crafts for technological backwardness,
piety and learning for obscurantism, appealing languor for sloth, manly
hunting and games-playing for childlike 'laziness', female elegance, repose
and self-expression for male dominance and possession, release into exciting
new emotional and physical sensations for primitive, animalistic responses.

Of course it is true that all of the cultural borrowings which constitute the widespread phenomenon of artistic Orientalism were secured in a political, social and economic atmosphere of unequal exchange. Few considered the ethics of trans- or interculturalism or sought to enhance and revive the donor culture. Most were egotistically involved in the single-minded pursuit of their own, often radical, artistic integrity. But the creative process is invariably a selfish one and this cannot nullify the value and power of the product. By the later nineteenth century, and with an increasingly sympathetic intensity in the twentieth, the first signs of collection and preservation, not just of cultural objects and the built environment, but also of the social, religious and philosophical contexts that engendered them, are on hand. Composers, for example, collected those elements of folk and exotic traditions that might be lost while still incorporating them into their own independent creative acts. This was as true of Béla Bartók in Europe and North Africa as it was of Colin McPhee in Bali. Other artists set about the same dual activity. They were still, it is true, responding to the needs of the West, often to destructive forces instituted by globalising cultures, but to suggest that they contributed to that destruction or failed to produce any preservation of lasting value is surely a counsel of despair.

Such attempts at conservation have not, however, been the subject of this book. I have not been concerned with Rustom Bharucha's anxieties about intercultural ethics, prescribing for mutually constructive cultural interaction in the future, however much I may feel sympathetic towards such an argument.[4] I have been concerned with what actually happened, with understanding Orientalism not only through the widest practical range of its manifestations, but also through the language and cultural contexts of its times and not ours. It has been, perhaps, an over-ambitious programme, but the whole point about responses to the East is that they have so often stimulated over-vaulting leaps of the imagination. Certainly the modern critics of Orientalism have been too procrustean. By creating a monolithic and binary vision of the past, they have too often damaged those intercultural relations which they seek to place on a more sympathetic basis for the future. In reality, Orientalism was endlessly protean, as often consumed by admiration and reverence as by denigration and depreciation. If these sensations were adopted solely to further the western arts, this does not invalidate the synthetic creative act which followed or the products which survive. Inevitably, some dross was produced in the process, but many masterpieces remain.

NOTES

1. Edward W. Said, *Musical Elaborations* (London, 1991), p. 52.
2. Quoted in Tomoko Sato and Toshio Watanabe (eds), *Japan and Britain: an Aesthetic Dialogue, 1850–1930* (London, 1991), p. 40.
3. G. S. Rousseau and Roy Porter (eds), *Exoticism in the Enlightenment* (Manchester, 1990), introduction, particularly p. 7.
4. Rustom Bharucha, *Theatre and the World: Performance and the Politics of Culture* (London, 1993).

PART XII
ORIENTALISM AND FEMINISM

34

ORIENTALISM, HINDUISM AND FEMINISM

Richard King

In Orientalism and Religion: Postcolonial Theory and the 'mystic East',
Richard King – reader in religious studies at the University of Stirling – after
identifying the genealogy of 'the mystical', the Christian category of 'religion'
and the modern concept of 'world religions', introduces the terms of the
'orientalist debate', as established by Said, and explores responses to Said's
work, with particular reference to South Asia. Then, in three specific case
studies, he examines the development of the notion of 'Hinduism' as a world
religion, the impact of colonialism on the study of Buddhism and the role played
by Western orientalists and Indian intellectuals in the construction of an image
of 'Hinduism' as a type of mysticism centred upon the philosophy of the
Vēdanta. It is in the first of these case studies, in a section entitled 'The
Relevance of Feminism to the Orientalist Debate', that he gives an account
of the relationship which many feminist writers believe exists between patri-
archalism and orientalism – that is to say, between the inferiorisation of the
woman in the West and the subjection of the Hindu/oriental in the East.

So far I have suggested that in the construction of 'Hinduism' as a single religion
the Orientalist creates a homogeneous picture of the world constructed according to Enlightenment (and ultimately Judaeo-Christian) presuppositions about
the nature of religion. Orientalist discourses, however, also tend to focus upon
the radical 'otherness' of Indian religion as a way of contrasting the Indian with

Richard King, *Orientalism and Religion* (London: Routledge, 1999), pp. 111–17.

the normative (i.e. Western) paradigm. At first sight this might seem to entail a contradiction. How can Orientalist discourses conceive of Indian religion in their own image and at the same time conceive of that same phenomena as the mirror-opposite of that image? In fact it is precisely because 'Hinduism' is conceived of in terms of Western conceptions of religion that it can then be meaningfully contrasted with the normative paradigm itself. In this sense, Orientalist discourses on Indian religion often become confined within a self-contained process of identification and differentiation constructed according to a normative paradigm (frequently modern, Western Christianity but sometimes secular liberalism). In the context of such discourses, the Indian subject remains trapped within the self-perpetuating logic of identity and difference, and thus remains subordinate to the normative paradigm. The complicity of identity and difference is an important feature of such discourses. Thus 'Hinduism' was conceptualized by Western Orientalists according to their own Western pre-suppositions about the nature of religion. It was precisely this that enabled them to construct an image of India that was the inverse of that paradigm.

As Kalpana Ram has pointed out:

> The logic of comparison – which is, on the face of it, concerned with difference – functions rather as a logic of identity, in which the Indian subject does not enjoy independent status, and is made intelligible only in opposition to the fundamental or privileged values of Western modernity ... In the hegemonic discourse of modernity and liberalism, the Western subject has been conceived as an individuated self-conscious authorial presence (the 'author' of his own activities) ... [T]he 'Indian' is not simply different from the 'Westerner', but is his exact inverse.[1]

This dilemma is reflected in the catch-22 situation in which the Indian colonial subject is placed. To agree with the colonial discourse is to accept one's sub-ordination in terms of a hegemonic Western paradigm. However, in rejecting such discourses one often perpetuates the paradigm itself, even if the categories are now inverted, reversed or revalorized. This, for instance, is the situation with regard to Hindu nationalist movements of the late nineteenth and early twentieth centuries. In their quest for home rule (*swaraj*) and freedom from imperial control, Hindus tended to perpetuate the nationalistic, romantic and homogenizing presuppositions of their British rulers.

As we have already seen, the manner in which Indological discourse has constructed India as the 'Other' or the 'shadow' of the West is a feature that is stressed in a number of critical accounts of Indological orientalism, e.g. the work of Ronald Inden (1985, 1990) and Ashis Nandy (1983). A number of scholars have pointed to work such as Louis Dumont's classic sociological study of the Indian caste system, *Homo Hierarchicus* (1970), as clear examples of this tendency. The hierarchical 'Indian' represented in this work comes to represent the antithesis of the ideal 'Western Man', or *homo aequalis*.[2] The essentialism endemic within such approaches necessitates a stereotypical representation of the Westerner in order that the Indian might reflect his polar opposite. The Westerner, presupposed as the normative paradigm in such analysis, tends to be idealized as modern, egalitarian, civilized, secular, rational and male. In contrast, the Indian is often represented as tied to tradition, primitive, hierarchical, uncivilized, religious, irrational and effeminate.

Rosalind O'Hanlon argues that the complicity between patriarchal and colonialist discourses has gone largely unnoticed by Edward Said and many of his followers, though Said has been quick to respond to this charge.[3] O'Hanlon suggests that the use of gender classifications to represent cultural differences and thus to establish the inferiority of the Orient:

> ... seems to me to run right through what he [Said] defines as the central principles of oriental representation from the late eighteenth century, almost as their natural substratum: the persistent reference to the effeminate sensuality of Asiatic subjects, their inertia, their irrationality, their submissiveness to despotic authority, the hidden wiles and petty cunning of their political projects. Implied in this femininity of weakness is also its opposite: an open dynamism and self-mastered rationality in colonial culture, what Said describes as 'the clarity, directness and nobility of the Anglo-Saxon race'.[4]

Similar criticisms have also been offered by Jane Miller and Reina Lewis.[5] Perhaps the most striking example of the feminization of Indians is to be found in British conceptions of the Bengali male as weak, docile and effeminate. Thus, in a work lucidly entitled *An Essay on the Best Means of Civilising the Subjects of the British Empire in India and of Diffusing the Light of the Christian Religion throughout the Eastern World* (1805), John Mitchell suggests that 'there seems to be a natural alliance betwixt the gentleness of the Hindoo, and the generosity of the Briton'.[6] Mitchell warns the reader, however, of the dangers of 'diluting' the manly virtues of the British by spending too long away from the homeland: 'there is danger lest the bold and somewhat rugged elements of our national spirit, should, instead of assimilating the Hindoo character to itself, be melted down into the softness of the country'.[7]

Mitchell's anxiety is grounded in a belief that national characteristics are at least partially a consequence of climatic conditions, and demonstrates British concerns about the threat of contamination by Indian sensibilities and characteristics as a result of one's isolation from the homeland. Similarly, Tejaswini Niranjana points out that British Orientalist William Jones usually represented the Hindus as:

> a submissive, indolent nation unable to appreciate the fruits of freedom, desirous of being ruled by an absolute power, and sunk deeply in the mythology of an ancient religion ... The presentation of Indians as 'naturally' effeminate as well as deceitful often go hand in hand in Jones' work.[8]

The passive, feeble and generally 'unmanly' nature of the Indian is highlighted in the following turn-of-the-century account of the Bengali people, taken from John Strachey's *India* – a standard text for English trainees in the Indian Civil Service.

> The physical organization of the Bengali is feeble even to effeminacy. He lives in a constant vapour bath. His pursuits are sedentary, his limbs delicate, his movements languid. During many ages he has been trampled upon by men of bolder and more hardy breeds ... His mind bears a singular analogy to his body: it is weak even to helplessness for purposes of manly resistance; but its suppleness and tact move the children of sterner climates to admiration not unmingled with contempt.[9]

It is here that we can see the ways in which notions of gender, race and nationality impinge upon each other in the colonial context. This is aptly demonstrated, for instance, in Mrinalini Sinha's analysis of the relationship between British 'colonial masculinity' and 'Bengali effeminacy'.[10] Such work opens up the possibility of a link between feminist critiques of Western patriarchal culture and postcolonial critiques of Western hegemony, since the colonial subjects of India and Africa have both been described in terms of the prevailing feminine stereotypes of the day. Indeed, one might even wish to argue, as Kalpana Ram, Veena Das and Rosalind O'Hanlon have, that the link between Western conceptions of India and of the female coincide to such a degree that:

> often, Indian male and female subjects are made to share a common subject position that is 'feminine' in relation to the Western model. The link explored here is not simply between Woman and Native, conceived in general terms, but between Western Woman (or Woman in Western discursive traditions) and the Indian Native. In Western discourses on modernity and subject-hood these terms have often been positioned in such a way that their attributes overlap and coincide.[11]

Just as the myth of India has been constructed as the 'Other' (i.e. as 'not-West') to the West's own self-image, women have been defined as 'not-male' or other in relation to normative patriarchal paradigms. The construction of images of the 'Other' has thus increasingly become a target of both the feminist critique of patriarchy,[12] and of postcolonial critiques of Orientalism. Indeed, it would seem that the patriarchal discourses that have excluded the 'feminine' and the female from the realms of rationality, subjectivity and authority have also been used to exclude the non-Western world from the same spheres of influence.

In this sense, one might wish to point out that colonialism, in the broadest sense of the term, is a problem for all women living in a patriarchal society, and not just for those living under the political domination of a foreign power. Thus French feminist Hélène Cixous's appeal to the body as a source of female awareness stems from the fact that women have been unable to conceptualize their own experience as females because their bodies have been colonized by patriarchal discourse.[13] The potential links between the feminist and 'Third World' agendas are noted by Veena Das, who argues that:

> Categories of nature and culture, emotion and reason, excess and balance were used to inferiorize not only women but also a whole culture. This means that if feminist scholarship is to claim for itself, as I believe it should, a potential for liberation ... , that there is the possibility of a natural alliance between feminist scholarship and knowledge produced by (and not *of*) other cultures.[14]

Another parallel worth exploring, though beyond the scope of this work, is the exclusion of women and the 'Third World' from the privileged domain of science and technology. The rhetoric of 'modernization' and 'development' theory, as enshrined, for instance, in the popular tripartite distinction between First, Second and Third World nations, perpetuates the belief that Western technological 'progress' is not only superior to that of the non-West, but also that the manner in which it transforms societies is a politically and culturally neutral process through which the non-Western world can 'catch up' with the West through modernization and development.[15]

The work of Claude Alvares provides a highly critical account of the ways in which European powers either appropriated or marginalized the indigenous agricultural, industrial and medical technologies of the Asian world. Despite its polemical nature, his analysis provides a useful corrective to the standard modernist historical accounts, which portray European technology as vastly superior to that of the East. Alvares argues that the imitation (and appropriation) of Indian craftwork practices was essential to the revolution of European textile industries, particularly from the sixteenth century onwards.[16] He also points to the Indian origins of plastic surgery, which, it is claimed, derives from the necessity to reconstruct noses as a result of an Indian custom of amputating the nose of criminals as a punitive practice, and to the effectiveness but eventual suppression of indigenous brahmanical inoculations against smallpox.[17] I am reminded here of Francis Bacon's famous remark that the three most important scientific discoveries in the history of the world have been paper and printing, gunpowder and the compass. These three discoveries have been instrumental in the development of the mass media of communication, the arms race, merchandising and the cultural interaction and exploration of the world. All three were, of course, initially discovered in Asia by the Chinese and not, as might be thought, in the West.

With regard to the status of women, feminists, from a number of different perspectives, have long argued that a similar position holds with regard to the subordination and exclusion of women from the realms of science and technology. Susan Hekman in a recent review of contemporary feminist theory writes:

Because only subjects can constitute knowledge, the exclusion of women from the realm of the subject has been synonymous with their exclusion from the realm of rationality and hence, truth ... [B]ecause women are defined as incapable of producing knowledge, they are therefore defined as incapable of engaging in intellectual, and specifically, scientific activities.[18]

In order to see the relevance of such statements to colonial discourses about India, one need only replace the term 'Indians' for 'women' in the above quote and then reread it. The context changes but the analysis of power relations remains just as appropriate. Thus, just as women are denied subjectivity and agency in history, so too are Indians in colonial discourses. In this sense both become dehumanized and silenced. Equally comparable is the association of the female with nature and the irrational in Western thought (themes taken up by ecofeminism and radical feminism), and the parallel equation of the colonized subject with the uncivilized and irrational savage. In this regard one is reminded of the time an English reporter asked Mahātma Gandhi what he thought of British civilization. Gandhi's reply – 'I think that it would be a good idea!' – provides a humorous example of the deliberate inversion of British colonial prejudices.

CONCLUSIONS

Let me sum up some of the strands of argument that I have been considering as they relate to the study of Hinduism in general. The study of Asian cultures in the West has generally been characterized by an essentialism that posits the existence of distinct properties, qualities or 'natures' which differentiate 'Indian' culture from the West. As Inden has shown, Western scholars have also tended to presuppose that such analysis was an accurate and unproblematic representation of that which it purported to explain, and that as educated Westerners they were better placed than the Indians themselves to understand, classify and describe Indian culture.

Simplistically speaking, we can speak of two forms of Orientalist discourse, the first, generally antagonistic and confident in European superiority, the second, generally affirmative, enthusiastic and suggestive of Indian superiority in certain key areas. Both forms of Orientalism, however, make essentialist judgements that foster an overly simplistic and homogenous conception of Indian culture.

However, Orientalist discourses are not univocal, nor can they be simplistically dismissed as mere tools of European imperialist ideology. Thus, the 'new' Indian intelligentsia, educated in colonially established institutions, and according to European cultural standards, appropriated the romanticist elements in Orientalist dialogues and promoted the idea of a spiritually advanced and ancient religious tradition called 'Hinduism', which was the religion of the Indian 'nation'. In this manner, Western-inspired Orientalist and nationalist discourses permeated indigenous self-awareness and were applied in anti-colonial discourses by Indians themselves. However, such indigenous discourses remain deeply indebted to Orientalist presuppositions and have generally failed to criticize the essentialist stereotypes embodied in such narratives. This rejection of British political hegemony, but from a standpoint that still accepts many of the European presuppositions about Indian culture, is what Ashis Nandy has called 'the second colonization' of India.

In this regard, the nature of Indian postcolonial self-identity provides support for Gadamer's suggestion that one cannot easily escape the normative authority of tradition, for, in opposing British colonial rule, Hindu nationalists did not fully transcend the presuppositions of the West, but rather legitimated Western Orientalist discourse by responding in a manner that did not fundamentally question the Orientalists' paradigm.

Through the colonially established apparatus of the political, economic and educational institutions of India, contemporary Indian self-awareness remains deeply influenced by Western presuppositions about the nature of Indian culture. The prime example of this is the development since the nineteenth century of an indigenous sense of Indian national identity and the construction of a single 'world religion' called 'Hinduism'. This religion is now the cognitive site of a power struggle between internationally orientated movements (such as ISKCON and the Rāmakṛṣṇa Mission) and contemporary Hindu nationalist movements (such as the Vishwa Hindu Parishad and the Rashtriya Svayamse-vak Sangh). The prize on offer is to be able to define the 'soul' or 'essence' of Hinduism. My thesis in this chapter has been that this 'essence' did not exist (at least in the sense in which Western Orientalists and contemporary Hindu movements have tended to represent it) until it was invented in the nineteenth century. In so far as such conceptions of Indian culture and history prevail and the myth of 'Hinduism' persists, contemporary Indian identities remain subject to the influence of a Westernizing and neo-colonial (as opposed to truly postcolonial) Orientalism.

NOTES

1. Kalpana Ram, 'Modernist anthropology and the construction of Indian identity', in *Meanjin* 51, 1992, pp. 589–90. See also Ashis Nandy, *The Intimate Enemy: Loss and Recovery of Self under Colonialism*, Delhi, Oxford University Press, 1983, pp. 71–4.
2. See Ram, 'Modernist anthropology and the construction of Indian identity', pp. 594–8; Gyan Prakash, 'Writing post-Orientalist histories of the Third World: perspectives from Indian historiography', in *Comparative Studies in Society and History* 32.2, 1990, p. 393; Ronald Inden, 'Orientalist constructions of India', in *Modern Asian Studies* 20.3, 1986, p. 440; Ronald Inden, *Imagining India*, Oxford, Basil Blackwell, 1990, especially p. 154, but see also pp. 201–4; Veena Das, *Critical Events: An Anthropological Perspective on Contemporary India*, Oxford, Oxford University Press, 1995, pp. 24–54; Declan Quigley, *The Interpretation of Caste*, Oxford, Clarendon Press, Oxford, 1994, ch. 3; Mary Searle-Chatterjee and Ursula Sharma (eds), *Contextualising Caste: Post-Dumontian Approaches*, Sociological Review monograph; Oxford, Blackwell, 1994, While it is true that Dumont's account of the centrality of caste in Indian culture does function as a means of contrasting Indian culture with modern Western conceptions of itself as socially fluid and

egalitarian, it is important to bear in mind that the emphasis upon caste as a defining feature of Indian culture did not begin with the Western Orientalists and was a major preoccupation of earlier accounts of India, such as that provided by the Muslim scholar al-Bīrunī.

3. See Edward Said, *Orientalism: Western Conceptions of the Orient*, London, Penguin, 1991, p. 188; 'Orientalism and after: an interview with Edward Said', in *Radical Philosophy* 63, Spring 1993, pp. 26–7.

4. [O'Hanlon, Rosalind, 'Cultures of rule, communities of resistance: gender, discourse and tradition in recent South Asian historiographies,' in *Social Analysis* 25, 1985, pp. 94–114.]

5. Jane Miller, *Seductions: Studies in Reading and Culture*, London, Virago, 1990, pp. 118–22. See also Reina Lewis, *Gendering Orientalism: Race, Femininity and Representation*, New York and London, Routledge, 1996.

6. John Mitchell, *An Essay on the Best Means of Civilising the Subjects of the British Empire in India and of Diffusing the Light of the Christian Religion Throughout the Eastern World*. Edinburgh, W. Blackwood, and London, T. Cadell & W. Davies, 1805, pp. 79–80. This work received an award from the University of Glasgow, bequeathed by the Rev. Claudius Buchanan, Vice-Provost of the College of Fort-William in Bengal.

7. Ibid.,pp. 88–9.

8. Tejaswini Niranjana, 'Translation, colonialism and rise of English', in *Economic and Political Weekly* 25.15, 14 April 1990, p. 774. See, for instance, Jones' approval of Henry Lord's (1630) description of the Banians as 'maidenly and well-nigh effeminate, of a countenance shy and somewhat estranged, yet smiling out a glazed and bashful familiarity'. See also Peter Marshall, *The British Discovery of Hinduism in the Eighteenth Century*, Cambridge, Cambridge University Press, 1970, p. 250.

9. John Strachey, *India*, 1888, cited in Claude Alvares, *Decolonizing History: Technology and Culture in India, China and the West. 1492 to the Present Day*, Goa, India, The Other India Press, and New York, Apex Press, 1991, p. 187. See Inden, *Imagining India*, pp. 86–7, 123 for a brief mention of the feminization of India in the Western imagination.

10. Mrinalini Sinha, *Colonial Masculinity: The 'Manly Englishman' and the 'Effeminate Bengali' in the Late Nineteenth Century*, Manchester, Manchester University Press, 1995, See also Nandy, *The Intimate Enemy*, 1983, ch. 1; Ann Laura Stoler, *Race and the Education of Desire: Foucault's History of Sexuality and the Colonial Order of Things*, London, Duke University Press, 1995.

11. Ram, 'Modernist anthropology and the construction of Indian identity', p. 590. See O'Hanlon, 'Cultures of rule, communities of resistance', p. 111.

12. See, for instance, Simone de Beauvoir, *The Second Sex*, Harmondsworth, Penguin, 1972; Dale Spender, *Man-Made Language*, London, Routledge & Kegan Paul, 1980, e.g., p. 23.

13. Hélène Cixous and Catherine Clement, *The Newly Born Woman*, translated by Betsy Wing, Minneapolis, University of Minnesota Press, 1986, p. 68.

14. Veena Das, 'Gender studies, cross-cultural comparison and the colonial organization of knowledge', in *Berkshire Review* 21, 1986, p. 73. For a psychoanalytically inspired account of the West's projection of the 'feminine' onto India, see Nandy, *The Intimate Enemy*, ch. 1.

15. For a critique of notions of 'modernization' and 'development' and the ideology of progress underlying them, see Mark Hobart (ed.), *An Anthropological Critique of Development: The Growth of Ignorance*, London, Routledge, 1993. See also Aijaz Ahmed, *In Theory: Classes, Nations, Literature*, London, Verso, 1992.

16. Alvares, *Decolonizing History*, pp. 55–64.

17. Ibid., p. 67.

18. Susan J. Hekman, *Gender and Knowledge: Elements of a Postmodern Feminism*, Cambridge, Polity Press, 1990, p. 94.

PART XIII
ORIENTALISM RECONSIDERED

35

ORIENTALISM RECONSIDERED

Edward Said

In the mid-1980s, at a conference held at the University of Essex, Edward Said was offered an opportunity to look again at the issues raised by his study of orientalism. This he did with both frankness and determination. He admitted that he had not yet fully digested or understood some of the criticisms made of his book Orientalism, *but he continued stubbornly to defend his thesis that orientalists, mainly nineteenth-century, had played a decisive part in the formation of negative images of the orient. Much of what he had written, in* Orientalism, *had been said before – by such writers as A. L. Tibawi, Abdullah Laroui and Anouar Abdel-Malek – but its significance remained undiminished, particularly in the field of women's studies, black and ethnic studies, and socialist and anti-imperialist studies. Many of these took as their 'point of departure' the right of formerly un- or mis-represented human groups to speak for and represent themselves in domains defined, politically and intellectually, by others.*

*The reader might also like to consult 'East Isn't East: The Impending End of the Age of Orientalism' (*Times Literary Supplement, 3 February 1995) and the Afterword of the 1995 Penguin edition of* Orientalism.

There are two sets of problems that I should like to take up, each of them deriving from the general issues addressed in *Orientalism*, of which the most

F. Barker, P. Hulme, M. Iverson and D. Loxley (eds), *Literature, Politics and Theory* (Methuen, 1986), pp. 210–29.

important are: the representation of other cultures, societies, histories; the relationship between power and knowledge; the role of the intellectual; the methodological questions that have to do with the relationships between different kinds of texts, between text and context, between text and history.

I should make two things clear at the outset. First of all, I shall be using the word 'Orientalism' less to refer to my book than to the problems to which my book is related; moreover, I shall be dealing, as will be evident, with the intellectual and political territory covered by *Orientalism* (Said 1978) as well as the work I have done since. This imposes no obligation on my audience to have read me since *Orientalism*; I mention it only as an index of the fact that since writing *Orientalism* I have thought of myself as continuing to look at the problems that first interested me in that book but which are still far from resolved. Second, I would not want it to be thought the license afforded me by the present occasion is an attempt to answer my critics. Fortunately, *Orientalism* elicited a great deal of comment, much of it positive and instructive, yet a fair amount of it hostile and in some cases (understandably) abusive. But the fact is that I have not digested and understood everything that was either written or said. Instead, I have grasped some of the problems and answers proposed by some of my critics, and because they strike me as useful in focusing an argument, these are the ones I shall be taking into account in the comments that follow. Others – like my exclusion of German Orientalism, which no one has given any reason for me to have *included* – have frankly struck me as superficial or trivial, and there seems no point in even responding to them. Similarly the claims made by Dennis Porter (1983), among others, that I am ahistorical and inconsistent, would have more interest if the virtues of consistency (whatever may be intended by the term) were subjected to rigorous analysis; as for my ahistoricity that too is a charge more weighty in assertion than it is in proof.

Now let me quickly sketch the two sets of problems I would like to deal with here. As a department of thought and expertise Orientalism, of course, refers to several overlapping domains: first, the changing historical and cultural relationship between Europe and Asia, a relationship with a 4000-year-old history; second, the scientific discipline in the west according to which, beginning in the early nineteenth century, one specialized in the study of various Oriental cultures and traditions; and, third, the ideological suppositions, images and fantasies about a currently important and politically urgent region of the world called the Orient. The relatively common denominator between these three aspects of Orientalism is the line separating Occident from Orient and this, I have argued, is less a fact of nature than it is a fact of human production, which I have called imaginative geography. This is, however, neither to say that the division between Orient and Occident is unchanging nor is it to say that it is simply fictional. It is to say – emphatically – that as with aspects of what Vico calls the world of nations, the Orient and the Occident are facts produced by human beings, and as such must be studied as components of the social, and not the divine or natural, world. And because the social world includes the person or subject doing the studying as well as the object or realm being studied, it is imperative to include them both in any consideration of Orientalism for, obviously enough, there could be no Orientalism without, on the one hand, the Orientalists, and on the other, the Orientals.

Far from being a crudely political apprehension of what has been called the problem of Orientalism, this is in reality a fact basic to any theory of interpretation, or hermeneutics. Yet, and this is the first set of problems I want to consider, there is still a remarkable unwillingness to discuss the problem of Orientalism in the political or ethical or even epistemological contexts proper to it. This is as true of professional literary critics who have written about my book, as it is of course of the Orientalists themselves. Since it seems to me patently impossible to dismiss the truth of Orientalism's political origin and its continuing political actuality, we are obliged on intellectual as well as political grounds to investigate the resistance to the politics of Orientalism, a resistance that is richly symptomatic of precisely what is denied.

If the first set of problems is concerned with Orientalism reconsidered from the standpoint of local issues like who writes or studies the Orient, in what institutional or discursive setting, for what audience, and with what ends in mind, the second set of problems takes us to wider issues. These are the issues raised initially by methodology and then considerably sharpened by questions as to how the production of knowledge best serves communal, as opposed to factional, ends, how knowledge that is non-dominative and non-coercive can be produced in a setting that is deeply inscribed with the politics, the considerations, the positions and the strategies of power. In these methodological and moral reconsiderations of Orientalism I shall quite consciously be alluding to similar issues raised by the experiences of feminism or women's studies, black or ethnic studies, socialist and anti-imperialist studies, all of which take for their point of departure the right of formerly un- or misrepresented human groups to speak for and represent themselves in domains defined, politically and intellectually, as normally excluding them, usurping their signifying and representing functions, over-riding their historical reality. In short, Orientalism reconsidered in this wider and libertarian optic entails nothing less than the creation of new objects for a new kind of knowledge.

But let me now return to the local problems I referred to first. The hindsight of authors not only stimulates in them a sense of regret at what they could or ought to have done but did not; it also gives them a wider perspective in which to comprehend what they did. In my own case I have been helped to achieve this broader understanding by nearly everyone who wrote about my book, and who saw it – for better or worse – as being part of current debates, conflicts and contested interpretations in the Arab-Islamic world, as that world interacts with the United States and Europe. Certainly there can be no doubt that – in my own rather limited case – the consciousness of being an Oriental goes back to my youth in colonial Palestine and Egypt, although the impulse to resist its accompanying impingements was nurtured in the heady atmosphere of the post-Second World War period of independence when Arab nationalism, Nasserism, the 1967 War, the rise of the Palestine national movement, the 1973 War, the Lebanese Civil War, the Iranian Revolution and its horrific aftermath, produced that extraordinary series of highs and lows which has neither ended nor allowed us a full understanding of its remarkable revolutionary impact.

The interesting point here is how difficult it is to try to understand a region of the world whose principal features seem to be, first, that it is in perpetual flux, and second, that no one trying to grasp it can by an act of pure will or of sovereign understanding stand at some Archimedean point outside the flux. That is, the very reason for understanding the Orient generally, and the Arab world in particular, was first that it prevailed upon one, beseeched one's attention urgently, whether for economic, political, cultural, or religious reasons, and second, that it defied neutral, disinterested or stable definition.

Similar problems are commonplace in the interpretation of literary texts. Each age, for instance, reinterprets Shakespeare, not because Shakespeare changes, but because, despite the existence of numerous and reliable editions of Shakespeare, there is no such fixed and non-trivial object as Shakespeare independent of his editors, the actors who played his roles, the translators who put him in other languages, the hundreds of millions of readers who have read him or watched performances of his plays since the late sixteenth century. On the other hand, it is too much to say that Shakespeare has no independent existence at all, and that he is completely reconstituted every time someone reads, acts or writes about him. In fact, Shakespeare leads an institutional or cultural life that among other things has guaranteed his eminence as a great poet, his authorship of thirty-odd plays, his extraordinary canonical powers in the west. The point I am making here is a rudimentary one: that even so relatively inert an object as a literary text is commonly supposed to gain some of its identity from its historical moment interacting with the attentions, judgements, scholarship and performance of its readers. But, I discovered, this privilege was rarely allowed the Orient, the Arabs, or Islam, which separately or together were supposed by mainstream academic thought to be confined to the fixed status of an object frozen once and for all in time by the gaze of western percipients.

Far from being a defence of the Arabs or of Islam – as my book was taken by many to be – my argument was that neither existed except as 'communities of interpretation' which gave them existence, and that, like the Orient itself, each designation represented interests, claims, projects, ambitions and rhetorics that were not only in violent disagreement, but were in a situation of open warfare. So saturated with meanings, so overdetermined by history, religion and politics are labels like 'Arab' or 'Muslim' as subdivisions of 'the Orient' that no one today can use them without some attention to the formidable polemical mediations that screen the objects, if they exist at all, that the labels designate.

I do not think that it is too much to say that the more these observations have been made by one party, the more routinely they are denied by the other; this is true whether it is Arabs or Muslims discussing the meaning of Arabism or Islam, or whether an Arab or Muslim disputes these designations with a western scholar. Anyone who tries to suggest that nothing, not even a simple descriptive label, is beyond or outside the realm of interpretation, is almost certain to find an opponent saying that science and learning are designed to transcend the vagaries of interpretation, and that objective truth is in fact attainable. This claim was more than a little political when used against Orientals who disputed the authority and objectivity of an Orientalism intimately allied with the great mass of European settlements in the Orient. At bottom, what I said in *Orientalism* had been said before me by A. L. Tibawi (1961, 1966), by Abdullah Laroui (1976, 1977), by Anwar Abdel Malek (1963, 1969), by Talal Asad (1979), by S. H. Alatas (1977a, 1977b), by Fanon (1969, 1970) and Césaire (1972), by Panikkar (1959) and Romila Thapar (1975, 1978), all of whom had suffered the ravages of imperialism and colonialism, and who in challenging the authority, provenance and institutions of the science that represented them to Europe, were also understanding themselves as something more than what this science said they were.

Nor was this all. The challenge to Orientalism, and the colonial era of which it is so organically a part, was a challenge to the muteness imposed upon the Orient as object. In so far as it was a science of incorporation and inclusion by virtue of which the Orient was constituted and then introduced into Europe, Orientalism was a scientific movement whose analogue in the world of empirical politics was the Orient's colonial accumulation and acquisition by Europe. The Orient was therefore not Europe's interlocutor, but its silent Other. From roughly the end of the eighteenth century, when in its age, distance and richness the Orient was rediscovered by Europe, its history had been a paradigm of antiquity and originality, functions that drew Europe's interests in acts of recognition or acknowledgement but *from* which Europe moved as its own industrial, economic and cultural development seemed to leave the Orient far behind. Oriental history – for Hegel, for Marx, later for Burkhardt, Nietzsche, Spengler and other major philosophers of history – was useful in portraying a region of great age, and what had to be left behind. Literary historians have further noted in all sorts of aesthetic writing and plastic portrayals that a trajectory of 'westering', found for example in Keats and Hölderlin, customarily saw the Orient as ceding its historical pre-eminence and importance to the world spirit moving westwards away from Asia and towards Europe.

As primitivity, as the age-old antetype of Europe, as a fecund night out of which European rationality developed, the Orient's actuality receded inexorably into a kind of paradigmatic fossilization. The origins of European anthropology and ethnography were constituted out of this radical difference and, to my knowledge, as a discipline anthropology has not yet dealt with this inherent political limitation upon its supposedly disinterested universality. This, by the way, is one reason Johannes Fabian's book, *Time and The Other: How Anthropology Makes Its Object* (1983), is both so unique and so important; compared, say, with the standard disciplinary rationalizations and self-congratulatory clichés about hermeneutic circles offered by Clifford Geertz, Fabian's serious effort to redirect anthropologists' attention back to the discrepancies in time, power and development between the ethnographer and his/her constituted object is all the more remarkable. In any event, what for the most part got left out of Orientalism was precisely the history that resisted its ideological as well as political encroachments, and that repressed or resistant history has returned in the various critiques and attacks upon Orientalism, which has uniformly and polemically been represented by these critiques as a science of imperialism.

The divergences between the numerous critiques made of Orientalism as ideology and praxis, at least so far as their aims are concerned, are very wide none the less. Some attack Orientalism as a prelude to assertions about the virtues of one or another native culture: these are the nativists. Others criticize Orientalism as a defence against attacks on one or another political creed: these are the nationalists. Still others criticize Orientalism for falsifying the nature of Islam: these are, *grosso modo*, the fundamentalists. I will not adjudicate between these claims, except to say that I have explicitly avoided taking stands on such matters as the real, true or authentic Islamic or Arabic world, except as issues relating to conflicts involving partisanship, solidarity or sympathy, although I have always tried never to forsake a critical sense or reflective detachment. But in common with all the recent critics of Orientalism I think that two things are especially important – one, a rigorous methodological vigilance that construes Orientalism less as a positive than as a critical discipline and therefore makes it subject to intense scrutiny, and two, a determination not to allow the segregation and confinement of the Orient to go on without challenge. My own understanding of this second point has led me to the extreme position of entirely refusing designations like 'Orient' and 'Occident'; but this is something that I shall return to a little later.

Depending on how they construed their roles as Orientalists, critics of the critics of Orientalism have either reinforced the affirmations of positive power lodged within Orientalism's discourse, or much less frequently alas, they have engaged Orientalism's critics in a genuine intellectual exchange. The reasons for this split are self-evident: some have to do with power and age, as well as institutional or guild defensiveness; others have to do with religious or ideological convictions. All, irrespective of whether the fact is acknowledged or not, are political – something that not everyone has found easy to acknowledge. If I may make use of my own example, when some of my critics in particular agreed with the main premises of my argument they tended to fall back on encomia to the achievements of what one of their most distinguished individuals, Maxime Rodinson, called '*la science orientaliste*'. This view lent itself to attacks on an alleged Lysenkism lurking inside the polemics of Muslims or Arabs who lodged a protest with 'western' Orientalism, despite the fact that all the recent critics of Orientalism have been quite explicit about using such 'western' critiques as

Marxism or structuralism in an effort to over-ride individious distinctions between east and west, between Arab and western truth, and the like.

Sensitized to the outrageous attacks upon an august and formerly invulnerable science, many accredited members of the certified professional cadre whose division of study is the Arabs and Islam have disclaimed any politics at all, while pressing a rigorous, but for the most part intellectually empty and ideologically intended counter-attack. Although I said I would not respond to critics here, I need to mention a few of the more typical imputations made against me so that you can see Orientalism extending its nineteenth-century arguments to cover a whole incommensurate set of late twentieth-century eventualities, all of them deriving from what, to the nineteenth-century mind, is the preposterous situation of an Oriental responding to Orientalism's asseverations. For sheer heedless anti-intellectualism unrestrained or unencumbered by the slightest trace of critical self-consciousness no one, in my experience, has achieved the sublime confidence of Bernard Lewis, whose almost purely political exploits require more time to mention than they are worth. In a series of articles and one particularly weak book (1982), Lewis has been busy responding to my argument, insisting that the western quest for knowledge about other societies is unique, that it is motivated by pure curiosity, and that in contrast Muslims neither were able nor interested in acquiring knowledge about Europe, as if knowledge about Europe was the only acceptable criterion for true knowledge. Lewis's arguments are presented as emanating exclusively from the scholar's apolitical impartiality whereas, at the same time, he has become an authority drawn on for anti-Islamic, anti-Arab, Zionist and Cold War crusades, all of them underwritten by a zealotry covered with a veneer of urbanity that has very little in common with the 'science' and learning Lewis purports to be upholding.

Not quite as hypocritical, but no less uncritical, are younger ideologues and Orientalists like Daniel Pipes whose expertise as demonstrated in his book *In the Path of God: Islam and Political Power* (1983) is wholly at the service not of knowledge but of an aggressive and interventionary state – the US – whose interests Pipes helps to define. Even if we leave aside the scandalous generalizing that allows Pipes to speak of Islam's anomie, its sense of inferiority, its defensiveness, as if Islam were one simple thing, and as if the quality of his either absent or impressionistic evidence were not of the most secondary importance, Pipes's book testifies to Orientalism's unique resilience, its insulation from intellectual developments everywhere else in the culture, and its antediluvian imperiousness as it makes its assertions and affirmations with little regard for logic and argument. I doubt that any expert anywhere in the world would speak today of Judaism or Christianity with quite that combination of force and freedom that Pipes allows himself about Islam, although one would have thought that a book about Islamic revival would allude to parallel and related developments in styles of religious resurgence in, for example, Lebanon, Israel and the US. For Pipes, Islam is a volatile and dangerous business, a political movement intervening in and disrupting the west, stirring up insurrection and fanaticism everywhere else.

The core of Pipes's book is not simply its highly expedient sense of its own political relevance to Reagan's America, where terrorism and communism fade imperceptibly into the media's image of Muslim gunners, fanatics and rebels, but its thesis that Muslims themselves are the worst source for their own history. The pages of *In the Path of God* are dotted with references to Islam's incapacity for self-representation, self-understanding, self-consciousness, and with praise for witnesses like V. S. Naipaul who are so much more useful and clever in understanding Islam. Here, of course, is perhaps the most familiar of Orientalism's themes – they cannot represent themselves, they must therefore be represented by others who know more about Islam than Islam knows about itself. Now it is often the case that you can be known by others in different ways than you know yourself, and that valuable insights might be generated accordingly. But that is quite a different thing from pronouncing it as immutable law that outsiders *ipso facto* have a better sense of you as an insider than you do of yourself. Note that there is no question of an *exchange* between Islam's views and an outsider's: no dialogue, no discussion, no mutual recognition. There is a flat assertion of quality, which the western policy-maker or his faithful servant possesses by virtue of his being western, white, non-Muslim.

Now this, I submit, is neither science, knowledge, or understanding: it is a statement of power and a claim for relatively absolute authority. It is constituted out of racism, and it is made comparatively acceptable to an audience prepared in advance to listen to its muscular truths. Pipes speaks to and for a large clientèle for whom Islam is not a culture, but a nuisance; most of Pipes's readers will, in their minds, associate what he says about Islam with the other nuisances of the 1960s and 1970s – blacks, women, post-colonial Third World nations that have tipped the balance against the US in such places as UNESCO and the UN, and for their pains have drawn forth the rebuke of Senator Moynihan and Mrs Kirkpatrick. In addition, Pipes – and the rows of like-minded Orientalists and experts he represents as their common denominator – stands for programmatic ignorance. Far from trying to understand Islam in the context of imperialism and the revenge of an abused, but internally very diverse, segment of humanity, far from availing himself of the impressive recent work on Islam in different histories and societies, far from paying some attention to the immense advances in critical theory, in social science and humanistic research, in the philosophy of interpretation, far from making some slight effort to acquaint himself with the vast imaginative literature produced in the Islamic world, Pipes obdurately and explicitly aligns himself with colonial Orientalists like Snouck Hurgronje and shamelessly pre-colonial renegades like V. S. Naipaul, so that from the eyrie of the State Department and the National Security Council he might survey and judge Islam at will.

I have spent this much time talking about Pipes only because he usefully serves to make some points about Orientalism's large political setting, which is routinely denied and suppressed in the sort of claim proposed by its main spokesman, Bernard Lewis, who has the effrontery to dissociate Orientalism from its two-hundred-year-old partnership with European imperialism and associate it instead with modern classical philology and the study of ancient Greek and Roman culture. Perhaps it is also worth mentioning about this larger setting that it comprises two other elements, about which I should like to speak very briefly, namely the recent (but at present uncertain) prominence of the Palestinian movement, and second, the demonstrated resistance of Arabs in the United States and elsewhere against their portrayal in the public realm.

As for the Palestinian issue, between them the question of Palestine and its fateful encounter with Zionism on the one hand, and the guild of Orientalism, its professional caste-consciousness as a corporation of experts protecting their terrain and their credentials from outside scrutiny on the other hand, these two account for much of the animus against my critique of Orientalism. The ironies here are rich, and I shall restrict myself to enumerating a small handful. Consider the case of one Orientalist who publicly attacked my book, he told me in a private letter, not because he disagreed with it – on the contrary, he felt that what I said was just – but because he had to defend the honour of his profession! Or, take the connection – explicitly made by two of the authors I cite in *Orientalism*, Renan and Proust – between Islamophobia and anti-Semitism. Here, one would have expected many scholars and critics to have seen the conjuncture, that hostility to Islam in the modern Christian west has historically gone hand in hand with, has stemmed from the same source, has been nourished at the same stream as anti-Semitism, and that a critique of the orthodoxies, dogmas and disciplinary procedures of Orientalism contribute to an enlargement of our understanding of the cultural mechanisms of anti-Semitism. No such connection has ever been made by critics, who have seen in the critique of Orientalism an opportunity for them to defend Zionism, support Israel and launch attacks on Palestinian nationalism. The reasons for this confirm the history of Orientalism for, as the Israeli commentator Dani Rubenstein has remarked, the Israeli occupation of the West Bank and Gaza, the destruction of Palestinian society and the sustained Zionist assault upon Palestinian nationalism have quite literally been led and staffed by Orientalists. Whereas in the past it was European Christian Orientalists who supplied European culture with arguments for colonizing and suppressing Islam, as well as for despising Jews, it is now the Jewish national movement that produces a cadre of colonial officials whose ideological theses about the Islamic or Arabic mind are implemented in the administration of the Palestinian Arabs, an oppressed minority within the white European democracy that is Israel. Rubenstein notes with some sorrow that the Hebrew University's Islamic studies department has produced every one of the colonial officials and Arabs experts who run the Occupied Territories.

One further irony should be mentioned in this regard: just as some Zionists have construed it as their duty to defend Orientalism against its critics, there has been a comic effort by some Arab nationalists to see the Orientalist controversy as an imperialist plot to enhance American control over the Arab world.

According to this seriously argued but extraordinarily implausible scenario, we are informed that critics of Orientalism turn out not to be anti-imperialist at all, but covert agents of imperialism. The next step from this is to suggest that the best way to attack imperialism is either to become an Orientalist or not to say anything critical about it. At this stage, however, I concede that we have left the world of reality for a world of such illogic and derangement that I cannot pretend to understand its structure or sense.

Underlying much of the discussion of Orientalism is a disquieting realization that the relationship between cultures is both uneven and irremediably secular. This brings us to the point I alluded to a moment ago, about recent Arab and Islamic efforts, well-intentioned for the most part, but sometimes motivated by unpopular regimes, who in attracting attention to the shoddiness of the western media in representing the Arabs or Islam divert scrutiny from the abuses of their rule and therefore makes efforts to improve the so-called image of Islam and the Arabs. Parallel developments have been occurring, as no one needs to be told, in UNESCO where the controversy surrounding the world information order – and proposals for its reform by various Third World and socialist governments – has taken on the dimensions of a major international issue. Most of these disputes testify, first of all, to the fact that the production of knowledge, or information, of media images, is unevenly distributed: the centres of its greatest force are located in what, on both sides of the divide, has been polemically called the metropolitan west. Second, this unhappy realization on the part of weaker parties and cultures has reinforced their grasp of the fact that although there are many divisions within it, there is only one secular and historical world, and that neither nativism, nor divine intervention, nor regionalism, nor ideological smokescreens can hide societies, cultures and peoples from each other, especially not from those with the force and will to penetrate others for political as well as economic ends. But, third, many of these disadvantaged post-colonial states and their loyalist intellectuals have, in my opinion, drawn the wrong set of conclusions, which in practice is that one must either attempt to impose control upon the production of knowledge at the source or, in the worldwide media economy, attempt to improve, enhance, ameliorate the images currently in circulation without doing anything to change the political situation from which they emanate and on which, to a certain extent, they are based.

The failings of these approaches strike me as obvious, and here I do not want to go into such matters as the squandering of immense amounts of petro-dollars for various short-lived public relations scams, or the increasing repression, human rights abuses and outright gangsterism that have taken place in many formerly colonial countries, all of them occurring in the name of national security and fighting neo-imperialism. What I do want to talk about is the much larger question of what, in the context provided by such relatively small efforts as the critique of Orientalism, is to be done, and on the level of politics and criticism how we can speak of intellectual work that is not merely reactive or negative.

I come now finally to the second and, in my opinion, the more challenging and interesting set of problems that derive from the reconsideration of Orientalism. One of the legacies of Orientalism, and indeed one of its episte-mological foundations, is historicism, that is, the view pronounced by Vico, Hegel, Marx, Ranke, Dilthey and others, that if humankind has a history it is produced by men and women, and can be understood historically as, at each given period, epoch or moment, possessing a complex, but coherent unity. So far as Orientalism in particular and the European knowledge of other societies in general have been concerned, historicism meant that the one human history uniting humanity either culminated in or was observed from the vantage point of Europe, or the west. What was neither observed by Europe nor documented by it was, therefore, 'lost' until, at some later date, it too could be incorporated by the new sciences of anthropology, political economics and linguistics. It is out of this later recuperation of what Eric Wolf (1982) has called people without history, that a still later disciplinary step was taken, the founding of the science of world history whose major practitioners include Braudel (1972–3, 1981–4), Wallerstein (1974–80), Perry Anderson (1974) and Wolf himself.

But along with the greater capacity for dealing with – in Ernst Bloch's phrase – the non-synchronous experiences of Europe's Other, has gone a fairly uni-form avoidance of the relationship between European imperialism and these variously constituted, variously formed and articulated knowledges. What, in other words, has never taken place is an epistemological critique at the most fundamental level of the connection between the development of a historicism which has expanded and developed enough to include antithetical attitutes such as ideologies of western imperialism and critiques of imperialism on the one hand and, on the other, the actual practice of imperialism by which the accumulation of territories and population, the control of economies, and the incorporation and homogenization of histories are maintained. If we keep this in mind we will remark, for example, that in the methodological assumptions and practice of world history – which is ideologically anti-imperialist – little or no attention is given to those cultural practices like Orientalism or ethnography affiliated with imperialism, which in genealogical fact fathered world history itself; hence the emphasis in world history as a discipline has been on economic and political practices, defined by the processes of world historical writing, as in a sense separate and different from, as well as unaffected by, the knowledge of them which world history produces. The curious result is that the theories of accumulation on a world scale, or the capitalist world state, or lineages of absolutism depend (a) on the same displaced percipient and historicist observer who had been an Orientalist or colonial traveller three generations ago; (b) they depend also on a homogenizing and incorporating world historical scheme that assimilated non-synchronous developments, histories, cultures and peoples to it; and (c) they block and keep down latent epistemological critiques of the institutional, cultural and disciplinary instruments linking the incorporative practice of world history with partial knowledges like Orientalism on the one hand and, on the other, with continued 'western' hegemony of the non-European, peripheral world.

In fine, the problem is once again historicism and the universalizing and self-validating that has been endemic to it. Bryan Turner's exceptionally important little book *Marx and the End of Orientalism* (1978) went a very great part of the distance towards fragmenting, dissociating, dislocating and decentring the experiential terrain covered at present by universalizing historicism; what he suggests in discussing the epistemological dilemma is the need to go beyond the polarities and binary oppositions of Marxist-historicist thought (voluntarism *v.* determinism, Asiatic *v.* western society, change *v.* stasis) in order to create a new type of analysis of plural, as opposed to single objects. Similarly, in a whole series of studies produced in a number of both interrelated and frequently unrelated fields, there has been a general advance in the process of, as it were, breaking up, dissolving and methodologically as well as critically reconceiving the unitary field ruled hitherto by Orientalism, historicism and what could be called essentialist universalism.

I shall be giving examples of this dissolving and decentring process in a moment. What needs to be said about it immediately is that it is neither purely methodological nor purely reactive in intent. You do not respond, for example, to the tyrannical conjuncture of colonial power with scholarly Orientalism simply by proposing an alliance between nativist sentiment buttressed by some variety of native ideology to combat them. This, it seems to me, has been the trap into which many Third World and anti-imperialist activists fell in supporting the Iranian and Palestinian struggles, and who found themselves either with nothing to say about the abominations of Khomeini's regime or resorting, in the Palestine case, to the time-worn clichés of revolutionism and, if I might coin a deliberately barbaric phrase, rejectionary armed-strugglism after the Lebanese débâcle. Nor can it be a matter simply of recycling the old Marxist or world-historical rhetoric, which only accomplishes the dubiously valuable task of re-establishing intellectual and theoretical ascendancy of the old, by now impertinent and genealogically flawed conceptual models. No: we must, I believe, think both in political and above all theoretical terms, locating the main problems in what Frankfurt theory identified as domination and division of labour and, along with those, the problem of the absence of a theoretical and utopian as well as libertarian dimension in analysis. We cannot proceed unless therefore we dissipate and redispose the material of historicism into radically different objects and pursuits of knowledge, and we cannot do that until we are aware clearly that no new projects of knowledge can be constituted unless they fight to remain free of the dominance and professionalized particularism that comes with historicist systems and reductive, pragmatic or functionalist theories.

These goals are less grand and difficult than my description sounds. For the reconsideration of Orientalism has been intimately connected with many other activities of the sort I referred to earlier, and which it now becomes imperative to articulate in more detail. Thus, for example, we can now see that Orientalism is a praxis of the same sort, albeit in different territories, as male gender dominance, or patriarchy, in metropolitan societies; the Orient was routinely described as feminine, its riches as fertile, its main symbols the sensual woman, the harem, and the despotic – but curiously attractive – ruler. Moreover Orientals, like Victorian housewives, were confined to silence and to unlimited enriching production. Now much of this material is manifestly connected to the configurations of sexual, racial and political asymmetry underlying mainstream modern western culture, as adumbrated and illuminated respectively by feminists, by black studies critics and by anti-imperialist activists. To read, for example, Sandra Gilbert's recent and extraordinarily brilliant study of Rider Haggard's *She* (1983) is to perceive the narrow correspondence between suppressed Victorian sexuality at home, its fantasies abroad and the tightening hold of imperialist ideology on the male late-nineteenth-century imagination. Similarly, a work like Abdul Jan Mohamed's *Manichean Aesthetics* (1983) investigates the parallel but unremittingly separate artistic worlds of white and black fictions of the same place, Africa, suggesting that even in imaginative literature a rigid ideological system operates beneath a freer surface. Or in a study like Peter Gran's *The Islamic Roots of Capitalism* (1979), which is written out of a polemically although meticulously researched and scrupulously concrete anti-imperialist and anti-Orientalist historical stance, one can begin to sense what a vast invisible terrain of human effort and ingenuity lurks beneath the frozen Orientalist surface formerly carpeted by the discourse of Islamic or Oriental economic history.

There are many more examples that one could give of analyses and theoretical projects undertaken out of similar impulses as those fuelling the anti-Orientalist critique. All of them are interventionary in nature, that is, they self-consciously situate themselves at vulnerable conjunctural nodes of ongoing disciplinary discourses where each of them posits nothing less than new objects of knowledge, new praxes of humanist (in the broad sense of the word) activity, new theoretical models that upset or at the very least radically alter the prevailing paradigmatic norms. One might list here such disparate efforts as Linda Nochlin's explorations of nineteenth-century Orientalist ideology as working within major art historical contexts (1983); Hanna Batatu's immense restructuring of the terrain of the modern Arab state's political behaviour (1984); Raymond Williams's sustained examination of structures of feeling, communities of knowledge, emergent or alternative cultures, patterns of geographical thought, as in his remarkable *The Country and the City* (1973); Talal Asad's account of anthropological self-capture in the work of major theorists (1979, 1983), and along with that his own studies in the field; Eric Hobsbawm's new formulation of 'the invention of tradition' or invented practices studied by historians as a crucial index both of the historian's craft and, more importantly of the invention of new emergent nations (1983); the work produced in re-examination of Japanese, Indian and Chinese culture by scholars like Masao Miyoshi (1969), Eqbal Ahmad, Tariq Ali, Romila Thapar (1975, 1978), the group around Ranajit Guha (*Subaltern Studies*), Gayatri Spivak (1982, 1985), and younger scholars like Homi Bhabha (1984, 1985) and Partha Mitter (1977); the freshly imaginative reconsideration by Arab literary critics – the *Fusoul* and *Mawakif* groups, Elias Khouri, Kamal Abu Deeb, Mohammad Banis, and others – seeking to redefine and invigorate the reified classical structures of Arabic literary performance, and as a parallel to that, the imaginative works of Juan Goytisolo (1976, 1980) and Salman Rushdie (1979, 1983) whose fictions and criticisms are self-consciously written against the cultural stereotypes and representations commanding the field.

It is worth mentioning here, too, the pioneering efforts of the *Bulletin of Concerned Asian Scholars*, and the fact that twice recently, in their presidential addresses, an American Sinologist (Benjamin Schwartz) and Indologist (Ainslee Embree) have reflected seriously upon what the critique of Orientalism means for their fields, a public reflection as yet denied Middle Eastern scholars; perennially, there is the work carried out by Noam Chomsky in political and historical fields, an example of independent radicalism and uncompromising severity unequalled by anyone else today (1969, 1983); or in literary theory, the powerful theoretical articulations of a social, in the widest and deepest sense, model for narrative put forward by Fredric Jameson (1981), Richard Ohmann's empirically arrived-at definitions of canon privilege and institution in his recent work (1976), his revisionary Emersonian perspectives formulated in the critique of contemporary technological and imaginative, as well as cultural ideologies by Richard Poirier (1971), and the decentring, redistributive ratios of intensity and drive studies by Leo Bersani (1978).

One could go on mentioning many more, but I certainly do not wish to suggest that by excluding particular examples I have thought them less eminent or less worth attention. What I want to do in conclusion is to try to draw them together into a common endeavour which, it has seemed to me, can inform the larger enterprise of which the critique of Orientalism is a part. First, we note a plurality of audiences and constituencies; none of the works and workers I have cited claims to be working on behalf of one audience which is the only one that counts, or for one supervening, overcoming truth, a truth allied to western (or for that matter eastern) reason, objectivity, science. On the contrary, we note here a plurality of terrains, multiple experiences and different constituencies, each with its admitted (as opposed to denied) interest, political desiderata, disciplinary goals. All these efforts work out of what might be called a decentred consciousness, not less reflective and critical for being decentred, for the most part non- and in some cases anti-totalizing and anti-systematic. The result is that instead of seeking common unity by appeals to a centre of sovereign authority, methodological consistency, canonicity and science, they offer the possibility of common grounds of assembly between them. They are therefore planes of activity and praxis, rather than one topography commanded by a geographical and historical vision locatable in a known centre of metropolitan power. Second, these activities and praxes are consciously secular, marginal and oppositional with reference to the mainstream, generally authoritarian systems from which they emanate, and against which they now agitate. Third, they are political and practical in as much as they intend – without necessarily succeeding in implementing – the end of dominating, coercive systems of knowledge. I do not think it too much to say that the political meaning of analysis, as carried out in all these fields, is uniformly and programmatically libertarian by virtue of the fact that, unlike Orientalism, it is not based on the finality and closure of antiquarian or curatorial knowledge, but on investigative open models of analysis, even though it might seem that analyses of this sort – frequently difficult and abstruse – are in the final account paradoxically quietistic. I think we must remember the lesson provided by Adorno's negative dialectics and regard analysis as in the fullest sense being *against* the grain, deconstructive, utopian.

But there remains the one problem haunting all intense, self-convicted and local intellectual work, the problem of the division of labour, which is a necessary consequence of that reification and commodification first and most powerfully analysed in this century by George Lukács. This is the problem sensitively and intelligently put by Myra Jehlen for women's studies (1981), whether in identifying and working through anti-dominant critiques, subaltern groups – women, blacks, and so on – can resolve the dilemma of autonomous fields of experience and knowledge that are created as a consequence. A double kind of possessive exclusivism could set in: the sense of being an excluding insider by virtue of experience (only women can write for and about women, and only literature that treats women or Orientals well is good literature), and second, being an excluding insider by virtue of method (only Marxists, anti-Orientalists, feminists can write about economics, Orientalism, women's literature).

This is where we are now, at the threshold of fragmentation and specialization, which impose their own parochial dominations and fussy defensiveness, or on the verge of some grand synthesis which I for one believe could very easily wipe out both the gains and the oppositional consciousness provided by these counter-knowledges hitherto. Several possibilities impose themselves, and I shall conclude simply by listing them. A need for greater crossing of boundaries, for greater interventionism in cross-disciplinary activity, a concentrated awareness of the situation – political, methodological, social, historical – in which intellectual and cultural work is carried out. A clarified political and methodological commitment to the dismantling of systems of domination which since they are collectively maintained must, to adopt and transform some of Gramsci's phrases, be collectively fought, by mutual siege, war of manoeuvre *and* war of position. Lastly, a much sharpened sense of the intellectual's role both in the defining of a context and in changing it, for without that, I believe, the critique of Orientalism is simply an ephemeral pastime.

BIBLIOGRAPHY

(Books already listed in the bibliography at the end of the anthology are not included here.)

Abdel-Malek, Anwar (1969), *Idéologie et renaissance nationale*, Paris.

Alatas, S. H. (1977a), *Intellectuals in Developing Societies*, London.

———— (1977b), *The Myth of the Lazy Native*, London.

Anderson, Perry (1974), *Lineages of the Absolute State*, London.

Asad, Talal (1979), 'Anthropology and the Analysis of Ideology', *Man*, n.s. XIV (4), pp. 607–27.

———— (1983), 'Anthropological Conceptions of Religion: Reflections on Geertz', *Man*, n.s. XVIII (2), pp. 237–59.

Batatu, Hanna (1984), *The Egyptian, Syrian and Iraqui Revolutions: Some Observations on their Underlying Causes and Social Character*, Washington.

Bersani, Leo (1978), *A Future for Astyanax: Character and Desire in Literature*, Cambridge.

Braudel, Fernand (1972–3), *The Mediterranean and the Mediterranean World in the Age of Philip II*, trans. Sian Reynolds, 2 vols, New York.

———— (1981–4), *Civilization and Capitalism*, trans. Sian Reynolds, 3 vols, London.

Césaire, Aimé (1972), *Discourse on Colonialism*, trans. J. Pinkham, New York.

Chomsky, Noam (1969), *American Power and the New Mandarins*, New York.

———— (1983), *The Fateful Triangle: Israel, the United States and the Palestinians*, New York.

Fabian, Johannes (1983), *Time and the Other: How Anthropology Makes its Object*, New York.

Fanon, Frantz (1969), *The Wretched of the Earth*, trans. Constance Farrington, Harmondsworth.

———— (1970), *Black Skin White Masks*, trans. Charles Lam Markmann, London.

Gilbert, Sandra (1983), 'Rider Haggard's Heart of Darkness', *Partisan Review*, 50, pp. 444–53.

Goytisolo, Juan (1976), *Revindicación del conde Julián*, Barcelona.

———— (1980), *Señas de identidad*, Barcelona.

Gran, Peter (1979), *The Islamic Roots of Capitalism: Egypt 1760–1840*, Austin.

Jameson, Fredric (1981), *The Political Unconscious: Narrative as a Socially Symbolic Act*, London.

Jan Mohamed, Abdul (1983), *Manichean Aesthetics: The Politics of Literature in Colonial Africa*, Amherst.

Jehlen, Myra (1981), 'Archimedes and the Paradox of Feminist Criticism', *Signs*, VI (4), pp. 575–601.

Laroui, Abdullah (1976), *The Crisis of the Arab Intellectuals*, trans. Diarmid Cammell, Berkeley.

———— (1977), *The History of the Maghrib*, trans. Ralph Manheim, Princeton.

Lewis, Bernard (1982), *The Muslim Discovery of Europe*, New York.

Mitter, Partha (1977), *Much Maligned Monsters: History of Europe's Reaction to India*, Oxford.

Miyoshi, Masao (1969), *The Divided Self: A Perspective on the Literature of the Victorians*, New York.

Ohmann, Richard (1976), *English in America: A Radical View of the Profession*, Oxford.

Panikkar, K. M. (1959), *Asia and Western Dominance: A Survey of the Vasco da Gama Epoch of Asian History, 1498–1945*. London.

Pipes, Daniel (1983), *In the Path of God*, New York.

Poirier, Richard (1971), *Performing Self: Composition and Decomposition in the Language of Contemporary Life*, Oxford.

Porter, Dennis (1983), 'Orientalism and Its Problems', in Barker, F. et al. (eds), *The Politics of Theory*, Colchester, pp. 179–93.

Rushdie, Salman (1979), *Midnight's Children*, London.

——— (1983), *Shame*, London.

Spivak, Gayatri Chakravorty (1982), '"Draupaudi" by Mahasveta Devi', in Abel, Elizabeth (ed.), *Writing and Sexual Difference*, Chicago, pp. 261–82.

——— (1985), 'The Rani of Sirmur', in Barker, F. et al. (eds), *Europe and its Others*, I, Colchester, pp. 128–51.

Thapar, Romila (1975), *Ancient India: A Textbook of History for Middle Schools*, New Delhi.

——— (1978), *Medieval India: A Textbook of History for Middle Schools*, New Delhi.

Tibawi, A. L. (1961), *British Interests in Palestine, 1800–1901*, London.

——— (1966), *American Interests in Syria, 1800–1901*, Oxford.

Wallerstein, Immanuel (1974–80), *The Modern World System*, 2 vols, New York.

Williams, Raymond (1973), *The Country and the City*, London.

Wolf, Eric (1982), *Europe and the People without History*, Berkeley.

PART XIV
BEYOND ORIENTALISM

Several writers have tried to bridge the gap between orient and occident, East and West. Among these, Fred Dallmayr – in his study of Indian and European philosophy, *Beyond Orientalism: Essays in Cross-Cultural Encounter* – and Bryan S. Turner – in his study of the economic relations of East and West, *Orientalism, Post-Modernism and Globalism* – have both made notable attempts.

36

EXIT FROM ORIENTALISM

Fred Dallmayr

In his chapter 'Exit from Orientalism' in Beyond Orientalism: Essay in Cross-Cultural Encounter, *Fred Dallmayr, a student of European and Indian history and philosophy, explains how* Wilhelm Halbfass, *a German-American philosopher and Indologist, attempted to transgress the 'essentialised' images of Western and Indian culture and 'exit from Orientalism'. Dallmayr surveys three aspects of Halbfass's work: his approach to cross-cultural understanding; his application of hermeneutical insights to the study of classical Indian texts; and his emphasis on the compatibility (or incompatibility) of classical Hinduism with modern Western conceptions of democracy and political equality.*

> Then there was not being nor non-being. ... Death was not, not was immortality. ... But the breathless one breathed by itself.
>
> *Rigveda*, Mandala 10

There was a time when cross-cultural understanding was largely a matter of expertise. Study and comprehension of non-Western cultures, including the 'Orient,' was consigned to an array of area specialists ranging from philologians to historians and cultural anthropologists. Armed with the arsenal of Western philosophical and scientific categories, area studies pursued a somewhat predatory aim, that of incorporating or assimilating non-Western life-forms into preestablished frames of reference (unless they were relegated to a mysterious

Fred Dallmayr, 'Exit from Orientalism', in his *Beyond Orientalism: Essays in Cross-Cultural Encounter* (New York: State University of New York Press, 1996), pp. 115–17 and 134.

otherness beyond the pale of knowledge). To be sure, incorporation of this kind was not a purely academic exercise, but was buttressed and fueled by concrete political and economic ventures of that time, especially the administrative needs of colonial empires. In Edward Said's formulation, this constellation of factors formed the backdrop of Western 'Orientalism,' a label highlighting the collusion of scholarship with the imperatives of colonial domination. In its distilled form, this kind of constellation is no longer prevalent today. Our age of post-colonialism has also given rise to forms of 'post-Orientalism,' that is, endeavors to rupture or transgress the traditional Orientalist paradigm. To the extent that Orientalist discourse was part and parcel of a 'Eurocentric' world view, transgression sometimes heralds a radical anti-Eurocentrism, perhaps even a dismissal of European scholarship as such; to the degree that the latter was tied also to 'logocentrism' (or a 'foundational' metaphysics), cognitive understanding tends to give way to constructivism, that is, the imaginative invention of traditions and life-forms. All along this trend is corroborated by the ongoing processes of globalization, processes which, in their pervasive effects, undermine the prerogatives of area specialists.

Clearly, the demise of Orientalism cannot be cause for lament. Still, even while welcoming new departures, one may plausibly be concerned about the manner of the demise, that is, the way in which the exit from Orientalism is sought and performed. Is it really possible to move briskly from Eurocentrism to anti-Eurocentrism (and from logos to antilogos)? Is it sensible to equate traditional learning – however flawed – simply with colonial oppression? Does the critique of cultural 'essences' and stable identities really warrant the claim that traditions and life-forms are 'up for grabs' and can be constructed *ad libidum*? In our globalizing context, is there not still room and need for cross-cultural understanding – beyond the confines of Eurocentrism and logocentrism? And does such understanding not involve or presuppose a patient learning process, a sustained effort of reciprocal interrogation, which, in turn, can hardly disdain some of the resources (philological, historical, anthropological) of traditional scholarship?

As it happens, the groundwork for such a post-Orientalist inquiry has already been laid in our time by a group of scholars from the West and the non-West, including such distinguished names as Wilfred Cantwell Smith, J. L. Mehta, and Raimundo Panikkar. A younger member of this group – but by no means 'junior' in terms of insights and achievements – is Wilhelm Halbfass whose work is the topic of the present chapter. In his outlook and background, Halbfass illustrates and exemplifies some of the important ingredients of the emergent post-Orientalist discourse. Thoroughly trained both in Western philosophy and in the specialized research tradition of Indology, Halbfass stands at the crossroads of interacting (sometimes conflicting) life-forms and language games, a position that enables him to act (at least in some respects) as a mediator or honest broker. While immersed in academic pursuits, Halbfass is also a clearheaded citizen of the world, completely attentive to the complexities of globalization, and especially to the persisting political and economic asymmetries between West and non-West (asymmetries which render the term *post-Orientalism* intrinsically ambivalent).

As it stands today, Halbfass's opus is already impressive by its range and subtlety; apart from a long string of journal articles, his scholarly reputation is particularly tied to three successive publications: *India and Europe: An Essay in Understanding* (1988); *Tradition and Reflection: Explorations in Indian Thought* (1991); and *On Being and What There Is: Classical Vaisesika and the History of Indian Ontology* (1992). Limitations of space as well as (more crucially) limits of my Indological competence militate against any attempt at surveying this vast field of scholarship. The following shall focus on three topical areas which appear to be particularly salient. First is Halbfass's approach to cross-cultural understanding and particularly to Indian culture and traditions. Next, attention shifts to one of the central concerns of traditional Indian thought: the status and meaning of being as articulated in Vedic and post-Vedic texts as well as in philosophical literature. Finally discussion turns to some political problems besetting the relation of India and the West: in particular the compatibility of *homo hierarchicus* with modern democracy and the role and prospects of Indian culture in the context of Western hegemony. These comments will lead me to some concluding remarks on the viability of cross-cultural scholarship, as epitomized by Halbfass's work, in a time of rapid globalization. . . .

[. . .]

What surfaces here are philosophical problems of considerable magnitude which resist easy settlement and which certainly cannot be adjudicated through the facile invocation of formulas (such as Eurocentrism or anti-Eurocentrism). In Indian thought, transcendence of difference (or equality) has itself to be justified in light of a differentiated *dharma*, which is precisely the opposite of modern Western thought where difference or distinction is radically put on the defensive (as in need of justification). What is called 'Europeanization' or 'Westernization' of the world is to a large extent the militant extension of egalitarianism or the principle of equivalence to other parts of the globe (with capital serving as the currency of equivalence). Liberty here is not adverse to equality, because it basically means freedom of choice (where all choices are equivalent or of equal value). Whatever their intrinsic merits may be, the principles of equality and equal liberty are today exported around the globe in a missionary and largely unthinking way, without much reflection on the premises of such principles and how they (and their consequences) might be vindicated. Non-Western societies, which are not readily swayed by these principles, are quickly dismissed as illiberal and undemocratic. India in particular – given the long legacy of 'homo hierarchicus' – is likely to be denounced as a major obstacle on the road to world democracy (in a not very subtle resurrection of Orientalism).

As it seems to me, exiting from Orientalism in our time requires more than an exchange of blind charges and counter-charges; above all, it requires a serious rethinking of such basic philosophical categories as equality (or sameness) and difference. Perhaps, in reacting against Buddhism, traditional Indian (or rather Hindu) thought has tended to privilege difference too much over sameness (and being over nonbeing), forgetting the more complex legacy of the 'ontology of openness' deriving from the Vedas. But the problems are reciprocal or cross-cultural. As Ernesto Laclau and Chantal Mouffe have persuasively pointed out, the two principles of equivalence and difference presuppose each other and need to be articulated jointly, but in a way that resists synthesis, yielding only reciprocal destabilization. What this points up is an enormous task looming ahead of us in the wake of Orientalism: the task of genuine dialogical learning on the level of basic frameworks, beyond the limits of assimilation and exclusion. By being willing to shoulder this task, Wilhelm Halbfass's work makes an important contribution to cross-cultural understanding which can serve as a guidepost illuminating future endeavors.

37

FROM ORIENTALISM TO GLOBAL SOCIOLOGY

Bryan S. Turner

In his chapter 'From Orientalism to Global Sociology', in Orientalism, Postmodernism and Globalism, *Bryan S. Turner, a Marxist sociologist, argues that the orientalist discourse is ultimately about the origins of the West, not the origins of the East. It involves a theory of power, an argument about social change, a perspective on sexuality, and a theory of rational bureaucracy. Whilst it is true that the actual role of the oriental scholar in relation to both colonial authorities and subordinate cultures was often highly problematic, it should not be assumed that Western analysis of oriental society invariably produced negative stereotypes. But the real problem with any critique of orientalism is an epistemological one.*

In this volume [*Orientalism, Postmodernism and Globalism*] I have discussed various components of the orientalist discourse, namely a theory of power, an argument about social change, a perspective on sexuality, and a theory of rational bureaucracy. This discourse in social science has two consequences. First, it provided a general perspective on social and historical difference which separated the Occident and the Orient. Indeed, in this framework the Orient became the negative imprint of the Occident. Secondly, it generated a moral position on the origins of modern culture, despite the fact that this social science language was couched in terms of value neutrality.

Bryan S. Turner, 'From Orientalism to Global Sociology', in his *Orientalism, Postmodernism and Globalism* (London: Routledge, 1994), pp. 100–4.

The orientalist discourse was ultimately about the origins of the West, not the origins of the East. Social theorists took very different positions on this issue in the nineteenth century. We have seen that Weber in his sociology of religion identified the origins of rationality in Western culture in the Christian tradition which he clearly regarded as occidental. By contrast, Nietzsche in *The Birth of Tragedy* in 1872 sought the origins of contemporary society in a Greek or classical legacy (Silk and Stern 1981). In this respect, Nietzsche shared in the enthusiasm for Hellenism which dominated German thinking in the nineteenth century, but Nietzsche's interpretation was also a radical departure from the conventional romantic position, since he argued that modern culture had its origin in the violence of the Greek tradition, not in its tranquillity and sanity (Stauth and Turner 1988). The question of origins raises serious difficulties for the orientalist tradition, since much of contemporary science and technology arose within Chinese civilization. Since China was, within the orientalist discourse, apparently a stagnant and stationary society, it was difficult to see how China could have produced major technological changes and scientific developments. This question about China has never been satisfactorily resolved and continues to be a major problem within the sociology of science (Needham 1954; Turner 1987). There is a similar debate about the origins of Japanese capitalism and its possible relation to Confucian values which has been central to recent attempts to rethink capitalism as a system.

The critical evaluation of orientalism has produced a new awareness of the underlying general assumptions of Western social science, history and literary criticism. The process of de-colonization clearly cannot be separated from the de-colonization of thought. However, there are a number of unresolved issues within the critique of orientalism itself. First, it is simplistic to see the Western analysis of oriental society in a completely negative light because the notion of 'oriental society' was not always used merely as a negative stereotype. We have seen for example that Nietzsche used Islam as the basis for a critique of Christianity and regarded the Greek legacy as a legacy of extreme violence. In fact, the orientalist tradition was often ambiguous in its assessment of oriental cultures, especially where orientalism adopted a romantic perspective on non-Western societies. The actual role of the oriental scholar in relation to both colonial authorities and subordinate cultures was often highly problematic. Thus conflicting interpretations of Christian Snouck Hurgronje's contribution to Dutch colonial policy in Indonesia provide a good illustration of these issues (Benda 1958; Niel 1956; Wertheim 1972). Snouck Hurgronje, whose study of Mecca deeply influenced Weber's views on Islam, especially on the role of the city in Islamic culture, posed as a Muslim scholar to study the holy places. His advice to the Dutch Government during the Acheh War was regarded by his informants as a terrible betrayal. While he advised the Dutch authorities that Islam was not a fanatical collection of 'priests' under the control of the Ottoman caliph, he had no doubts as to the superiority of Western values. This confident belief in the superiority of the West served to justify the betrayal.

We can note that the critique of orientalism often somewhat naïvely criticizes orientalism as racist. This critique of racism would be true for example of V. G. Kiernan's *The Lords of Human Kind* (1972). Racism, however, is endemic to human society, since it is part of a basic 'we – other' problematic. That is, the problem of 'other cultures' is a universal problem, given the very existence of norms and values in human society. There are good reasons for believing that all societies create an 'insider – outsider' division and in this sense orientalism is not a problem peculiar to the Occident.

The issues are however somewhat trivial. As we have argued, the main problem with the critique of orientalism is a problem around epistemology. It is difficult for critics of orientalism to confront the issue of the 'real Orient', particularly if they adopt an anti-foundationalist position on discourse. Postmodern epistemologies do not promise an alternative orthodoxy and reject the possibility of 'true' descriptions of the 'real' world. This epistemological scepticism does not lend itself either to political action or to the development of alternative frameworks (Rorty 1986). If discourse produces its own objects of enquiry and if there is no alternative to discourse, then there is little point in attempting to replace oriental discourse with some improved or correct analysis of 'the Orient'. There is no neutral ground from which to survey the possibilities of an alternative analysis. This problem seems to be a particular difficulty for Said since he often appears to be merely recommending an improvement in our account of Islam. This appeared to be his position in *Covering Islam* (1978). Do we want a better description or an alternative description? Or is it the case that contemporary theories of epistemology would rule out such a set of questions? These difficulties are not confined to the study of Islam. One finds that similar attempts to develop new, postcolonial frameworks for the study of Indian history have not proved to be especially productive or significant (O'Hanlon and Washbrook 1992).

We clearly need a more positive and less pessimistic outcome to the critique of orientalism. By way of conclusion to these chapters on orientalism, I shall suggest four intellectual responses which might point to a more conclusive outcome to this debate. First, it appears to be obvious that the sociological value of the concept 'oriental society' is zero. The ideal type of oriental society is too limited, too prejudicial and too shallow in historical terms to be of any value in contemporary social science. However, the debates which have surrounded this conflict and the critique of orientalism have been theoretically productive and beneficial, regardless of its moral merits. One can detect in contemporary writing on Islam, for example, a far more self-reflexive and self-critical attitude towards Western constructions of Islam. In particular, there is now far greater awareness of the diversity and complexity of Islamic traditions which preclude an essentialist version of a monolithic 'Islam' (Lubeck 1987). Second, we should also note that the orientalist discourse was based upon the problem of difference (we *versus* them, East *versus* West, rationality *versus* irrationality). Perhaps an alternative to orientalism is a discourse of sameness which would emphasise the continuities between various cultures rather than their antagonisms. For example, in the case of Islam it is clear that we may regard Islamic cultures as part of a wider cultural complex which would embrace both Judaism and Christianity. We need therefore a new form of secular ecumenicalism. This type of historical and moral sensitivity clearly underlined the work of Marshall G. S. Hodgson, whose *The Venture of Islam* (1974) is a magisterial contribution to the historical sociology of religions, despite my criticism of his view of conscience and piety. Third, and following from this comment, we should recognize the fact that the most recent developments in historical sociology have been focused on the idea of a world-system or the political and cultural importance of globalism. We live culturally and economically in a world which is increasingly unified in terms of the emergence of a world-system by common forces, at least in the economic field. Our awareness of globalism should begin to transform the character of social science. There is now an important body of literature focused on the idea of the obsolescence of the nation-state and the growing self-consciousness of the world as a world-system (Chirot 1986; Mann 1986;). While the theory of a global order has theoretical and moral problems of its own, it does represent a significant shift away from the traditional ethnocentricity of the orientalist debate. Indeed, these cultural developments (specifically the emergence of a global communications system) make 'the development of a form of global sociology' (Robertson 1987: 37) increasingly important. The traditional forms of 'society-centred' analysis in sociology are hopelessly out of date. Equally the sharp contrast between Occident and Orient is an anachronism of the nineteenth-century imperial legacy. Fourth, there is considerable intellectual merit in the methodological strategy of treating our own culture as strange and as characterized by a profound otherness. One practical technique here is to turn the anthropological gaze onto the history of our own religions and cultural practices. Since anthropology emerged originally as a response to cultural colonization of other cultures, the application of anthropology to modern industrial society and to the Western forms of modernization has a radical effect on the consciousness of Western scholars. Perhaps the primary example of this approach is to be found in Talad Asad's *Genealogies of Religion: Discipline and Reasons of Power in Christianity and Islam* (1993). Asad argues that in order to understand how local people enter or resist the process of modernization, anthropology must also study the West. In applying anthropology to Western processes of development Asad explains how religion was fundamental to the emergence of disciplines and rational values in the West. In modern times, he also demonstrates how the reaction to the Salman Rushdie affair has been crucial for a defence of Britishness in a society which is increasingly multicultural. Here again, the reaction to Islam has been a major part of the reshaping of British conservative thought.

One problem for contemporary scholarship is that, if orientalism was itself part of a project of modernity which has now terminated (Kellner, 1988), it is difficult to establish a clear alternative. The dominance of postmodernist perspectivism tends to make one nervous about definite or universalistic stand points. It is clear that banal recommendations to merely scrutinize our own value positions when conducting empirical research on alternative cultures are pointless. The critique of orientalism leaves us open to two dangers. The first is a naïve trust in the 'native' or the pre-modern as a form of humanity which is not corrupted by Westernization or modernization. Basically there are *a priori* no privileged moral positions. It would be nice however to follow the recommendation that the social researcher has one, prior and decisive commitment, namely 'solidarity with the wretched of the earth' (Wertheim 1972: 328), but we also have to take note of the problem of excessive anthropological charity when understanding alien beliefs in their context (Gellner 1962).

Another problem is that the critique of orientalism leaves us open to a peculiar form of indigenous conservatism posing as progressive anti Westernism. In some Arab intellectual circles, Foucault has been stood virtually on his head. The argument goes like this. If the critique of orientalism is true, then all Western observations are a distortion of the real nature of Islam. Therefore, our own version of ourselves is true. While it is clear that what Muslims say about themselves, 'must have a central role in the enquiry' (Roff 1987: 1) into Islam, the 'internal' evidence cannot have an exclusively privileged position. We do not want to exchange an outdated orientalism for an equally prejudicial occidentalism. The importance of the current epistemological scepticism is that it precludes such discursive privileges.

Four lines of development are important as an alternative to orientalism. The first is to abandon all reified notions of 'Islam' as an universal essence in order to allow us to study many 'Islams' in all their complexity and difference. Such a move would at least avoid the unwarranted essentialism of the old scholarly orthodoxy. Second, we need to see these Islams within a global context of interpenetration with the world-system. We need to understand Islamic debates in a deeply global context. This perspective avoids the limitations of dichotomous views of East and West, or North and South. Third, sociology itself has to break out of its nationalistic and parochial concerns with particular nation-states from a society-centred perspective. Over twenty years ago, W. E. Moore (1966) challenged sociologists to abandon their narrow nationalistic perspectives in order to develop the (largely implicit) global sociology of the classical tradition. My argument is that a satisfactory resolution to the many problems and limitations of the orientalist tradition ultimately requires a genuinely global perspective. Fourth, the anthropological gaze should be also directed towards the otherness of Western culture in order to dislodge the privileged position of dominant Western cultures.

BIBLIOGRAPHY

Benda, H. J. (1958), 'Christiaan Snouck Hurgronje and the foundations of Dutch Islamic policy in Indonesia', *Journal of Modern History*, 30, pp. 228–37.
Chirot, D. (1986), *Change in the Modern Era*, San Diego: Harcourt Brace Jovanovich.

Gellner, E. (1962), 'Concepts and society', *Transactions of the Fifth World Congress of Sociology Louvain* 1, pp. 153–83.

Kellner, D. (1988), 'Postmodernism as Social Theory: Some Challenges and Problems', *Theory, Culture and Society* 5, pp. 239–70.

Lubeck, P. M. (1987), 'Structural Determinants of Urban Islamic Protest in Northern Nigeria', in W. R. Roff (ed.), *Islam and the Political Economy and Meaning: Comparative Studies of Muslim Discourse*, Berkeley and Los Angeles: University of California Press.

Mann, M. (1986), *The Social Sources of Power* Volume 1: *A History of Power from the Beginning to AD 1760*, Cambridge University Press.

Moore, W. E. (1966), 'Global Sociology: The World as a Singular System', *American Journal of Sociology*, 71, pp. 475–82.

Needham, J. (1954), *Science and Civilisation in China*, Cambridge University Press.

Niel, R. van (1956), 'Christian Hurgronje: In memory of the Centennial of His Birth', *Journal of Asian Studies*, 16, pp. 591–4.

O'Hanlon, R. and Washbrook, D. (1992), 'After Orientalism: Culture, Criticism and Politics in the Third World', *Comparative Studies in Society and History*, 34, 1, pp. 141–67.

Robertson, R. (1987), 'Globalisation and Societal Modernisation: A Note on Japan and Japanese Religion', *Sociological Analysis*, 46, 5, pp. 35–42.

Roff, W. R. (1987), editor's introduction, in W. R. Roff (ed.), *Islam and the Political Economy of Meaning: Comparative Studies of Muslim Discourse*, Berkeley and Los Angeles: University of California Press.

Rorty, R. (1986), 'Foucault and Epistemology', in B. Hoy (ed.), *Foucault: A Critical Reader*, Oxford: Basil Blackwell.

Said, E. W. (1978), *Covering Islam*, New York: Pantheon.

Silk, M. S. and Stern, J. P. (1981), *Nietzsche on Tragedy*, Cambridge University Press.

Stauth, G. and Turner, B. S. (1988), *Nietzsche's Dance: Resentment, Reciprocity and Resistance in Social Life*, Oxford: Basil Blackwell.

Turner, B. S. (1987), 'State, Science and Economy in Traditional Societies: Some Problems in Weberian Sociology of Science', *British Journal of Sociology*, 38, 1, pp. 1–23.

Wertheim, W. F. (1972), 'Counter-Insurgency Research at the Turn of the Century – Snouck Hurgronje and the Acheh War', *Sociologische Gids*, 19, pp. 320–8.

BIBLIOGRAPHY

(The place of publication is London except where otherwise specified.)

BOOKS

Ahmed, A., *Postmodernism and Islam* (Routledge, 1992).
Araf Hussein, Robert Olson, *Orientalism, Islam and Islamists* (Amana Books, 1984).
Arberry, Arthur John, *British Orientalists* (Collins, 1943).
Archer, Mildred, *Indian Architecture and the British, 1780–1830* (Felthem: Country Life Books, 1968).
Archer, Mildred and Lightbown, Ronald, *India Observed: India as Viewed by British Artists, 1760–1860* (Trefoil Books, 1982).
Aziz al-Azmeh, *Islams and Modernities* (Verso, 1993).
Bailey, A. M. and Llobera, J. K. (eds), *The Asiatic Mode of Production* (Routledge and Kegan Paul, 1981).
Barker, Francis et al. (eds). *The Politics of Theory* (Colchester, 1983).
Barker, F., Hulme, P., Iverson, M. and Loxley, D. (eds), *Literature, Politics and Theory* (Methuen, 1986).
Barthold, Vasilli Vladimirovitch, *La Découverte de l'Asie: Histoire de l'orientalisme en Europe et en Russe*, French translation by Basile Nikitone (Paris: Payot, 1947).
Bassnett, S. and Trivedi, Harish, *Post-colonial Translation* (Routledge, 1999).
Bayly, C. A. (ed.), *The Raj, India and the British, 1600–1947* (National Portrait Gallery, 1990).
Behdad, A., *Belated Travelers* (Cork University Press, 1994).
Bhabha, Homi K., *The Location of Culture* (Routledge, 1994).
Bhabha, Homi K. (ed.), *Nation and Narration* (Routledge, 1990).
Bharucha, Rustom, *Theatre and the World: Performances and the Politics of Culture* (Routledge, 1993).
Black, Jeremy, *The British and the Grand Tour* (Croom-Helm, 1985).
Bolt, Christine, *Victorian Attitudes to Race* (Routledge and Kegan Paul, 1971).

Brantlinger, Patrick, *Rule of Darkness: British Literature and Imperialism 1830–1914* (Ithaca: Cornell University Press, 1988).

Bratton, J. S. and Jacqueline Susan (eds), *Acts of Supremacy: The British Empire and the Stage, 1790–1930* (Manchester University Press, 1991).

Breckenridge, C. A. and van der Veer, P. (eds), *Orientalism and the Postcolonial Predicament* (Philadelphia: University of Pennsylvania Press, 1993).

Cannon, Garland, *The Life and Mind of Oriental Jones* (Cambridge University Press, 1990).

Carrott, Richard, *The Egyptian Revival: Its Sources, Monuments and Meanings, 1808–1858* (Berkeley: University of California, 1978).

Clarke, J. J., *Oriental Enlightenment* (Routledge, 1997).

Clifford, J., *The Predicament of Culture* (Harvard University Press, 1988).

Codwell, J. F. and Macleod, D. S., *Orientalism Transposed: The Impact of the Colonies on British Culture* (Aldershot: Ashgate, 1998).

Colebrooke, Henry Thomas, *Essays on the Religion and Philosophy of the Hindus*, 2 vols (W. H. Allen, 1937).

Conner, Patrick, *Oriental Architecture in the West* (Thames and Hudson, 1977).

Conner, Patrick (ed.), *The Inspiration of Egypt: Its Influence on British Artists, Travellers and Designers, 1700–1900* (Brighton: Brighton Museum, 1983).

Dallmayr, Fred, *Beyond Orientalism* (New York: State University of New York Press, 1996).

Daniel, N., *Islam and the West: The Making of an Image* (Edinburgh University Press, 1960).

Davies, Philip, *Splendours of the Raj: British Architecture in India, 1660–1947* (Murrayi, 1985).

Deherain, Henri, *Silvestre de Sacy et ses correspondants* (Paris: Hachette, 1919).

Drew, John, *India and the Romantic Imagination* (Oxford University Press, 1987).

The Fine Art Society, *Eastern Encounters: Orientalist Painters in the Nineteenth Century* (David Hughes and Louise Whitford, 1978).

The Fine Art Society, *Travellers beyond the Grand Tour* (1980).

Foucault, M., *Power/Knowledge* (New York: Pantheon Books, 1980).

Gramsci, A., *The Modern Prince* (International Publishers, 1957).

Guha, Ranajit and Spivak, Gayatri Chakravorty (eds), *Selected Subaltern Studies* (Oxford University Press, 1988).

Head, Raymond, *The Indian Style* (Allen and Unwin, 1986).

Hegel, G. W. F., *The Philosophy of History* (New York: Dover Publications, 1956).

Herold, J. Christopher, *Bonaparte in Egypt* (New York: Harper and Row, 1962).

Hobsbawm, Eric and Ranger, Terence (eds), *The Invention of Tradition* (Cambridge University Press, 1983).

Hutchins, Francis G., *The Illusion of Permanence: British Imperialism in India* (Princeton, NJ: Princeton University Press, 1987).

Hyam, Ronald, *Empire and Sexuality* (Manchester University Press, 1990).

Impey, Oliver, *Chinoiserie: The Impact of Oriental Styles on Western Art and Decoration* (Oxford University Press, 1977).

Inden, Ronald, *Imagining India* (Oxford: Blackwell, 1990).

Kabbani, Rana, *Europe's Myths of the Orient: Devise and Rule* (Macmillan, 1986).

King, Donald and Sylvester, David, *The Eastern Carpet in the Western World from the Fifteenth to the Seventeenth Century* (Arts Council of Great Britain, 1983).

King, Richard, *Orientalism and Religion* (Routledge, 1999).

Kopf, David, *British Orientalism and the Bengal Renaissance: The Dynamics of Indian Modernisation, 1773–1835* (Berkeley: University of California Press, 1969).

Leask, Nigel, *British Romantic Writers and the East: Anxieties of Empire* (Cambridge University Press, 1992).

Lewis, R., *Gendering Orientalism* (Routledge, 1969).

Llewellyn, Briony, *The Orient Observed: Images of the Middle East from the Searight Collection* (Victoria and Albert Museum, 1989).

Lockett, Terence A., *Oriental Expressions: The Influence of the Orient on British Ceramics* (Stoke-on-Trent: Northern Ceramic Society, 1989).

Longford, Elizabeth, *A Pilgrimage of Passion: The Life of Wilfred Scawen Blunt* (Weidenfeld and Nicolson, 1979).

Lowe, Lisa, *Critical Terrains: French and British Orientalisms* (Ithaca: Cornell University Press, 1991).

MacKenzie, John M., *Orientalism: History, Theory and the Arts* (Manchester University Press, 1995).

Majeed, Javed, *Ungoverned Imaginings: James Mill's The History of British India and Orientalism* (Oxford University Press, 1992).

Martino, Pierre, *L'Orient dans la littérature française aux XVIIe et au XVIIIe siècle* (Paris: Hachette, 1906).

de Meester, Marie E., *Oriental Influences in English Literature of the Nineteenth Century* (Heidelberg: C. Winter, 1915).

Melman, Billie, *Women's Orients: English Women and the Middle-East, 1718–1918* (Macmillan, 1992).

Mill, James, *The History of British India* (Baldwin, Cradock and Joy, 1820).

Mills, Sara, *Discourses of Difference: Women's Travel Writing and Colonialism* (Macmillan, 1990).

Moore-Gilbert, B. J., *Kipling and Orientalism* (Croom-Helm, 1986).

Mukherjee, S. N., *Sir William Jones: A Study in Eighteenth-Century British Attitudes to India* (Cambridge University Press, 1968).

Nasir, Sari Jamil, *The Arabs and the English* (Longman, 1976).

Nerval, Gerard de, *Voyage en Orient*, ed. Henri Clouard, 3 vols (Paris: Le Divan, 1927).

Nietzsche, Friedrich, *Human All Too Human* (University of Nebraska Press, 1986).

Porter, Dennis, *Haunted Journeys: Desire and Transgression in European Travel Writing* (Princeton, NJ: Princeton University Press, 1991).

Renan, Ernst, Oeuvres complètes, 7 vols (Paris: Calmann-Levy, 1947).

Rosenthal, Donald A., *Orientalism: The Near East in French Painting, 1800–1880* (Rochester; NY: Memorial Art Gallery, 1982).

Sacy, Silvestre de, *Mélanges de littérature orientale* (Paris: E. Docrocq, 1861).

Said, Edward W., *Orientalism* (Pantheon Books, 1978).

Said, Edward W., *Culture and Imperialism* (Chatto and Windus, 1993).

Schacht, S. and Bosworth, C. (eds), *The Legacy of Islam* (Oxford University Press, 1979).

Schlegel, Friedrich, *Über die Sprache und Weisheit der Indier* (Heidelberg: Mohr and Zimmer, 1808).

Schneider, William H., *An Empire for the Masses: The French Popular Image of Africa, 1870–1900* (West Port, CT: Greenwood Press, 1982).

Schwab, R., *La Renaissance Orientale* (Paris: Editions Payot, 1950).

Sharafuddin, Mohammed, *Islam and Romantic Orientalism* (Tauris, 1993).

Spivak, Gayatri Chakravorty, *In Other Worlds: Essays in Cultural Politics* (Methuen, 1987).

Sprinker, Michael, *Edward Said: A Critical Reader* (Oxford: Blackwell, 1992).

Stevens, Mary Anne, *The Orientalists: Delacroix to Matisse, European Painters in North Africa and the Near East* (Weidenfeld and Nicolson, 1984).

Stokes, Eric, *The English Utilitarians and India* (Oxford University Press, 1959).

Suleri, Sara, *The Rhetoric of English India* (Chicago: University Press, 1992).

Sullivan, Michael, *The Meeting of Eastern and Western Art* (Thames and Hudson, 1973).

Summers, Vera A., *L'Orientalisme d'Alfred de Vigny* (Paris: H. Champion, 1930).

Taylor, Philip M., *The Projection of Britain: British Overseas Publicity and Propaganda, 1919–1939* (Cambridge University Press, 1981).

Thompson, James, *The East: Imagined, Experienced, Remembered: Orientalist Nineteenth-Century Painting* (Dublin: National Gallery of Ireland, 1988).

Thornton, A. P., *Doctrines of Imperialism* (Wiley, 1963).

Thornton, Lynne, *The Orientalists: Painters- Travellers, 1828–1908* (Paris: ACR Edition International, 1983).

Turner, B. S., *Marx and the End of Orientalism* (George Allen and Unwin, 1978).

Turner, B. S., *Orientalism, Postmodernism and Globalism* (Routledge, 1994).

Verrier, Michelle, *The Orientalists* (New York: Brizzolli, 1979).

Wilson, Horace Hayman, *The History of British India from 1805 to 1835*, 2 vols (J. Madden & Co., 1845–6).

Windshuttle, K., *The Killing of History* (New York: Free Press, 1996).

ARTICLES, PAMPHLETS AND THESES

Abdel-Malek, Anouar, 'Orientalism in Crisis', *Diogenes*, no. 44, winter 1963, pp. 103–40.

Ahmad, Aijaz, 'Between Orientalism and Historicism', *Studies in History*, 7, 1, n.s., 1991, pp. 135–63.

Alexander, Edward, 'Professor of Terror', *Commentary*, August 1989, pp. 49–50.

Arberry, Arthur G., 'British Contributions to Persian Studies' (Longmans, Green & Co., 1942).

Beckingham, C. F., 'Review of Orientalism', *Bulletin of the School of Oriental and African Studies*, 42, 1979, pp. 38–40.

Benda, H. J., 'Christiaan Snouck Hurgronje and the Foundations of Dutch Islamic Policy in Indonesia', *Journal of Modern History*, 30, 4, 1958, pp. 338–47.

Bhabha, Homi K., 'Of Mimicry and Man; Ambivalence of Colonial Discourse', *October*, 28, spring 1984, pp. 125–33.

Bhabha, Homi K., 'Signs Taken for Wonders: Questions of Ambivalence and Authority under a Tree Outside Delhi, May 1817', *Critical Inquiry*, 12, 1, 1985, pp. 144–65.

Bhatnagar, R., 'Uses and Limits of Foucault: A Study of the Theme of Origins in Said, "Orientalism"', *Social Scientist*, 158, 1986, pp. 3–22.

Bowen, Harold, 'British Contributions to Turkish Studies' (Longmans, Green & Co., 1945).

Brockington, J. L., 'Warren Hastings and Orientalism', in G. Carnall and C. Nicholson (eds), *The Impeachment of Warren Hastings* (Edinburgh University Press, 1989).

Cahen, C., Letter to the Editor, *Diogenes*, no. 49, spring 1965, pp. 135–8.

Clifford, J., 'Review of *Orientalism*,' *History and Theory*, 19, 2, 1980, pp. 204–23.

Gabrieli, F., 'Apology for Orientalism', *Diogenes*, no. 50, summer 1965, pp. 128–36.

Gellner, E., 'In Defence of Orientalism', *Sociology*, 14, 2, 1980, pp. 295–300.

Halliday, F., 'Orientalism and its Critics', *British Journal of Middle Eastern Studies*, 20, 2, 1993, pp. 145–163.

Hourani, A., 'The Road to Morocco', *New York Review of Books*, 8 March 1979.

Inden, R., 'Orientalist Constructions of India', *Modern Asian Studies*, 20, 3, 1986, pp. 401–48.

Kopf, David, 'Hermeneutics versus History', *Journal of Asian Studies*, 39, 3, 1980, pp. 495–506.

Lewis, Bernard, 'British Contributions to Arabic Studies' (Longmans, Green & Co., 1941).

Lewis, Bernard, 'The Question of Orientalism', in B. Lewis, *Islam and the West* (Oxford University Press, 1993).

Little, D. P., 'Three Arab Critiques of Orientalism', *Muslim World*, 69, 2, 1979, pp. 110–31.

MacKenzie, John M., 'Occidentalism: Counterpoint and Counter-polemic', *Journal of Historical Geography*, 19, 3, 1993, pp. 339–44.

MacKenzie, John M., 'Scotland and the Empire', *International History Review*, 15, 1993, pp. 714–39.

MacKenzie, John M., 'Edward Said and the Historians', *Nineteenth-Century Contexts*, 18, 1994, pp. 9–25.

Mani, L. and Frankenberg, R., 'The Challenge of Orientalism', *Economy and Society*, 14, 2, 1985, pp. 174–92.

Marshall, P. J., 'Warren Hastings as Scholar and Patron' in Anne Whiteman, J. S. Bromley and P. G. M. Dickson (eds). *Statesmen, Scholars and Merchants: Essays in Eighteenth-Century History Presented to Dame Lucy Sutherland* (Oxford University Press, 1973).

Nasir, Sari Jamil, 'The Image of the Arab in American Popular Culture', Ph.D. thesis (University of Illinois, 1962).

Netton, George Henry, 'The Mysteries of Islam', in G. S. Rousseau and Roy Porter (eds), *Exoticism in the Enlightenment* (Manchester University Press, 1990).

Nochlin, Linda, 'The Imaginary Orient', *Art in America*, May 1983, pp. 118–31, 187–91.

O'Hanlon, R. and Washbrook, D., 'After Orientalism: Culture, Criticism and Politics in the Third World', *Comparative Studies in Society and History*, 34, 1, 1992, pp. 141–67.

Parry, Benita, 'Problems in Current Theories of Colonial Discourse', *Oxford Literary Review*, 9, 1987, pp. 27–58.

Rendall, Jane, 'Scottish Orientalism from Robertson to James Mill', *The Historical Journal*, 25, 1, 1982, pp. 43–69.

Richardson, M., 'Enough Said', *Anthropology Today*, 6, 4, 1990, pp. 16–19.

Sadik Jalal al-'Azm, 'Orientalism and Orientalism in Reverse', *Khamsin*, 8, 1981, pp. 5–26.

Schaar, Stuart, 'Orientalism at the Service of Imperialism', *Race and Class*, 21, 1, 1979, pp. 67–80.

Sivan, Emmanuel, 'Edward Said and His Arab Reviewers', in E. Sivan, *Interpretations of Islam: Past and Present* (Princeton, NJ: Darwin Press, 1985).

Spivak, Gayatri Chakravorty, 'Can the Subaltern Speak?', in Cary Nelson and Lawrence Gossberg (eds), *Marxism and the Interpretation of Culture*, (Basingstoke: Macmillan Education, 1988).

Spivak, Gayatri Chakravorty, 'Poststructuralism, Marginality, Postcoloniality and Value', in Peter Collier and Helga Geyer-Ryan (eds), *Literary Theory Today* (Cambridge University Press, 1990).

Tibawi, A. L., 'English-Speaking Orientalists', *Islamic Quarterly*, 8, 1–4, 1964, pp. 25–45 and 73–88.

Tibawi, A. L., 'Second Critique of the English-Speaking Orientalists', *Islamic Quarterly*, 23, 1, 1979, pp. 3–54.

Tibawi, A. L., 'On the Orientalists Again', *Muslim World*, 70, 1, 1980, pp. 56–61.

Weiner, Justus Reid, '"My Beautiful Old House" and Other Fabrications by Edward Said', *Commentary*, September 1999, pp. 23–31.

Wilson, Ernest J., 'Orientalism: A Black Perspective', *Journal of Palestine Studies*, 10, 2, 1981, pp. 59–69.

Wilson, W. Daniel, 'Turks on the Eighteenth-Century Operatic Stage and European Political, Military, and Cultural History', *Eighteenth-Century Life*, 9, 2, 1985, pp. 79–92.

ACKNOWLEDGEMENTS

Grateful acknowledgement is made to the following sources for permission to reproduce material previously published elsewhere. Every effort has been made to trace the copyright holders, but, if any have been inadvertently overlooked, the publisher will be pleased to make the necessary arrangements at the first opportunity.

1. 'The Indian Form of Government' by James Mill, *The History of British India*, 1820.
2. 'Gorgeous Edifices' by G. W. F. Hegel, *The Philosophy of History*. Translated by S. Sibree, P. F. Collier & Sons, New York, 1902.
3. 'The British Rule in India' by Karl Marx, *New York Daily Tribune*, 25 June 1853.
4. 'Les Commencements de l'Orientalisme' by Pierre Martino, *L'Orient dans la Littérature Française*, Librarie Hachette, Paris, 1906.
5. 'The Asiatic Society of Calcutta' by Raymond Schwab, *The Oriental Renaissance*, Columbia University Press, New York, 1984. Copyright © Les Editions Payot.
6. 'Appearance and the Thing-in-itself' by F. Nietzsche, *Human, All Too Human*. Reprinted from *Human, All Too Human*, permission of the University of Nebraska Press. Copyright © 1984 by the University of Nebraska Press.
7. 'On Hegemony and Direct Rule' by Antonio Gramsci, *The Modern Prince*, International Publishers, 1957.
8. 'Truth and Power' by Michel Foucault, from Colin Gordon (ed.) *Power/Knowledge*, Pantheon Books, 1980. Copyright © 1972, 1975, 1976, 1977 by Michel Foucault. Collection copyright © 1980 by The Harvester Press. Reprinted by permission of Pantheon Books, a division of Random House, Inc.
9. 'Orientalism in Crisis' by Anouar Abdel-Malek, *Diogenes*, No. 44, Winter, 1963.
10. 'English-Speaking Orientalists' by A. L. Tibawi, *Islamic Quarterly*, 8, 1–4, 1964, pp. 25–45.
11. 'Apology for Orientalism' by Francesco Gabrieli, *Diogenes*, No. 50, Summer, 1965.

12. 'Shattered Myths' by Edward Said, from *Middle East Crucible*, by Naseer H. Aruri (ed.), Medina University Press, 1975. Reprinted by permission of the Association of Arab-American University Graduates Press, www.aaug.org

13. 'Arabs, Islam and the Dogmas of the West' by Edward Said, *The New York Times Book Review*, 31 October 1976. Copyright © 1976 by the New York Times Co. Reprinted by permission.

14. 'My Thesis' by Edward Said, *Orientalism*, Pantheon Books, 1978. Copyright © 1978 by Edward W. Said. Reprinted by permission of Pantheon Books, a division of Random House, Inc.

15. 'On Flaubert' by Edward Said, *Orientalism*, Pantheon Books, 1978. Copyright © 1978 by Edward W. Said. Reprinted by permission of Pantheon Books, a division of Random House, Inc.

16. 'Latent and Manifest Orientalism' by Edward Said, *Orientalism*, Pantheon Books, 1978. Copyright © 1978 by Edward W. Said. Reprinted by permission of Pantheon Books, a division of Random House, Inc.

17. 'Marx and the End of Orientalism' by Bryan S. Turner, *Marx and the End of Orientalism*, George Allen and Unwin, 1978.

18. 'Three Arab Critiques of Orientalism', D. P. Little, *Muslim World*, No. 69, 1979.

19. 'Second Critique of English-Speaking Orientalists' by A. L. Tibawi, 'Second Critique of English-Speaking Orientalists and the Approach to Islam and the Arabs', *Islamic Quarterly*, 23: 1, 1979.

20. 'On the Orientalists Again' by A. L. Tibawi, *Muslim World*, No. 70, 1980.

21. 'Orientalism at the Service of Imperialism' by Stuart Schaar, *Race and Class*, 21: 1, 1979.

22. 'Hermeneutics versus History' by David Kopf, *Journal of Asian Studies*, 39: 3, 1980. Reprinted with the permission of the Association of Asian Studies, Inc.

23. 'Enough Said' by Michael Richardson, *Anthropology Today*, 6: 4, 1990, Royal Anthropological Institute of Great Britain and Ireland.

24. 'Orientalism and Orientalism in Reverse' by Sadik Jalal Al-'Azm, *Khamsin*, No. 8, 1981.

25. 'Orientalism: A Black Perspective' by Ernest J. Wilson III, *Journal of Palestine Studies*, 10: 2, 1981.

26. 'The Question of Orientalism' by Bernard Lewis, *Islam and the West*, Oxford University Press, 1993.

27. 'Gorgeous East' by B. J. Moore-Gilbert, *Kipling and 'Orientalism'*, Croom-Helm, 1986.

28. 'Orientalist Constructions of India' by Ronald Inden, *Modern Asian Studies*, 20: 3, 1986.

29. 'Between Orientalism and Historicism' by Aijaz Ahmad, *Studies in History*, 7: 1, 1991. Copyright © Jawaharla Nehru University, New Delhi, 1991. All rights reserved. Reproduced with the permission of the copyright holder and the publisher, Sage Publications India Pvt Ltd, New Delhi, India.

30. 'Humanising the Arabs' by Billie Melman, *Women's Orients*, Macmillan, 1992.

31. 'Indology, Power, and the Case of Germany' by S. Pollock from Carol A. Breckenridge and Peter van der Veer (eds) *Orientalism and the Postcolonial Predicament*, University of Pennsylvania Press, 1993.

32. 'Turkish Embassy Letters' by Lisa Lowe, *Cultural Critique*, Vol. 15, Spring, 1990.

33. 'History, Theory and the Arts' by John MacKenzie, *Orientalism: History Theory and the Arts*, Manchester University Press, 1995.

34. 'Orientalism, Hinduism and Feminism' by Richard King, *Orientalism and Religion*, Routledge, 1999.

35. 'Orientalism Reconsidered' by Edward Said, from F. Barker and P. Hulme (eds) *Literature, Politics and Theory*, Methuen, 1986. Reproduced with permission from Taylor and Francis.

36. 'Exit from Orientalism' by Fred Dallmayr, *Beyond Orientalism*, State University of New York Press, 1996. Reprinted by permission of the State University of New York Press, from *Beyond Orientalism: Essays on Cross-Cultural Encounter* by F. Dallmayr (ed.) © 1996. State University of New York. All rights reserved.
37. 'From Orientalism to Global Society' by Bryan S. Turner, *Orientalism, Postmodernism and Globalism*, Routledge, 1994.